History of London

HANOVERIAN LONDON
1714–1808

History of London

HANOVERIAN
LONDON
1714-1808

George Rudé

LONDON
SECKER & WARBURG

First published in England 1971
by Martin Secker & Warburg Limited
14 Carlisle Street, London W1

Copyright © 1971 by George Rudé

436 43700 7

Printed in Great Britain
by Richard Clay (The Chaucer Press) Ltd
Bungay, Suffolk

Contents

List of Illustrations

Introduction

HANOVERIAN London was unique among the cities of the world. In the first place, she acquired the largest population (though there is a possibility that this was exceeded before 1800 by Eddo, the future Tokyo). In 1700, if we accept the figures put forward by Mr Wrigley, her population was second, in Europe at least, to that of Paris.[1] But, during the century, the population of Paris remained largely stagnant, whereas London's did not; in the next fifty years, Paris had almost certainly been overtaken. Yet the statistical calculations of the period were notoriously defective, and we can only assert, with some degree of confidence, that by 1801, the year of the first census in either country, the population of London exceeded that of Paris by one-third or more – a fact all the more remarkable as at this time the population of England and Wales was little more than one-third of that of France.

So there may be some doubt as to the point at which London became Europe's (if not the world's) largest city; but there can be no doubt at all that, throughout the century, Londoners formed a larger proportion of the national population than the inhabitants of any other major city. In 1750, for example, about one Englishman (and Welshman) in ten lived in London, whereas one Dutchman in eleven may have lived in Amsterdam and no more than one Frenchman in forty lived in Paris. A consequence of this concentration was that London formed a vast consumers' market and was able to exercise a quite disproportionate influence on the economy of Britain as a whole. Professor F. J. Fisher's researches have shown that, in the seventeenth century, London's food market was responsible for a major part of the 'revolutionary' changes taking place in agriculture; and, in Daniel Defoe's *Tour Through the Whole Island of Great Britain*, we read that, in the 1720s, every part of the Kingdom was 'employ'd to furnish something to supply the city of London with provisions'.

So London, in addition to being a great centre of population, was also a great emporium, an economic octopus 'that sucks [again to quote Defoe] the vitals of trade in this island to itself'. And, conversely, as a great port,

[1] See page 4 below.

London became not only the great point of exodus for the whole nation's produce, but the point of entry for a large part of the world's trade which she, in turn, distributed both to her own citizens and to the country at large. London was, in fact, not only by far the greatest port in Britain (handling over three-quarters of the nation's trade in 1700), but she remained, throughout the century, the largest centre of international trade, the largest ship-owner and the largest ship-builder in the world; through her markets, her trade and her shipping, she became, in the course of it, the world centre of insurance and banking and, by the end of the Napoleonic Wars, she had even eclipsed Amsterdam, for long her rival, as the money market of the world.

It was natural, therefore, that the great London merchants, who had their offices, banks and warehouses at the centre of this great emporium, in the City of London, should also be quite unique, many having become (in Defoe's words) 'princes, greater and richer, and more powerful than some sovereign princes'. But England's – and, in this respect, she was broadly similar to other European countries – was still a predominantly 'aristocratic' society, in which political authority was firmly vested in the landed classes, who controlled both Houses of Parliament and from whom alone governments were formed. This aristocratic domination went much further: it permeated the cultural and religious life of the nation, and therefore also of its capital city, where the wealthiest and most powerful resided. As they settled down, after the rough-and-tumble of Queen Anne's declining years, to a relatively calm and unruffled existence under the first Hanoverians, they developed, equally, a dull, tolerant, conformist, but frequently indifferent attitude towards religion, an attitude that was reflected in the small number of churches that were built in these hundred years. The aristocracy also patronized the arts, and it was to the aristocratic houses of St George's and St James's ('the polite end of the town') that aspiring poets, writers and painters came in search of patrons. In this sense, the prevailing trend in the arts, and in London's whole cultural life, was aristocratic rather than plebeian; and this was as true, for a great part of the century, of architecture and the fine arts as it was of literature and music. Yet, here again, Hanoverian London was unique among the great cities of the age – among those, at least, in which an aristocracy played so large a part in the nation's affairs. For one thing, the aristocratic patrons most often chose to live in fairly simple terrace houses, which contrasted oddly with the opulent city residences of their fellow-noblemen on the continent of Europe. (There were, of course, exceptions, like the stately mansions of the Earl of Chesterfield, the Duke of Richmond, the Royal princes, and perhaps a score of others.) For another thing, by the middle of the century the prevailing aristocratic patronage and culture, based on the more fashionable quarters of Westminster and the Court of St James's, was already being challenged by a new 'rich' or 'middling' culture and patronage based on the City and the Strand. These 'middling' classes found a painter of their own in Hogarth; and the novel, one of the great cultural innovations of the century, was essentially an *urban* product which drew its inspiration and its 'values' more from the coffee-houses of the City than from the aristocratic or 'genteel' houses of St James's. Moreover, from the 1760s, middle-class patrons began to make their presence felt in the theatres of the Haymarket and Covent Garden, and it was David Garrick's realization of this fact and his willingness to come to terms with it that accounted, in part at least, for his enormous popularity.

Even more remarkable was the emergence in London, far earlier than elsewhere, of the elements of a genuine citizens' democracy. In its most advanced form, it was found on the hustings of Westminster, where every householder, or 'pot-walloper', had the parliamentary franchise. But, in local affairs, Westminster was oligarchic; besides, parliamentary contests were rare (there were perhaps twenty in the Hanoverian period), and the electors, even if 'popular' themselves, had to choose between candidates who were aristocratic or 'genteel'. In the City of London, the situation was different, and here there had grown up, over the centuries, what Sydney and Beatrice Webb called a 'rate-payers' democracy'. For the government of the City, which exercised important privileges and carried influence in both national and local affairs, was vested not so much in the great 'moneyed companies' and wealthy merchants (though these carried some weight in the Court of Aldermen) as in the smaller merchants and 'middling' shopkeepers and tradesmen who, as freemen of the Livery Companies, formed the Court of Common Hall and were strongly represented in the governing Court of Common Council. This citizens' democracy was a unique phenomenon: even Republican Amsterdam was ruled by oligarchs and Paris had no elective municipal government at all. Moreover, it had certain remarkable consequences. One was that the City of London, through its mouthpiece, the City Corporation, was almost always in opposition to the Court and to the governments of the day for the greater part of the eighteenth century, and almost continuously from about 1730 to the mid-1780s. This was in itself of some political importance, as the City could not be ignored and its opposition played a part in moulding national policies and in persuading governments (like that of Sir Robert Walpole in the 1730s) to attune their policies more to the City's wants. Another consequence was that the City, to lend strength to its opposition, began to call for a reform of parliament and to court the favours of a wider public. In this way, City 'Radicalism', as it emerged in the 1760s, acquired a popular base, for the unenfranchised citizens – vulgarly known as 'the Mob' – were drawn into political activity as the junior partners of the City and its leaders. In Paris, a similar educative role was performed by the Parlement, which, in its disputes with the King's ministers, gave the 'lower order' of Parisians their first lessons in political ideas and political agitation. But in Paris the association was never so close and, before the Revolution, there was never a popular fermentation of the scope and depth of that roused by John Wilkes and the City Radicals in the 1760s and 1770s. And London's 'working trades' (as Defoe called them) took a further step forward in the 1790s when, under the impact of the revolutionary events in France, they formed a political association of their own – the London Corresponding Society – in which can already be seen the germs of the nineteenth-century working-class movement.

These, then, are some of the distinguishing features of Hanoverian London, features which mark her off not only from other cities of the time but from other stages in her own earlier, and later, history. But to leave it at that – as a kind of 'Portrait of an Age' – would be to give the entirely erroneous impression that nothing much changed and that London, in 1808 (the terminal date of this volume), was much the same as she had been when the first Hanoverian came to the throne in 1714. This, of course, was far from being the case, and it is possible to pin-point certain approximate land-marks in London's evolution over these hundred years. In 1714, she was already the largest centre of shipping and international trade in Europe; she already dominated (to a degree never equalled since) the nation's whole economic and political life, and was the Mecca of its artists and men of letters. But the new dynasty was not yet securely founded and the landed classes, still strictly divided between Whigs and Tories, were licking their wounds after their internecine struggle in the last years of Anne. By the 1750s, the picture had greatly changed. London had become the largest city in Europe; she had prospered through the long years of peace, which had only recently been disturbed. The Jacobite challenge had been finally defeated, and the landed classes, relatively undivided, shared the spoils of office, built their squares and terrace houses, and basked in social and religious peace. Rents and prices remained relatively stable.

The arts flourished: it was the age of Hogarth, of the first novelists and Dr Johnson, and it would soon be that of Reynolds and Chippendale, of Adam's Neo-Classical houses and the smug complacency of Blackstone's *Commentaries*.

By the 1780s the picture had changed again. The social and international peace had gone and the complacency and toleration were no longer the same as before. The political crises of the 1760s and the war with the American colonists had once more divided the landed classes. Middle-class Radicalism, emanating from the City of London, had made its first great challenge to the aristocratic control of Parliament. Meanwhile, a new popular Radicalism, politically inspired by the City but exacerbated by rising prices, had made its appearance in the city's streets: at first as the champion of 'liberty' in the Wilkite disturbances of the 1760s and 1770s, and later as the illiberal opponent of Roman Catholicism in the Gordon Riots of 1780. The 'No Popery' riots put a brake on the City's Radicalism and drove a wedge between the City and the 'mob', and the City, as well as the bulk of the merchants and landed classes, soon rallied to the 'New' Tory government of the younger Pitt, an alliance that was at first strengthened by the French Revolution and the long wars with France.

The wars brought even greater changes. The docks were built and London's economy (like that of the nation as a whole), though shaken by periodical crises, expanded and generally prospered. Though architecture was in the doldrums, the other arts and sciences flourished; yet the war saw an exodus of the poets and writers (soon to be followed by the artists) from the metropolis. London's population grew to a million and, for the first time, the increase was due as much to an excess of births over deaths as to an influx from the country outside. Fashions changed; men's wigs were abandoned and trousers were being worn in the place of breeches, and women's clothes became lighter and simpler. The London square, built for the aristocracy and gentry, was becoming increasingly invaded by the 'middling' and commercial classes. City Radicalism revived and, from 1808 onwards, the City went once more into opposition to government. Yet here there were two important changes: the journeymen and small master craftsmen had begun, through the London Corresponding Society, to form a Radical movement of their own; and, with Sir Francis Burdett's election to Parliament in 1807, it was Westminster and not the City that became the new springboard of a middle-class Radical revival.

It is with these changing trends and with these general features of Hanoverian London that this book is mainly concerned. It is not an

original book, in that it does not seek to overthrow the accepted conclusions
of others or to venture on a wide new trail of uncharted discovery. It
draws heavily – perhaps too heavily – on the work of other writers in the
field: on Sir Walter Besant's history (though he posed some very different
questions) of over sixty years ago; on Wrigley, Spate and Glass for London's topography and population; on Defoe and a host of later writers for
her economy; on Summerson and Pevsner for her buildings and her architecture; on Turberville for her culture and entertainments; on Habbakuk
and Mingay for her landed classes; on the Webbs for her government and
Marshall for her Poor Law; on Christie and Maccoby for middle-class
Radicalism; on Sharpe, Sutherland and Beaven for the City's politics;
on Robbins for Middlesex; and, most heavily of all, on Dorothy George's
great work on the life of London's 'working trades', the poor and labouring
classes. To these I have added, from my own researches, the picture here
presented of London's rents and rates, of the London 'mob' and war-time
volunteers, of popular Radicalism and social protest movements.

So it is, in the main, a work of synthesis, of 'putting together', rather
then one of exploration or of original research. Yet it may perhaps claim
the virtue of having attempted to impose some order on the pieces in the
jig-saw, of drawing some scattered threads together and weaving them
into a more or less intelligible pattern of the life and history of a great city
over the span of a hundred years.

Abbreviations

Add. MSS.	Additional Manuscripts, British Museum
B.M.	British Museum
Corp. Lond. R.O.	Corporation of London Records Office
E.H.R.	*English Historical Review*
G.L.	Guildhall Library
H.O.	Home Office
H.P.L.	Holborn Public Library
M.P.L.	Marylebone Public Library
Old Bailey *Proceedings*	*The Whole Proceedings upon the King's Commission of Oyer and Terminer and Gaol Delivery for the City of London and . . . for the County of Middlesex*
P.A.R.	Papers, Acts, Reports (miscellaneous), in Corporation of London Records Office
P.R.O.	Public Records Office
W.P.L.	Westminster Public Library

Beaven	A. B. Beaven, *The Aldermen of the City of London*
Besant	Sir Walter Besant, *London in the Eighteenth Century*
Georgian London	Sir John Summerson, *Georgian London*
London Life	M. Dorothy George, *London Life in the Eighteenth Century*
Sharpe	R. R. Sharpe, *London and the Kingdom*

Strype, *Survey*	John Strype, *A Survey of the Cities of London and Westminster*
A Tour	Daniel Defoe, *A Tour Through the Whole Island of Great Britain*
Three Tours	W. S. Lewis, *Three Tours through London in the Years 1748, 1776, 1797*
Wesley's *Journal*	*The Journal of the Rev. John Wesley, A.M.,* ed. N. Curnock
Wheatley and Cunningham	H. B. Wheatley and P. Cunningham, *London Past and Present*
Wilkes and Liberty	George Rudé, *Wilkes and Liberty. A Social Study of 1763 to 1774*

1

The Growth of the
Metropolis

AMONG THE significant features of London's development during
the eighteenth century was its continued growth into a compact
metropolis extending ever farther beyond its original City boundaries; so that by 1801 the population of the City of London represented no
more than one-sixth of that of the new 'greater' London where, a hundred
years before, it had represented between one-third and a quarter.[1] This
had, of course, been a long and continuous process extending over more
than two hundred years; yet a map dating from Elizabeth's day (1563)
shows how far the City at that time still dominated the whole conurbation
of London: the villages and hamlets to the east lay scattered to the north
and east of the Tower; only Finsbury and Clerkenwell lay north of the
City walls; and even Westminster formed a mere narrow strip along the
river, bounded by the as yet undeveloped 'Convent Garden', Charing
Cross and St James's Park.

But gradually there had emerged the reality of a 'greater' London enclosed within the so-called 'Bills of Mortality'; and the great enumerators
of the seventeenth century – John Gaunt in 1631 and 1661, Sir William
Petty in 1682 and Gregory King in 1695 – made substantial allowance for
this larger area beyond the City of London which, in addition to the City
'without the Walls', included Westminster, the Borough (the five parishes
of old Southwark) and the contiguous or out-parishes of Middlesex and
Surrey.

Since Gregory King's time, considerable additions had been made to
this greater London with its fluid, constantly expanding frontiers. John

---

[1] William Robson, *The Government and Misgovernment of London*, 1939, pp. 42–5;
M. Dorothy George, *London Life in the Eighteenth Century*, 1966, p. 319.

B

Strype, writing in 1720, called the London that had emerged from the reigns of William and Anne 'the Metropolis and Glory of the Kingdom';[1] and Daniel Defoe, in his *Tour* of 1724, took careful note of the changes which had taken place in the past thirty years and others that were taking place before his very eyes. 'London,' he wrote, 'as a city only, and as its walls and liberties line it out might, indeed, be viewed in a small compass; but, when I speak of London, now in the modern acceptation, you expect I shall take in all that vast mass of buildings, reaching from Black-Wall in the east, to Tot-Hill Fields in the west; and extended in an unequal breadth, from the bridge, or river, in the south, to Islington north; and from Peterburgh House on the bank side in Westminster, to Cavendish Square, and all the new buildings by, and beyond, Hanover Square, by which the city of London, for so it is still to be called, is extended to Hide Park Corner in the Brentford Road, and almost to Marylebone in the Acton Road; and how much farther it may spread, who knows?' Though filled with admiration, he was not altogether enchanted by what he observed, for he saw it as a 'disaster' that London was 'thus stretched out in buildings, just at the pleasure of every builder, or undertaker of buildings, and as the convenience of the people directs, whether for trade or otherwise; and this has spread the face of it in a most straggling, confus'd manner, out of all shape, uncompact, and unequal'. So much so that while in some places, as from St George's in Southwark to Shoreditch in Middlesex, London was three miles broad, in others, as from Peterburgh House to Montague House, its breadth was only two miles; while in others again, as at Wapping, it was only half a mile broad, and at Redriff (Rotherhithe) 'much less'. He calculated that the whole extent of the new circumference of London might stretch for thirty-six miles, enclosing the cities of London and Westminster, the borough of Southwark, and such newly absorbed villages as Deptford, Islington and Newington – though he excluded Poplar, Blackwall, Greenwich, Chelsea, Marylebone and Knightsbridge. Yet he foresaw that London would rapidly extend much farther; for 'Westminster is in a fair way to shake hands with Chelsea, as St Gyles's is with Marylebone; and Great Russel Street by Montague House, with Tottenham-Court'. And 'whither,' he asked, 'will this monstrous city then extend?'[2]

We shall see that Defoe somewhat exaggerated the degree of London's

[1] John Strype, *A Survey of the Cities of London and Westminster*, 1720, p. 1.
[2] Daniel Defoe, *A Tour Through the Whole Island of Great Britain*, 1966, vol. 1, pp. 314-24.

unplanned sprawl, but he had shrewdly noted the main trends. London, in fact, during the next forty years spread and sprawled more or less as he had forecast, and if we compare John Strype's map of 1720 (contemporary with Defoe's own *Tour*) with that contained in 'The City Guide of London, Westminster and Southwark with the New Buildings to the Year 1761', we shall see how many of the gaps in Defoe's 'line of circum-vallation' had been filled in by a combination of planned development, speculative building and simple economic pressure. To the east, Wapping, Shadwell, Stepney and Bethnal Green had been considerably extended and joined more firmly to the City; to the south, Blackman Street linked the Borough with Newington Butts; to the south-west, Tothill Fields at the extremity of Westminster now reached, as Defoe had foretold, almost to Chelsea; Knightsbridge, though its approaches were still infested with highwaymen and footpads, had become more closely linked with Hyde Park Corner; and Hammersmith, Paddington, Marylebone and St Pancras already formed with Chelsea the 'five villages beyond the Bills' that were becoming recognized as an integral part of the metropolis. Of these Hammersmith, Paddington and St Pancras remained small villages (even in 1801 St Pancras had no more than 357 houses); but Chelsea and Marylebone were developing into flourishing townships, the number of houses in Chelsea rising from 350 in 1717 to 1,350 in 1795 and those in Marylebone from 317 in 1723 to 577 in 1739 and 7,764 in 1801.[1]

Even more important for London's future had been the opening of Westminster Bridge in 1750, thus linking Westminster directly with Southwark and St George's Fields; and the construction in 1756–7 of the New Road (forming the present Marylebone, Euston and Pentonville Roads), running north of Marylebone and St Pancras and stretching eastwards from Paddington to the Angel at Islington. These new arteries, far more than any haphazard sprawl, played a significant part in filling up some of London's internal gaps both north and south. New buildings would soon fill up whole empty spaces on both sides of Westminster Bridge (to which Blackfriars Bridge would be added in 1769), and the New Road set the pace and direction of future building plans between Oxford Street and a $1\frac{1}{4}$-mile front running north and east of Marylebone. As London thrust northwards and as Portman, Manchester and Bedford Squares followed one another in quick succession in the 1770s and 1780s, Horace Walpole wrote to Miss Berry from Berkeley Square (in April

[1] H. B. Wheatley and P. Cunningham, *London Past and Present*, 1891, vol. 2, p. 511; vol. 3, pp. 1–3.

1791) that 'the town is so extended the breed of chairs is almost lost, for Hercules and Atlas could not carry anybody from one end of this enormous capital to the other'.[1] Moreover, as the gaps were progressively filled up, 'the Metropolis of Great Britain', as Dean Tucker termed it in a letter to the Earl of Shelburne in the eighties, was losing some of its self-contained community life and acquiring a new compactness unknown to Daniel Defoe.[2] In Defoe's day, Joseph Addison had looked on London as 'an aggregate of various nations, distinguished from each other by their respective customs, manners, and interests';[3] but when Boswell, in belated response to Dr Johnson's advice, visited Wapping in 1792, he found the experience disappointing, 'whether from that uniformity which has in modern times, in a great degree, spread through every part of the Metropolis, or from our want of sufficient exertion'.[4] To those, like Boswell and Walpole, who cherished the London of the 1760s, the city's new metropolitan appearance seemed hardly reassuring. But to others, as London stood on the threshold of a new century, it appeared as a monument to man's material achievement; for it was, so the census of 1801 described it, 'the Metropolis of England, at once the Seat of Government and the greatest Emporium in the known world'.[5]

Meanwhile, the population of the expanding metropolis had nearly doubled; yet the increase had not been at the pace of a hundred years before. According to Mr Wrigley, the various calculations made in the seventeenth century suggest that it rose from about 200,000 in 1600 to 400,000 in 1650 and 575,000 in 1700; and, in the next hundred years, it rose to 675,000 in 1750 and to 900,000 in the census of 1801.[6] The last figure alone may be accepted as reasonably reliable, as it was based on an enumeration of the inhabitants, whereas earlier calculations had depended on the Bills of Mortality, or records of burials and baptisms kept by the parish clerks, which by their very nature, as Defoe rightly pointed

[handwritten marginal note: NB— population]

[1] W. S. Lewis, *Three Tours through London in the Years 1748, 1776, 1797*, 1941, p. 93.
[2] *London Life*, p. 73.
[3] M. Dorothy George, 'London and the Life of the Town', in *Johnson's England*, ed. A. S. Turberville, 1965, vol. 1, p. 163.
[4] *London Life*, p. 78.
[5] W. G. East, 'England in the Eighteenth Century', in *An Historical Geography of England before A.D. 1800*, ed. H. C. Darby, 1948, p. 494.
[6] E. A. Wrigley, 'A Simple Model of London's Importance in Changing English Society and Economy 1650–1750', *Past and Present*, no. 37, 1967, p. 44. Dr George, however, has 674,350 for 1700, thus showing virtually no increase between 1700 and 1750 (*London Life*, p. 319).

out, omitted from their reckoning not only Jews and Roman Catholics but also Protestant dissenters, the children of foreigners and those who were too poor to have their children registered. And Thomas Pennant, writing eighty years later, added his comment on their deficiencies: why, he asked, should it be assumed that Londoners should be buried (let alone baptized) *within* rather than *without* the Bills?[1] Yet for purposes of comparison with other cities, these deficiencies may not be so grave as they appear in retrospect. Paris, for example, appears, by a variety of calculations, to have added next to nothing to its population in the course of the century (and certainly not between 1760 and 1801), while London's increased by nearly two-thirds. Even more striking is the fact that, during this period, London's population formed a steady 10 per cent of the population of England and Wales, while that of Paris remained at one in forty or fifty of the population of France. And, to underline the relative dominance of London, Mr Wrigley makes the further point that, around the middle of the century, about one in six of all English men and women were either living in London or had once lived there and had thus been directly exposed to the social, political and cultural influence of the capital.[2]

So much for the bald facts of London's spread and its growth of population in the eighteenth century. But these tell us little of the actual manner or *dynamics* of London's growth; and we shall still have to enquire further as to how the population grew, how it was distributed over the different parts of the capital, and how and why London tended to project itself into the neighbouring rural areas of Essex, Middlesex and Surrey.

The first thing to note is that the growth in London's population was due far more to a continuous immigration from the provinces than from any natural increase from within the metropolis itself. In fact, during the first half of the century, the annual number of deaths fairly consistently, and often substantially, exceeded the number of births. This 'shortfall' of births appears to have been at its greatest between 1727 and 1750, when the waste of lives recorded in the Bills of Mortality exceeded any that had been known since the great Plague. Between 1724 and 1742, annual baptisms fell from 19,370 to 13,571; burials rose to their highest point just when baptisms were at their lowest, rising to 32,167 in 1741; and, most significant of all, the greatest mortality was among children of under five years of age, reaching a figure of three in four of all children that had

[1] *A Tour*, vol. 1, p. 376; Thomas Pennant, *Some Account of London*, 1805, p. 272.
[2] E. A. Wrigley, *Past and Present*, no. 37, 1967, pp. 45, 49–50, 70.

been christened between 1730 and 1749. Historians have naturally specu-
lated about the reasons for this excessive mortality: was it due to insanitary
conditions, to epidemics or to a deterioration in the standard of living?
None of these factors appears to offer a satisfactory explanation. Public
health was no worse than it had been in the reigns of William and Queen
Anne; fever, the greatest killing disease of the day, showed no signs of
being particularly virulent, apart from a sharp epidemic in 1741; and the
price of corn and wheat was considerably lower at this time than it had
been in the lean years under William and Anne. So it seems reasonable to
accept the explanation usually given by contemporaries and adopted
subsequently by historians, notably by Dr George: the excessive consumption of spirits, particularly of gin, between the 1720s and 1740s, to
which a representation to the House of Commons in 1751 attributed the
deaths over the past dozen years of 9,323 children per annum.[1]

Baptisms in London continued to be at a relatively low level until about
1760, when they began to increase; and from that time onwards the
shortfall in births ceased to be a regular feature, and by the 1790s it could
reasonably be expected that, in normal years, the number of baptisms
should exceed the number of burials; and this tendency continued beyond
the end of the century.[2] Yet the margin was generally a small one, and,
even after the 1760s, accounted for a small part of the continuous growth
in population. This could only be made up by a steady inflow of new
settlers from the provinces. This immigration, Mr Wrigley estimates,
must have reached a net figure (that is, after allowing for the *outflow*) of
8,000 per annum towards the 1750s.[3] No similar estimates have been made
for the latter part of the century, but there is other evidence to suggest
that the annual inflow must have continued: there is, for example, the
view expressed by a contemporary in 1757 that two-thirds of London's
adults were born in the provinces or had come 'from distant parts'; while
the records of the Westminster General Dispensary between 1774 and
1781 show that only a quarter of 3,236 married persons treated in those
years were born within the Bills.[4]

Who were these new arrivals? Mr Wrigley supposes that the provincials
were mainly young persons (he suggests an average age on arrival of

[1] *London Life*, pp. 38–41. See also E. A. Wrigley, 'London and the Great Leap
Forward', *The Listener*, 6 July 1967, p. 7.

[2] For shortfalls in 1770 and 1791, see Sir Walter Besant, *London in the Eighteenth
Century*, 1902, pp. 637–8; and Thomas Pennant, *Some Account of London*, pp. 412–13.

[3] E. A. Wrigley, *Past and Present*, no. 37, 1967 p. 46.

[4] *London Life*, p. 118.

twenty years) and largely composed of 'household servants of both sexes, apprentices and labourers [who] came to London in large numbers, together with girls in trouble, younger sons without local prospects, fugitives from justice, those unable to find work, the restless, and those attracted by the scale and consequence of city life'.[1] The City of London would generally be barred to them, because, through poverty or origin, they would be ineligible for admission to the City's freedom or to exercise a City craft. So they tended to crowd into the districts adjoining the City, such as the precinct of St Katherine's by the Tower, the liberty of East Smithfield, into parts of Southwark, or into the waterside parishes and hamlets east of the Tower of London. To this eastern region, in particular, they would be drawn by the demands of London's growing port and shipping industries; Mr Ralph Davis, the historian of Britain's merchant navy, suggests that, by 1700, one-quarter of London's population depended directly on employment in port trades.[2]

But, of course, these immigrants were not exclusively composed of English provincials; apart from the Scots and Welsh and Irish, there were growing numbers of Germans, Dutchmen, Frenchmen and Jews, many of whom formed their own communities when they settled in the capital. The Irish were probably the most numerous; they were for the most part unskilled labourers, engaged in building, portering, hawking, retailing and coal-heaving, and settled mainly in St Giles in the Fields, Whitechapel, St George in the East, Holborn and Marylebone. Their numbers have never been exactly recorded, but they must have formed the great majority of the 14,000 Roman Catholic households included in the returns of Papists for 1767 and 1780.[3] Jews, many of them Poles and Germans (the so-called Ashkenazim) who had escaped from persecution, began to arrive in London in considerable numbers after the 1750s. In 1753, both they and the older-established Sephardic Jews were believed to number 5,000 in the country as a whole; but, fifty years later, according to Patrick Colquhoun, they numbered 15,000 to 20,000 in the capital alone. The wealthier settled in the City (and a few like the financiers Joseph Salvador and Sampson Gideon off the Strand, in Leicester Fields, or Arlington Street); but mainly – and the Ashkenazim in particular – they set up house and shop in humble quarters in Whitechapel, Houndsditch, Mile End or Petticoat Lane. One such concentration lay in the relatively poor parish of

[1] E. A. Wrigley, *The Listener*, 6 July 1967, p. 7.
[2] Ralph Davis, *The Rise of the English Shipping Industry*, 1962, p. 390.
[3] House of Lords Record Office, Returns of Papists for 1767, 1780.

St James, Duke's Place, on the northern fringe of the City 'within the Walls'. Already accounting for a quarter of the inhabitants in 1695, their number had risen to more than one-half the population by the early nineteenth century. The parish contained the chief Ashkenazi synagogue (the 'Great Synagogue') and it was there that Jews, in spite of their continuing civic disabilities, first began to play a part in London public life. After 1748, Jews were beginning to attend the vestry meetings, the first Jewish overseer was elected in 1751, and, from the early 1780s onwards, Jews were regularly filling the post of constable, head-borough and scavenger (though not yet of juror or foreman) on the Leet Jury.[1]

Among smaller groups of immigrants were Frenchmen, Germans, Dutch and Portuguese. French immigration dated from the 1680s, when, following Louis XIV's revocation of the Edict of Nantes, Huguenots sought a sanctuary in London and brought their native silk-weaving to Spitalfields; they continued to play a prominent part in the weaving districts throughout the eighteenth century. Germans, Dutchmen and Portuguese added comparatively little to London's population, though their presence may have added to the hostility displayed to foreigners during such popular outbursts as the Gordon Riots of 1780. More significant, particularly in the poorer and more crowded districts, were the increasing numbers of Negroes. They were mainly from the West Indies and (after 1783) from the southern states of North America; but there were also Indian lascar seamen recruited by the East India Company. These various groups may have accounted for 10,000 or more of the population of the capital in the last quarter of the century.[2]

In addition to this movement of population into London from without there was the parallel movement of population from within. In the City of London itself, there had long been a tendency for the poorer tradesmen to move towards the periphery or to the City 'without the Walls' from the City 'within'. This migration was reflected in the wide gap separating the prosperity of some of the parishes from others; so we find that, in 1695, whereas 65 per cent of the inhabitants of St Botolph Billingsgate and nearly 70 per cent in St Matthew Friday paid a surtax on properties of an annual value of £50 and more, the proportion fell to 1.1 per cent in St

---

[1] Alfred Rubens, 'The Jews of the Parish of St James, Duke's Place, in the City of London', in *Remember the Days: Essays on Anglo-Jewish History presented to Cecil Roth*, ed. J. M. Shaftesley, 1962, pp. 181–205.

[2] *London Life*, pp. 116–45.

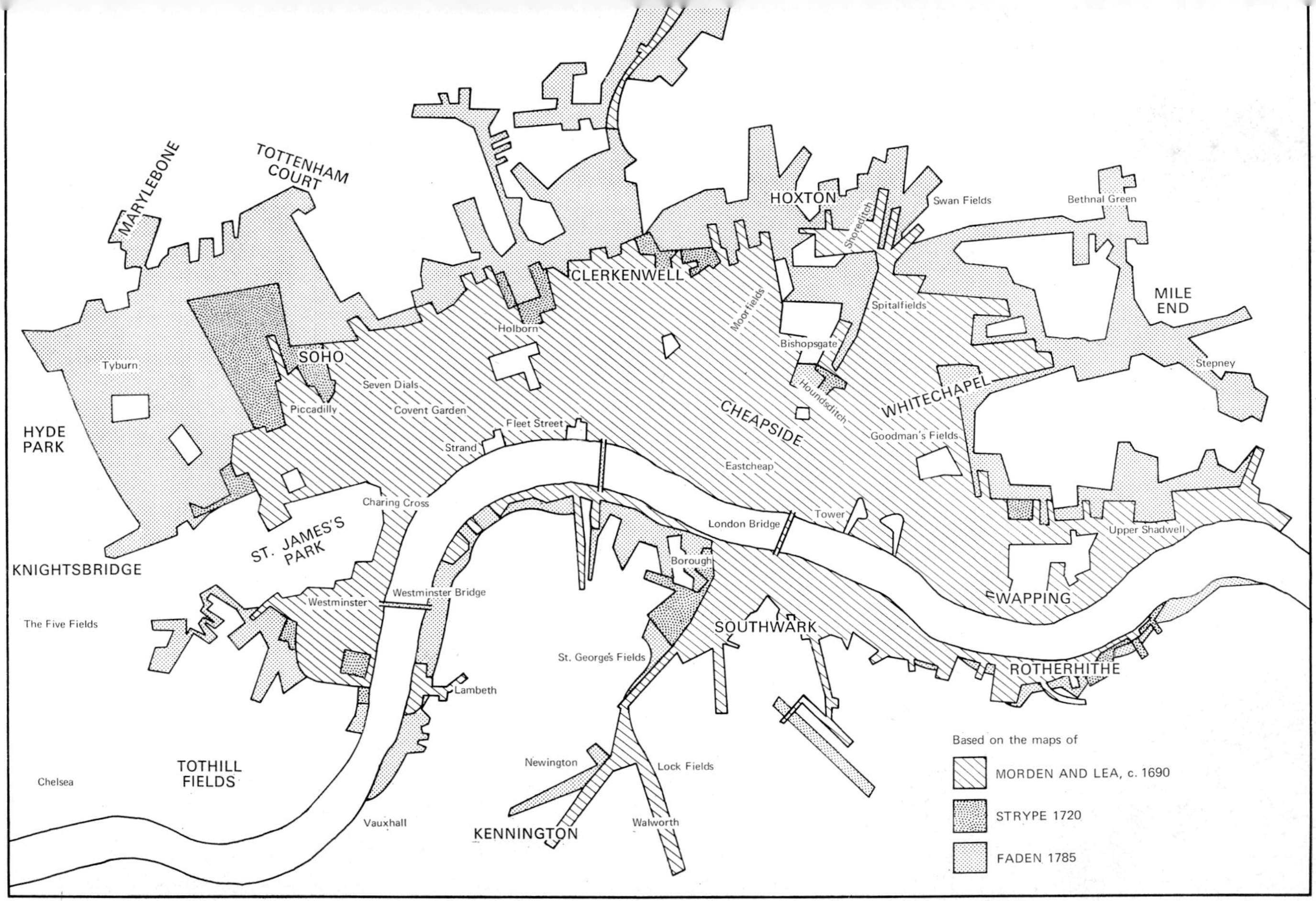
MARYLEBONE
TOTTENHAM COURT
HOXTON
Swan Fields
Bethnal Green
MILE END
Stepney
Tyburn
HYDE PARK
SOHO
CLERKENWELL
Holborn
Moorfields
Shoreditch
Spitalfields
Bishopsgate
Houndsditch
Seven Dials
Piccadilly
Covent Garden
Fleet Street
Strand
CHEAPSIDE
WHITECHAPEL
Goodman's Fields
Eastcheap
Charing Cross
London Bridge
Tower
Upper Shadwell
ST. JAMES'S PARK
KNIGHTSBRIDGE
Westminster
Westminster Bridge
Borough
WAPPING
The Five Fields
SOUTHWARK
St. George's Fields
ROTHERHITHE
Lambeth
Newington
Lock Fields
Chelsea
TOTHILL FIELDS
Vauxhall
KENNINGTON
Walworth
Based on the maps of
MORDEN AND LEA, c. 1690
STRYPE 1720
FADEN 1785

1 The growth of London from 1690 to 1785

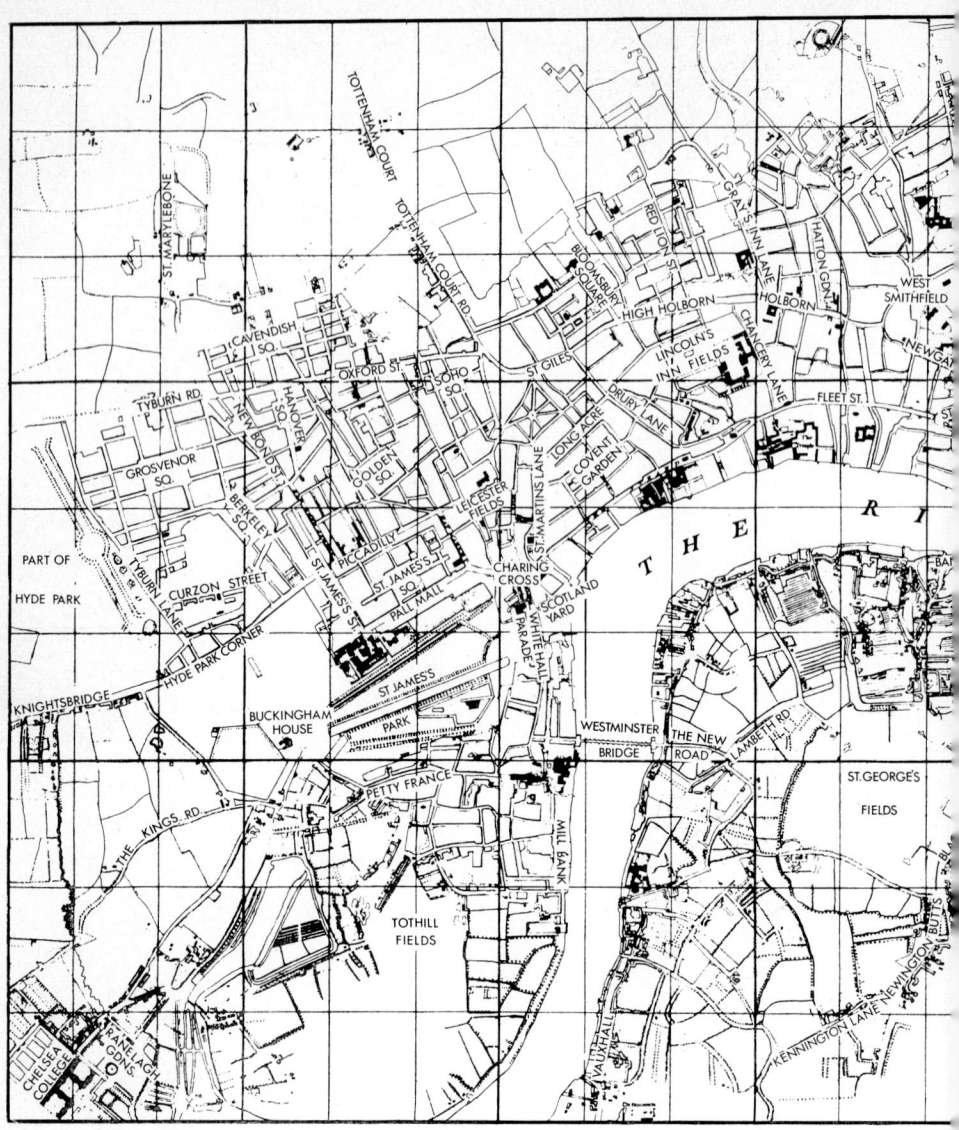

2 London in 1746 (*Based on John Roque's* Plan of the Cities of London and Westminster and Borough of Southwark, *begun in 1737 and published in 1746*)

3 East London in 1746 (*Based on John Roque's* Plan of the Cities of
London and Westminster)

Anne Blackfriar and 0.7 per cent in Allhallows London Wall.[1] Many of these poorer craftsmen left the City altogether and settled in the poorer, but economically 'freer', adjoining districts, some of which had from Elizabeth's time onwards begun to assume the appearance of urban slums. Meanwhile, some of the wealthier citizens migrated from the City westwards, either following the Court to the vicinity of St James's or, increasingly as the eighteenth century advanced, establishing themselves in roomier and more modern houses in Marylebone or Chelsea. The gentry did the same, and there was a parallel and far more considerable migration from the once fashionable *piazzas* and precincts of Covent Garden, Soho and St Giles's into the more newly developed aristocratic quarter at 'the polite end of the town', in St James's or Piccadilly. Henry Fielding gave a spirited, if somewhat exaggerated, picture of this process in 1752:

> Within the memory of many now living the circle of the people of Fascination included the whole parish of Covent Garden and a great part of St Giles in the Fields; but here the enemy broke in and the circle was presently contracted to Leicester Fields and Golden Square. Hence the People of Fashion again retreated before the foe to Hanover Square; whence they were once more driven to Grosvenor Square and even beyond it, and that with so much precipitation, that had they not been stopped by the walls of Hyde Park, it is more than probable they would by this time have arrived at Kensington.[2]

This whole westward movement had reached far greater proportions by the time Archenholtz, a German visitor, wrote, thirty years later, that there had been, 'within the space of twenty years, truly a migration from the east end of London to the west, thousands passing from that part of the city, where new buildings are no longer carried on, and to this end, where fertile fields and the most agreeable gardens are daily metamorphosed into houses and streets'.[3] One consequence of these various migrations was that London's population growth was anything but uniform and that the newer districts expanded rapidly while the older (as Archenholtz

[1] D. V. Glass, 'Notes on the Demography of London at the End of the Seventeenth Century', *Daedalus*, Spring 1968, p. 583; P. E. Jones and A. V. Judges, 'London Population in the late Seventeenth Century', *Economic History Review*, vol. 6, 1935–6, pp. 45–63.

[2] M. Dorothy George, in *Johnson's England*, vol. 1, p. 163.

[3] J. W. Archenholtz, *A View of the British Constitution and of the Manners and Customs of the People of England*, 1794, p. 119.

a demographic constant; an outflow from city interior to outlying districts

had noted) tended to decline. So we find, in the figures published by Dr George, that the population of the City (both 'within' and 'without' the Walls) fell from an estimated 208,300 in 1700 to 134,300 in 1801 and that of the Borough (or Southwark) from 100,000 to 98,700; while Westminster's population increased from 130,000 to 165,000, that of the out-parishes of Middlesex and Surrey from 226,900 to 379,000; and (most sensational of all) that of the five parishes not included in the Bills – Marylebone, St Pancras, Hammersmith, Kensington and Chelsea – increased theirs from a combined total of 9,150 in 1700 to 123,000 in 1801.[1]

A further consequence of these movements was that a growing gulf was drawn between the eastern and western districts of London. Where, earlier, citizens had sought their recreations and country retreats almost indiscriminately either east or west, the east was now becoming more and more the sole preserve of the industrious and poor and the west that of the fashionable and rich. The sharpness of this contrast did not escape Archenholtz when he wrote in the 1780s:

NB – use

> The east end, especially along the shores of the Thames, consists of old houses, the streets there are narrow, dark and ill-paved; inhabited by sailors and other workmen who are employed in the construction of ships and by a great part of the Jews. The contrast between this and the West end is astonishing: the houses here are mostly new and elegant; the squares are superb, the streets straight and open. . . . If all London were as well built, there would be nothing in the world to compare with it.[2]

A similar gulf would soon divide the north from the south. Already the South Bank was becoming a refuse dump for some of the dirtier trades that had been kept out of the City: the tanneries of Bermondsey, for example, and the sprawling timber yards of Lambeth. The process would be carried much further with the building of railways and goods yards in the following century, and the consequent further deformation of the residential areas of South London. Professor Spate has underlined the social distinctions thus increasingly tending to separate the west from the east and south in his picture of London's water supply in the eighteenth and early nineteenth centuries. At the beginning of the eighteenth century, new water companies had been formed to supplement the services performed by the New River Company (formed in 1609–13) up to the time of

[1] *London Life*, p. 319.
[2] J. W. Archenholtz, *A View of the British Constitution*, p. 119.

Queen Anne. The companies took their water direct from the Thames, from the Lea or the springs issuing from the Bagshot sands at Hampstead. Steam engines were introduced in 1754 and 1774, allowing the Shadwell service to be extended; and the West Ham company set up an engine at Old Ford in 1754; but, in these areas, it was only the basements that were generally supplied. In contrast, in the West End, the Chelsea Water Company had been formed, under an Act of 1723, with the specific task of supplying water at an expanding rate as new buildings went up. Here, too, iron pipes were introduced in 1756, while not generally supplied until after 1810. So, with this one-sided development, the west prospered while the south and east stagnated; by 1837 the daily supply of water to each West End house was 218 gallons and 182 gallons to each house in the north, whereas the east received only 143 and the south a mere 93 gallons.[1]

The contrast between east and west, between the poorer and richer districts, was further reflected in the degree of planned development or haphazard sprawl that attended London's eighteenth-century expansion. Such planning as there was was concentrated almost without exception in the west, while in the east, if we except the repeated attempts made by the City authorities to arrest the growth of building, there was virtually none at all.[2] For, to quote Dr George once more: 'While West London was developed largely by the laying out of streets and squares on long leases, regulated by private and local Acts, East London grew obscurely, its development apparently influenced by the customs (confirmed by statute) of the great liberty of the manors of Stepney and Hackney, by which the copy-holders were empowered to grant leases of thirty-one years without fine to the lord of the manor, under penalty of forfeiture of the copy-hold if a longer lease was granted.'[3] Copyhold was not universal in East London, but it was in this and similar ways that Stepney, Spitalfields, Ratcliffe, Limehouse, Wapping, St George in the East (a more recently created parish), Shadwell, Mile End Old Town and Bethnal Green were progressively developed or merely 'filled out' in that 'straggling, confus'd manner', without plan or purpose, so thoroughly deplored by Defoe in his description of London in 1724. But, of course, it was not only the poor who crowded into these districts as the city spread eastwards. They at-

[1] O. H. K. Spate, 'The Growth of London, A.D. 1600–1800', in *An Historical Geography of England before 1800*, pp. 539–41.

[2] *London Life*, pp. 78–82; R. J. Mitchell and M. D. R. Leys, *A History of London Life*, 1963, pp. 179–80.

[3] *London Life*, p. 75.

tracted shipbuilders and brokers, merchants, tradesmen and manufacturers as well; and it was in these eastern out-parishes of Middlesex that the Radical candidates, John Wilkes and John Glynn, were to draw their main support among the wharfingers, lightermen, warehousemen, importers, coal-merchants, shopkeepers and victuallers in the Middlesex elections of 1768 and 1769.[1]

But Defoe exaggerated, of course, when he saw the whole of London's development in these terms: 'out of all shape, uncompact and unequal' and 'just at the pleasure of every builder'. Long before he wrote, the City had been rebuilt after the Fire in accordance with the provisions of a statute jointly devised by the City authorities and the Privy Council, which included an important new prescription: the standardization of new buildings; and already, three years after the Fire, 1,600 houses had been begun or been completed and fourteen churches were in the process of construction. Shortly after, speculators like Nicholas Barbon (the son of the famous Praise-God Barbon – or 'Barebones' – of Cromwell's Parliament of 'saints') had taken over the building of whole new streets on the western and northern outskirts of the City. Barbon had had a large share, for example, in the development of the Bedford estate, adjoining Gray's Inn in Holborn, where land had been let for building in support of local charities and where new streets, such as Bedford Street, Bedford Row, Princes Street and Theobald's Road, had emerged at the end of the old century and in the early years of the new. Meanwhile the London square, the joint creation of the great landlord and the speculative builder, had also begun to provide for the more elegant housing of the aristocracy and gentry. It was a rich field for investment, as the practice was to let land in plots on long leases and at a low ground rent, but on two conditions: that houses of a prescribed type and value should be built and that both houses and land should revert to the ground landlord when the lease expired. Thus enterprising aristocrats lucky enough to own, or shrewd enough to buy, sites suitable for development, became owners of much of the most profitable real estate in London.[2]

The square had made its first appearance (though it was not yet so called) in the Covent Garden *piazza*, promoted by the 4th Earl of Bedford and designed by Inigo Jones, under Charles I in 1631. It had been followed by Leicester Fields (today's Leicester Square) in 1635; and, during the

[1] George Rudé, *Wilkes and Liberty*, 1962, p. 84.

[2] Thomas Pennant, *Some Account of London*, pp. 154–5; Dorothy Marshall, *Dr Johnson's London*, 1968, p. 19.

Restoration, by the Earl of Southampton's Bloomsbury Square (laid out in 1665), Soho Square (1681), Lincoln's Inn Fields and Red Lion Square (1684) and St James's Square (planned for the Earl of St Albans in 1663 and completed in 1684). All these developments resulted, as we have said, from the combined enterprise of noble patrons and speculative builders (men such as Nicholas Barbon, Sir Thomas Bond, Richard Frith, Sir Thomas Neale and Gregory King); but the two building schemes centred round Bloomsbury and St James's Squares, and successively promoted by the Earls of Southampton and St Albans, went further. They firmly established two important new principles of urban development: the presence of the landlord's own house in the square (this had already been seen in the Covent Garden *piazza*), and the principle of a complete unit of development, comprising square, secondary streets, markets and even a church. Thus, though planned in the first place for the greater glory of the aristocratic patron, these schemes became snowballs for further plans of development, including not only shops, inns and markets but also the erection of smaller houses and dwellings for the nobleman's retainers or others of the 'middling' or 'lower sort' of people.[1]

Similar ventures were continued after the Hanoverian Succession, some of them even before Defoe completed his tour of London. Hanover Square and its adjoining streets were promoted and built by the Earl of Scarborough in 1717–19; the Earl of Burlington launched his building projects around his house in Piccadilly at about the same time, and Cavendish Square, the creation of the Harley–Cavendish estate, began to be inhabited in 1724. Shortly after Defoe wrote, these schemes were followed by the Grosvenor estate project, culminating in the emergence of Grosvenor Square between 1725 and 1753, and, after a building 'lull' in the 1730s, by the piecemeal and desultory construction of Berkeley Square in 1739–47.[2]

The succession of wars in which the country engaged in the middle years of the century laid a blighting hand on building and development; and after the Grosvenor and Berkeley Square projects, begun in the 1720s and 1730s, there was little new to record until the next big building boom of the 1760s and 1770s. Among its earliest products were Portland Place, and Portman and Manchester Squares (completed about 1774),

[1] Sir John Summerson, *Georgian England*, 1962, pp. 31–54; Steen Eiler Rasmussen, *London the Unique City*, 1961, pp. 152–8; Donald J. Olsen, *Town Planning in London in the Eighteenth and Nineteenth Centuries*, 1964, pp. 39–42.

[2] *Georgian London*, pp. 98–112.

which began to rise from the fields north of Oxford Street. But these projects were not solely inspired by aristocratic enterprise: they were given more than a merely casual impetus by the completion, nearly twenty years before, of the New Road which, by linking Paddington and Islington and skirting St Pancras and Marylebone, provided a standing invitation to the planned development of northern London. To the same period belong the laying-out of Finsbury Square to the north of the City by George Dance (1777), and two prestigious enterprises carried through on Thames-side: the Adam Brothers' Adelphi (begun in 1768) and Sir William Chambers' Somerset House (in 1776).

The same year saw the first stage of what proved to be the most ambitious, the most protracted and probably the most important of the planned aristocratic building ventures of the century. This was the further development of Bloomsbury by the creation of Bedford Square with its adjoining streets after 1776. Today Bedford Square has the architectural distinction of being the only eighteenth-century square in London that survives virtually intact. At the time it was built, it was the first square since the *piazza* in Covent Garden to be planned and carried through as a single unit; and the contractors were obliged to make footways, pave the streets, lay sewers and to build their houses according to a uniform design, in which the dimensions of each storey and the quality of the materials used in the construction of every part of each house were rigorously prescribed. As the builders' plans proceeded, the Square itself served as a focal point from which a network of streets radiated outwards: following 1776, Charlotte (today's Bloomsbury) and Caroline (today's Adeline) Streets to the south, Bedford (now Bailey) and Tavistock Streets to the west, and Gower, Store and Chenies Streets to the north all began to take shape; and – another novelty – the agreements covering their construction, as those covering the Square itself, provided for leases extending over ninety-nine years. And while the Duke of Bedford himself deserted his Square for Arlington Street, St James's, in 1810, the original development plan continued, with amendments, and went on until the building of Gordon Square rounded off the whole venture in 1860.

A parallel scheme was that launched, as an eastward projection of the Bedford estate, by the Foundling Hospital estate in 1790. It eventually spread over an area bounded on the west by the Bedford estate, on the south by Guilford Street, on the east by Gray's Inn Road and on the north by Tavistock Place, and, over a period of a little over thirty years, came to include Guilford, Millman, Doughty and Grenville Streets, Caroline

Place and Brunswick Square (by 1797), and Bernard, Coram, Kenton, Compton, Henrietta (now Handel), Hunter and Wakefield Streets and Tavistock Place (between 1796 and 1823). These were the last two great projects of urban development until John Nash began, in 1811, to lay the stamp of his genius on Regency London.[1]

With all these extensions and developments, which were so radically transforming the face of the metropolis, one might reasonably suppose that rents and property values rose appreciably, and on occasion sharply, as the century went on; except, of course, in those parts of Southwark or the City in which population stagnated or declined. William Maitland, in his *History of London*, basing his calculations on the sums for which the greater part of the city's buildings were insured with the Fire Offices, believed that the 'constructive' value of the 95,958 houses within the Bills of Mortality amounted, in 1739, to a total of £28,562,463 16s. 10½d. Using these figures and what he knew of the average rent in a number of City wards (£4 8s. 7½d. in a poor district such as East Smithfield, compared with £48 in Cheap and £56 in Langbourn Ward), he made the further calculation that the sum total of annual values, or rents, in London amounted to £1,919,380, corresponding to an average rent of £20 per house.[2] Unfortunately, owing to the vagaries and complexities of the eighteenth-century rating system, it is difficult to arrive at entirely satisfactory conclusions by other means. It might seem useful, for instance, to compare the assessments for the county rate in different parishes and at different times. But, in Middlesex, the proportion levied on the parishes remained fixed according to custom until an Act of 1797.[3] Another tantalizing source of enquiry is provided by the annual assessments for the land tax; but this, too, proves to be of little use, as these were 'block' assessments which took no account of individual properties or streets and, like the tax assessments of eighteenth-century France, were based more on abstract and traditional assumptions than on the current realities of urban growth. So we find that the quotas levied on the City's twenty-eight wards, after remaining constant or slightly falling at ten-year intervals between 1722 and 1783, actually took a sharp downward turn after the greater part of the Tower Ward was transferred to Stepney in the early 1790s.[4]

[1] Donald J. Olsen, *Town Planning in London*, pp. 44–57, 74–84.
[2] William Maitland, *The History and Survey of London*, 1760, pp. 753–6.
[3] *London Life*, pp. 413–14.
[4] G[uildhall] L[ibrary], MSS. 11295/1–20, 11316/69–71, 121–3, 168–70.

It is rather more rewarding to take samples from the tax or rate-collectors' books, as these usually give the current annual values (or 'rents') of individual properties street by street. But these, too, have to be used with the greatest caution and do not necessarily provide us with the information that the entry in the 'Rents' column would appear to indicate. For one thing, as in the City, new occupants frequently paid a 'fine' in order to secure their lease; thus the figure in the 'Rents' column may be greater than the nominal rent or the rent that was actually paid.[1] A more serious obstacle is that, in Marylebone certainly and probably elsewhere, the so-called 'rent' is not, strictly speaking, a rent at all but the 'rateable value' on which the local assessment was made, and thus liable to fluctuate with any change in its rating procedures made by the authority concerned. (Mr Francis Sheppard gives the example of a house in Queen Anne Street, Marylebone, whose 'rent' – alias 'assessment' – was reduced from £60 to £49 in the space of a couple of years.)[2]

So even the rate books, for all the value of the information they provide, are no sure and infallible guide to the actual variations in rents and property values as between one parish and another or between one decade and the next. Yet, with this important qualification, they may serve a useful purpose all the same. They can help us to distinguish a wealthy mansion from a 'middling' house and a 'middling' house from a poor man's tenement or cottage, or to distinguish a prosperous street or neighbourhood from one that was poor or going to seed. Moreover, they can help us to determine by and large whether rents or property values were, over a given period, rising or falling or merely stagnating. From such records we can tell, for example, that, in the City, even after the 1760s (when prices generally rose), the annual values of properties remained remarkably constant and that such changes as took place usually went with a change of ownership or tenancy or with an extension or development of the property concerned. (The value of large businesses, for instance, tended to rise: thus the 'rents' of the offices and warehouses of the East India Company in Fenchurch Street and Crutched Friars rose steeply, and possibly trebled, between 1771 and 1807.)[3]

But the City was, generally speaking, an area of residential decline

---

[1] I am indebted to Mr P. E. Jones, Deputy Keeper of Records at the London Guildhall, for this information.

[2] F. H. W. Sheppard, *Local Government in St Marylebone 1688–1835*, 1958, pp. 151–2. See also pp. 205–6.

[3] G.L. MSS., Sewer Rate, 2137/1–4 (1771), 33–6 (1791), 65–8 (1807).

rather than one of rapid development or 'improvement'. The case was, of course, different with the fashionable parishes of Westminster, the development areas of Holborn, and the expanding new villages 'beyond the Bills'; so, in their case, the pattern, as might be expected, varied somewhat from that described above. Yet, here again (as noted of the City by Maitland), it appears that property values stagnated, or even fell, before the middle of the century – and even before the sixties: prosperous residential districts such as St George's and St James's and Cavendish Square, Marylebone, seem to be cases in point. But after the 1760s, values in these areas, unlike those in the City of London, appear to have risen steadily, and even sharply. Once more the advance seems to have been greatest where properties changed hands, leases were renewed, or where existing owners or occupiers made improvements or extensions; and it was most marked of all in areas that were becoming fashionable, like the Grosvenor estate or Cavendish Square, or which were part of a general area of development, like most of the parish of Marylebone. In some cases, the increase was greatest between the 1750s and the 1780s or early nineties; this appears, for example, to have been so with Leicester Fields and Cavendish Square. In others, as on the Grosvenor estate in St George's and the Bedford estate in Holborn, the increase was noticeably greater in the ten to twenty years of inflation between the early 1790s and the opening decade of the nineteenth century. On the Bedford estate values appear, during this period, in some cases to have doubled and, in others, to have risen by one-half or one-third; and from another source we learn that the income from rents on the Grosvenor estate rose from £7,500 in 1795 to £12,000 in 1802.[1]

Something more remains to be said about London's expansion into the surrounding countryside. We have already noted two ways in which this expansion might take place: the gradual and haphazard filling-up of the riverside districts to the east, mainly in response to commercial and economic needs; and the more organized expansion northwards (and to a lesser degree south-westwards) prompted by the building of the New Road, the new bridges across the Thames and the enterprises of such

[1] W[estminster] P[ublic] L[ibrary], Rate Books, St Anne, A. 91, 216, 1619, 1655; St George, C. 1, 137, 296, 393, 540, 553; St James, D. 48, 68, 116, 129. H[olborn] P[ublic] L[ibrary], Rate Books, St Andrew and St George the Martyr, 1730, 1760, 1788, 1808. M[arylebone] P[ublic] L[ibrary], Rate Books, 1683–1728, 1730, 1752, 1788, 1807. G. E. Mingay, *English Landed Society in the Eighteenth Century*, 1963, p. 58.

C

noble patrons as the Duke of Bedford in Bloomsbury. But there was a
third way, as piecemeal, involuntary and unplanned as the first. This was
the gradual conversion of Thames-side villages and rural districts of Essex,
Surrey and Middlesex first into rural retreats, subsequently into residential suburbs, for Church of England prelates, aristocrats and City merchants. Of the first, the Bishops of London, as lords of the manors of
Stepney and Hackney, long had a country residence at Bethnal Green;
while the Bishops of Winchester had, since the 1660s, had a palace in
Cheyne Walk, in Chelsea. John Strype, in 1720, gives an enthusiastic
account of the aristocratic penetration into the 'towns seated on the
Thames': he mentions, in particular, the Duke of Beaufort's and Lord
Cheyne's mansions (the latter soon to be sold to Sir Hans Sloane) at
Chelsea; the Earl of Peterborough's 'stately' house at Parsons Green; the
Earl of Falconbergh's seat at Chiswick; the Earl of Bradford's mansion at
Twickenham; the Earl of Torrington's at Weybridge; the Duke of
Northumberland's majestic seat at Sion House, near Brentford, and
numerous houses built for London gentry at Fulham, Isleworth and
Richmond. Defoe, not to be outdone, writes of 3,000 houses, mainly built
since the Restoration, of which many 'would pass for palaces', lying west
and north and within a radius of a dozen to twenty miles from London;
and he instances Lord Halifax's seat at Bushy Park; the country homes of
the Earls of Marr, Bradford, Strafford, Shrewsbury and Burlington, and
of Lords Brook and Dunbar; and, among the gentry, those of Sir Thomas
Frankland, Sir Godfrey Kneller and Sir Stephen Fox, the latter's house
at Chiswick being described as 'the flower of all the private gentlemen's
palaces in England'.[1]

Meanwhile, the City's merchants had not been slow to follow suit.
Already in the fifteenth century, we read of City butchers and bakers as
tenants of the manor of Tooting Bec and of a dozen Lord Mayors of
London buying country properties, mainly in Essex, which was then the
most fashionable of the City's rural outposts. Sir Josiah Child, wealthiest
of London's merchants and company directors of the late seventeenth
century, built Wanstead House, near Leytonstone; and Defoe writes of
'several very considerable estates purchas'd and now enjoy'd' by London
tradesmen in this part of Essex: he makes particular mention of Mr
Western, an iron merchant, near Kelvedon; Mr Cresnor, a wholesale

---

[1] *London Life*, p. 77; Wheatley and Cunningham, vol. 1, pp. 375–80; Strype, *A Survey*, pp. 44–5; *A Tour*, vol. 2, pp. 12–13.

grocer, at Earl's Colne; Mr Olemus, near Braintree; and Sir Thomas Webster, at Copthall.[1]

Middlesex, too, was being opened up as a 'dormitory' for London merchants. Mr Michael Robbins tells us of a City haberdasher who, in 1709, regularly commuted between his City shop and his home in Enfield and of a stage-coach proprietor of South Mimms who, a few years later, claimed exemption from serving as high constable of Edmonton on the grounds that he spent most of his time at his place of business in Goswell Street, Clerkenwell! He also quotes Thomas Coxe writing of Middlesex in 1724: 'We may call it almost all London, being inhabited chiefly by the citizens, who fill the towns in it with their county houses, to which they offer resort that they may breathe a little sweet air, free from the fog and smoke of the City.' This was, no doubt, an exaggeration, for even in 1793 only 300 of London's 16,000 merchants and tradesmen listed in *The Universal British Directory* appear to have held Middlesex freeholds. But even this marked a considerable penetration of the country by the town. The 'urban' out-parishes (a recognized part of the metropolis) in the 1760s already accounted for nearly half the county's voters; and even the mainly rural parishes of Brentford, Chiswick, Edmonton, Highgate, Isleworth and Tottenham were already well on the way to being fully 'colonized' by Londoners and to being incorporated within their city. The point is emphasized by the rapid rise in the population of the Middlesex parishes, some of them nearly doubling in size (including Brentford and Tottenham) between the 1730s and 1780s.[2]

The census of 1801 took stock of these realities and included in its return for London such Surrey parishes as Putney, Clapham, Wandsworth, Streatham and Richmond, and extended the out-parishes of Middlesex to embrace Chiswick, Ealing, Edmonton, Tottenham, Enfield, Harrow, Twickenham, Staines and Uxbridge.[3] Thus, by varied and devious means, the metropolis of London had considerably extended its boundaries since Defoe's account of almost eighty years before.

[1] *A Tour*, vol. 2, p. 15.
[2] Michael Robbins, *Middlesex*, 1953, pp. 190–1, 365–7; *Wilkes and Liberty*, p. 80.
[3] Besant, p. 76.

2

Economic Life

THE CENSUS, as we saw, spoke of late eighteenth-century London as 'the greatest Emporium in the known world'. It was no exaggeration; and, with its rapidly rising population, London was also a vast consumers' market, a considerable manufacturing city, the largest centre of international trade and shipping in the country, and was already well on the way to supplanting Amsterdam as the leader of the world's insurance and money market.

It was natural that with a population rising during the century from 575,000 to 900,000 (and, even in 1801, twelve times the size of any other city), London should have provided the biggest and most important consumers' market in the Kingdom. It had to be supplied daily with such quantities of water, fuel, food and other necessities of life, not to mention the luxuries that its wealth demanded, as imposed problems of distribution and economic organization not only on the metropolis itself but on almost every part of the country. The magnitude of this problem can be measured by the fact that, in the year 1725 alone, London consumed 369,000 quarters of flour, 60,000 calves, 70,000 sheep and lambs, 187,000 swine, 52,000 sucking pigs, 115,000 bushels of oysters, 14,750,000 mackerel, 1,398 boatloads of cod, haddock and whiting, 16,366,000 lb of butter, 21,066,000 lb of cheese, 5 million gallons of milk, 475,000 chaldrons of coal – not to mention 1,970,989 barrels of beer, 30,000 tuns of wine, 11,200,000 gallons of spirits, and vast quantities of hay and oats for the 22,639 horses which, by 1739, were housed in her mews and stables. And, as the population grew, these figures naturally tended to expand with it: the amount of bread that was baked, for example, was based on an annual consumption of a quarter of wheat per head, and the number of chaldrons of coal consumed rose from 475,000 in 1726 to over a million in 1800.[1]

The point was well taken by Daniel Defoe, who, in his *Tour Through the Whole Island of Great Britain*, continually returns to the theme that 'this whole Kingdom, as well as the people, as the land, and even the sea, in every part of it, are employ'd to furnish something, and I may add the best of every thing, to supply the city of London with provisions; I mean by provisions, corn, flesh, fish, butter, cheese, salt, fewel, timber, &c. and cloths also; with every thing necessary for building, and furniture for their own use, or for trades'.[2] And, as he travelled, he methodically noted the products that found their way from the provinces to the London markets. From Suffolk came butter, cheese and corn, partly shipped from the old and decaying port of Dunwich and its small auxiliary, Walberswick, and partly direct from the great corn and butter market of Woodbridge. From Suffolk, too, and from Norfolk came turkeys, chickens, geese and mutton; Yarmouth also sent herrings and supplied, besides, a great part of the barges for the coal trade. Essex sent mutton and large consignments of fish – sole, turbot, whiting, codling and flounder – from Shoeburyness, at the mouth of the Thames. Sea fish – herrings, flat fish and mackerel – came from the Sussex and Kentish coast; and salmon from the Severn and Trent. Cheshire, Gloucester and Somerset sent cheese; and faggots and 'bavins' for fuel came from Shooter's Hill, in Kent, and 'sea-coal' from Newcastle. Sheep came from Lincoln and Leicestershire, bullocks from Kent, cattle from Wales and the Highlands of Scotland, those from Anglesea and Skye having to swim the first part of their journey to the mainland. Paving stones for London's houses came from the quarries of Dorset and Kent (and also from Aberdeen). Hereford sent bacon and both Hereford and Devon sent cider. From Surrey came Dorking capon and oats and meal from the Croydon market and vegetables from the Lambeth market-gardens. Chichester, in Sussex, sent corn and meal. The largest supplier of all was Kent which, in addition to its fish, fire-wood, bullocks and paving stones, sent corn, timber, the best oysters from Faversham and Swale, and great quantities of cherries and apples from the rich orchards around Maidstone.[3]

[1] Besant, pp. 299–301; Raymond Smith, *Sea-Coal for London*, 1961, pp. 141; Steen Eiler Rasmussen, *London the Unique City*, p. 119.

[2] *A Tour*, vol. 1, p. 12. See also vol. 1, pp. 3, 55, 59.

[3] *A Tour*, vol. 1, pp. 9, 11–12, 45, 53, 55, 58–60, 67, 100, 112–14, 135, 157, 209; vol. 2, pp. 49, 131.

This gives us a useful picture of how London was provided in the early eighteenth century, and much of it remained valid for the period as a whole. Later, she also became the largest market for Lancashire cottons, for the lace made in Buckinghamshire, Bedfordshire and Devon, and for the gloves made around Worcester, Hereford and Ludlow. And it is noticeable that the produce of Middlesex gets little or no mention in Defoe's account. It was, in fact, not until the 1750s and the Enclosure Acts of the 1760s that the county began to play a significant part in supplying London's markets. Not so much in grain; for, even in 1798, wheat was grown on only 7,000 acres (notably at Hendon, Cranford and Norwood). But the northern parishes became the chief supplier of London's hay, and also sent her plentiful consignments of barley, beans and peas; and three-quarters of the fruit sold in Covent Garden, towards the end of the century, came from a seven-mile stretch of road, lined with orchards, running through Hammersmith, Chiswick and Brentford to Isleworth and Twickenham.[1]

How did all this richly varied produce reach the London markets? Fish and coal came to Billingsgate; fruit and vegetables to Covent Garden, to the Borough Market (closed in 1755), or to the open cherry and apple market at the Three Cranes Wharf. Corn came to the riverside markets at Bear Quay and Queenhithe, or even was sold 'on the pavement' at Newgate, until the Corn Exchange began to supplant them in 1760. Poultry, game and eggs, and hides and skins were sent to Leadenhall; broad-cloth to Blackwell Hall, meal and malt to Queenhithe, and cattle, sheep and horses to the great Metropolitan cattle market at Smithfield. Hay, next to coal the bulkiest cargo of all, was delivered at four markets (at one time six), strategically placed at four widely separated corners of the city – the Haymarket, Smithfield, Whitechapel and the Borough (to which Paddington was added after 1801). Yet roads were notoriously bad in the early eighteenth century, both those within the capital and those converging on it. In London they were ill-paved and heavily congested, for in 1739 there were already 2,484 private carriages and 1,100 carriages for hire. Besides, the main thoroughfares (along Fleet Street and the Strand and along High Holborn and Oxford Street) ran east to west rather than north to south: the one exception was the southern projection of the old Ware Road, which meandered through Shoreditch and the City over London Bridge to the Borough and Newington Butts. The roads radiating out from London were considerably worse, except those few

[1] Michael Robbins, *Middlesex*, pp. 25, 35–8.

constructed by the turnpike commissioners since 1697; and Defoe, having taken careful stock of the roads to Harwich, to York and Scotland, Baldock and Bedford, Derby, Worcester and Holyhead, and having noted such improvements as had been made, concludes nevertheless sadly that 'the land trade of England has been greatly obstructed by the exceeding badness of the roads'.[1]

But bad as they were, the roads carried a large volume of this traffic. Cattle from Scotland, Wales and Kent and sheep from Lincoln and Leicester trudged many a weary mile to market; and, in one of his most colourful and most quoted passages, Defoe describes the great droves of turkeys that marched for seventy or eighty miles from villages in Norfolk or 'High' Suffolk, via Sudbury and Clare or Newmarket Heath, or 'over Stratford-Bridge on the River Stour' along the Ipswich–London road, to Leadenhall Market. In Defoe's day, too, the roads were used to convey geese and chickens by carriage from East Anglian farms and (more surprisingly) bacon and cider from Hereford; and, later in the century, convoys of horses brought hay to the London markets, and corn from the east midlands counties was carried by road to the mills at Hertford and Ware, whence it continued its journey down the Lea to the wharves at Queenhithe and Bear Quay.

But inevitably, and not only because of the poor state of the roads, the greater volume of goods arrived by sea and river: Defoe instances fish, butter, cheese and corn from Suffolk; cheese from Cheshire, Gloucester and Warwick; meal from Chichester; coals from Newcastle; faggots and bavins from Shooter's Hill; and cherries, oysters and apples from Kent; though he regrets, in particular, that herrings, mackerel, whiting and sprats from the East Anglian coast have to travel by sea rather than by road. Communications improved considerably in the second half of the century: the New Road and its extensions, after 1756, and the two new bridges at Westminster and Blackfriars (not to mention the paving of streets after 1762) all served to relieve the congestion of London's internal traffic; and, between 1760 and 1809, 1,514 further laws were passed relating to turnpikes, many of which brought welcome improvements to the roads leading in and out of London. But sea and river continued to be the main channels of supply. Of the bulkiest goods delivered, hay alone was

[1] O. H. K. Spate, 'The Growth of London', in *An Historical Geography of England before A. D., 1800*, pp. 541–2; Steen Eiler Rasmussen, *London the Unique City*, pp. 119–21; T. C. Barker and Michael Robbins, *A History of London Transport*, 1963, vol. 1, pp. 1–10; *A Tour*, vol. 1, pp. 117–32, 343–6.

entirely dependent on horse transport. Corn from the granaries of the Upper Thames basin, the Farnham area of Surrey, the east midlands counties, Kent and East Anglia came variously down the Wey, the Lea, up the Thames estuary, or by the 'long sea' route around the Kentish coast. And the largest consignments of all – 'sea-coal' from Newcastle – continued to arrive, in ever larger quantities, by coastwise shipping and river barge: the value of cargoes was said to be £1,800,000 in 1796, and that year there were 1,200 barges employed in the delivery of coal out of a total of 2,500 lighters and 1,000 other small craft afloat on London's river. A part of this traffic was diverted to inland waterways after the London branch of the Grand Trunk Canal opened in 1801, thus allowing coal to come direct from the Staffordshire pits to north London – and thus also denting the monopoly hitherto enjoyed in the London market by Newcastle and Durham and the Northumberland coal-owners.[1]

But, of course, while she drew heavily on the provinces for her basic means of subsistence, London also contributed substantially from her own resources for her material needs as a great urban community. Like every major city, she had a wide multiplicity of trades and crafts, variously engaged in producing, retailing and distributing, within her metropolitan boundaries. How many 'trades' were there? To the traditionalist who still looked back to the days when every form of economic activity was regulated by gilds and 'companies', remarkably few: John Strype, for example, writing in 1720, appears only to pay serious attention to the sixty trades represented by the old City Companies, which he solemnly lists in strict order of precedence. More realistically, a 'General Description of all Trades', published in London in 1747, accounts for 135 crafts and 80 other occupations, and accompanies the record with a statement of the numbers employed, their hours of work and wages, the capital needed to start up in them, the conditions and cost of apprenticeship, and other useful information of the kind. But even this extended list was inclined to limit its conception of a 'trade' to one which was organized in the traditional way, with small master-craftsmen employing a small number of journeymen and a couple of apprentices serving a fixed term. Yet there were by now innumerable trades and occupations which had grown up outside or had long outlived the traditional framework of 'company' or

[1] *A Tour*, vol. 1, pp. 53–5, 100, 112–14, 131–2, 135, 147; Steen Eiler Rasmussen, *London the Unique City*, pp. 121–3; O. H. K. Spate, in *An Historical Geography of England*, pp. 542–5; Raymond Smith, *Sea-Coal for London*, pp. 51, 141. See also H. L. Beales, 'Travel and Communications', in *Johnson's England*, vol. 1, pp. 125–59.

gild. Of the first were the growing number of productive and servicing trades, which had developed on almost modern capitalist lines, recognizing no limit to the number of workpeople they employed and no economic laws other than those of supply and demand. Of the second, there were old trades like silk-weaving, which, though nominally organized on the old craft basis and nominally subscribing to the regulations of the gild, in practice paid little more than lip-service to the old rules prescribing the number of apprentices and journeymen they might employ. So in 1745, when the Young Pretender threatened to march on London, we find 133 master weavers in Spitalfields pledging the military service of their journeymen, who, on average, numbered twenty-three, but in six cases numbered over sixty and in two cases over a hundred![1]

These new realities were the subject of constant complaints by the more conservative-minded, but they were rarely methodically recorded, even in the directories of the day. For a faithful record (though it only covers a part of the capital) we must look to the occasional Westminster poll book. That of 1749, for example, classifies its 9,465 voters in 395 trades and occupations, of which the most numerous are victuallers (846), tailors (491), carpenters (379), peruke-makers (300), shoemakers (285), butchers (271), chandlers (269), bakers (183) and distillers (141). The list tended, as we should expect, to grow longer as the century progressed; and the London Directory of 1791 (covering a wider field, though most certainly incomplete) accounted for no fewer than 492 occupations practised by the tradesmen and shopkeepers of the capital.[2]

There are, of course, numerous ways in which one might attempt to classify so wide a range of occupations: by their wealth and profitability, by their social status, the degree of skill required for their exercise, their numerical importance (note the number of victuallers and distillers in Westminster!), by their geographical distribution, the type of service they performed, their presumed importance to the economy or by the broader 'industry' to which they belonged. Here, in a brief survey, it may be best to confine oneself to the three broad categories, based on industry and type of service, adopted by Dr George in her *London Life*:

First, trades catering for London's position as an important national and international market and the chief *entrepôt* for Britain's coastwise and

[1] *London Gazette*, 5 October 1745.
[2] Strype, *A Survey*, p. 165; *A General Description of all Trades*, 1747; *Alphabetical List of those who Polled in the Westminster By-Election of 1749* (MS. transcript in W.P.L.); London Directory, 1791.

overland trade. Such trades include ship-, boat- and barge-building and their subsidiaries, cooperages, breweries, distilleries, sugar-refiners and other enterprises catering for export as well as for the home market.

Secondly, trades providing high-class goods for which London enjoyed (in Great Britain, at least) a high reputation: trades such as clock and watchmaking, cutlery (especially surgical instruments), plate, jewellery, furniture, saddlery and coach-building.

Thirdly, an allied or overlapping group of trades supplying the wants of a large luxury-loving part of the population: coffee-houses, chocolate-makers, peruke-makers and barbers, shoemakers and tailors, silk-weavers, mantua-makers and milliners, and the various branches of the building trade.[1] And we might add, and distribute over all three groups, a number of other trades that figure prominently in the Westminster poll book: food-retailers (bakers, butchers, grocers, victuallers and chandlers), men engaged in the carrying trades (coachmen and coach-makers, porters and watermen), booksellers, stationers, surgeons and apothecaries.

Of course, a great many of these trades and services had, by their very nature, to be within easy reach of the whole community and were therefore found fairly evenly distributed over the residential parts of London. But, even among the comparatively petty trades practised by the electors of Westminster in 1749, we find a certain regional distribution and the tendency of some trades to belong to one parish rather to another. For example, clockmakers and poulterers were nearly all to be found in St George's; cheesemongers and cabinet-makers in St James's; watermen and builders' labourers in St Margaret's; card-makers, booksellers and lace-men in St Martin's; and brokers tended to congregate in St James's, St Margaret's and St Martin's (while being conspicuously absent from St Anne's Soho, St Clement Dane's, St George Hanover Square and St Paul Covent Garden). But these are relatively minor variations and can largely be explained in terms of the social and economic differences of the parishes concerned: thus, wealthy residential parishes like St George's and St James's would stimulate a larger demand for luxury products, watermen would naturally be found in the largest numbers on the Thames-side near what soon became Westminster Bridge, while card-makers or booksellers would be more inclined to set up shop in the commercial quarter formed by the streets around the Strand.

But, in the case of the large productive trades, regional distribution was bound to be more pronounced, either because of their local, tradi-

[1] *London Life*, p. 162.

tional associations, or because they had been excluded from the City as being obnoxious or obstreperous, or because they had deliberately chosen to free themselves from the 'freedom' and regulations of City Company, gild or Common Council. Thus, clockmakers and jewellers were to be found mainly in Clerkenwell and the neighbouring parish of St Luke's. In 1798 there were said to be 7,000 watchmaking artisans in Clerkenwell alone, and a further 1,000 in St Luke's; at this time, 120,000 watches were being made each year in Clerkenwell, 70,000 of them for export. Potters were concentrated in three districts: Chelsea, Lambeth and Bow. Silk-weaving, originally established in small groups in Whitechapel and Shoreditch, had spread in the late seventeenth century to Stepney and, with the arrival of the French Huguenots, to Spitalfields; and from there, again, it had more recently spread farther to Bethnal Green, Moorfields and Mile End Old Town. 'Cow-keeping', not surprisingly, was centred on Islington, which supplied most of the city's milk. Timber yards were mainly to be found in Lambeth, soap-makers in Southwark, and the metal trades to the north of Smithfield. Tanners and leather-dressers (like slaughterers) tended, because of the obnoxious nature of their craft, to be confined to the misty wasteland of Bermondsey; others, together with glue-makers, were drawn to the cattle market at Smithfield. Other subsidiary trades, like starch-making, might be centred around London's grain markets. The large brewers and distillers (unlike the petty beermen and spirit-makers of the Westminster poll book) had set up their shops and warehouses at some distance from the centre. So, in 1769, we find Henry Thrale, Dr Johnson's friend, established in Park Street, Southwark; Sir Joseph Mawbey, M.P., in Vauxhall; Sir Ben Trueman in Brick Lane, Spitalfields; and Samuel Whitbread in Chiswell Street, St Luke's. Brewing had become a major business and was rapidly expanding. Pennant lists the twenty-four largest brewers of 1786, together with their annual output of strong beer, ranging from 10,000 barrels at the lowest to 150,000 barrels in the case of Samuel Whitbread. That year, they and all the other brewers between them brewed a total of nearly 5 million barrels of porter (much of it for export), $1\frac{1}{2}$ million barrels of small beer and over $\frac{1}{2}$ million barrels of table beer.[1]

But, impressive as was the range of London's craftsmanship and the volume of her industry, as a manufacturing centre she was gradually being challenged. At the time of the Restoration she was outstanding as

[1] O. H. K. Spate, in *An Historical Geography of England*, p. 534; Thomas Pennant, *Some Account of London*, pp. 266–7; *London Life*, pp. 175–9; *Wilkes and Liberty*, p. 4.

by far the largest industrial producer in the country. Her pre-eminence remained, but as the Industrial Revolution took root in the midlands and the north, it was no longer as conspicuous as it had been a hundred years before. One feature of her relative decline was the flight of established trades from London into midlands towns and country districts, either to escape the stricter craft regulations of the capital or to seek cheaper food and fuel, lower wages and rents, or closer proximity to raw materials. A case in point is shoemaking, which, by 1738, was already beginning to migrate to Northampton; a dozen years later, it was said that shoes sold in London were chiefly made in the country where labour was cheaper. Similarly, framework knitting, which became so conspicuously associated, during the Industrial Revolution, with the 'hosiery' counties of Leicester, Derby and Nottingham, had at first been firmly centred in London – largely in Shoreditch and Norton Folgate. In 1660 London's 400 knitting frames contrasted with the 250 frames scattered over the rest of the country. As the industry grew at the turn of the century, there was a general expansion, but the balance had decisively shifted: in 1727 there were 2,500 frames in London and 4,600 frames in the rising 'hosiery' counties. Between 1732 and 1750, 800 frames were removed from London to Nottingham, which, by 1789, already eclipsed the London stockingers with its 3,000 frames. By 1750 only 1,000 frames remained in London, and by 1782 a mere 500 of a national total of 20,000 frames.[1]

But if London's eminence as a manufacturing centre was no more conspicuous than that of any other large north-European capital, such as Paris, her position as an international port and a centre of trade was quite unique. It was, in fact, trade rather than manufacture that dominated her economy in the eighteenth century, as it had done in the latter part of the seventeenth.[2] In the first chapter we noted the suggestion that perhaps one-quarter of London's population, at the beginning of the century, depended for their livelihood on one or other of the numerous trades associated with the port of London. It is also remarkable to note the high proportion of the nation's trade and shipping that passed through London's Pool. By the end of the seventeenth century, which had witnessed a phenomenal expansion in her foreign trade, England was importing nearly £6 million and exporting over £7 million of goods a

[1] *London Life*, p. 199; J. D. Chambers, *Nottinghamshire in the Eighteenth Century*, 1966, pp. 92–5, 111–14; E. Lipson, *The Economic History of England*, 1947, vol. 1. pp. 106–8, 343.

[2] E. A. Wrigley, *Past and Present*, no. 37, July 1967, p. 62.

year. Her trade was divided, in varying and changing proportions, between half a dozen trading areas: Northern Europe (the so-called 'Baltic trade', covering Norway, North Russia, Denmark and the Baltic coast); 'Nearby' Europe (Holland, France, Germany, Flanders, Ireland); Spain and Portugal, including the Canaries, Madeira and the Azores; the Mediterranean countries other than Spain and France; East India (the world east of the Cape); the West Indies and the slave coast of Africa; and North America. In almost all these areas and in the trade associated with them, London had played a dominant and pioneering role; the exceptions were long-distance fishing, coal exporting and the Irish trade. Since the Restoration, an increasing proportion of England's trade had been with the Baltic nations, whose timber was imported in growing quantities both for shipbuilding and house-building and, in London's case, for the rebuilding of the City; and, even more strikingly, in the rapidly expanding colonial trade with America and the West Indies. Four-fifths of the increase in England's shipbuilding during this period has been attributed to the expansion in these trades; and of this increase London had the lion's share, as she had of the new colonial products – sugar, tobacco, rice and ginger – which (with tea from India and wines from Portugal and France) catered for a rising demand among her expanding population. In return, she increased the exports of her own woollens, cloths, leather, metals, fish, corn and porter, and the re-exports of colonial products to her European neighbours. In short, by 1700, London handled no less than 80 per cent of England's imports, 69 per cent of her exports, 86 per cent of her re-exports and 77 per cent of the combined foreign trade of the Kingdom. She also outmatched all other English ports in terms of shipping: in 1702 she owned far more than the combined tonnage of the rest of the nation's ports (140,000 against 103,000 tons), and eight times that of her nearest rival, Bristol. This volume of shipping delighted Daniel Defoe when he visited the Pool and found in it 'above two thousand sails of all sorts, not reckoning barges, lighters or pleasure-boats, and yachts; but of vessels that really go to sea'.

The new century saw a general increase in England's foreign trade, and of this London continued to hold a substantial share. The West Indies trade, in particular, continued to expand at a rapid pace: the import of sugar multiplied five times over, and of the 153,000 hosgheads imported into England in 1792, 105,000 were landed in the port of London. More generally, the value of foreign imports brought to London rose from £4·8 million in 1700 to £5·5 million in 1750 (after a decline in the war years 1739–48) and to £12·3 million in 1790; and exports from £5·4 to £8·4 and £10·7 million; and the tonnage of London-based ships engaged in foreign trade rose from 157,000 in 1705 to 235,000 in 1751 and 620,000 in 1794. At this time, she was still pre-eminent among England's ports, but *relatively* her position had gradually declined. Liverpool built new docks between 1710 and 1721, and soon an increasing proportion of American cotton, which had previously been handled by London, would be directed to Liverpool for the growing textile industries of Manchester. The western ports, too, were gaining a monopoly of the slave trade and an increasing share of West Indian sugar and tobacco, and, as the Industrial Revolution took root in the midlands and the north, the bulk of the Baltic and Norwegian trade was veering towards Newcastle and the north-east coast. It was a gradual process and Defoe, in 1724, still wrote of London 'that sucks the vitals of trade in this island to itself'. But London's predominance was already well past its peak; her percentage of the tonnage of ships entering English ports had already declined from 59 in 1686 to 54 in 1718, and would decline to 49 in 1772; while her share of the nation's foreign trade fell from 77 per cent in 1700 to 67 per cent in 1737 and 65 per cent in 1792.[1]

Yet London remained throughout a great and expanding port, and Pennant noted approvingly, soon after the turn of the new century, how 'the whole river, from the bridge, for a vast way, is covered with a double forest of masts, with a narrow avenue in mid-channel'. And, naturally, all this traffic, from both the coastwise and the foreign trade, put an increasing strain on London's river and port facilities. But these were still generally adequate for her needs when, early in the 1720s, Defoe observed in the Pool three wet docks, twenty-two dry docks and thirty-three yards for laying up, repairing and building merchant ships – and this was 'exclusive of all boat-builders, wherry-builders, and above-bridge barge-builders'. Besides, at this time, the river itself was navigable enough, as few ships drew more than 11 or 13 feet of water, and they generally came up with the flood and down with the ebb, except in the broader reaches below Gravesend where smaller ships had room to tack. The only serious obstacle was that caused by the material scoured out from the breach at Dagenham, which blocked navigation and made it

[1] Sir Joseph G. Broodbank, *A History of the Port of London*, 1921, vol. 1, pp. 74–81; Ralph Davis, *The Rise of the English Shipping Industry*, pp. 16–18, 33–5; *A Tour*, vol. 1, pp. 43, 48; Theodore Barker, 'London and the Great Leap Forward', *The Listener*, 29 June 1967, p. 846; O. H. K. Spate, in *An Historical Geography of England*, p. 543.

necessary to remove the three-decker moorings at Woolwich some 20 fathoms into the channel. But more serious still, as trade and tonnage expanded, was the inadequacy of the quays and wharves. The so-called 'legal quays' (where alone the bulk of dutiable goods could be landed) were only 500 yards long and, by the end of the century, were only sufficient to handle about one-third of the traffic that had to land there; and even when supplemented by the 'sufferance wharfs' on both sides of the Upper Pool, they caused irritating delays, particularly to the great West Indian fleet, and provoked complaints which long remained unheeded. Moreover, the size of ships had substantially increased: in 1732 there had been only 205 ships belonging to London of over 200 tons, but by 1792 this had become 751; and, to add to the problem, there came increasing complaints that, from Deptford upwards, the depth of the channel had been reduced by as much as 4 or 5 feet, possibly from the overflow of mud and silt from the city's sewers. In addition, the river was heavily congested with small craft, colliers and coasters, two or three hundred of which often arrived in the Pool at the same time. So the volume of protest mounted, and Parliament at last agreed to set up a Committee in 1796; at the end of a four-year enquiry, it adopted a proposal by the West Indian 'lobby' to remove three or four hundred of the most valuable ships and cargoes out of the river into docks. Wapping and the Isle of Dogs were alternately proposed as the most suitable site; Parliament decided on the Isle of Dogs; and here, in July 1800, the first stone of the West India Dock was laid. Other docks followed in rapid succession: the London Dock was opened in Janaury 1805 and the East India Dock, spread over a 32-acre expanse at Blackwall, in August 1806. So the foundations were laid, after much delay, argument and tribulation, for the modern Port of London.[1]

The shipping and the trade of the port of London naturally brought subsidiary and associated services in their train. In the first place, there were the shipbuilders, coopers, wharfingers, lightermen, warehousemen, sugar-refiners and importers, who established themselves in the riverside parishes and of whom mention has already been made. There was also a rising army of factors and brokers, some of whom, at least, soon began to operate from the City. At a higher level there were the great trading companies, with headquarters in the City of London, of which the most

[1] Thomas Pennant, *Some Account of London*, pp. 269–70; Daniel Defoe, *A Tour*, vol. 1, p. 348; O. H. K. Spate, in *An Historical Geography of England*, pp. 543–7; Raymond Smith, *Sea-Coal for London*, pp. 141–2.

important at this time were the East India Company (incorporated in 1600 and established in Leadenhall Street in 1726), the South Sea Company (created by Parliament in 1711 and based on Threadneedle Street), the African Company (founded in 1673 and also in Leadenhall Street), and the Russia, Levant and Hudson Bay Companies. These 'moneyed companies' were immensely wealthy: the combined volume of bonds issued by the East India and South Sea Companies in the early 1720s amounted to over £7 million. Moreover, they enjoyed great prestige and continued, during the century, to exercise a virtual monopoly (much resented by the challenging, or 'interloping', traders) in the area allotted to them in their charters.[1] But equally significant for the future development of the City was the emergence of a new service, also centred on the City and directly associated with its port – marine insurance. This was a direct offshoot of the great expansion of England's foreign trade after the Restoration and the increasing demand for security against risk voiced by the overseas merchants. Even before 1700, a small group of professionals – 'brokers' or 'office-keepers' – had begun to specialize in receiving premiums, making payment for losses and collecting 'lines' for merchants and others with whom they had connections. But the business only became firmly established on a durable basis with the founding, in 1720, of the two first marine insurance houses – the London Assurance and the Royal Exchange. At this time, the insurable risks in English foreign trade have been estimated as amounting to £20·3 million, of which some £2·3 million only was insured by the two companies. But after this London's insurance market grew continuously, and by the middle of the century she had become the most important insurance centre in western Europe. Business grew with the personal contacts made in the City's numerous coffee-houses, such as the Jerusalem and the Jamaica, where a large part of the business was transacted, and with the establishment of Lloyd's famous list of ships in 1734 and of Lloyd's Register thirty years later. It was through Lloyd's, too, that the specialist underwriter made his appearance in the 1780s. By 1810 the volume of business was such that the chairman of Lloyd's was able to report that, in the previous year, private insurers had underwritten risks to the value of £140 million and the two companies an additional £6 million – which, at an average premium of 7½ per cent, meant that the total premium income was upward of

[1] See L. S. Sutherland, *The East India Company in Eighteenth Century Politics*, 1952, pp. 14–48; and P. G. M. Dickson, *The Financial Revolution in England. A Study in the Development of Public Credit 1688–1756*, 1967, p. 407.

4 Leicester Square, by T. Bowles, 1750 (*British Museum*)

5 The Hyde Park Corner Turnpike, with a view of St George's Hospital, 1798
(*British Museum*)

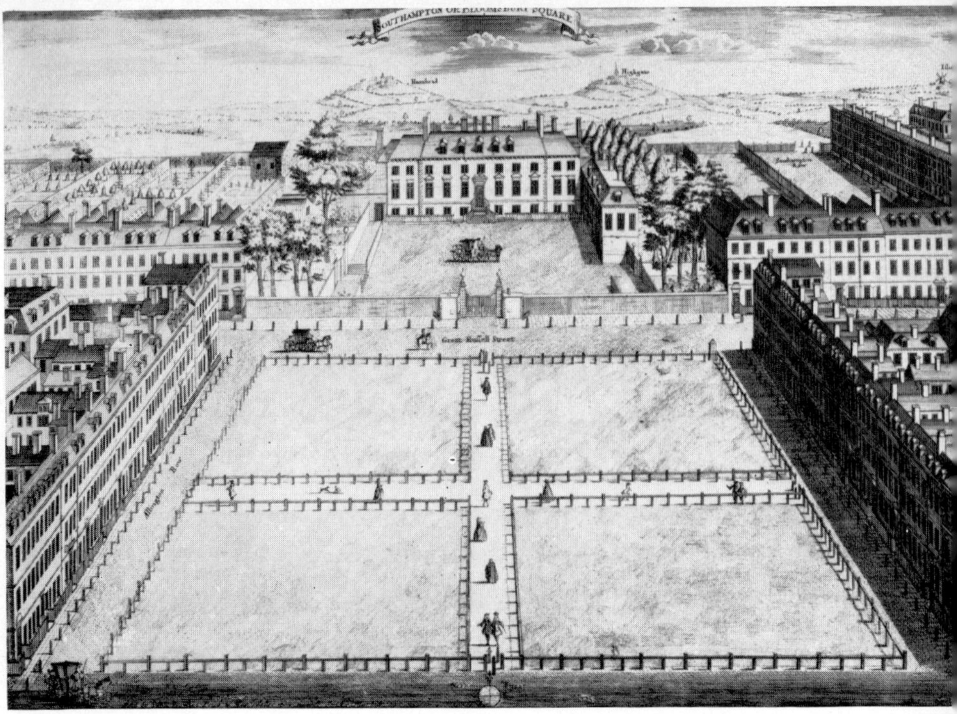

6 Bloomsbury Square (*British Museum*)

7 Great Russell Street and Montague House (the site of the present British Museum entrance) in 1778, by Michael Angelo Rooker (*British Museum*)

8 Hanover Square, by Dayes (*Mansell Collection*)

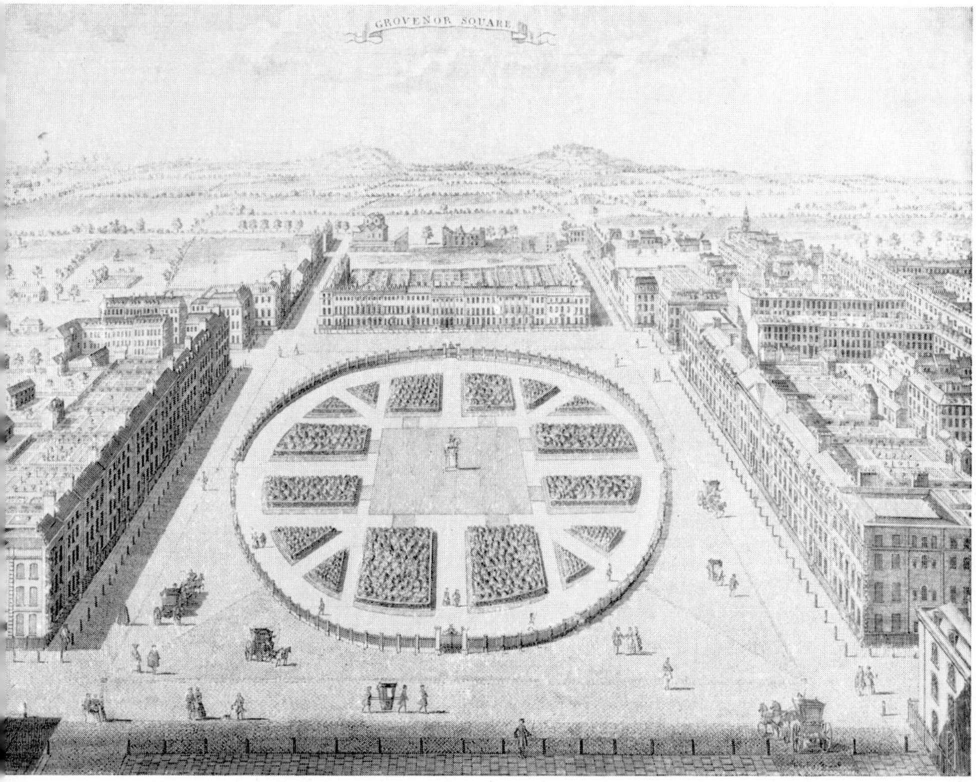

9 Grosvenor Square (*Mansell Collection*)

10 View of Whitehall from Richmond House, by Canaletto
(Collection of His Grace the Duke of Richmond)

£10 million. This, however, was a war-time peak from which there was a sharp fall with the return of peace.[1]

A parallel development was the emergence of insurance companies specializing in giving cover against fire, and later against early death. The earliest fire offices in London were, in addition to the London Assurance and the Royal Exchange, the Westminster (1717), the Hand in Hand (1719) and the Sun Fire Offices (1710): these were already established in Defoe's time. By 1791 another half-dozen offices had made their appearance, either in the City or in Westminster: among these were the Union, Phoenix, Equitable and Amicable insurance offices; to which were further added, in the next fifteen years, Imperial Insurance, the British Fire Office, Globe Insurance, and the Albion Fire and Life Insurance Office. Besides the Albion, the Royal Exchange, Amicable and Equitable societies now also provided life insurance.[2]

An even more important consequence of London's commercial pre-eminence was that she gradually evolved, by a process that was not completed until the end of the Napoleonic Wars, into the world's leading financial centre. Banking naturally followed in the wake of commerce. The earliest of the City's private bankers was Sir Thomas Gresham, the founder of the Royal Exchange. He had been followed, in the 1670s, by Sir Josiah Child, and further banks, Stone's, Hoare's and Martin's, had been established in the City of London by the time of Queen Anne, to say nothing of goldsmiths like Mocatta and Goldsmid, who had, since the 1680s, engaged in banking as a side-line to their regular business. Child's Bank alone had assets of over £175,000 in 1704 and of £734,000 fifty years later. These private bankers had begun by advancing loans and discounting commercial bills for London merchants, but they later extended their business to the provinces, acting as agents both for individual clients and for country banks, of which there were 150 by 1776 and 280 by the early 1790s. Through these operations, they helped to develop the manufactures of the northern and midlands counties, and London (it has been said) 'served as a sort of natural balance to establish an equilibrium of supply and demand between the banks of the agricultural and those of the manufacturing districts'.[3] As the volume of banking expanded, London's

---

[1] A. H. John, 'The London Assurance Company and the Marine Insurance Market of the Eighteenth Century', *Economica*, vol. 25, 1958, pp. 126–31.

[2] Besant, p. 392; London Directories, 1789, 1795; *Kent's Directory*, 1806.

[3] Elie Halévy, *A History of the English People in the Nineteenth Century. England in 1815*, 1961, p. 342; P. G. M. Dickson, *The Financial Revolution in England*, p. 437;

D

banks grew in number from 35 to 40 (in and around Lombard Street) in the 1760s to 56 in 1789, 60 in 1791, 70 in 1795, 72 in 1806 and 77 in 1808.[1]

But considerable as was the business of these banks – particularly after they set up a central clearing house in Lombard Street in 1775 – the range of their activities was comparatively limited; above all, they were purveyors of strictly private, not public, credit. Public credit, involving the active and regular intervention of the State as borrower and debtor (not to mention as protector), only became institutionalized after the Bank of England was founded by a group of London merchants, based on Grocers' Hall, in 1694. In return for a loan of £1,200,000 at 8 per cent, the Whig government of the day allowed these merchants to form a corporation; the new society, by making itself indispensable to a series of governments, acquired a monopoly of the issue of bank notes in the capital, which, though constantly challenged by its opponents, survived a succession of parliamentary debates and threats of termination. The Bank's main activity, as it developed, was to issue notes, to discount bills issued by the Treasury – Navy bills bearing interest after six months, Exchequer bills from the day of issue – and to act as guardian of the Consolidated Fund and other balances deposited by the State. The enormous capital thus accumulated it was free to lend at interest to other parties, and this was further supplemented by the reserve deposited with it by both country and London bankers, a large part of which it employed in discounting commercial bills on behalf of British and overseas merchants.

The Bank took some time to disarm its critics: as late as 1781 Parliament decided that its monopoly should expire in 1812. (This, however, was followed by a series of reprieves.) But, before this, as searching a critic as Adam Smith had written in his *Wealth of Nations* that 'the Stability of the Bank of England is equal to that of the British Government. It acts not only as an ordinary bank, but as a great engine of State.'[2] Yet in the process of building up this excellent public image, the Bank had had its ups and downs, not least in the great 'Bubble Year' of 1720, when, in unwisely bidding against its rival, the South Sea Company, it had lent money too freely and had heavily depleted its

---

D. M. Joslin, 'London Private Bankers 1720-1785', in *Essays in Economic History*, ed. E. M. Carus-Wilson, 1962, vol. 2, pp. 340-59.

[1] Sir John Clapham, *The Bank of England, A History*, 1944, vol. 1, pp. 163-5; London Directories, 1789-95; *Kent's Directory*, 1806.

[2] Adam Smith, *Wealth of Nations*, Book II, chap. 2, ed. Thorold Rogers, 1880, vol. 1, p. 320; quoted by Elie Halévy, *England in 1815*, p. 346.

stocks. Its loans, in August that year, stood at £948,000 and its reserves of bullion at a little over £1 million. The bursting of the 'Bubble' dealt a severe blow to public credit and to public confidence in general; in the course of a spirited account of it, the historian Maitland tells how, in the atmosphere of panic and suspicion of all types of speculation that followed, the Privy Council rejected no less than 156 other 'villanous Projects set on Foot', including one 'for inoffensively emptying Bog-houses'![1]

The Bank, however, survived, in spite of further depletions of its holdings in bullion in the war years and end-of-war years 1748, 1763, 1783 and 1793 and, with minor set-backs, steadily increased its business. The balance on its profit and loss account, standing at £145,000 in the 'Bubble Year' and still only at £297,000 in 1760, rose briskly after this to reach £3,471,000 in 1797. By 1815 it was paying an interest of 10 per cent on a capital of £11,642,400.[2]

Meanwhile, the bonds and stock of the Bank of England and of the other great 'moneyed companies' in the City of London, not to mention the bonds and short-term loans issued by the government itself, were being increasingly subscribed to by big foreign investors and creditors in Holland, France, Switzerland and other countries. Moreover, London had also, since the 1750s, become an international market for gold and precious stones and, during the long wars with France at the end of the century, she was able to provide long-term capital at low rates of interest on a scale that had only been attempted by the Bank of Amsterdam before. Meanwhile, the Dutch suffered a succession of financial disasters as the result of Holland's involvement, on the eventually losing side, in the Napoleonic Wars: in 1798 the monopoly of the Dutch East India Company was ended, and the prestigious Bank of Amsterdam itself failed four years after the wars were over. Its recovery came too late to offer a serious challenge to London's newly won position as the world's leading banking and financial centre, and a historian of the 'money market' has written that 'twenty years of war had made Britain the one country in the world where capital might be invested with the maximum of contemporary safety'.[3]

[1] W. Maitland, *An Account of the Rage for Public Speculations, which existed in, and about, the year 1720* (extract from Maitland's *History of London*), 1806, pp. 8–21.

[2] Sir John Clapham, *The Bank of England*, vol. 1, pp. 224–9, 295–7, 301–2; Elie Halévy, *England in 1815*, pp. 344–6.

[3] E. T. Powell, 'Evolution of the Money-Market, 1315–1815', *The Financial Times*, 1915. See also P. G. M. Dickson, *The Financial Revolution in England*, pp. 320–4; William M. Clarke, *The City in the World Economy*, 1967, pp. 18–20.

So London, at the turn of the century, was on the eve of becoming the recognized headquarters of world banking and credit, where she was already established as its leading port and leading centre of shipping and insurance. Meanwhile, she played an even more remarkable role at home. She was, at once, the nation's banker, chief centre of overseas trade, a major manufacturing centre, and the largest consumer of her agricultural and industrial products. Her multiform activities as trader, banker, producer and consumer radiated outwards and vitally affected the development of the nation's whole economy. The work of Professor E. J. Fisher shows that, in the seventeenth century, London's food market had been a major factor in promoting technical changes and specialization in England's main agricultural districts; Mr Wrigley's observations on the early eighteenth century suggest that, by 1750, something like 200,000 rural families were being fully employed in supplying London with bread alone. She promoted further change as the country's largest consumer of coal, meat, shoes, butter, clocks, leather, gloves, lace, cloth and luxury goods of every kind; and it has been said that, besides its grip on foreign trade, the City of London, through its brokers, factors, markets and Exchanges, 'controlled the wool and woollen trades, the coal trade, the livestock trade, and it affected considerably the trade in butter, cheese, fish, poultry, wine, horses, tin and linen'. London also played an outstanding part in promoting the Industrial Revolution in the midlands, the north and the south-west; for, to take two examples alone, her banks provided the working capital required to develop the iron industry in South Wales and the new machine-manufactured textiles of Lancashire and Yorkshire. In short, her position in the economic life of the nation during the eighteenth century was unique.[1]

[1] E. A. Wrigley, *Past and Present*, no. 37, pp. 55–63; O. H. K. Spate, in *An Historical Geography of England*, p. 547; Theodore Barker, *The Listener*, 29 June 1967, pp. 845–7.

3

Men of Property

DANIEL DEFOE, in attempting to classify Englishmen in their appropriate social classes, divided the nation into seven major groups:

The *great*, who live profusely.
The *rich*, who live very plentifully.
The *middle sort*, who live well.
The *working trades*, who labour hard but feel no want.
The *country people*, farmers, &c., who fare indifferently.
The *poor*, that fare hard.
The *miserable*, that really pinch and suffer want.[1]

Such a classification, if we leave aside the country people who do not concern us here, may serve as a useful model for the social divisions between Londoners in the eighteenth century, at a time when the modern class structure deriving from the Industrial Revolution had not yet taken shape. It has the disadvantage of not taking account of the intermediate group of gentry between 'the great' (landed magnates or aristocracy) and 'the rich' (wealthy merchant class) and of making it necessary to squeeze the considerable class of professional people and those engaged in the arts and sciences – artists, writers, doctors, lawyers – in among those of 'the middle sort'; moreover, it bases class almost exclusively on wealth. Yet it has the advantage over the two other well-known classifications that span the century – that of Gregory King in 1696 and of Patrick Colquhoun in 1805 – of attempting a division by classes rather than by occupations.[2] And even if there cannot be said to be any clear-cut division between 'the great' and 'the rich' or between 'the middle sort' and 'the

[1] Daniel Defoe, *The Review*, 25 June 1709, cited in *London Life*, p. 363.
[2] M. Dorothy George, *England in Transition*, 1953, pp. 150-5.

working trades', there may seem to be a fairly clear dividing line between those who live 'profusely', 'plentifully' and 'well' and those who 'labour hard', 'fare hard' and 'really pinch and suffer want'. In this chapter, we are concerned with the first of these two main groups, with the wealth and style of living of the owners of great, substantial or 'middling' property.

To start at the top of Defoe's social pyramid: how many of 'the great' were there in Hanoverian London, and how wealthy were they? Unfortunately, neither the hearth-tax returns of 1694 (used by Gregory King) nor the census returns of 1801 (used by Colquhoun) provide for any separate estimates for London. But if we take King's *national* figure of 186 lords, both temporal and spiritual, and Colquhoun's of 313, and if we assume that nearly all of these were fully or partly resident in the capital, we must conclude that some 180 to 300 noble families had, at one time or another during these hundred years, some sort of establishment, permanent or other, in the metropolis. Again, King estimated that the average yearly income of the family of a temporal lord was £2,800 and that of a bishop £1,300, while Colquhoun, writing a century later, raised these to £8,000 in the first case and £4,000 in the second. Both men put these incomes considerably higher than those of any other groups in their descending social ladder. King gives his baronets an income of £880 and his wealthier merchants one of £400; Colquhoun gives them respectively £3,000 and £2,600. If we accept their calculations as reasonably accurate for the nation as a whole, we should perhaps raise them in the case of London, which was likely to attract the wealthier rather than the poorer members of 'the great'. But, even so, a mere *average* would not take us far, as it would not tell us who was getting richer or who was getting poorer, and it would tend to blanket the very real distinctions in both wealth and social status dividing the ordinary aristocrat from the great landed magnates and leaders of political factions and 'connections', such as the Dukes of Bedford, Devonshire, Newcastle and Richmond, the Marquis of Rockingham, or Lord Holland.

How did this aristocracy derive its wealth? In the first place, from the land: even those long established in the metropolis continued to draw incomes from rents or tolls or from the sale of grain or wool or cattle. The 'broad acres' of the Marquis of Rockingham, for example, were the main basis of the fortune of the Wentworth Woodhouse family; the Duke of Kingston's scattered estates yielded a net income of nearly £14,000 in 1726, £19,000 in 1731, £22,000 in 1740, and more after the 1760s – and

such rises were far more spectacular after the outbreak of the Revolutionary and Napoleonic Wars. Secondly, from real estate: we have already
noted the building schemes and the investments in real estate promoted
by noble landlords like the 4th Duke of Bedford, Lord Oxford (the
former Robert Harley), Lord Grosvenor, the Earls of Southampton and
St Albans and the adventurous and highly intelligent young Earl of
Burlington. It was a lucrative business. The Bloomsbury estate of the
Dukes of Bedford yielded a gross return of £8,000 in 1771 where it had
yielded £3,700 in 1732; and Lord Grosvenor's London estate yielded
£2,000 in 1722, £7,000 in 1779 and £12,000 in 1802. Thirdly, by inheritance or inter-marriage with the mercantile plutocracy: such as the alliance
cemented in 1695 between the future 2nd Duke of Bedford and the
granddaughter of the fabulously wealthy London banker and East India
merchant, Sir Josiah Child. (Yet, admittedly, such cases were still rare.)
Fourthly, from place and politics, which continued to provide exceptional
financial opportunities (as well as power and prestige) to members of the
landed classes. The office of Secretary of State, in particular, yielded
handsome profits. In 1762 its value was put at £8,000 or £9,000 a year;
it might yield even more and, fifty years earlier, Daniel Finch, 2nd Earl
of Nottingham, is reputed to have accumulated £50,000 in half-a-dozen
years. When the 3rd Earl of Sunderland, Walpole's great rival, died in
1722, he left £75,000 in stocks and shares, which had been largely derived
from 'office'. And Walpole himself, through his long tenure of high
offices of State, was able to make ample provision for his offspring. His
eldest son drew £7,000 a year from the Auditorship of the Exchequer;
his second son enjoyed an income of £3,000 from his office of Clerk of
the Pells; and Horace Walpole, although not strictly a 'politician', held
offices which, on his father's death, are said to have been worth £3,400 a
year. Such proceedings were not unusual; it was, in fact, accounted an
exceptional virtue of William Pitt, the Great Commoner and future Earl
of Chatham, that he refused to accept the usual perquisites when he held
the traditionally lucrative post of Paymaster of the Forces.[1]

And, fifthly, they derived wealth, like the mercantile *bourgeoisie* itself,
from trade, financial speculation and their holdings in the banks and
'moneyed' trading companies. Among the original proprietors of Bank of
England Stock before the turn of the century were the Dukes of Leeds

[1] J. H. Plumb, *Sir Robert Walpole*, vol. 1, 1956, pp. 6–8; G. E. Mingay, *English
Landed Society in the Eighteenth Century*, pp. 58, 70; H. J. Habbakuk, 'England', in
The European Nobility in the Eighteenth Century, ed. A. Goodwin, 1953, pp. 5–11.

and Devonshire, the Earls of Pembroke and Bradford, the (later) Duke of Marlborough and the Earl of Portland (who, like King William, held £10,000 or more), and Lord Edward Russell and the Marquis of Normanby (£4,000). In 1721 the Marlborough and Godolphin families had combined holdings of £104,600, Lady Elizabeth Germain held £11,700, the Duchess of Devonshire £11,600 and the Duchess of Kendall, a mistress of George I, £10,000. Lady Elizabeth Germain, at this time, also held £25,000 East India stock and £50,520 South Sea stock. Other large South Sea proprietors were the Earl of Pembroke (£69,000) and the Duchess of Kendall (£47,000); and among noble ministers (some of whom were badly caught out in 'the Bubble') were the Duke of Argyll (£8,500), Lord Stanhope (£10,000), Lord Townshend (£2,500) and the Earl of Sunderland (£13,000).

Wealthy noblemen, ministers among them, were also among the heaviest subscribers to government loans. The Duke of Newcastle and Lord Parker, the Lord Chancellor, both subscribed £10,000 to the loan raised on the land tax of 1720. The largest subscribers to the 3 per cent loan of 1742 included Lord William Manners and the Dukes of Rutland and Somerset, each of whom had holdings of £20,000; and to the loan of 1748 Lords Anson and Ilchester subscribed £20,000 and Henry Fox, the future Lord Holland, £15,000. Bank of England proprietors of 1751 included twenty-nine noblemen, their widows or their wives (most of them Londoners), bearing such names as Argyll, Lonsdale, North, Palmerston, Shelburne, Stanhope and Vere. At mid-century, too, the records of holdings of combined stock in the principal 'moneyed companies' reveal the considerable sums accumulated in the hands of certain aristocratic families: the Marlboroughs held £276,154; Francis, Earl of Godolphin £71,763; Lady Elizabeth Germain £83,400; the Duchess of Montague £20,000; the Duke of Leeds £22,627; Francis, Lord North and Guildford £20,500 (shared with three other members of the family); while the Earl of Pembroke's South Sea holdings (£69,000 at their peak in 1723) had shrunk to a mere £8,000. And, finally, one of the most consistently wealthy of all these aristocratic stockholders, Lady Elizabeth Germain, left her heir, Lord George Sackville, a legacy of £120,000 in funds when she died in 1769. (He had to change his name to Lord George Germain, but perhaps it was not too heavy a price to pay!)[1]

Where did the aristocracy reside? From the Restoration up to the

[1] Sir John Clapham, *The Bank of England*, vol. 1. pp. 274-85; P. G. M. Dickson, *The Financial Revolution in England*, pp. 109, 278-81, 288-96.

reign of Queen Anne their houses had been dispersed over the more
fashionable streets and *piazzas* of Westminster: Covent Garden, in particular, after the enterprising venture of the Earl of Bedford, had become
the acknowledged centre of fashion. Others (they included the Earls of
Sunderland, Ailesbury and Rockingham) were established in Leicester
Fields, and more in Soho; some, after the opening of St James's Square,
began slowly to move westwards into the parishes of St James's and St
George's. At the turn of the century we still find in the rate books the
heaviest concentration of aristocratic names in Soho Square, lying south
of Oxford Street, and Golden Square, to the north of Piccadilly; while St
James's Square was, at this time, only beginning to assume something of
its later aristocratic complexion. Golden Square included among its
residents in 1707 a duchess, six present and future peers, and a bishop;
John Strype, writing of Soho Square as late as 1720, described it as
having 'very good buildings on all Sides, especially the East and South,
which are all inhabited by Nobility and Gentry'. With the Hanoverian
Succession, however, Covent Garden, Leicester Fields and Soho Square
began to be deserted by the more elegant society: Hanover Square, built
in 1717–19, soon replaced Golden Square as a centre of the aristocracy,
and the number of noble patrons in Golden Square, while still six in
1720, had fallen to two in 1730 and to one in 1740.[1]

Meanwhile, St James's Square and the streets off Piccadilly (Arlington
Street, for example) were improved and developed; so the 'polite end of
the town' tended to become centred in the neighbouring parishes of St
James's and St George's, where the large landowners and party managers,
Cabinet ministers, and seekers after preferment and offices of State had
easy access to the Court of St James's, which continued to be the main
fount of Royal and ministerial favour even after George III, soon after
his accession, acquired Buckingham House (the future Buckingham
Palace). Already in the 1720s there were thirteen aristocrats out of twenty-
five residents in Hanover Square, and in St James's Square no fewer than
twenty out of twenty-three: the first included the Dukes of Bolton,
Roxburgh and Montrose, the Earls of Essex and Pontefract, and Lords
Hilsborough and Londonderry, and the second the Dukes of Norfolk
and Chandos, the Earls of Bristol, Pembroke, Clarendon, Chesterfield
and Portmore, the Countess of Bradford, Viscount Palmerston and Lady

[1] *Survey of London*, ed. F. H. W. Sheppard, vols 29 (St James Westminster, Part 1,
1960), pp. 78–81; 31 (St James Westminster, Part 2, 1963), pp. 143–5; 33 (St Anne
Soho, Part 1, 1966), pp. 45–50; 34 (St Anne Soho, Part 2, 1966), pp. 428–31.

Elizabeth Germain. Meanwhile, Arlington Street had developed (as the ever-observant Horace Walpole later noted) the complexion of a 'ministerial' rather than of a purely aristocratic street: there were eight aristocrats among twenty-nine residents in 1728 (the latter including Lord Carteret, William Pulteney and Sir Robert Walpole). And this, broadly, appears to have remained the social pattern of these squares and streets for the rest of the century.[1]

Also at 'the polite end of the town' lay the streets and squares to the north of Piccadilly, which began to be improved and developed to suit the new aristocratic taste in the 1720s to 1750s. Lord Chesterfield's house, for example, before he moved to Grosvenor Square, lay behind Shepherd's Market, with Lord Eglington, James Boswell's patron, close by in Queen Street. Devonshire House lay off Berkeley Street and Burlington House a few blocks farther east. The Duke of Queensberry's mansion was in the Gardens behind and, in Berkeley Square, Robert Adam built for the Earl of Bute (until then resident in South Audley Street close by) what later became known as Lansdowne House. Farther north, in Grosvenor Square, completed in 1753, lay the residences of Lord North, the Earl of Hardwicke and the Marquis of Rockingham, all of whom played important political roles in the early years of George III.

Some aristocrats, however, either from choice or circumstance, lived, or continued to live, outside the immediate orbit of the Court. Between 1717 and 1751 two successive heirs to the Throne, the future George II and his son, Frederick Prince of Wales, made Leicester House, in Leicester Fields (the 'pouting place of princes', as Pennant called it), the centre of opposition to their Royal father. The Duke of Northumberland resided at Charing Cross; it was here that he successfully warded off the rioters, who were celebrating Wilkes's election victory of March 1768, by promptly 'putting out lights' and ordering the neighbouring Ship Alehouse to fill the intruders with beer. On the same occasion, the Duke of Newcastle's house, off Leicester Fields, was also visited but did not escape so lightly. Soho Square still continued to retain a small number of aristocratic patrons, such as Earl Tilney and the Earl of Carlisle in the 1740s, the Duchess of Wharton and Lord Chedworth in the 1750s, the Duke of Argyll and Lord Pigot in the 1760s, Lord Knollys in the 1770s and 1780s, and the Bishops of Peterborough, Salisbury and Winchester

[1] W.P.L., Poor Rate, St Anne Westminster, 1722; St George Hanover Square, 1725, 1728; St James's, 1729. See also Hugh Phillips, *Mid-Georgian London*, 1964, pp. 65, 287-8, 301-2.

between 1752 and 1761. Meanwhile, Cavendish Square had been completed in 1724 and was filled up with a long succession of aristocratic and episcopal occupants, among the more famous of whom were the Duke of Argyll, the Earl of Bessborough, the Duke of Beaufort, the Duke of Chandos, Viscount Barington, the Duke of Bolton, the Bishop of Durham, the Princess Amelia and Lady Mary Wortley Montagu.

Bloomsbury Square, however, though it housed the 2nd Earl of Chesterfield, appears to have attracted mainly dignitaries of the Church and the Law. The Bishop of Chester and the Archbishop of York were successive inmates of No. 9 in the 1770s; earlier, Baron Thompson and Lord Chief Justice Wills had followed one another at No. 3. Chief Justice Lee and Mr Baron Smythe were contemporaries at Nos. 22 and 23. But the most eminent resident of all was the Earl of Mansfield, whose house at No. 11, which he had occupied since 1751, was destroyed, with its valuable library and furniture, by the 'No Popery' rioters of June 1780. Meanwhile, Marylebone, lying on the northern fringe of the built-up area of London, had drawn a solid influx of aristocratic residents. That same year, its nobility and principal inhabitants, having decided to form a voluntary association for self-protection against future riots, appointed a committee composed of the Dukes of Portland, and Manchester, the Earls of Macclesfield, Harcourt, Sussex and Bessborough, Viscounts Townshend, Cranbourne and Mahon, Lord de Ferrers, Lord Duncannon, the Dean of Windsor, seven baronets and forty other notables.[1]

Some of these aristocratic houses were princely mansions rivalling (or almost rivalling) those built by the Duke of Bedford at Woburn, the Duke of Kingston at Thoresby, the Duke of Devonshire at Chatsworth, or the Marquis of Rockingham at Wentworth Woodhouse. There were, perhaps, a score of these. They included Bedford House, off Bloomsbury Square; Burlington House, off Piccadilly; Montague House (merged with the British Museum in 1755), in Russell Street; Chesterfield House, in South Audley Street; Devonshire House, in Piccadilly; Richmond House, in Whitehall; Holland House, in Kensington; Northumberland House, at Charing Cross; Craven House, in Drury Lane; Powys House, in Great Ormond Street; Lansdowne House, in Berkeley Square; Norfolk House, in St James's Square; Newcastle House, in Leicester Fields; and the successive residences of the Princes of Wales: first Leicester House and later Carlton House, in Pall Mall, which Henry Holland rebuilt for the

[1] *Wilkes and Liberty*, p. 3; Hugh Phillips, *Mid-Georgian London*, p. 295–8, 302–3.

future Prince Regent and which (in 1795) was assessed for rates at the considerable sum of £1,000 a year.

These great houses varied greatly in their degree of elegance or modernity and in the style of living that was conducted within them. Among the most magnificent were those of the Earl of Chesterfield and the Duke of Richmond. Chesterfield House, built in the Palladian style to Isaac Ware's design for the 4th Earl, was ready for occupation in March 1749. At this time, the Earl wrote to a friend: 'I have yet finished nothing but my *boudoir* and my library; the former is the gayest and most cheerful room in England, the latter the best. My garden is now tufted, planted and sown, and will, in two months more, make a scene of verdure and flowers not common in London.' The Earl had systematically furnished his mansion by collections and purchases from other noble houses: from Canons, the seat of the Duke of Chandos, he had acquired a magnificent set of columns and a grand staircase of marble; from Houghton, Sir Robert Walpole's old house, a lantern of copper-gilt for eighteen candles, which Henry Fielding commemorated in a ballad that he wrote for the *Craftsman*. The garden was reputed the finest of its kind in London; and 'on the mantelpieces and cabinets [to quote from the *Quarterly Review* of a century later, when the house was sold for £175,000] stand busts of old orators, interspersed with voluptuous vases and bronzes, antique or Italian, and airy statuettes in marble or alabaster, of nude or semi-nude Opera nymphs'.

A few months after Chesterfield moved into his mansion in South Audley Street, Horace Walpole sent Sir Horace Mann an account of a party given at Richmond House, in Whitehall, which had been built for the 2nd Duke by the Earl of Burlington (it was subsequently altered and enlarged for the 3rd Duke by James Wyatt).

The night before last the Duke of Richmond gave a firework: a codicil to the Peace. The garden lies with a slope down to the Thames, on which were lighters, from whence were thrown up, after a concert of music, a great number of rockets. Then from boats on every side were discharged water-rockets and fires of that kind; and then the wheels which were ranged along the rails of the terrace were played off; and the whole concluded with the illumination of a pavilion on the top of a slope, of two pyramids on each side, and the whole length of the balustrade to the water. You can't conceive a prettier sight; the garden filled with everybody of fashion, the

Duke [of Cumberland], the Duke of Modena and the two black Princes [of Anamaboe]. The King and Princess Emily were in their barge under the terrace; the river was crowded with boats, and the shores and adjacent houses with crowds.[1]

The London aristocracy employed a succession of builders and architects to build and design their houses for them in a changing variety of styles: whether Dutch (as at the time of Anne) or Italian or French (as under the earlier Georges), or (and this became long the most fashionable of all) what was termed Palladian. Among these architects were Nicholas Hawksmoor, James Gibbs, Henry Holland, George Dance (father and son), Isaac Ware, Sir William Chambers and William Kent. But none achieved the renown of Robert and James Adam, and it was the Adam house which, after the early 1760s, became the hallmark of aristocratic elegance and fashion. Among the houses that the brothers Adam (it was mainly Robert) built for the nobility at this time were Lansdowne House, begun for the Earl of Bute in 1765; Chandos House, in Chandos Street, Cavendish Square, built for the Duke of Buckingham in 1770–1; Derby House, at 23 Grosvenor Square, for Lord Stanley in 1773–4; and Home House, at 20 Portman Square (now the Courtauld Institute), for the Countess of Home in 1775–7. These Adam houses, constructed in the Neo-Classical grand style, were dominated by their public rooms: the parlour, the Great Eating Room, the Library (in the centre of the ground floor), not to mention the spacious kitchen and stables. Sir John Summerson has written: 'They were not built for domestic but for public life – a life of continual entertaining in drawing-rooms and ante-rooms and "eating rooms" where conversation would not be wholly ephemeral, where a sentence might be delivered which would echo round political England, where an introduction might mean the beginning of a career or a deft criticism the dethronement of a policy.'[2]

In addition to the princely mansions and the Adam houses, there were perhaps another thirty or forty houses of the nobility that, at any one time, were assessed for rates at £200 or more. Such was the Duke of Norfolk's house on the fashionable east side of St James's Square, which, after it had been extended by the addition of the house next door in the 1740s, was assessed for rates at £525. Also in St James's Square were the houses of the Earl of Bristol (£216), Lady Elizabeth Germain (£200),

---

[1] Wheatley and Cunningham, vol. 1, p. 388; vol. 3, pp. 162–3.
[2] *Georgian London*, p. 144.

the Bishop of London and the Earl of Buckingham (£250), Lady Decker (£300), Lord Royston (£350) and the Duke of Leeds (rising from £250 to £525 between the 1750s and the 1790s). In Arlington Street the Marquis of Bath's house, the Earl of Ossory's, the Duke of Kingston's and the Earl of Granville's (the latter believed to have provided the setting for the second scene in Hogarth's 'Marriage à la Mode') were assessed respectively at £260, £250 and £200. Lord Mansfield's house in Bloomsbury Square had an annual value of £230; while, in Pall Mall and Spring Gardens, Whitehall, in 1795, Carlton House was assessed at £1,000, the Duke of Marlborough's mansion at £600, Lord Berkeley's at £240, and Lady Godolphin's and the Earl of Harrington's at £268. Yet these were the exception rather than the rule. The majority of London's aristocratic dwellings did not rise to such palatial grandeur and (to quote Sir John Summerson once more): 'The members of the aristocracy were not interested in their town houses to anything like the same extent that they were in their country dwellings.'[1] There were few, in fact, even among the wealthiest of London's aristocrats, who would have entertained the notion of investing such great sums in their town houses as those spent in building, extending or rebuilding their country seats by the Duke of Devonshire at Chatsworth (over £40,000), the Duke of Kingston at Thoresby (over £34,000), Lord Malcombe at Eastbury (£140,000) or the Marquis of Rockingham at Wentworth Woodhouse and Audley End (respectively £83,000 and £100,000). Notable exceptions were the Earl of Chesterfield and the Dukes of Devonshire and Richmond, known for their 'continental' tastes. The great majority, however, were content with the standard product of the time, the Georgian terrace house, whose graceful but simple vertical lines can still be admired in many a London (or Dublin) street or square. Typical of this kind of house is that classified by the Building Act of 1774 as 'First Rate', costing more than £850 to build and assessed for rates at £60 to £100. (Even the house of the late King's mistress, the Duchess of Kendall, in Portugal Row had, in 1728, a rentable value of no more than £90 a year.) To the astonishment of visiting foreigners there was no *porte-cochère* and no surrounding garden wall, such as distinguished the houses of their own privileged classes. St James's Palace, in particular, aroused amusement mingled with contempt, and provoked Bielfeld's quip: 'Les Rois de Grande Bretagne sont logés au Palais de St James comme des invalides, et

---

[1] *Georgian London*, pp. 110-11.

les invalides de l'Armée et de la Marine comme des Rois à Chelsea et à Greenwich!'[1]

For some aristocrats their London house was almost a *pied à terre*, which they used mainly for special occasions such as the London season, for settling old bills or for placing orders with their tailor, dressmaker, coach-maker, wine merchant or grocer. It could be a costly experience. The 1st Duke of Devonshire, on one such visit, spent £1,000 on a supper and masked ball, and the Duke of Bedford, to prepare for similar occasions, kept over forty servants at his London residence, their wages alone amounting to £860 a year. The 2nd Duke of Kingston spent over £2,000 during a fortnight's stay in the summer of 1752; while Lord Ashburnham spent an average of £4,321 a year on his personal expenditure alone on annual visits to London between 1710 and 1716.[2]

There was a similar traffic in reverse when London aristocrats took time off from their London duties or social round to seek the relative peace and quiet and the more salubrious air of the surrounding countryside. One of the most splendid of all these extra-metropolitan retreats was the 1st Duke of Northumberland's palatial residence, Syon House at Isleworth, whose Jacobean gallery was remodelled by Robert Adam at a cost of £5,000. The Earl of Burlington employed William Kent to design his sumptious Palladian Chiswick Villa (1720–5), and the Duke of Chandos employed a succession of architects, including James Gibbs, to design his mansion of Canons, at Stanmore (1713–25), which Defoe called 'the most magnificent house' in England. Later in the century the Earl of Chesterfield bought the Ranger's House at Blackheath (1753), the Earl of Chatham moved from St James's Square to Hayes (1761) and Robert Adam rebuilt Kenwood House, near Hampstead Heath, for the Earl of Mansfield (1767–9). Meanwhile the mercurial Lord Bolingbroke had retired to his ancestral manor house at Battersea, where he died in 1751. And these were only some of the mainly eighteenth-century additions to the 'many noble seats' of which Defoe had written so eloquently in his *Tour*: 'in Istleworth, Twittenham, Hamersmith, Fullham, Puttney, Chelsea, Battersea, and the like'.[3]

But one further 'noble seat' deserves a mention, if not so much for its

[1] G. E. Mingay, *English Landed Society in the Eighteenth Century*, p. 160; Hugh Phillips, *Mid-Georgian London*, pp. 55, 65; W.P.L., Rate Books, 1722–95; *Georgian London*, p. 126; M. Dorothy George, in *Johnson's England*, vol. 1, p. 170.

[2] G. E. Mingay, *English Landed Society*, pp. 157–8.

[3] G. E. Mingay, *English Landed Society*, p. 160.

elegance or architectural splendour as for the interest that it has aroused. Strawberry Hill, at Twickenham, was bought by Horace Walpole (who later became the 1st Earl of Orford) in 1748 and extended and designed for him in the 'Gothick' style that had already been made fashionable by William Kent and his pupils. 'Every true Goth,' wrote its owner, 'must perceive that [the rooms] are more the work of fancy than of imitation.' Yet they were carefully and systematically constructed, incorporating themes culled from the ceiling of Henry VII's Chapel at Westminster, the tomb of Archbishop Warham in Canterbury, and the choir of Old St Paul's, lined with a medley of contrasting wall-papers and set in lath and plaster that has, mysteriously, stood the test of time. The younger Beckford, the author of *Vathek* (surely an expert in 'Follies'!), called it 'a Gothic mouse-trap'; but Walpole himself was delighted with it and wrote enthusiastically of a visit paid by distinguished foreign notables in the summer of 1764: 'Strawberry . . . has been more sumptuous today than ordinary and banqueted their respective majesties of France and Spain. I had Monsieur and Madame de Guerchy, Mademoiselle de Nangis, their daughter, two other French gentlemen, the Prince of Masserano, his brother and secretary, Lord March, George Selwyn, Mrs Anne Pitt, and my niece Wardegrave. The refectory never was so crowded; nor have any foreigners been here before that comprehended Strawberry.'[1]

Defoe, in his list of social categories, makes no provision for the gentry; King and Colquhoun divide them into four separate groups. First, in order of precedence, come the Baronets (with average incomes of £880 in 1696 and £3,000 in 1805); then come the Knights (£650 and £1,500), followed by the Esquires (£450 and £1,500) and, last, the mere 'Gentlemen' (£280 and £700); thus all four groups rank substantially, in terms of wealth, beneath the aristocracy. In number, of course, they far eclipse them: 800 families of Baronets in 1696, falling to 540 in 1805; 600 Knights, falling to 350; 3,000 (6,000) Esquires; and 12,000 (20,000) Gentlemen; thus, a combined total of 16,400 'gentle' families at the end of the seventeenth century and one of 26,890 at the end of the eighteenth, compared with a mere 186 and 313 in the case of the lords temporal and spiritual. On this reckoning, we might reasonably suppose that there were around 3,000 to 4,500 'gentle' families resident in Hanoverian London.

How did the gentry derive their wealth? The more prosperous differed little in this from many of 'the great': from rents, tolls and landed estates, trade in cattle and corn, even by marriage and inheritance. Professor

[1] *Three Tours*, pp. 112-16.

11 Burlington House, Piccadilly (*Mansell Collection*)

12 Burlington House

13 Devonshire House

14 View of Westminster from the parapet of the Banqueting Hall, Whitehall, by J. T. Smith in 1807 (*British Museum*)

16 Elevation of the house of Sir Watkin Williams Wynn in St James's Square (*British Museum*)

15 Doctor Johnson and his servant Francis in Bolt Court, Fleet Street

17 Interior of the Bank of England (*Mansell Collection*)

18 The Royal Exchange, 1788 (*Guildhall Library*)

Plumb has observed that 'as the cousinage of the aristocracy covered the whole of England in a network of blood-relationship', so the squirearchy (he was thinking in particular of wealthy, ambitous squires like Sir Robert Walpole) extended theirs over the counties and neighbourhoods.[1] The poorer landed gentry – the Squire Westerns and their like – who accounted for perhaps three-quarters of the 'esquires' and 'gentlemen' noted by King and Colquhoun, would not be likely to be found in significant numbers in the capital, except perhaps among those whom Colquhoun describes as 'living on incomes'. There would, however, in London be a disproportionate number of gentry who sat in parliament, held Cabinet posts or lucrative offices of State. Others, again, would be connected with the arts or sciences or with the law: directly as judges and senior counsel or, indirectly, through the many gentlemen's sons who studied at the Inns of Court.[2]

Some of the gentry (though they were far fewer than among the aristocracy) had financial interests in the City of London or contributed substantially to government loans. Among the first 500 subscribers to Bank of England stock in the 1690s were 150 'esquires' and 'gentlemen' resident in London or in its immediate suburbs; a few of these were men of wealth. The largest holders of Bank stock in 1709 included two prosperous gentlemen with London addresses: Sir Francis Dashwood (£12,000) and Sir Stephen Fox (£5,000). The governors and twenty-nine directors of the East India Company in 1720 included, among a majority of London business men and merchants, a rich landowner and diplomat, Sir Lambert Blackwell, who became Sheriff of Nottingham, and owned land worth £40,000. Listed among the large East India proprietors of 1724 were Sir Isaac Newton, the distinguished scientist (£11,000), Sir Littleton Powys, a judge of the King's Bench (£15,000), and Sir Thomas Colby, Bart, of Kensington (£10,000 or more). Dudley North held over £31,000 of East India stock in 1723. Among the largest subscribers to the government loan of 1748 were a number of Members of Parliament, including George Grenville, a younger brother of the Earl Temple (£10,000), who also appears among the large corporate owners of stock in 1750 with a holding of over £15,000. Some gentlemen continued to figure among the more substantial proprietors of Bank of England stock

[1] J. H. Plumb, *Sir Robert Walpole*, vol. 1, p. 15.
[2] Robert Robson, *The Attorney in Eighteenth-Century England*, 1959, pp. 15, 167; Wilfrid Prest, 'Legal Education of the Gentry at the Inns of Court, 1500–1640', *Past and Present*, no. 38, December 1967, pp. 20–39.

E

after the mid-century; but they were few. By and large, the gentry played only a minimal part in the activities of the City of London.[1]

Where, and in what style, did the gentry live? A few, presumably those most closely connected with trade, lived in the City: Sir John Major, Bart, for example, was living in Savage Gardens, in the Tower Ward, in 1771, when he was assessed for the sewer rate at £60. A few, too, rivalled the really 'great' among the aristocracy in their style of living. None more successfully than Sir Robert Walpole, who was Chief Minister to the first two Georges for over twenty years and had previously held a succession of government posts that brought him a fortune (as well as a spell in the Tower of London), which he largely invested in his mansion and art treasures at Houghton, on the Norfolk coast. He moved into 17 Arlington Street in 1716 and remained there until 1731 (his house was assessed at £135). He next spent four years in St James's Square before becoming, in September 1735, the first First Lord of the Treasury to take up permanent residence at 10 Downing Street. On leaving office in 1742, he returned to another house in Arlington Street and died there in 1746. Meanwhile, he had bought a house and a garden, as a rural retreat, at Chelsea for £1,100.[2]

Another wealthy landowner and baronet, who lived in considerable style in London, was Sir George Savile, Member for Yorkshire and long one of the Marquis of Rockingham's principal lieutenants in the House of Commons. In 1755 he was living in the most expensive house in Hanover Square (assessed at £200) and moved, in 1764, to Savile House, an even more lavish mansion (though assessed at the same rent), on the north side of Leicester Fields, where he remained till his death in 1783; three years before, when the 'No Popery' rioters were on his trail, he had his railings torn down and his house was threatened. Among other distinguished gentry was Sir Joseph Banks, the botanist, who returned from a famous voyage to the Pacific in 1771 to take up residence in New Burlington Street; he moved in 1775 and spent twenty years in a handsome Adam-style house at 29 (later 32) Soho Square. There was also Sir Watkin Williams Wynn, for whom Robert Adam built a house at 20 St James's Square in the early 1770s; it was assessed at £300 in 1795. There

[1] Sir John Clapham, *The Bank of England*, vol. 1, pp. 275–89; P. G. M. Dickson, *The Financial Revolution in England*, pp. 112–17, 263–4, 279–300.

[2] G.L., Sewer Rate, 1771, MSS. 2137/1–4; W.P.L., St George Hanover Square, Poor Rate, 1728; Hugh Phillips, *Mid-Georgian London*, pp. 71, 288; Wheatley and Cunningham, vol. 1, p. 380.

was Robert Clive, who returned from India to live in Berkeley Square; he took his life there in 1774. A few of the gentry lived in the overwhelmingly aristocratic St James's Square: among them, in the latter half of the century, were the Hon. Sir George Lee (£170), Sir Orlando Bridgman (£187), Sir Thomas Webb (£180), George Byng, M.P. (£250), Richard Barwell (£300), Admiral Anson (£250) and Sir Philip Francis (£200), who died there in 1818 after being a resident for over twenty years. A few more lived in Hanover Square, including the Rt Hon. Welbore Ellis (£200); and others on the fashionable Park-side of Arlington Street, where rents ranged from £60 to £240 in 1755 and £160 to £325 forty years later. But these were all among the wealthiest. For most the typical residence was the 'First' or 'Second' class terrace house in Baker Street, Bedford Row, Soho Square, Golden Square or parts of Marylebone, where rents might be at £40 to £60, and rarely over £100.[1]

Some country gentry, like the aristocracy, came to London for the season, to pass the day at Ranelagh or Vauxhall, to discharge their parliamentary duties, or to do the annual shopping. Their expenses naturally varied with their taste and the size of their bank balance. So Squire Blundell spent no more than £25 3s. 2d. on a fifteen-week visit; but he lodged with friends and ate at inexpensive taverns. Sir Thomas Chester, M.P. for Gloucestershire, on the other hand, spent £371 on lodgings during a four-months' residence, and a further £384 on clothes, wines, food and fuel; in 1789, Lady Blois paid £250 a year for a three-years' lease in Harley Street, while Sir Walter Calverley spent £260 on furniture and on the purchase of a 'chariot'.[2]

Some, like the aristocracy, sought an occasional or prolonged escape from London to the neighbouring countryside. We have noted Sir Robert Walpole's residence at Chelsea. Other Londoners, who lived in or retired to Chelsea were Sir Isaac Newton (1709–10), Sir Richard Steele, who rented a house by the waterside for £14 a year, and Sir Hans Sloane, the eminent physicist and President of the Royal Society, who bought the manor house from Lord Cheyne in 1712 and retired there with his library and collections thirty years later; on his death in 1753, his collection of antiquities was sold to Parliament for £20,000 and became the nucleus of that in the British Museum. Farther afield, there was the landscape designed by William Kent for Miss Pelham at Esher, whose

[1] Hugh Phillips, *Mid-Georgian London*, pp. 290–304; W.P.L., Rate Books, 1722–95; *Georgian London*, pp. 126, 143.
[2] G. E. Mingay, *English Landed Society*, p. 157.

cave (wrote Horace Walpole) 'was overhung to a vast height with wood-bines, lilacs, and laburnums, and dignified by those tall shapely cypresses . . . it was Parnassus, as Watteau would have painted it'. Among Palladian mansions was Wrotham Park, in South Mimms, designed for George Byng by Isaac Ware in 1754 (rentable value £475); earlier, we have Defoe's rhapsodies about Sir Stephen Fox's 'palace' and gardens at Chiswick, Baron Temple's 'fine seat and garden' at Sheen, Sir Richard Temple's house near Croydon and many others among the two thousand houses (in Middlesex alone) 'which in other places would have passed for palaces'.[1]

Those whom Defoe termed 'the rich' were essentially the great mercan-tile and financial *bourgeoisie* of the City of London. Enriched by the commercial and colonial expansion and wars of the Commonwealth and Restoration, they had been the close allies of aristocracy and gentry in carrying through the 'glorious revolution' of 1688. As founders of the Bank of England, they had identified their interest more closely with that of the Crown, and, with few exceptions, they remained throughout this period stalwart supporters of the Hanoverian monarchy through all its tribulations. They had, in some cases, become directly linked with 'the great' through the marriage of a son or a daughter. We have already referred to the alliance thus made between the Duke of Bedford and the London banker, Sir Josiah Child; and among the City aldermen and wealthy merchants of Hanoverian London there were several whose families, through intermarriage, moved into the aristocracy: among them, Sir James Bateman (Lord Mayor in 1717), whose son became the 1st Viscount Bateman; Sir John Fryer (Lord Mayor in 1721), whose widow married the 1st Viscount Palmerston; Sir Peter Delmé (1724), father-in-law of the 1st Lord Ravensworth; Thomas Harley (1768), brother of the 3rd Earl of Oxford; and perhaps there were a dozen others.[2] Moreover, their wealth was, perhaps inevitably, considerably greater as a rule than that of the aristocratic families that sought their alliance; and Defoe spoke no more than the truth when he wrote that 'our merchants are princes, greater and richer, and more powerful than some sovereign princes', and contrasted the 'immense wealth' of men enriched 'behind the counter' with the declining fortunes of the gentry and many 'ancient families'.[3]

---

[1] Wheatley and Cunningham, vol. 1, p. 380; Geoffrey Webb, 'Architecture and the Garden', in *Johnson's England*, vol. 2, pp. 117–18; *A Tour*, vol. 1, pp. 166–8; vol. 2, pp. 12–13.

[2] A. B. Beaven, *The Aldermen of the City of London*, vol. 1, 1908, pp. 195–203.

[3] Daniel Defoe, *The Complete English Tradesman*, 1726, pp. 240–2.

These were the men whom Gregory King included under his rubric 'merchants and traders by sea' and Colquhoun termed more specifically 'eminent merchants, and bankers'; they both numbered them at 2,000 and attributed to them an average yearly income of £400 and £2,600 respectively. In London, there may have been 1,000 such men among the 10,000–15,000 merchants and 'principal tradesmen' of the metropolis and among the increasingly prosperous Sephardic Jewish community, who, though mainly resident in the City of London, were excluded from all civic rights within it. The wealth of this *bourgeoisie* was largely derived from overseas trade and banking, and through their close association with the Bank of England, the private banks, and the great trading 'moneyed companies' whose boards they dominated and largely controlled. To cite a few examples. Among the founders of the Bank of England were 250 London merchants and tradesmen, including Sir Theodore Jannsen, who, like King William and the Earl of Portland, held £10,000 of the original stock. Jannsen, who was three times elected director of the Bank in its first twenty-five years, had increased his holding to £25,000 by 1707–9, when, among the Bank's principal proprietors, there were several other London merchants including two future Lord Mayors: Sir Peter Delmé (£14,300) and Sir James Bateman (£10,000); two aldermen: Sir Henry Furnese (£10,000) and Sir John Lethieullier (£6,500); also John Francis Fauquier (£26,400), Jacob Jacobson (£40,289) and Peter Fabrot (£5,885). Jannsen was also a director of the South Sea Company in the year of the Bubble and forfeited his holdings as a result of the scandal that ensued; yet he could well afford it, having previously estimated his fortune at £300,000 ('which I thought enough, and therefore took no measures to increase it'). Sir Peter Delmé, too, acquired a considerable fortune. In the year of his mayoralty (1724), he was holding no less than £118,358 of Bank stock, £47,700 of East India stock and over £122,000 of South Sea stock (in addition to a further £150,000 which he shared with a fellow-director in trust for the Bank of England).

Among the largest of these stockholders were a group of Sephardic Jews, all of whom had offices in the City of London; and the names of da Costa, de Medina, Henriquez, Rodriguez, Salvador, Pereira, Ximenes and de Mattos were to become famous in London banking and commerce during the eighteenth century. Anthony da Costa held £7,700 of Bank of England stock in 1709 and £31,331 of East India stock in 1724; the equivalent holdings of Francis Pereira were £13,200 and £85,075; by 1726 Pereira's holding of Bank stock, £104,625 16s. 8d., almost equalled the combined holdings of the Marlborough and Godolphin families. An operator on an even larger scale was the financier Samson Gideon who, with £35,000, was the largest single subscriber to the 3 per cent loan of 1742 and who, as government loan agent and 'stag', initially subscribed £300,000 to the loan of 1744 and £590,000 to that of 1750, while, on his own account, he held £76,450 of corporate stock in March of that year. He died, nearly forty years later, leaving a fortune of half a million pounds.[1]

And there was certainly no tendency for this 'financial revolution' (as Dr Dickson has called it) of the first half of the eighteenth century to go into reverse during the second. In fact, it was rather the other way, as merchants, who had made their money in trade, turned more and more 'from commercial pursuits proper to those of pure finance'. Dr Sutherland gives us the comparatively humble example of William Braund, who, beginning as a merchant in the Portugal trade, and connected by business and marriage with banking and insurance, became progressively an East India shipowner, a manager of the Sun Fire Office and a director of the East India Company. He died in 1774, after spending most of his life in the City – 'on 'Change, in Lloyd's Coffee-house, in City offices' – leaving an estate of £45,000.[2]

Braund may perhaps only marginally qualify as one of 'the rich'; he is certainly not so by the standards of some we have mentioned before. And it is, therefore, not surprising that he preferred to live in the City, migrating from Rood Lane, Fenchurch Street, in the 1730s, settling in Tokenhouse Yard in 1744, moving to Throgmorton Street in the mid-fifties, to Coleman Street or Broad Street in 1763, to Russia Court, Leadenhall Street, in 1766, and returning finally to Fenchurch Street in 1768, before retiring to die on his property at Hacton, Essex. Other, wealthier City men also chose to live within the City: there was no compulsion to do so, for, even if they were aldermen, they were not bound by any residential qualification. At the end of the century, for example, we read of the noted engraver and print-publisher, John Boydell, alderman of Cheap, who, although he had had a gallery built for him by George Dance in Pall Mall, continued to live over his shop at 90 Cheapside, where he rose every morning at five and washed himself at the pump in Ironmonger Lane. And, a generation earlier, several of

[1] Sir John Clapham, *The Bank of England*, vol. 1, pp. 275–82; P. G. M. Dickson, *The Financial Revolution*, pp. 112–18, 249–314, 445; Beaven, vol. 1, pp. 121–3.
[2] Lucy S. Sutherland, *A London Merchant 1695–1774*, 1962, pp. 4–16.

the wealthy aldermen most actively engaged, on one side or the other, in the affair of John Wilkes, resided within the City of London. Such were Richard Oliver, West India merchant, of 107 Fenchurch Street; William Nash, wholesale grocer, of Cannon Street; Frederick Bull, tea merchant, of Threadneedle (later Leadenhall) Street; James Townsend, of 6 Austin Friars; and even the Rt Hon. Thomas Harley, merchant and banker, of Aldersgate Street. But Wilkes himself (who belonged more to the 'lesser' gentry than to the wealthy merchant class) lived consecutively in St James's Place, at 13 Great George Street, at 7 Princess Court, and at 30 Grosvenor Square; while one of his principal associates, William Beckford, a wealthy West India merchant, who was twice Lord Mayor of London and had an income of £36,000, lived for nineteen years in Soho Square at the comparatively modest 'rent' of £68 a year.[1]

Some of the wealthiest merchants, however, had both the means and the ambition to live, like the aristocracy, at 'the polite end of the town'. Among these, in the 1750s and 1760s, were a number of directors of the big 'moneyed companies'. Two South Sea directors, William Fauquier and John Warde, lived respectively in Stratton Street, Piccadilly, and in Duke Street, St James's; Luke Scrafton, a director of the East India Company, lived in Grosvenor Square; and both Peter du Cane, a Bank of England director, and Sir Charles Asgill, Lombard Street banker and alderman of Candlewick Ward, had houses in St James's Square. Another of Wilkes's associates, John Sawbridge, grandson of Jacob Sawbridge, from whom he had inherited a fortune, lived in Burlington Street, off Piccadilly. Earlier, Sir Theodore Jannsen had been one of the original residents of Hanover Square, where he lived from 1720 to 1723; while Samson Gideon, wealthiest of London's Jewish financiers, having spent many years in Leicester Fields, moved at the end of a long life (in 1787) to Arlington Street, Piccadilly. Yet these were a small number compared with those who preferred to live out their lives within the limits of the City. And we must remember, too, that, in spite of the intermarriage and social integration, there was still a lingering gulf separating the everyday manner of life of the mere 'rich', who had made their money from trade, from that of the gentry or 'the great'. Archenholtz shrewdly noted that

> This difference which holds even in the hours of eating and drinking, in the kind of amusements, the dress and manner of speaking etc.

[1] Lucy S. Sutherland, *A London Merchant*, p. 4; Wheatley and Cunningham, vol. 1, p. 251; vol. 2, p. 263; *Wilkes and Liberty*, pp. 2–5.

has given rise to a degree of mutual contempt by the inhabitants of each of these quarters for the other. Those of the city reproach them of the other end for their idleness, manner of living, and desire to imitate everything that is French: these in their turn never mention an inhabitant of the city but as an animal gross and barbarous, whose only merit is his strong box.[1]

But if wealthy merchants preferred the comparative austerity of Soho Square, Leicester Fields and the City to the aristocratic neighbourhood of St James's, they certainly had no inhibitions about emulating the nobility and gentry in building properties and retreats in the rural areas beyond the metropolis. Defoe, as we saw, makes frequent reference to the fashionable houses established by City merchants in Essex, Surrey and Middlesex: in Surrey he noted, in particular, the mansions of Sir Theodore Jannsen at Wimbledon and of Sir James Bateman at Tooting. He also noted that wealthy Jewish merchants had 'fixt upon' Highgate as their favourite country retreat and had built a synagogue. We saw, too, that a directory of 1793 claimed that, at this time, there were 300 London merchants with freeholds in Middlesex alone. Among such Londoners, twenty-five years before, were two of Wilkes's staunchest, and certainly the wealthiest, supporters in the county elections of 1768–9: Alderman John Sawbridge, who owned land in Edmonton and Tottenham (the latter alone of an annual value of £480), and Alderman James Townsend, the proprietor of Bruce Castle, Tottenham, which was assessed for land tax at the very considerable sum of £806 a year. Even more elegant and costly was Osterley Park, once Sir Thomas Gresham's home, which had been acquired by Sir Thomas Child, the banker, in 1711, and was decorated for Robert Child by Robert Adam half a century later. Adam's work was spread over twenty years and resulted in a mansion which, with its splendid portico and slim Ionic columns, challenges even the splendour of nearby Syon House.[2]

Defoe's 'middle sort' were the medley of social groups sandwiched between the rich merchant *bourgeoisie* and 'his working trades, who labour hard but feel no want'. They were the people whom William Beckford, in a speech in Parliament in 1761, championed as 'the middling classes of England' and whom John Wilkes, two years later, termed 'the middling

[1] Hugh Phillips, *Mid-Georgian London*, pp. 288, 302; W.P.L., St James's, Poor Rate, 1775, 1769, 1774; J. W. Archenholtz, *A View of the British Constitution*, p. 122.

[2] Daniel Defoe, *A Tour*, vol. 1, p. 168; vol. 2. pp. 2–3; *The Universal British Directory*, 1793; Nikolaus Pevsner, *Middlesex*, pp. 128–30; *Wilkes and Liberty*, p. 87.

set of people' whom (with those of 'the inferior set') he considered to stand 'most in need of protection'. In Gregory King's list of 1696 they are made up of such varied elements as 'merchants and traders by land', 'persons in the law', 'clergymen', 'persons in sciences and liberal arts' and 'shopkeepers and tradesmen'. But Patrick Colquhoun, while adopting King's categories up to this point, took account of the great social and industrial changes of the past hundred years by adding new groups such as shipowners and manufacturers, clothiers, technicians, innkeepers, dissenting clergymen and teachers – swelling King's total of 'middling' families from 82,000 to 254,000, or more than trebling their numbers at a time when the national population had less than doubled.[1]

How far such a development was reflected in London it would, for lack of precise information, be impossible to say with any certainty. Yet we may, with such facts as are available, hazard an estimate of the number of Londoners formed by these 'middling' groups by the end of the century. Before that, the numbers of merchants and tradesmen listed in the directories are quite insufficient to afford us any clue. Thus, the *London Guide* for 1749 lists a little over 4,000 tradesmen and merchants, *Mortimer's Universal Directory* for 1763 a mere 3,000 and *Baldwin's Complete Guide* for 1770 some 6,000 to 6,500. In 1791 the *London Directory* lists some 14,750 tradesmen and master craftsmen (including manufacturers and innkeepers) in the Cities of London and Westminster; from other sources we learn that there were at this time some 500 counsel and 1,840 attorneys (or solicitors), 640 sworn brokers and perhaps 1,000 civil servants, 81 rectors and vicars in the City of London, and 479 surgeons and 86 apothecaries. But the gaps are, even now, far too evident to provide us with an answer. We appear, however, to be on more certain ground with *Holden's Triennial Directory* of 1805–7, which, among its 140,000 names, lists those of 49,900 London business and professional men, covering every sort of trade and drawn from the out-parishes and Southwark as well as the City of Westminster. Yet this, in contrast to the rest, is too high a figure, as it includes not only the wealthier merchants (Defoe's 'rich') but also many belonging, more properly, to the 'working trades'. But if we deduct an adequate proportion for these higher and lower groups and take note of the numbers of voters in London, Westminster and the out-parishes (about 20,000 at this time), we may arrive at a figure of some 30,000 families of the 'middle sort', accounting for

[1] M. Dorothy George, *England in Transition*, pp. 150–5.

perhaps 125,000 persons, or 1 in 7 of the population of London according to the census of 1801.[1]

How and where did the 'middling' people live? It was rarely in the manner of the gentry, let alone of the aristocracy or 'the rich'. Gregory King attributes to the highest group among them, the 'lesser' merchants, an average income of two-thirds that of a mere 'gentleman', while Colquhoun gives them slightly more (£800 against a gentleman's £700). But, after that, the proportions fall off steeply: 'lesser' clergy's incomes are, in both cases, only one-sixth of those of 'gentleman'; arts and sciences between one-quarter and one-fifth in the one case and one-third in the other; while shopkeepers and tradesmen fall somewhere between the two.

Yet these 'middling' groups, though their incomes might be broadly similar, led such different lives, resided in such different parts of the town, and engaged in such a wide variety of occupations that it will be best to consider them, briefly, in three separate categories: the tradesmen and shopkeepers of the Cities of London and Westminster; the manufacturing, carrying and servicing trades, based on the port and the out-parishes of Surrey and Middlesex; and, finally, the professional men and artists, whose lives, though not their incomes, were often nearer to those of the gentry than to the tradesmen or lesser merchants. In the case of the first, their lives were centred on their shops and offices (which also served as homes). The rents they paid, or on which they were assessed for rates, might range between £8 or £10 at the lower end of the scale and £40 or £50 at the upper. These are the tradesmen and householders who appear in such large numbers in the rate books or poll books of Westminster, in the rate books of the City, and – if freemen of the City Companies – in the occasional printed polls of the livery of London. In Westminster they were scattered over the nine parishes, though with occasional heavy concentrations in certain streets, as in the 471 households appearing in the rate books for the Strand. Here Mr Hugh Phillips has used the rate books and Horwood's map of 1799 to reconstruct the addresses and occupations of a little under half the occupants (228) of 1750. Though some are more prosperous, most are typical of the tradesmen of Westminster such as we saw them represented in the poll book of 1749: lacemen (a fair number), cheesemongers, confectioners, watchmakers, stationers, book and print-sellers, publicans, cabinet-makers, hosiers, haberdashers, mercers, druggists, toymen, perfumers, oilmen, pawnbrokers, ironmongers, linen drapers, grocers, apothecaries, tobacconists, pastrycooks, jewellers and a

[1] Besant, pp. 391-3; London Directories of 1749, 1763, 1770, 1791, 1805-7.

score or more of others. These are, on the whole, substantial tradesmen. Their rents varied between a minimum rent of £7 and a maximum of £135, and the average ranged, according to the ward they lived in, between £38 and £48.[1]

For the City of London, let us take samples of rents from two parishes, neither of which are among either the poorest or the wealthiest picked out by P. E. Jones and A. V. Judges in their study of the City's population in the late seventeenth century.[2] In Aldgate (6th precinct), in 1771, fourteen houses in Crutched Friars paid 'rents' ranging between £10 and £45 with an average of £22; in Gun Powder Alley, six properties paid £4 and one paid £6; in John Street, four properties paid an average of £17 5s. od.; in Gould Square, eight properties paid between £30 and £50, an average of £37 10s. od.; in Cooper's Row, a dozen properties paid between £18 and £80, an average of £22; and, on Tower Hill, eleven paid between £8 and £60, an average of £33. In Aldersgate Within (St Leonard's precinct), forty-three properties were assessed for rates at an average of £17 15s. od.[3]

The second group were, in essence, the 'middling' element among the freeholders of the out-parishes, of whom a particularly useful record survives in the Middlesex poll books of the 1760s. The 40s. freeholders of Middlesex, who alone were eligible to vote in the county elections, numbered at this time between 3,500 and 4,000; and, of these, about 1,000 (or 28 per cent) occupied properties whose annual value ranged between £10 and £49, and may therefore be included among 'the middle sort'. Of these, in turn, a little under one-half belonged to the out-parishes of London in which they exercised such occupations as wharfingers, lightermen, warehousemen, importers, coal-merchants, victuallers and shopkeepers of every sort.[4] Though their occupations often differed from those of the tradesmen, shopkeepers and master craftsmen of Westminster and the City of London, it may be supposed that their standard and manner of living was broadly similar.

Of course, among these tradesmen and shopkeepers there were men who, while not aspiring to be counted among 'the rich', rose considerably

[1] Hugh Phillips, *Mid-Georgian London*, pp. 119–84, 289–91; W.P.L., Poor Rate, 1750, F.525 (St Martin's).
[2] P. E. Jones and A. V. Judges, *Economic History Review*, vol. 6, 1935–6, pp. 58–62.
[3] G.L., Sewer Rate, 1771, MSS. 2137/1–4.
[4] George Rudé, 'The Middlesex Electors of 1768–1769', *E.H.R.*, vol. 75, 1960, pp. 601–17.

in wealth and status above the level of their fellows. Sir John Summerson gives us the example of William Tufnell, a bricklayer of Millbank working for the New River Company, who had the skill and opportunity to make a small fortune which, on his death in 1733, was valued at £30,000.[1] Moreover, shopkeeping was becoming a specialized occupation, and London's shops, in the more fashionable districts at least, were acquiring a reputation for the excellence of their window-dressing and the rich luxuries of the goods they offered for sale. Defoe, writing in 1713, displays a sort of fascinated horror at this new-fangled development in 'painting and gilding'; ''tis a small matter,' he observes, 'to lay out two or three hundred pounds, nay, five hundred pounds, to fit up a pastry cook's, or a toy shop. . . .' And, later in the century, visiting foreigners were amazed at the number and the magnificence of London's shops, whether in Pall Mall or at St Paul's, with their large glass windows and elegant displays, and considered them infinitely superior to those in the fashionable Rue St Honoré in Paris.[2]

Such success stories as that of William Tufnell were more dramatically repeated in the case of several of the writers, artists and 'professional' men, whose activities, more than those of any others, have shed such an aura of glamour over Hanoverian London. A relatively minor example from the earlier years was that of Nicholas Hawksmoor, the architect, who, from humble beginnings, rose through the patronage of wealthy patrons to acquire the suffix of 'Esquire' and to leave a country estate and considerable property in London. A more sensational rise to fame was that of Sir Joshua Reynolds, the price of whose painted heads rose from 5 guineas in 1753 to 25 in 1760, who was making £6,000 a year by 1762, was admitted to the fashionable Brooks' Club in 1764, became President of the Royal Academy in 1769, and held the office without a challenger for fifteen years. But London could equally be the graveyard of a young artist's dreams, as illustrated by the tragic story of Thomas Chatterton, the poet, who, coming to London in search of fame in May 1770, took his life in his Holborn lodgings a mere four months later.[3]

For such young artists or writers of 'the middle sort' it was essential, particularly in the earlier part of the century, to win the benevolence of a

[1] *Georgian London*, p. 71.

[2] M. Dorothy George, *England in Transition*, pp. 33-4; and in *Johnson's England*, vol. 1, pp. 175-6.

[3] *Georgian London*, p. 71; Andrew Shirley, 'Painting and Engraving', in *Johnson's England*, vol. 1, p. 58; Wheatley and Cunningham, vol. 1, pp. 285, 480; vol. 3, p. 245.

wealthy patron. John Gay, the author of *The Beggar's Opera*, was living in Burlington Gardens in 1729 in the London residence of his patrons, the Duke and Duchess of Queensbury, and was a frequent visitor to Burlington House. Handel, the musician, had a succession of patrons: at first he was attached to the household of the Duke of Chandos, subsequently he spent three years in Burlington House, and later he enjoyed the personal favour of George II. Alexander Pope, in 1729, was a regular guest at the Dover Street house of Edward Earl of Oxford. James Boswell, when he first came to London in 1762, was sheltered by the Earl of Eglington in his house in Queen Street, Mayfair. Even the formidable Samuel Johnson, who thought that £50 a year 'was undoubtedly more than the necessities of life require', made an unsuccessful attempt to woo the patronage of the Earl of Chesterton, then living in Grosvenor Square; and like Hogarth and Smollett, he later became a pensioner of the Earl of Bute. Joseph Addison, the founder of *The Tatler*, did better: he married the Countess of Warwick (in 1716) and went into permanent residence at Holland House.[1]

Some artists and writers established themselves, when the opportunity arose, in Mayfair or St James's, or in other fashionable parts of the town. George Romney, the portrait painter, lived for several years in Cavendish Square and John Zoffany in Albemarle Street and Bennet Street, St James's. John Gray, the author of the 'Elegy in a Country Churchyard', lodged in Jermyn Street in 1753; and John Hoppner, the artist, died at 18 Charles Street, St James's. Richard Brinsley Sheridan lived successively in Hertford Street, Mayfair, and in George Street, Hanover Square, while Boswell lived, at various times, in Bond Street, Conduit Street, Half Moon Street and Queen Anne Street, Cavendish Square. Some preferred rural retreats: Pope had a weakness for Twickenham; William Godwin lived for several years in St Pancras and Somers Town; Charles Lamb, in 1800, was living in Chapel Street, Pentonville (then still a village). For many artists the Mecca, often after various peregrinations around the town, was Leicester Fields. William Hogarth resided there from 1733 to 1756 (his house was assessed at £60). Sir Joshua Reynolds, a later resident, moved in 1761 from Great Newport Street (with a rent of £60) to a larger establishment (£110) at 47 Leicester Fields, where he lived until his death in 1792. Sir Thomas Lawrence lived in the Fields

[1] Sir Henry Hadow, 'Music', in *Johnson's England*, vol. 2, p. 194; R. W. Chapman, 'Authors and Booksellers, in *Johnson's England*, vol. 2, p. 318n; Wheatley and Cunningham, vol. 1, pp. 13, 148, 305.

in 1787 and John Copley from 1785 to 1812. William Hillman, the portrait painter, died there in 1741, and Louis-François Roubiliac, the sculptor, moved in the same year to St Martin's Lane, close by. Others, again, preferred the coffee-house life and bustle of Fleet Street and the Strand. David Garrick, like other actors, favoured Covent Garden or the Strand: after a succession of lodgings in Goodman's Fields and Covent Garden, he lived, at the height of his fame (between 1749 and 1772), at 27 Southampton Street, Strand, and moved from there to the Adelphi, where he died in 1779. Oliver Goldsmith spent the last sixteen years of his life at a number of addresses in and about the Temple – finally, after several years at Garden Court and King's Bench Walk, at No. 2 Brick Court, in the Middle Temple. But the most inveterate resident of all in this quarter of London was Samuel Johnson, who resisted all temptations to move into a more fashionable part of the town: the decision was made the easier, no doubt, by the fact that he rarely earned more than £300 a year. After early lodgings in Exeter Street, Little Britain, Greenwich, Woodstock Street and Castle Street (both off Oxford Street), he came to live, more or less permanently, in and around the Strand in the late 1740s. Successively, he migrated to lodgings in Boswell Court, Gough Square (where he compiled his Dictionary), Inner Temple Lane, Johnson's Court, Fleet Street; and, finally, to 8 Bolt Court, Fleet Street, where he rented a house and garden from Allen, the printer, for £40 a year and died in 1784.[1]

Like the merchants and the gentry, several of the writers and artists sought a prolonged or occasional escape from London in the countryside. Johnson spent many summers with his friends, the Thrales, at Streatham Park. George Romney had a retreat at Pine Apple Place, Maida Vale, where he went for 'rural breakfasts'. Reynolds occupied Wick House, on Richmond Hill, between 1772 and 1792. Garrick had an 'airy portico' at Hampton, designed by Robert Adam, and became lord of the manor of Heston. Pope owned a villa and 5 acres of land at Twickenham, where he was visited by Swift, who also rented a room for 6s. a week in Chelsea. Many artists sought rustic themes at Paddington, in whose churchyard several painters, engravers and sculptors of the late eighteenth century lie buried. Henry Fielding lived on Ealing Common in 1754, and Oliver Goldsmith lived at Edgware in 1768 and at Kingsbury from 1771 to 1774.

---

[1] Wheatley and Cunningham, vols 1-3, various; Hugh Phillips, *Mid-Georgian London*, pp. 79, 278; R. W. Chapman, 'Authors and Booksellers', in *Johnson's England*, vol. 2, p. 318; W.P.L., St Anne Westminster, Poor Rate, 1755, 1762.

Leigh Hunt was born at Southgate (with 'its pure sweet air of antiquity') in 1784, and J. M. W. Turner, the painter, was at school at Brentford. Among other artists connected with Middlesex were William Hogarth, who regularly visited Chiswick between 1749 and 1764 and was buried in the churchyard, and John Zoffany, the portrait painter, who lived in the fishing village of Strand on the Green, died there in 1810, and lies buried in the churchyard on Kew Green across the river.[1]

[1] Wheatley and Cunningham, vol. 3, pp. 1–3; Michael Robbins, *Middlesex*, pp. 149–154.

4

Social Life, the Arts and Entertainment

IN HANOVERIAN ENGLAND, London was the centre of the nation's culture, fine arts, intellectual pursuits, taste and fashion, as it was the centre of government and economic life. These had a certain stability in that they closely reflected the needs of the largely aristocratic society of which we have written in the previous chapter. Nevertheless, fashion, whether in dress or manners, whether in the arts, literature or ideas, underwent considerable changes during the span of years separating the death of Queen Anne from the long reign of George III. At the most superficial level, it can be seen in the gradual shortening of the male peruke from the shoulder-length periwig that was still fashionable under Anne and George I to the short pig-tail peruke of the 1750s to 1780s and to its eventual disappearance during the wars with France; and, conversely, in the evolution of the female head-dress from the simplicity of the earlier years to the 'walking steeples' of the 1770s, which prompted Hannah More, after a dinner party, to describe the ladies' head-gear as being composed of 'an acre and a half of shrubbery besides slopes, grass-plats, tulip-beds, clumps of peonies, kitchen gardens, and green-houses'![1] It could also be seen in the progressive refinement of manners of both Court and aristocracy. It was a long cry to the muted refinement and decorum of the Court of George III or the sophisticated elegance of the Regency from the barrack-room explosions of the first two Georges, the earthy obscenities of Sir Robert Walpole, and the note that Queen Anne is reported to have sent Sir Robert, when a young minister, that 'the fat

[1] *Three Tours*, pp. 55–6.

19 A general prospect of Vauxhall Gardens in 1751, from a drawing by Samuel Wale
(*Victoria and Albert Museum*)

21 The Rotunda at Ranelagh Gardens, 1751, from a drawing by Canaletto
(*British Museum*)

22 The tavern and tea garden at Bagnigge Wells, 1772, from a drawing by F. Sanders
(*British Museum*)

old bitch' had decided to forgive him![1] At a more exalted level, it was also a long trek from the satire of Swift and Gay or the self-conscious classicism of Pope to Percy's *Reliques* and the sentimental drama of Hannah More; from the Neo-Classical serenity of the Adam house to the Gothic fantasies and *chinoiseries* of Strawberry Hill; or from the smug acceptance of Blackstone's *Commentaries* to the radical challenge implicit in Bentham's *Fragment on Government* or the *Wealth of Nations* by Adam Smith.

Among the more reputable entertainments of the day, the theatre was continuously popular with the fashionable classes and, increasingly, with 'the middle sort' of people as well. The Italian Opera House, in the Haymarket, alone drew almost exclusively 'genteel' patrons and, even among them, as the century progressed, its stilted elegance and patently foreign imitation gradually lost their appeal. In the early years of the century, the most popular theatres were the Lincoln's Inn Fields Theatre, in Portugal Row, and the Theatre Royal in Drury Lane. The Lincoln's Inn theatre virtually closed down after 1732, when its highly successful and enterprising manager, John Rich, moved to the Covent Garden Theatre, which opened a year later, and under Rich's management became the rival of the Drury Lane as the most fashionable and popular playhouse of the middle years of the century.

John Rich owed his translation to the Covent Garden to two outstanding successes. One was his revival of the pantomime of *Dr Faustus*, in which he played the part of Harlequin and drew away the public from every other theatre: Hogarth depicts the scene in his 'Masquerades and Operas'. The other success was of greater consequence: his production of John Gay's *Beggar's Opera* in 1727. The play, based on familiar (and seamy) London life, was a refreshing novelty and ran for sixty-two nights, a record for its day. Both manager and playright did well out of the venture and the wits wrote that the play 'made Gay rich and Rich gay'. It also made the fortune of Lavinia Fenton, who played the part of Polly Peachum, for she caught the eye of the Duke of Bolton, who first set her up as his mistress at £400 a year and later made her his wife.

At the Covent Garden Playhouse in the 1730s, Rich paid his actors a basic salary of £1 a night, so they might earn between £150 and £180 a year. But stars earned more. Mrs Heron drew £250 in 1735–6; Lavinia Fenton earned 30s. a night as Polly Peachum; and Garrick, in his first

[1] Dorothy Marshall, 'Manners, Meals, and Domestic Pastimes', in *Johnson's England*, vol. 1, p. 336.

F

major London role (in 1741) was paid £2. But salaries tended to rise. During the 1742-3 season at the Covent Garden, players were paid 7 guineas a week where they had previously been paid 5, while stars like Garrick and Kitty Clive earned twice that amount; and Rich's salaries bill rose from £6,104 in 1740-1 to £7,379 in 1746-7. Other costs tended to rise as well, 'scenes and machines' rising meanwhile from £100 to £253, 'wardrobe' from £522 to £1,064, music from £206 to £680, and heating and lighting from £62 to £100 in the one case and from £85 to £350 in the other. For their seats, the public paid 3s. in a box off-stage, 2s. in the pit and 1s. in the gallery at the Lincoln's Inn Fields and the New Theatre, Goodman's Fields, in the 1730s, and twice as much at the Covent Garden after 1792. Receipts and profits naturally varied with the theatre, the play and the season. Rich's opening night at the Covent Garden yielded £115 in receipts, where a good opening night at the larger Lincoln's Inn Fields had yielded £180. The Covent Garden was considered to have a maximum earning capacity of £220 a night, but Garrick, on his 'benefit' night in the spring of 1747, brought in £274. Rich's profits for the first thirty performances at the Covent Garden were about £33 a night. But profits varied greatly. A one-night run like *The Provok'd Husband*, when played for the first time, raised only £10; whereas *The Beggar's Opera*, when revived and co-billed with *Europa* in 1735, made a clear profit of £97 13s. 5d.; and the outstanding success of the 1730s – a two-feature programme combining *The London Cuckolds* (a comedy) with *Apollo and Daphne* (an opera) – yielded a profit of £157.[1]

It was an age of considerable acting talent: among men, there were Garrick, Quin, Foote, Kemble and Spranger Barry; and, among women, Mrs Cibber, Kitty Cliff and Peg Woffington. But none achieved the fame and popularity of David Garrick. Garrick's first London appearance was in the part of Richard II at the Goodman's Fields Theatre, in Great Alie Street, in October 1741. His success outmatched that of the first production of *The Beggar's Opera* of fifteen years before, as he played the part for 150 consecutive nights and earned £300. He went on to play leading roles for the next thirty-five years, alternating between the Covent Garden Theatre and the Theatre Royal in Drury Lane. He played and produced Shakespeare (often with considerable emendation), the comedies of Sheridan and the new sentimental comedies which, in the 1760s, became

---

[1] Arthur H. Scouten (ed.), *The London Stage 1660-1800*, Part 3, *1729-1747*, Carbonade (Illinois), 1961, pp. xix-clxxxviii; Hugh Phillips, *Mid-Georgian London*, pp. 146-51, 192-3.

popular with middle-class audiences. Among his finest and most applauded performances were those in *The Clandestine Marriage, The School
for Scandal* and *The Belle's Strategem*. But the most moving occasion of
all was when Garrick made his last appearance at the Drury Lane, in
The Wonder, a comedy by Mrs Centlivre, on 10 June 1776. Normally,
seats could not be booked in advance, though doors opened at five o'clock,
one hour before the curtain was due to rise. This time, to mark the
occasion, the whole proceedings were delayed by half an hour and the
playbill added: 'Ladies are desired to send their servants a little after 5 to
keep places, to prevent confusion.' But Garrick was as popular with the
groundlings as he was with the occupants of the boxes; and when the
play ended, there was a general feeling of deprivation (for, as a contemporary wrote: Garrick's loss 'impoverished the publick stock of harmless
pleasure') and both actors and audience dissolved in tears.[1]

But while the theatre, both by its nature and its long tradition, was
always susceptible to the demands of a wider audience, the patronage of
the visual arts remained, far longer, almost exclusively aristocratic. One
result was the preoccupation with portraiture, which dominated painting
(if not sculpture) for the greater part of the century. And portraits were,
almost inevitably, expected to be flattering to the patrons who commissioned them. It was rare indeed for the aristocratic patron to take
the attitude reported of the Duke of Hamilton by Jonathan Richardson
in his *Essay on the Theory of Painting* (1715). The Duke, who had been
painted by Sir Godfrey Kneller, the fashionable portraitist of the day,
gazed alternately into the mirror and at the canvas and said: 'Zounds,
when I look in the glass I am a poltroon, when I look there I am a man
of quality.' Consequently, the one great English artist of the century who
painted his subjects 'warts and all' – William Hogarth – was dismissed
by even a fashionable *connoisseur* like Horace Walpole as a painter of
'slender merit'; and his famous set of six pictures, the 'Marriage à la
Mode', was sold in 1750 for only 120 guineas (from which 24 guineas
must be deducted for the cost of the frames). Another reason why
Hogarth, among others, was never seriously considered as an artist (while
his engravings sold in thousands and appeared on the walls of many a
'middling' household) was his complete failure to respond to the call of
Antiquity. The Grand Tour, by sending the sons of the nobility to enlarge
their horizons in Rome and Florence, brought home a slavish devotion to

[1] W. J. Lawrence, 'The Drama and the Theatre', in *Johnson's England*, vol. 2,
160-89; W. S. Lewis, *Three Tours*, pp. 70-6.

the 'classical', as seen through the eyes of the Italian painters of the Renaissance, from Michaelangelo and Raphael onwards, and through those of English painters like Reynolds and Wilson after their visits to Rome. The mood was reinforced when Winckelmann, the noted German antiquarian, whose essays were published in 1756, proclaimed, hot on the heels of the discovery of the ruins of Herculaneum and Pompeii, that 'imitation of the Ancients is the shortest way to perfection in the fine arts'. Meanwhile, a third preoccupation had crept in, and became the stronger with the succession of wars with France and Spain in the 1750s to 1780s: the theme that the artist must elevate the mind by a continual evocation of the heroic and the moral. So a high premium was placed on historical portraiture, and Reynolds' *Discourses* before the Royal Academy reveal the strong influence on him of Richardson's view that 'a painter should read the best writers – such as Homer, Milton, Virgil, Spenser, Thucydides, Livy, Plutarch, etc.; but chiefly the Bible'. And all three of these attitudes were clearly evident in the catalogue prepared for the sale of Dr Mead's great collection of paintings in 1754: it announced the sale of 45 portraits, 23 landscapes and sea pieces, 13 architectural and 'ruin' pictures, 14 Dutch still-lives and animal pictures and 55 historical pictures by a score of artists; but not one was English or Spanish, and while several were Italian not one was a primitive.[1]

But already, in spite of the current preoccupations with Greece and Rome, British artists were beginning to be taken seriously by their aristocratic patrons. The new attitude took time to develop. In George I's day, Sir Godfrey Kneller was one of a handful of English painters who could compete successfully with foreigners for the most important commissions. Yet, by 1748, a list of eminent artists published by the *Universal Magazine* included the names of 42 Englishmen or Scots (Hogarth, Gainsborough, Reynolds and Wilson are among them), 9 Dutchmen, 3 Frenchmen and one German. The scales were turned even more decisively in favour of the native artist by the founding of the Royal Academy, with Reynolds as its first president, on 2 January 1769. From now on, aristocratic patronage, with George III setting the example, was assured for British painters and sculptors. The new trend is reflected in the rising prices that the artists were able to command from their patrons. Reynolds, as we noted in an earlier chapter, was charging 25 guineas for a head in 1760 where, seven years before, he had charged only 5, and (according to Johnson) he was already making an income of £6,000 a couple of years

[1] Osbert Sitwell and Margaret Barton, 'Taste', in *Johnson's England*, vol. 2, pp. 1–26.

later. He continued for long to hold a dominant position, and in the Academy's exhibition of 1776, in which neither Gainsborough nor Romney were represented, he displayed no fewer than thirteen of his own portraits. But Gainsborough had sixteen pictures (including five landscapes) in the exhibition of 1780 and, in 1786, was asking 40 guineas for a head, 80 for a half-length and 160 for a full-length portrait; and even George Romney, who held no official position, made a professional income, in the same year, of £3,504. Moreover, a wider public was becoming involved, particularly through the sale of engravings and the holding of exhibitions on historical themes. William Woollett's engraving of 'The Death of Wolfe' (after Benjamin West, 1776) made £15,000 in fourteen years; and Jonathan Copley's 'Death of Chatham' (1781), which he displayed in his own gallery at an entrance fee of 1s., drew over 20,000 spectators.[1]

More deliberately refined and more consciously imitative of foreign models was the London *salon*. The *salon* had begun to emerge in the 1750s but only reached its full flowering in the 1770s and eighties. Its presiding genius was Mrs Elizabeth Montagu, a 'female Macaenas', who had visited the reigning Queen of French literary hostesses, Madame du Deffand, in Paris and held her own French-imitated *salon* of letters and literary breakfasts alternately in her house in Hill Street and her mansion in Portman Square. The meetings were almost entirely composed of literary ladies, or 'blue-stockings', with a sprinkling of male writers and gossips, among whom Horace Walpole was a notable 'catch'. The tone was refined and aristocratic and the business was polite conversation and the patronage of letters. Mrs Montagu's principal rival among the 'blues' was Mrs Elizabeth Vesey, who was attached to Lawrence Sterne, the author of *Tristram Shandy*, and, unlike her colleagues, had a reverence for Voltaire and the French agnostics. Other 'blue-stockings' were Mrs Boscawen, wife of the admiral; Hannah More, who specialized in 'sensibility'; Elizabeth Carter, who translated Epictetus; Mrs Mary Grenville Delaney, who had known Swift; Fanny Burney, 'the mouse-like young lady of St Martin's Street' and author of *Evelina*; and Mrs Hester Thrale, who wrote an unsuccessful play, and some years later left *Anecdotes of the Late Samuel Johnson*. Only Hannah More and Fanny Burney have left their mark in literary anthologies; yet others among these ladies were greatly admired in their day. Mrs Delaney was described

[1] Andrew Shirley, 'Printing and Engraving', in *Johnson's England*, vol. 2, pp. 41–60; *Three Tours*, pp. 68–70.

by Edmund Burke as 'the highest bred woman in the world'; and Mrs Elizabeth Carter's erudition was commended by Johnson, who also thought Fanny Burney's *Evelina* the equal of Fielding.[1]

Of the more mundane pleasures, for the men, at least, drinking and gambling held pride of place. It was only during the French Revolutionary wars, and after some years of evangelical campaigning, that such vices, together with irreligion and irregular unions, began to be generally condemned. Drunkenness was considered a normal and satisfactory condition as much by Defoe or Sir Robert Walpole as it was later by Johnson or Wilkes. It was a Bow Street tavern that proudly proclaimed: 'Here you may get drunk for a penny, dead drunk for twopence, and get straw for nothing'; and Johnson expressed the opinion that 'a man is never happy in the present unless he is drunk'. In the first half of the century there was a tidy class division in drinking: the poor drank gin or cheap brandy, 'the middle sort' drank porter or ale and the wealthier classes drank French or Portuguese wine; when gin-drinking was discouraged and declined after 1750, the drinking of ale and wine continued unabated. At the end of Anne's reign, ordinary French claret sold at 4s. to 6s. a gallon, and good bottled claret at 3s., 4s. or even 10s. a bottle; a cheap port (introduced by the Methuen Treaty of 1703) sold for as little as 5s. a gallon; and Rhenish wine at 1s. 8d. a quart or 6s. a gallon. In the 1730s British brandy cost 4s. a gallon, Old Cognac 7s. 9d. and Jamaica rum 7s. At this time, the quantities of liquor consumed in London in a single year were enormous: 11,200,000 gallons of spirits (or 14 gallons per adult male), nearly 2 million barrels of ale and 30,000 tuns of wine. And to dispense this liquor there were in London, according to Maitland, 207 inns, 447 taverns, 5,875 beerhouses and 8,659 brandy shops.

Ale and porter (and also wine) were regularly drunk in taverns, which ranged from the common beerhouse or ale-house, or 'taverns of the second rank', to the more dignified middle-class affair like the Turk's Head in Gerrard Street, the Mitre in Fleet Street, the Crown and Anchor in the Strand, the Bedford Arms and the Shakespeare's Head in Covent Garden, and the Devil (or Old Devil) at Temple Bar. The larger taverns, or inns, were social centres not only used for drinking but also for concerts, formal dinners, political reunions or meetings of clubs and societies. Dr Johnson was a great tavern man and had a regular chair at the Turk's Head, where he presided over 'The Club', which he had founded with Reynolds in 1764 and whose members supped weekly at seven; he was

[1] Chauncy Brewster Tinker, *The Salon and English Letters*, 1915, pp. 134-65, 257.

equally at home in the Mitre, the Devil, and the Crown and Anchor where he sometimes dined with Boswell. Wine was drunk both in taverns and in the houses of the aristocracy and gentry. Yet here the richer 'citizens' could hold their own, and some of the biggest orgies of wine-drinking took place at the Mansion House which, built to George Dance's design, was first occupied as the Lord Mayor's residence by Sir Crisp Gascoigne in 1753. From the accounts of a generation later, we learn that over the dozen years 1774–85 the amount consumed at the annual dinners varied between a 'low' of 389 dozen bottles (in 1782) and a 'high' of 626 dozen bottles (in 1774), with an average of 481![1]

Gambling was, to a degree, officially encouraged, as a £1,500,000 Lottery Bill (an annual affair until 1824) was first adopted by Parliament in 1709; prizes were high and a lucky ticket-holder in 1713 drew £36,000. It began as an aristocratic vice which spread to other classes; and in the 1770s Horace Walpole ascribed the growth of crime, in part at least, to 'the outrageous spirit of gaming [which has] spread from the fashionable young men of quality to the ladies and to the lowest rank of the people'. Long before this, the Old Club at White's, in St James's Street, had established itself as the most fashionable gaming house in town and, according to Swift, Robert Harley, when Chief Minister under Anne, had cursed it as 'the bane of half the English nobility'. White's was joined, some years later, by Boodle's and Crockford's, both in St James's Street; and by Almack's in Pall Mall, which moved in 1778 to St James's Street under the new name of Brooks's. This became the greatest gambling den of all, and it was here that the largest stakes were placed and the largest fortunes were lost and won. Charles James Fox, when only twenty-four, lost £140,000 and had his debts paid for him by his wealthy father, Lord Holland. Lord Lauderdale once spoke of £5,000 being staked on a single card at faro and of £70,000 being lost and won in a single night; while Horace Walpole, himself a member of Brooks's, wrote of it as a place 'where a thousand meadows and cornfields are staked at every throw, and as many villages lost as in the earthquakes that overwhelmed Herculaneum and Pompeii'.[2]

Others forms of entertainment might be looked for in Covent Garden,

---

[1] *Three Tours*, p. 58; J. Ashton, *Social Life in the Reign of Queen Anne*, vol. 1, 1882, pp. 199–201; Besant, pp. 289–300; Bryant Lillywhite, *London Coffee Houses*, 1963, p. 23; M. Dorothy George, in *Johnson's England*, vol. 1, pp. 180–2.

[2] J. Ashton, *Social Life in the Reign of Queen Anne*, vol. 1, pp. 114–16; *Three Tours*, pp. 32, 44, 61; Wheatley and Cunningham, vol. 1, pp. 286–7.

which, since the aristocracy migrated west, had become the main centre of the city's night life. This was the area of the more fashionable 'disorderly houses' or 'houses of ill-fame', some of which are depicted by Hogarth, who knew the district well, in his 'Rake's Progress'. 'One would imagine,' mused Sir John Fielding sadly, 'that all the prostitutes in the kingdom had picked upon that blessed neighbourhood for a general rendezvous, for here are lewd women enough to fill a mighty colony.' To evade the law, the houses masqueraded under the ostensibly respectable (and legitimate) labels of tavern, coffee-house or 'bagnio'. Among the most popular were 'The Rose', in Drury Lane, Tom and Moll King's and Mother Douglas's (the former Betty Careless's) in the Covent Garden *piazza*. Tom King, an Eton scholar, received a mixed *clientèle*, including noblemen and *beaux*, who went to his tavern 'after Court in full dress, with swords and bags, and in rich brocaded coats and walked and conversed with persons of every description'; his death in 1737 was commemorated in a satirical broadsheet bearing the inscription, 'For thee, all bawds and pimps lament, from every bagnio sighs are sent.' Mother Douglas knew even greater fame; for not only was she portrayed by Hogarth in his 'Industry and Idleness' and in 'The March to Finchley', but she appeared in two contemporary plays and may have been the model for John Cleland's Mrs Cole in the *Memoirs of Fanny Hill*.[1] But this was a period when public morality and conjugal fidelity, as displayed by the fashionable classes, were at a low ebb. Prostitutes openly advertised their wares; gentlemen kept mistresses as a matter of course, if not as a matter of honour: George II set the example (after having been set it, in turn, by his father) by taking his mistress, the Countess of Yarmouth, with him on State visits to Hanover.[2] The fashion would gradually change, though slowly, as the Court itself under George III, became impregnated with 'middle-class' virtues, particularly after the American war; though, admittedly, the tide turned again with the Regency and the reign of George IV.

It was also an age of open-air life and 'outings', in which both sexes took part. The London parks were considered as much a part of London life as its coffee-houses or taverns. Walking in the Park was a favourite social pastime. St James's Park, in particular, was the public place among all public places where men and women of fashion paraded in order to see and to be seen. But Kensington Gardens was the more exclusive after

---

[1] Hugh Phillips, *Mid-Georgian London*, pp. 142-5; E. Beresford Chancellor, *The Annals of Covent Garden*, 1930, pp. 64-5.

[2] *Three Tours*, pp. 59-63.

Queen Caroline had it fenced round; and it was noted in 1774 that 'for the better regulating the company, servants are placed at the different entrances to prevent persons meanly clad from going into the garden'. Londoners also liked to go farther afield: a favourite excursion was to go to Epsom and Tunbridge, or to Dulwich and Sydenham Wells, to drink the waters. But Defoe observed that the more serious water-drinkers went to Dulwich and Sydenham, whereas to Epsom and Tunbridge people went 'more for the diversion of the season, for the mirth, and the company, for gameing, or intriguing, and the like'. In consequence, he noted a tendency for the aristocracy and gentry to go to Epsom, and the common people (by which he meant 'the middle sort') to go chiefly to Dulwich and Streatham – all the more readily 'because it lyes so near London, that they can walk to it in the morning, and return at night'.[1]

Of all short outings the favourite were visits to the fashionable pleasure gardens of Vauxhall and Ranelagh, which lay within easy reach of Westminster. Vauxhall Gardens (known as Spring Garden till 1785) was the older and the more popular and amusing. It was also the cheaper, the price of entry being 1s. until 1792, when it was raised to 2s. It had the larger gardens and could seat three to four hundred people at a time for supper. When the Gardens reopened, after a brief closure, in 1732, Hogarth was commissioned to paint the rooms and Roubiliac's first work in England, a statue of Handel, was put on display. One of the largest gatherings was in 1749, when a hundred musicians played to an audience of 12,000: it caused (wrote the *Gentleman's Magazine*) such a stoppage on London Bridge that no carriage could pass for three hours. The gardens continued to be fashionable until early in the next century; and one of its last great displays was when a M. Garnerin, in September 1802, landed there from a great height in a parachute.

Ranelagh, at Chelsea, opened as a pleasure garden in 1742. The price of entry was 2s. 6d. ('tea and coffee included') and 5s. on fireworks nights. It normally had no suppers and served no wines, and was the smaller and more sedate of the two. Its chief attraction was its round room, or Rotunda, 150 feet in diameter, with an orchestra in the centre and tiers of boxes all round; and Walpole, a regular visitor to both gardens, wrote to General Conway in 1744: 'Every night I constantly go to Ranelagh, which has totally beat Vauxhall. Nobody goes anywhere else – everybody goes there.' Both gardens staged balls, masquerades and other elegant *divertissements*. Of the latter, one of the most splendid and original was the

[1] M. Dorothy George, in *Johnson's England*, vol. 1, pp. 182–6; *A Tour*, vol. 1, p. 157.

regatta held on the Thames, followed by a supper and ball at Ranelagh, in June 1775. It was presented by all the most fashionable clubs and gaming houses of St James's, and 1,300 tickets were sold – to club members only. It was suggested that guests should wear fancy costume and the most fortunate were given seats on barges loaned or hired from the Lord Mayor and the City Companies. The race itself was rowed by twelve 'race-boats', each manned by two young watermen, from Westminster to Waterman's Hall, off London Bridge, and back. But there was unutterable confusion as barges clogged the path of the competitors and women and children, caught by a low tide, waded in the mud. Besides, it rained and blew; and Horace Walpole, having escaped home to Arlington Street before the supper, wrote to the Countess of Upper Ossory: 'There are such tides of people in the street, that I could scarce pass home. I feel as glad to be returned home as I did from the Coronation, and I think I will go to no more sights.'[1]

Other fashionable sports of the day, involving Londoners, were cricket and boxing. Cricket had an ancient history, going back to 1640 at least, and was at first played only by the humbler classes. Lord John Sackville rescued it for the gentry at Laleham Burley, in Kent, early in the eighteenth century. The first recorded match was that between the Gentlemen of Sevenoaks and the Gentlemen of London in July 1734; and, in 1746, Kent (captained by Lord John Sackville's gardener, Rumney) defeated an All-England eleven, recruited in the immediate 'home' counties, at the Artillery Ground in Finsbury by 111 runs to 110 before a large audience attended by the Prince of Wales and the Duke of Cumberland. Cricket was being played at Harrow in 1772, the earliest recorded school match was between Eton and Westminster on Hounslow Heath in 1796, and Eton and Harrow began their annual contests in 1800. While cricket might be a gentlemen's game – or a game where masters and servants met briefly on common ground – boxing was strictly for the prize-fighter or professional pugilist, whose task it was to batter his opponent senseless with his naked fists. Yet a first step was taken to tame the sport, and even to open it to the gentlemanly amateur, when Jack Broughton, Champion of England since 1740, three years later opened an academy for boxers in the Haymarket, where he provided his pupils, including 'persons of quality and distinction', with 'mufflers that will effectively secure them from the

[1] Wheatley and Cunningham, vol. 3, pp. 147-9, 427; M. Dorothy George, in *Johnson's England*, vol. 1, 188-90; F. H. W. Sheppard, 'An Eighteenth-Century Regatta on the Thames', *History Today*, December 1959, pp. 823-9.

inconveniency of black eyes, broken jaws, and bloody noses'. Broughton, while champion, enjoyed the patronage of the Duke of Cumberland; but when he was defeated for the title by Jack Slack, a Norfolk butcher, in 1750, the Duke, who had lost heavily on the contest, withdrew his patronage and later transferred it to the victor. Prize-fighting, in fact, provided one more opportunity for men of fashion to place a bet. In July 1764, runs a press report, Chairman Brooker and Brick-Street Jack fought it out in a field near Knightsbridge. 'The battle was the most desperate ever known, and, during the contest, several hundred pounds were won and lost.'[1]

Among the more violent sports on which gentlemen betted for high wagers were cock-fighting, and bull- and bear-baiting. There were bear-gardens in Marylebone Gardens and at the more disreputable Hockley-in-the-Hole, at Clerkenwell, where, in 1715, the sum of 2s. 6d. gave access to a combined performance of bull- and bear-baiting or to a contest between battling women or between a dog and a man. The fashionable set tended to desert these cruder sports before the middle of the century, but cock-fighting continued in vogue and, in the 1760s, gentlemen might wager as much as 40 guineas a battle on the success of their birds at the Royal Cockpit in St James's Park. When Boswell first came to London he was, on one such occasion, 'sorry for the poor cocks' and 'looked round to see if any of the spectators pitied them when mangled and torn in a most cruel manner'. But, he adds, 'I could not observe the smallest relenting sign in any countenance.'[2]

Nor need Boswell's experience surprise us, as violence was as much a characteristic of the age as powdered wigs and 'walking steeples'. Sons of the gentry were schooled in violence from tender years. Mrs Harris, mother of the 1st Earl of Malmesbury, describes, in February 1770, a drunken brawl followed by a riot at Winchester College, in the course of which the young gentlemen broke out of Hall, sallied forth 'with weapons of all kinds', and fought the townsmen with such vigour that the magistrates were compelled to read the Riot Act.[3] It was a period, too, when affairs of honour were still settled with sword or pistol, sometimes ending in farcical anti-climax and sometimes in injury or death. One duel

[1] Michael Robbins, *Middlesex*, pp. 144–5; E. D. Cuming, 'Sports and Games', in *Johnson's England*, vol. 1., pp. 376–80; Jack Lindsay, *1764*, 1959, p. 188.

[2] E. D. Cuming, in *Johnson's England*, vol. 1, pp. 372–5; Wheatley and Cunningham, vol. 2, pp. 216–18, 509–10; *Boswell's London Journal 1762–1763*, ed. F. A. Pottle, 1966, p. 113.

[3] *The Letters of the First Earl of Malmesbury from 1745 to 1820*, ed. J. H. Harris, 1870, vol. 1, pp. 194–7.

which achieved notoriety was that fought in Marylebone Fields, in 1748, between Lord Coke, son of the Earl of Leicester (a Whig), and Harry Bellenden (a Tory) over the alleged slight done by the former to a lady related to the latter; neither party was scathed. On another occasion (in 1779), Charles James Fox was wounded in a contest with a nephew of Robert Adam in Hyde Park. In its grimmer manifestations, this violence was reflected in the barbarities inflicted on the believed enemies of society or of the State. The most notorious was the public execution of the thirty-eight rebel prisoners after the Jacobite rising of Forty-five, who were drawn on hurdles to Kennington Common, hung for six minutes, cut down while still alive, decapitated and disembowelled, and their heads placed on Temple Bar; the last of these trophies was still grinning down on the citizens in 1772. Meanwhile, the bodies of highwaymen hung in chains on the highways and commons, women were flogged in Bridewell and soldiers in Hyde Park, and public executions at Tyburn were maintained by Parliament as an instrument of policy until 1783, when they were transferred to the more sheltered seclusion of Newgate Prison yard. To Francis Place's disgust, the former practice met with Johnson's approval; for (he said) 'the public was gratified by a procession; the criminal was supported by it. Why is all this to be swept away?'[1]

Yet it would be misleading to suggest that London's intellectual and cultural life, or even its fashions, its sports and entertainment, were solely dictated by the nobility and gentry or by 'the polite end of the town'. If we allow ourselves to be too much influenced by the smooth pen of Horace Walpole, the greatest gossip of the age, this must indeed appear to be the case. But London was, in this respect, quite different from Paris and other Continental cities, whose cultural and social life was dominated by the Court and the landed classes; whereas in London, the 'life of the town' (to borrow Dr George's phrase) bore almost as much the stamp of the City, with its commercial and middle-class values, as it did that of the Court of St James's. This is hardly surprising in view of the economic domination of the City, which we have already noted, and the extraordinary vitality and independence of its political institutions which we shall discuss in a later chapter. It was an influence, extending not only over the capital but over the nation as a whole, that Voltaire noted when he visited London in the 1720s; and he commended to his countrymen the

---

[1] *Three Tours*, pp. 15, 31–2; *Wilkes and Liberty*, p. 12; *A Narrative of the Trials of the Rebel Prisoners on the King's Commision of Oyer and Terminer, at the Court-House on St Margaret's Hill, Southwark*, 1746.

example of England, where, in contrast to his own country, he saw commerce, prosperity, religious toleration, scientific experiment and political
and intellectual freedom going hand in hand.[1]

It is possible that Voltaire, dazzled by the freshness of his experience,
overstated the case; but it is probably no exaggeration to say that such
important institutions and innovations as the coffee-house, the newspaper,
and even the novel, were the product of the City and of a commercial and
middle-class, rather than of an aristocratic, way of life. The first coffee-
house was opened in St Michael's Alley in the City in 1652 and was
quickly followed by others, both within the City and beyond Temple Bar;
but during the Restoration, the largest concentration lay within the square
mile around the Royal Exchange. Unlike their later Parisian counterparts,
they rapidly became centres of political discussion and, because of this,
they were briefly closed by Royal Proclamation in 1675. But they revived
and flourished and, in Anne's time, there were 450 coffee-houses and, by
1739, 551; at this time, 144 of them lay within the City walls (including
the Tower and London Bridge), while the rest were fairly evenly divided,
within Westminster, between the east and west sides of the Strand. There
was a further slight shift away from the City after a fire, in 1748, destroyed a large number of coffee-houses, enclosed between Cornhill and
Lombard Street and Birchin Lane and 'Change Alley, of which several
were reopened on other sites.

The coffee-house remained essentially a meeting-place where the events
of the day were discussed, papers were read and news and gossip were
exchanged; but they early divided on functional lines. Thus the Stock
Exchange emerged from the Stock Exchange Coffee-house or Tavern,
opened in Sweeting's Alley in 1773; the Jerusalem in Cornhill (a victim of
the 1748 fire) was frequented by merchants and captains in the China and
Indies trade; the Virginia and Maryland Coffee-house in Threadneedle
Street became the *venue* for shippers engaged in the Baltic trade and, in
1744, changed its name to the Virginia and Baltick; Lloyd's (or New
Lloyd's), which moved from Abchurch Lane to Pope's Head Alley in
1712, became the acknowledged centre of underwriting for marine insurance; Garraway's, in Cornhill, and Jonathan's and the Amsterdam, at
Temple Bar, were frequented by merchant bankers; and Batson's, in
Cornhill, was used as a consulting-room by physicians to receive their
City clients. Others achieved fame through their association with political
parties or writers and artists. Thus White's Chocolate House, in St

[1] Voltaire, *Letters concerning the English Nation*, 1759.

James's Street, the fashionable gaming house, was, in Swift's day, a Tory meeting-place, while Whigs favoured the St James's or Button's in Covent Garden. Will's Coffee-house, in Russell Street, Covent Garden, made famous by Dryden, was later patronized by Addison and Steele who also, with Swift and Gay, met at Garraway's in the City; while the artists Roubiliac, Wilson and Wilkie went to 'Old' Slaughter's in St Martin's Lane; David Garrick to Tom's in Birchin Lane; Goldsmith and Thomas Chatterton to the Chapter Coffee-house in Paternoster Row; and a plethora of notables, including Pope, Sheridan, Garrick, Fielding, Quin, Foote and Charles Churchill, favoured the Bedford Coffee-house in Covent Garden.[1]

As the coffee-house arose in response to the City's commercial and political needs, so the coffee-house, in turn, engendered the newspaper. The first daily newspaper, the *Daily Courant*, appeared in London in 1702. (In Paris, there was no daily press until the *Journal de Paris* was issued in 1777.) A more influential paper, the *Evening Post*, was first published in 1706, and Steele's and Addison's illustrious weeklies, the *Tatler* and the *Spectator*, were founded, respectively, in 1709 and 1711. There was a comparative lull during the first ten years of the Hanoverian Succession, at the end of which the *London Journal* appeared in 1725 and the *Craftsman*, which voiced the main opposition to Sir Robert Walpole, in 1727. There followed, in more or less rapid succession, the *Daily Advertiser* in 1730-1, the *Westminster Journal* in 1741, *Lloyd's Evening Post* in 1757, the *St James's Chronicle* in 1761 and the *Middlesex Journal* and the *Morning Chronicle* in 1769. Two years later, the London press fought its great duel, with City support, with Parliament and Lord North's first ministry over the right to publish parliamentary proceedings and debates. In the so-called 'printers' case' (1771), the editors and printers of eight London newspapers – including the *Middlesex Journal*, the *Gazetteer*, the *Morning Chronicle*, *St James's Chronicle* and the *London Evening Post* – were summoned to the bar of the Commons to answer for their conduct, and Lord Mayor Crosby and Alderman Oliver, their City champions, spent some weeks in the Tower of London; but the printers won their point and the papers continued, without further interference, to offer their readers the tenor of parliamentary debates. After this, the *Morning Post* appeared in 1780, *The Times* in 1785, and the Sunday *Observer* in

---

[1] Aytoun Ellis, *The Penny Universities. A History of the Coffee-Houses*, 1956, pp. 58-133; Bryant Lillywhite, *London Coffee Houses*, p. 23. (Mr Lillywhite lists 2,032 London coffee-houses in existence between 1652 and 1852.)

1791. By 1800 there were 278 newspapers, journals and periodicals where there had been only twenty-five when the *Daily Courant* made its first appearance a hundred years before.

Many of these papers were ephemeral and others had a strictly limited circulation, yet in the mass it is evident that they exerted a considerable influence both in moulding public opinion and in harnessing it as a political force. How many readers did these newspapers have? We can only guess the answer from such meagre evidence as we possess. In the eighteenth century, a circulation of 2,500 to 3,000 was reasonably satis-factory, though in periods of war or crisis it might rise to 4,500 or even 5,000: the *Craftsman* may have reached this figure in 1740, *The Times* in 1795 and the *Morning Post* in 1803. So perhaps after 1760 (in a period when there were never fewer than a hundred journals of all kinds circu-lating in the capital) the aggregate of their readers may have amounted to twelve times this number, and considerably more at moments of crisis. If so, the press was clearly a powerful factor in forming and expressing the opinions of a politically literate middle class.[1]

As the London coffee-house and the London press offered their own particular type of challenge to the Court and to an aristocratic way of life, so we find a similar challenge, although assuming different forms, in the impact of middle-class values on literature and the arts; and this was increasingly the case as the century went on. In their most sophisti-cated form these values were expressed in the novel, which was not merely an old medium into which a new content had been poured, but a new art form altogether. There is a world of difference between the mood expressed (let alone in the plot) by Daniel Defoe in *Moll Flanders* (1722), Samuel Richardson in *Pamela* (1740), Henry Fielding in *Joseph Andrews* (1742), and Tobias Smollett in *Roderick Random* (1748). But they all have in common, in addition to their literary innovations, a new realism and the assertion of a new middle-class morality as an antidote, or challenge, to the aristocratic traditions and assumptions, and the anomalies, in-sensibility and amorality of the society of their day. Moreover, these authors are essentially the product of the new urban society, the highest expression of which was, in their day, to be found in London; and in their

[1] D. Nicholl Smith, 'The Newspaper', in *Johnson's England*, vol. 2, pp. 331–67; R. S. Crane and F. B. Kaye, *A Census of British Newspapers and Periodicals 1620–1820*, 1927, pp. 182–201; *Handlist of English and Welsh Newspapers, 1620–1920*, 1920; Peter D. G. Thomas, 'John Wilkes and the Freedom of the Press (1771)', *Bulletin of the Institute of Historical Research*, May 1960, pp. 86–98.

books they present – and notably in Defoe's *Moll Flanders*, Smollett's *Roderick Random* and *Humphrey Clinker*, and Fielding's *Joseph Andrews* – a picture of the metropolis of London as seen through the eyes of their heroes and heroines. So the novel, with its urban message and its appeal to mainly urban readers, was, in its way, as much a product of the city and as much a vehicle for the propagation of middle-class values and middle-class social attitudes as the newspaper and the coffee-house.[1]

In the pictorial arts, a similar realism and didactic purpose imbue the work of William Hogarth; and we have seen how little his art had in common with that practised by the more fashionable artists of his times. Again, we saw how, a generation later, the aristocratic patron was beginning to be pushed aside by a new 'middling' or 'popular' patron, who welcomed the new school of historical painting but demanded, as in the case of Copley's painting of 'The Death of Chatham', that the heroes should be of the present rather than of ancient Greece or Rome. Equally, in the drama, actors and managers like Garrick and Colly Cibber owed a part, at least, of their great success to their ability to respond to the needs of a growing middle-class audience, to whom it was imperative that virtue should triumph and crime be punished, and to their willingness to adapt or 'doctor' the old plays (Shakespeare's included) where they fell short of the new moral standards. In this way, as it has been said, even 'Comedy had grown, like Niobe, all tears'.[2]

The process was taken a stage further when writers appeared who expressed directly, in their own work, the new 'sensibility' and the craving for middle-class respectability. In London, there was Hannah More who wrote not only a treatise on 'Sensibility' (1782) for her 'blue-stocking' friends but also a sentimental drama called *Percy* (1777), which ran for twenty-one nights and won its author both acclaim and a sum of £600. It contained, as an illustration of the new trend, the following remarkable passage:

PERCY: Am I awake? Is that Elwina's voice?
ELWINA: Percy, thou most adored and most deceived! . . .
              If thou canst be so wondrous merciful,
              Do not. O do not curse me! – but thou wilt,
              Thou must – for I have done a dreadful deed,
              A deed of wild despair, a deed of horror.
              I am, I am –

[1] Ian Watt, *The Rise of the Novel. Studies in Defoe, Richardson and Fielding*, 1966.
[2] W. J. Lawrence, in *Johnson's England*, vol. 2, pp. 160–6.

24 The Imports of Great Britain from France, by L. P. Boitard, 1757
(*Guildhall Library*)

25 Blackfriars Bridge, July 1766
(*British Museum*)

26 River shipping near the Tower, 1793 (*British Museum*)

27 London Bridge, 1760 (*Victoria and Albert Museum*)

29 The new front of the Theatre Royal, Drury Lane, designed by R. and J. Adam in 1775 (*Victoria and Albert Museum*)

28 Spranger Barry and Miss Nossiter in the Balcony Scene of Romeo and Juliet (*Victoria and Albert Museum*)

30 The riot at Covent Garden Theatre, 24 February 1763

31 The Beggar's Opera, by Hogarth (*Mansell Collection*)

PERCY: Speak, say, what art thou?
ELWINA: Married.
PERCY: Oh![1]

This was by no means a purely British phenomenon: we find a similar trend, in Germany, in Goethe's *Sorrows of Young Werther* and, in France, in the '*comédie larmoyante*' and Greuze's sentimental paintings. Nor was it limited to the arts and literature. Already in 1758, a whole generation before, we find Sir John Fielding, the Bow Street magistrate, commending a plan for 'preserving deserted girls' by employing them in public laundries in the following, almost 'Victorian' terms: 'And who will not rejoice to see this happy Change of Barrow Women, miserable Prostitutes, &c., converted into modest, decent, happy Women, and useful domestic Servants!'[2] To adopt an even wider perspective, it was, in fact, part of a far broader movement, which, in other fields, embraced the preaching of the Wesleys, the work of the humanitarians and the writings of Jeremy Bentham and Adam Smith. Collectively and in association with an industrial revolution, they would serve, in the course of time, to sap the foundations and undermine the props of Hanoverian England.

[1] Chauncy Brewster Tinker, *The Salon and English Letters*, p. 184.
[2] John Fielding, *A Plan for the Asylum for Orphans and other deserted Girls of the Poor of this Metropolis*, 1758.

G

5

The 'Other' London

WE HAVE yet to consider the great majority of London's population – that other London of Defoe's 'working trades', his 'poor' and his 'miserable' – whom historians, with the notable exception of Dr Dorothy George, have largely neglected. These were they who have been given a variety of composite names, sometimes purely descriptive, sometimes contemptuously derogatory. Wilkes, who had a certain sympathy for them, termed them 'the inferior set of people'; more commonly they were called 'the lower orders' or 'the meaner sort'; and Henry Fielding once referred to them as 'that very large and powerful body which forms the fourth estate in the community and has long been dignified by the name of the Mob'.[1]

Such collective labels have their uses, particularly as this was a period when more exact classifications were not as appropriate as they had been in the medieval past or as they were to become in the industrial society of the future. But Francis Place, who had known London from the 1760s onwards, was not merely voicing the prejudices of the respectable craftsmen when he objected to 'the working-people (being) all jumbled together as the "lower orders", the most skilled and the most prudent workmen, with the most ignorant and imprudent labourers and paupers'.[2] For indeed, although they might collectively be distinguished from 'the great', 'the rich' and the gentry, and even from 'the middle sort', there were, in London as in other great cities, important differences separating what Dr Dorothy Marshall has called 'the aristocrats of the working world' from the common labourers and urban poor.[3] Gregory King, in his census of 1696, draws a similar line between his 'artisans' and his

[1] J. P. de Castro, *The Gordon Riots*, 1926, p. 249.
[2] *London Life*, p. 209.
[3] Dorothy Marshall, *Eighteenth-Century England*, 1962, p. 36.

'labouring people and outservants'; and P. J. Grosley, who made a 'tour to London' in 1765, thought that 'we should properly distinguish the porters, sailors, chairmen and the day-labourers who work in the streets not only from persons of condition, most of whom walk a-foot, but even from the lowest class of shopkeepers'. Others, looking back from the nineteenth century or later, might see the main dividing line as between the small employers – the master craftsmen and lesser shopkeepers – and the mass of the wage-earners, or the 'industrious labouring poor'. But this, again, blankets the distinction between the skilled and the unskilled worker, on which Place so rightly insisted, as it blankets that between the more or less regularly employed labourers and the 'improvident' or indigent poor. There is, therefore, some point in drawing a broad line of distinction between as many as four groups within these 'lower orders', somewhat as follows:

1. The master craftsmen and small shopkeepers of the Cities of London and Westminster and the petty tradesmen with stalls in the Boroughs and the markets. These, while bordering often on Defoe's 'middle sort', more properly belong to his 'working trades'.

2. The skilled journeymen and apprentices, whom Defoe called the 'topping workmen' and whom Place, writing in the 1830s, numbered at some 100,000. The dividing line between these groups was extremely fluid (though becoming increasingly less so): a journeyman might still become a master, as Place himself became in the 1790s.

3. The mass of unskilled and semi-skilled: the daily labourers, porters, chairmen, servants, fell-mongers and tanners, riverside workers, sailors and coal-heavers, who, nominally at least, were in regular receipt of wages and of fixed abode.

4. Finally, the 'submerged' and floating population of vagrants and beggars, the 'miserable', the destitute, the unemployed and unemployable, the indigent, the aged, the part-time domestic workers, the casual workers, the poorest of the immigrant Irish and Jews, in fact all those whom Patrick Colquhoun, with his 'middling'-sort prejudices, tended to identify with London's 'underworld' or 'criminal classes' which he reckoned at 115,000 persons, or one-eighth of the city's population in 1797.[1]

---

[1] M. Dorothy George, *England in Transition*, p. 151; *London Life*, pp. 158–62; Besant, p. 383; E. P. Thompson, *The Making of the English Working Class*, 1963, pp. 55–6.

If we except the small employers and better-paid craftsmen, life for the mass of these citizens was hard, brutal and violent and a constant struggle against disease, high mortality and wretched economic conditions. 'The waste of life,' writes Dr George, 'was at its worst since the plague between 1727 and 1750.' But, although this wastage fell off, almost dramatically (particularly in relation to young children), during the second half of the century, the expectation of life remained low and it was not until 1790 that baptisms began, almost as a matter of course, to exceed burials.[1] The diseases which, year by year, claimed the largest number of victims were, in order of their frequency, 'convulsions', 'consumption', 'fevers or purple' and small-pox, and just being 'aged'; and this pattern remained constant for the greater part of the century. In addition, hairdressers, bakers, masons, bricklayers' labourers, labora-tory men, coal-heavers, and chimney-sweeps, in particular, were subject to serious pulmonary infection. And even in 1771, when the chances of survival had long since begun to improve, a newspaper advertisement illustrates the persistence of certain types of illness and of popular faith in quack remedies:

> Dr James's Powder, for Fevers, the Small Pox, Measles, Pleurisies, Quinsies, Acute Rheumatism, Colds, and all Inflammatory and Epidemical Disorders, as well as for those which are called Nervous, Hypochondriac and Hysteric.[2]

Yet, by this time, in addition to the determined legislative measures taken to stamp out gin-drinking, nearly a dozen hospitals and infirmaries had been built or extended to arrest the ravages of disease among the poor. St Bartholomew's, on the outskirts of the City, the oldest hospital in London which went back to 1123, ran courses in anatomy from 1738 and in surgery from 1765, and built a large new lecture theatre in 1791. St Thomas's, in Southwark, founded as an almonry in 1213, had been rebuilt as a hospital, by public subscription, between 1701 and 1706. The Westminster Hospital was founded in Petty France in 1720, and moved to a larger site in Chapel Street four years later. The Foundling Hospital, in Holborn, was built for Thomas Coram in 1739 as a 'hospital for exposed and deserted children'. Guy's, generously endowed by a Lombard Street bookseller as a hospital for 'incurables', opened, with

---

[1] *London Life*, pp. 25, 39.

[2] Besant, p. 637; Thomas Pennant, *Some Account of London*, p. 414; *Public Advertiser*, 27 March 1771; W. S. Lewis, *Three Tours*, p. 65.

sixty patients, in 1725. St George's Hospital stood then, as it does now, at Hyde Park Corner. It was founded in 1734 'for the relief of poor, sick and disabled persons'; the site was chosen (so Maitland tells us) 'on account of its Air, situation and Nearness to Town'; and by 1790, according to Pennant, no fewer than 173,217 patients had passed through its wards. At the other end of the town, the London Hospital had its first site in Prescott Street, Goodman Fields; it opened in 1740 as an infirmary for the relief of 'the sick and injured poor', and, more specifically, for 'Manufacturers, seamen in the Merchant Service and their Wives and Children'; it moved to Whitechapel Road in 1752, and between 1758 and 1781 three extensions were added at a cost of £60,000. A similar venture had been launched off Tottenham Court Road in 1745, when the Middlesex Hospital opened modestly in Windmill Street as an infirmary with eighteen beds for the sick and lame and cancer patients; ten years later, it began its move to Marylebone Fields, where the number of its beds grew to seventy by 1800 and to 179 by the end of the wars.

The hospitals found no difficulty in attracting patients; as new buildings went up and new wards were opened, they flocked in to fill them. In May 1748 the *Gentleman's Magazine*, reporting on 'the Numbers of Objects under Cure' in the metropolitan infirmaries in the course of the previous year, gave a total of 32,552 patients who had undergone treatment. They were dispersed as follows: 7,298 at the London, 7,243 at St Thomas's; 7,193 at St Bartholomew's; 5,436 at St George's; 2,336 at the Westminster; and 2,242 at Guy's. By modern standards, the treatment was primitive: hygiene and sanitation were patently neglected and little understood; beds were bug-ridden; nurses were untrained; and Guy's and the Middlesex were exceptional in admitting patients whose diseases were likely to be incurable. But, with all the hazards, a remarkably high proportion of the sick were patched up and restored to the community as cured or sound in limb. In 1734 Guy's, for instance, discharged 1,524 patients and buried 277, while in 1747 the Westminster cured 705 and buried a mere 48. But the hospitals were not only places of cure; they were also, in accordance with the current tenets of social morality, charitable and 'reforming' institutions in which the poor were constantly reminded of their lowly station in life and of their obligations to God and to their social betters. St George's forbade its patients 'to go out of the Hospital without Leave in Writing', but no such leave would be given in the case of St James's or Green Park! Guy's was more severe and threatened to withhold the next day's food from any patient 'found strolling about the Streets, or frequenting Publick Houses, or Brandy Shops'. At St Thomas's, a patient might be expelled if he swore, took God's name in vain, abused his neighbour, stole, or in any way acted 'immodestly'. The London Hospital would only issue certificates of discharge (which entitled the holder to further relief) to patients who attended chapel to 'return Thanks' for their cure. And it was the London, too, that admirably summed up this dual-purpose role of the eighteenth-century hospital in its claim that its patients, after their discharge, had been

> re-instated in their honest and industrious Capacities of working, and, so far as our Observation reaches, their Morals much amended, whereby the Publick again enjoy the Benefit of their Labours, and they and their poor Families are preserved from perishing, and prevented from being an Incumbrance to the Community.[1]

At this time, there were no clearly identifiable working-class districts, and small employers and their workpeople lived cheek by jowl often on the fringe of the most fashionable residential districts. It might even happen that wealth and squalor rubbed shoulders in uneasy association in the same street or alley – at least in the earlier part of the century – as noted in the following newspaper comment on the City in 1748:

> If we look into the Streets, what a Medley of Neighbourhood do we see! Here lives a Personage of high Distinction; next Door a Butcher with his stinking Shambles! A Tallow-chandler shall front my Lady's nice *Venetian* Window; and two or three brawny naked curriers in their Pits shall face a fine Lady in her back Closet, and disturb her spiritual Thoughts.

Yet this 'medley' was by no means universal and was becoming less so; and certain districts had already long taken on the appearance and acquired the reputation of urban slums and 'dangerous districts', unfrequented by the fashionable or rich. Some of the oldest of these, going back to Elizabethan times, lay in the belt around the City, in St Katherine by the Tower, East Smithfield and around the Mint in Southwark. Others developed later: east of the City in Shadwell, Whitechapel and Bethnal

[1] Wheatley and Cunningham, vol. 1, pp. 117–20; vol. 2, pp. 72–3, 100–1, 175–6, 428–9, 537–8; vol. 3, pp. 373–4, 486–7; Thomas Pennant, *Some Account of London*, p. 110; *Three Tours*, p. 30n; William Maitland, *History of London*, vol. 2, pp. 1304, 1313; Dorothy Marshall, *Dr Johnson's London*, pp. 255–66.

Green and, to the west, around Drury Lane, Clare Market, the Fleet
Ditch and, fairly generally, in the parish of St Giles in the Fields. There
were, in addition and overlapping with these, a network of rookeries and
'thieves' kitchens' – later dramatized by Dickens and Henry Mayhew –
in the courts and alleys off Holborn and Gray's Inn Lane, off Queen
Street and Long Acre, in Covent Garden; and a police detachment, sent
out on a night search at the end of the Gordon Riots, noted in particular
Chick Lane, Field Lane and Black Boy Alley, in Holborn and the Liberty
of Saffron Hill. These were the districts, with their insalubrious hovels
and tenements, in which cheap lodgings might be had for 2*d*. a night or a
garret at 1*s*. or 1*s*. 6*d*. a week, and in which the toll of disease and hunger
was above the normal: Saunders Welch, the magistrate, told Dr Johnson
in 1779 that more than twenty persons died from starvation every week
in London in streets and alleys such as these.[1]

The more respectable and 'settled' workers, whether labourers or
craftsmen, commonly lived in furnished rooms. There were certainly
some who had a hearth or a household of their own: thus, there appear
among the Westminster voters of 1749 the names of 83 labourers, 88
chairmen and 41 watermen, not to mention those of numerous craftsmen
of whom several must have been wage-earners. Again, there were trades
in which the journeyman was still commonly housed and boarded by his
master; as in the case of chemists, grocers, drapers, mercers, barbers,
jewellers, butchers, skinners, upholders, and perhaps a dozen or a score
of others; and such masters, if Freemen of the City, were still pledged, as
Lord Mayor Harley reminded them on a notable occasion in May 1768,
to keep their journeymen 'from going abroad' in times of riot and disorder. But such customs were dying out and the workers generally rented
lodgings, sometimes occupying a single room above a craftsman's shop
and sometimes sharing a tenement with other lodgers, in which (as in
contemporary Paris) the craftsman (the 'housekeeper') might live on the
ground floor and his sub-tenants on the upper storeys, rising the higher in
inverse proportion to their income or status. Rents naturally varied according to the street, the neighbourhood or the comforts provided, but, overall,
they might take up one-eighth of a working man's earnings. In a poor
district, during the greater part of the century, they appear to have
ranged from 2*s*. to 3*s*. 6*d*. a week, but they rose considerably, with the
French wars, after 1795. Benjamin Franklin, when a journeyman printer
in 1725, lodged in Duke Street, St James's, for a weekly rent that was

[1] *Three Tours*, p. 13; *London Life*, pp. 78–105.

reduced from 3s. 6d. to 1s. 6d.; a £50-a-year clerk was paying 2s. 6d. a week for lodgings in a mean part of the town in 1767; and Francis Place tells us that, twenty years later, he paid 3s. 6d. for his lodgings near Butcher Row, behind St Clement's Church, at a time when he was earning 14s. a week as a journeyman tailor.[1]

Wages varied widely according to occupation, sex and skill; but, in terms of the cost of food and lodging, they were generally low and changed little during the fifty years following the Hanoverian Succession. In these early and middle years of the century, labourers' weekly earnings ranged between 9s. and 12s.; and those of the lower-paid journeymen (such as stay and breeches-makers, glaziers, cabinet-makers and chairmakers) between 12s. and 15s., or between 2s. and 2s. 6d. a day if on piece-work; while silk-weavers, in one of the most chronically depressed of the skilled occupations of the day, normally earned as little as 10s. or 12s. a week. 'Middling'-paid craftsmen, like tailors and masons, earned 14s. to 15s.: in 1768 we find a Member of Parliament complaining to the Duke of Newcastle of the 'impudence' of tailors who 'set forth their inability to live on two shillings and sevenpence a day, when the common soldier lives for under sixpence'. On the other hand, a compositor might earn up to 21s. or 22s. a week; a jeweller, an instrument-maker, or a chair-carver as much as £3 or £4; and the East London coal-heavers, whose riotous proceedings caused the authorities considerable concern, were reputed to earn up to 10s. a day (though, no doubt, their work was irregular). At the bottom of the scale were the women domestic workers: while a female labourer might earn 7s. or 8s., we read of a silk-winder being hired at Spitalfields Market in 1760 for a mere 3s. a week. Meanwhile, working hours were long and generally continued to be so. Tailors worked from six in the morning till seven or eight at night, with an hour's break for dinner; bookbinders from six to nine, and from six to seven after 1785; building workers from six to six, or as daylight permitted; and a journeyman shipwright, sentenced in the Gordon Riots, told the Court that he worked from five in the morning till eight at night. Shop-workers' hours appear, if anything, to have got longer: in 1747, in the City, they were nominally from seven till eight; but Robert Owen, when a London draper's assistant in 1786, worked from eight till ten or ten-thirty at night.

While working hours generally remained constant, wages tended to

[1] W.P.L., Westminster Poll Book, 1749; Besant, p. 248; *Lloyds Evening Post*, 11–13 May 1768; *London Life*, pp. 96–101; Add. MSS. 3514, fo. 197.

rise with the cost of living after the 1770s. In 1775 a mason's labourer, previously earning 9s. to 12s., was said to be earning 12s. to 14s. a week. Among lower-paid craftsmen, masons complained of earning only 15s. in 1775, and saddlers, in 1777, of earning 12s. to 15s. (this had risen by 1786 to 14s. to 16s.). By this time, tailors and other 'middling'-paid craftsmen were earning 18s. to 22s. weekly; among more highly paid journeymen, compositors were earning up to 24s. in 1777 and 27s. in 1785; while the most highly paid of all, the jewellers and chair-carvers, appeared to be earning the same as before.

It was natural that wages should rise more sharply during the inflationary war years of 1794–1815. At this time, labourers' earnings appear to have risen to 2s. or 3s. a day or 15s. to 18s. (or even 22s.) a week. Saddlers' wages (among the lower-paid craftsmen) were up to 25s. in 1811, and Francis Place describes in detail the upward progression of tailors' weekly earnings to 25s. in 1795, 27s. in 1802, 30s. in 1807, 33s. in 1810 and 33s. in 1816. Compositors, meanwhile, were earning 36s. in 1800 and 48s. in 1805; and, according to Place, there were proportionate increases in other skilled trades whose workers (in defiance of the Combination Laws) were able to make their demands felt through their trade societies. In brief, then, during the second half of the century (including the period of the wars), the nominal wages of labourers rose by about one-half and those of all but the least organized among the craftsmen by 60–75 per cent.[1]

But, of course, for the workers and the small consumers in general everything depended on what their earnings would buy: on the price of meat and ale or clothes and lodgings; and above all on the price of bread, which, throughout the eighteenth century, formed by the far the most important item in the poor man's budget. In the 1760s, at least, it was assumed by the London bakers that the average Londoner – man, woman and child – consumed a quarter of wheat per year, or eight pounds of bread per week – that is, thirty-two pounds for an average family of four; and it must be remembered that, in London, even the poorest insisted on eating at all times the best wheaten loaf, largely undiluted with barley or rye.[2] And, in 1779, when the saddlers were arguing for a substantial rise in wages, they assumed that a journeyman, with a wife and three children,

[1] *London Life*, pp. 161–9, 205–7, 360–2; *Wilkes and Liberty*, pp. 7–8; G. D. H. Cole and Raymond Postgate, *The Common People, 1746–1946*, 1956, pp. 69–77.

[2] W. G. East, 'England in the Eighteenth Century', in *An Historical Geography of England before A.D. 1800*, p. 505; Walter M. Stern, 'The Bread Crisis in Britain, 1795–96', *Economica*, vol. 36, 1964, pp. 183–4.

would, in a weekly budget of 20*s.* (which was considerably more than the saddlers were then earning), spend 4*s.* 11*d.*, or nearly a quarter, on bread. For the lower-paid workers this proportion would, of course, be substantially higher (possibly as much as 50 per cent in the case of a low-paid labourer) and, for all, it would rise appreciably in times of bad harvests or national crises, when rising bread-prices would leave the small consumer correspondingly short of the other necessities of life. In the first half of the century, the price of wheat was low and might, in a normal year, fluctuate between 30*s.* and 36*s.* a quarter and the price of bread (regulated by the Assize of Bread according to the current price of wheat or flour) between 1¼*d.* and 1½*d.* a pound. There were only three bad seasons – in 1727, 1728 and 1740; but between 1756 and 1773 crops tended to be poor; prices were high again in 1775 and 1777, and after 1793 the French wars brought prolonged inflation and shortage. So we find the price of bread in London rising to 2*d.* a pound in 1768, 1773 and 1777; to 3*d.* in 1795 and 3½*d.* in 1796; while, in 1799, it reached the then fantastically high price of 4*d.* a pound. Meanwhile, wages, as we have seen, had risen, but in relation to the price of bread they lagged far behind; and it may be readily imagined what catastrophic effects such sharp increases in the basic means of life had on the incomes and budgets of the wage-earners, street-sellers and other small consumers. To the thousands of women domestic workers, the aged, infirm and parish poor who, even in normal times, lived on the border-line of bare subsistence, it meant utter destitution, and even starvation and death. But, at such times, as we shall see in later chapters, even journeymen and labourers of settled occupation found it impossible to make ends meet and, in order to maintain their standards, resorted to riots, strikes and violent disputes with their employers.[1]

Yet there were other means of seeking compensation or an escape from poverty, drudgery, and destitution, and many observers and commentators have agreed that the seamier side of eighteenth-century London life, which so outraged the sensibilities of the virtuous Francis Place (as he looked back from the comparative respectability of the 1820s and 1830s), sprang as much from the social conditions of the day as from the settled policy, indifference or bad example of the governing classes. Crime,

[1] *London Life*, pp. 169–70; D. G. Barnes, *A History of the English Corn Laws from 1660 to 1846*, 1965, pp. 13, 31–7, 53–6, 72, 297–8; S. and B. Webb, 'The Assize of Bread', *Economic Journal*, vol. 14, 1904, pp. 196–218; Walter M. Stern, *Economica*, vol. 36, p. 168; *Wilkes and Liberty*, pp. 8–9; Besant, pp. 303–7.

drunkenness, prostitution and violence thrived during the greater part of this period, though they appear to have diminished, to Place's considerable satisfaction, during the latter years of the century. Gin had come in from Holland with King William, had taken firm root among the poor and, for sixty years, became both a source of profit to farmers and distillers and a social evil of incalculable consequences. This was the age when every fourth house in St Giles's was a dram-shop and when a working man or woman could get into a drunken stupor for $1d.$ or $2d.$ The sale of spirits rose from $3\frac{1}{2}$ million gallons in 1727 to nearly $6\frac{1}{2}$ million gallons in 1735 and to over 8 million in 1743; while, by this date, more than 7,000 shops, both licensed and unlicensed, were selling gin and brandy in the metropolitan area of Middlesex alone. As late as 1751, after a still-born Gin Act in 1736 and another attempt by Parliament in 1743 to stamp out the grosser excesses of gin-drinking, Henry Fielding wrote in his *Enquiry into the Causes of the late Increase of Robbers*:

> A new kind of drunkenness, unknown to our ancestors, is lately sprung up amongst us, and which if not put a stop to, will infallibly destroy a great part of the inferior people. The drunkenness I here intend is . . . by this Poison called Gin . . . the principal sustenance (if it may be so called) of more than a hundred thousand People in this Metropolis.

Soon after, with the aid of Hogarth's pictorial propaganda and the further Gin Act of 1751, the London of 'Gin Lane' began to be a thing of the past; and, seven years later, Sir John Fielding wrote gratefully that 'Gin is now so dear . . . that good Porter shews the Pre-eminence'. Yet gin took a long time a-dying and revived remarkably when the occasion offered; in June 1780, at the height of the Gordon Riots, Horace Walpole was able to write, with reasonable accuracy, in relating the drunken scenes enacted outside Thomas Langdale's gutted distilleries in Holborn, that 'as yet there are more persons killed by drinking than by ball or bayonet'.[1]

Meanwhile, as Sir John Fielding had noted, a salutary switch had been made from the dram-shop to the tavern, where strong beer could now be had for $3d.$ a quart. (In Anne's time, the cheapest beer appears to have

[1] Add. MSS. 27825-30; Lord Kinross, 'Prohibition in Britain', *History Today*, July, 1959; George Rudé, '"Mother Gin" and the London Riots of 1736', *The Guildhall Miscellany*, no. 10, September 1959, pp. 53-63; *London Life*, pp. 41-55.

cost 2*d*.) The ale-house was a favourite resort of journeymen and apprentices from an early age. Even the unctuous Sir John Fryer, a dissenter who became Lord Mayor of London in 1720, relates how, as a young man, when apprenticed to a pewterer in the City, he played truant from church and 'once or twice' frequented 'a Public House on ye Sabbath Day'! The ale-house served a dual purpose: a place to get drunk (which was considered an Englishman's natural privilege) and to associate with one's fellows and discuss the news and business of the day. And so it became the natural meeting-place for workers' box clubs and benefit societies and often served as a 'house of call' for hatters, tailors, carpenters, plumbers and other tradesmen, who thereby laid the basis for their 'combinations' and trade union organization among the skilled. With all this went a great deal of tippling and drinking into which the new apprentice or workman was initiated from the day of his arrival on the job. Benjamin Franklin, when a compositor in London in the 1720s, thought his companions 'great guzzlers of beer' and, being a water-drinker, tried in vain to convert them. Francis Place was less strong-minded and wrote years later that, as a young apprentice, he went out with 'other lads' and 'spent many evenings at the dirty public houses frequented by them'. He gives us a picture of the activities and entertainments practised in these houses, all of which were 'immediately connected with drinking – chair clubs, chanting clubs, lottery clubs' and 'games of chance or dexterity, skittles, dutch pins, bumble-puppy, drafts, dominoes, etc., all provided by the publicans'. The picture is confirmed by Sir John Fielding who, for all his gratification at the turn from gin to beer, was even more censorious than Place of the excesses of the ale-house. Among the pastimes he considered the most time-consuming and money-wasting were 'Cards, Dice, Draughts, Shuffle-boards, Mississippi Fables, Billiards and cover'd Skittle-grounds', and, in arguing that greater discrimination should be shown in the issue of licences to publicans, he added in a fine flourish of rhetoric:

> At the Ale-House the Idle meet to game and quarrel; here the Gamblers form their Stratagems; here the Pick-pockets hide themselves till Dusk, and Gangs of Thieves form their Plots and Routs; here Conspirators contrive their hellish Devices; and here the Combinations of Journeymen are made to execute their silly Schemes.

And, forty years later, we find Patrick Colquhoun, in his famous *Treatise on the Police*, equally inveighing against the temptations and dissipations and invitation to crime afforded by 'disorderly' and 'ill-regulated Public Houses'.[1]

But it was not only drinking that, in Fielding's phrase, 'slackened the Industry of useful Hands'. Equally reprehensible (he considered) were such popular pastimes as 'Bull-baitings, Bear-baitings, Cock-matches, and such Races as are contrary to Law', all of which he condemned as 'inhuman' and calling for 'redress'. And so insidious were these habits that even Place admits that, as a young man, he frequented cock and hen clubs and became acquainted, in the company of 'other lads', with the lowest prostitutes in Wapping and St Katherine's. With cock- and dog-fighting, badger- and bull-baiting held price of place among the more violent of popular sports. The bear garden and cock pits and rotundas for fighting dogs in Marylebone Gardens had their popular as well as their aristocratic clients, and Hockley-in-the-Hole, after it ceased to attract the gentry and young *beaux* about the town, continued to cater for the 'meaner sort', offering them bull- and bear-baitings as well as firework displays and bouts between battling women. For this was also an age of female prize-fighters, whose contests were followed with almost as much enthusiasm as those between the professional males. There was, for example, the redoubtable Bruising Peg who, in June 1768, fought an opponent in Spa Fields for a new shift and (a newspaper tells us) 'beat her antagonist in a terrible manner'. Another pastime was to pelt the poor wretches sitting in the stocks at Charing Cross with rotten eggs or anything else (stones alone were forbidden) that came to hand. But the pillory could be a two-edged weapon, as the authorities discovered when they chose a victim whose fate moved the crowd to sympathy rather than to violent reprobation. It was one thing to expose a rogue like Titus Oates to popular vengeance of this kind in the 1670s, or the four 'thief-takers' of 1756, who received such a battering at the hands of the crowd that they were carried away half dead after an hour in the stocks. On other occasions, the crowd's reaction was totally different; as when Daniel Defoe, in 1703, sentenced to the pillory for writing a satirical tract at the expense of the Church, was pelted with flowers, or when the Radicals of

---

[1] Besant, pp. 300–1; J. Ashton, *Social Life in the Reign of Queen Anne*, vol. 1, p. 197; *London Life*, pp. 166–93; G.L., MS. 12,017; Sir John Fielding, *An Account of the Origin and Effects of a Police set on Foot by his Grace the Duke of Newcastle in the Year 1753, upon a Plan presented to his Grace by the late Henry Fielding Esq.*, 1758, pp. ix–x; Patrick Colquhoun, *Treatise on the Police of the Metropolis*, 1797, pp. 324–5.

1794, Thomas Hardy and Horne Tooke, were lustily cheered and carried from the stocks in triumph.[1]

But the greatest sport of all was to go to 'Tyburn Fair' on the eight 'hanging-days' of the year and to toast the more popular victims in beer or gin as they were carried along Holborn, St Giles's and Oxford Street to the place of execution. These were public holidays for all journeymen until the practice was discontinued in 1783; and Francis Place wrote that, within his recollection, 'a *hanging day* was to all intents and purposes a fair day. The streets from Newgate to Tyburn were thronged with people, all the windows were filled.' The scene has been captured for us, not without sympathy for the bystanders, by Hogarth in his final episode in the life of the luckless 'Idle Apprentice'. The crowd certainly showed, as it did around the pillory, a fair sense of discrimination. Child and wife murderers and 'thief-takers' received no sympathy and were treated with universal reprobation; and the notorious Jonathan Wild, whose record as an informer did not save him from the noose as a 'receiver', was carried, when justice caught up with him in April 1725, to the gallows to the accompaniment of derisive cheers and demands that he be 'promptly despatched'. Highwaymen, however, and those whose only crime was to have robbed the rich, were often cheered and toasted as heroes of the day – and none more than the fabulous John Rann, alias Sixteen-String Jack, who was hanged in 1774 for robbing Dr William Bell of his watch in Gunnersbury Lane; a showman to the last, he was hanged in a pea-green coat with a huge nosegay in his button-hole. But to Place all such 'brutalizing occasions' were, without exception, utterly distasteful; and he no doubt exaggerated when he wrote of the onlookers as composed of 'the whole vagabond population of London, all the thieves, and all the prostitutes, and all those who were evil-minded and some, a comparatively few, curious people'.[2]

Yet all popular pastimes were not of this 'brutalizing' kind. There was the traditional May Day, when the milkmen and women and the chimney-sweeps held a masquerade of their own, in which the women trundled a huge pyramid of flowers, festooned with kettles and salvers and pieces of silver, through the streets, while the chimney-sweeps, their faces whitened with meal and their heads framed in periwigs, banged their brushes and scrapers in discordant accompaniment. There were the

[1] *London Life*, pp. 105–6; Besant, p. 559; Wheatley and Cunningham, vol. 2, 216–17; *Wilkes and Liberty*, p. 11.
[2] Add. MSS. 27826, f. 107.

numerous fairs which, between them, took up eighty-two days of the year
from early May to late October: the May Fair and St Bartholomew's Fair
at Smithfield, the Whit Monday Fair at Greenwich, the Lady Fair at
Charlton, the Tothill Fair, the 'Gooseberry' Fair, and the fairs at Stepney,
Peckham, St James's and Camberwell Green. There were also the London
parks, which became so infested with 'the inferior set' that the leisured
classes took steps to ensure their greater privacy. In George II's time,
Queen Caroline spoke to Walpole of closing down St James's Park and
'converting it into a noble garden for the palace of that name'. It came to
nothing; and forty-five years later the Bow Street magistrates were still
considering means to clear its paths of 'beggars, gamblers, and other
disorderly persons'. Among popular Sunday resorts were Marylebone
Gardens, Highgate, Greenwich Park and St George's Fields (until they
were enclosed by Parliament in 1768). To some observers, such activities,
however peaceful and innocent, were reprehensible as they seemed to be
conducive to sloth and extravagance. Among such critics, we find the
Connoisseur testily observing in July 1754:

> Our common people are very observant of that part of the command-
> ment which enjoins them to do no manner of work on that day;
> and which they also seem to understand as a licence to devote it to
> pleasure. They take this opportunity of thrusting their heads into the
> pillory of *Georgia*, being sworn at Highgate, and rolling down Flam-
> stead Hill in the park at Greenwich. As they all aim at going into the
> country, nothing can be a greater misfortune to the meaner part of
> the inhabitants of London and Westminster than a rainy Sunday.

To such persons the pleasures of the poor appeared, almost without
discrimination, to be a general 'nuisance' and as such to be strenuously
discouraged. Magistrates worked hard to put down not only common
gaming houses, ale-houses, bull-baitings and cock-fighting, but fairs, tea-
gardens and every sort of popular entertainment. Even the theatre was
suspect; and when Thomas Odell, in 1729, opened a play-house in Great
Alie Street, in Goodman's Fields – where Garrick later won his laurels
in the part of Richard II – there was a clamour of protest supported by
the plea that the theatre would have 'very uncomfortable effects' on the
health, industry and thrift of the working people, who inhabited the
district in large numbers. The protesters won their point, and the theatre
remained closed for a dozen years.[1]

[1] *Three Tours*, p. 78; Besant, pp. 465–71; M. Dorothy George, in *Johnson's England*,
vol. 1, pp. 184–5; Wheatley and Cunningham, vol. 2, p. 99; *London Life*, p. 279.

Another, and more valid, complaint of magistrates was the increase in crime. In 1731 the author of an anonymous pamphlet related how highwaymen and criminals, no longer content to practise their skills on Hounslow Heath or on the outskirts of the capital, were brazenly moving in to the centre: he instanced cases of stage coaches being robbed in High Holborn, Whitechapel, Pall Mall and Soho, and of citizens being held up in their carriages in Cheapside, St Paul's Churchyard and the Strand. One witness at this time told the court at the Old Bailey how he had seen William Gordon, a noted highwayman, actually sitting on horseback in the kitchen of a tavern between Kensington and Knightsbridge! In 1751 Henry Fielding, as the senior Bow Street magistrate, wrote his famous *Enquiry into the Causes of the late Increase in Robbers*; he ascribed the rise in crime to gambling, gin and 'the increase in luxury among the lower orders of the people'; and he proposed a number of remedies, including the recruitment of a special police at Bow Street, the offer of £100 rewards, and a concerted plan to break the gangs of robbers, bring highwaymen and house-breakers to exemplary justice, and to clear the streets of beggars, prostitutes and homeless children. Writing in pious memory of his brother in 1758, Sir John Fielding claimed that a considerable success had been achieved during the intervening years: that the robbers had been dispersed, scarcely a highwayman had escaped his just deserts, house-breaking and shop-lifting were under control, juvenile crime was on the wane; and he pointed, in particular, to the Sessions Papers for 1755 and 1756, which revealed that 'gangs of friendless boys, from 14 to 18 years of age, were transported, indeed I may say by wholesale, for picking of pockets and pilfering from Shops'; and he added that scarcely a session passed 'without indictments being found against porters, and such lower sorts of men, for ravishing the infants of the poor'.[1]

Yet Sir John's picture proved to be over-optimistic. With London's rising population and the increasing frequency of harvest failures, the volume of crime, far from abating, continued to rise after the 1760s. The Old Bailey *Proceedings* of 1763 record the trial of 433 persons for murder, burglary, robbery and theft, of whom 243 were convicted and 47 were sentenced to death. The *Proceedings* of 1768 record the trial of 613, the conviction of 246 and 54 death sentences; by 1770, the number of capital convictions had risen to 61. In these last four years, there was, besides, a remarkable increase in the number of burglaries committed in London

[1] Besant, pp. 494–533; A. P. Herbert, *Mr Gay's London*, 1948, p. 13; Sir John Fielding, *An Account of the Origin and Effects of a Police*, pp. 15–40.

32 Hogarth's drawing for Plate IV of 'Industry and Idleness'
(*Mansell Collection*)

33 Interior of a sealing-wax factory (*Mansell Collection*)

34 The sailors' Fleet Wedding entertainment, 1747 (*British Museum*)

35 Plate II of Hogarth's 'Marriage à la Mode', 1745 (*Victoria and Albert Museum*)

36 High Life Below Stairs, 1772 (*British Museum*)

37 Stage coach at the Angel Inn, 1747, Hogarth (*British Museum*)

38 English silver with London hall marks: coffee-pot by W. Shaw and W. Priest, 1754–5, candlesticks (from a set of fourteen), 1768–9 (*Victoria and Albert Museum*)

39 Painted and gilt bookcase William Kent, *c.* 1730 (*Victoria Albert Museum*)

and Westminster: according to a parliamentary Report of 1812, there were 13 houses broken into between Michaelmas 1766 and Lady Day 1767, 36 houses between Lady Day and Michaelmas 1767, 52 in 1767–8, 62 in the middle months of 1769, and 104 between Michaelmas 1769 and Lady Day 1770. Four years later the *Gentleman's Magazine* reported: 'The papers are filled with robberies and breaking of houses, and with the recital of the cruelties committed by the robbers, greater than ever known before.' There was, equally, no relaxation in armed hold-ups or in the daring activities of highwaymen, which were still being carried out in the heart of the metropolis. In 1773 a mounted highwayman robbed Sir Francis Holbourne and his sisters in their coach in St James's Square; the Lord Mayor was held up at pistol-point at Turnham Green in 1776; and, in the 1780s, not only were the Prince of Wales and the Duke of York robbed in broad daylight in Hill Street, Berkeley Square, but the Great Seal of England was stolen from Lord Chancellor Thurlow's house in Ormond Street and melted down for silver![1]

The long wars with France brought another upward swing in the incidence of crime, and the Old Bailey *Proceedings* of 1794 reveal that the number of persons brought to trial that year had risen to 1,060 (over twice the number of thirty years before), of whom 493 were convicted and 68 were held for execution. It was against this background that Patrick Colquhoun wrote the second of the great police reports of the century, his *Treatise on the Police of the Metropolis*. In a much-quoted passage, he claimed that no fewer than 115,000 persons in London were regularly engaged in criminal pursuits: half of them prostitutes or 'lewd and immoral women'; with 8,500 cheats, swindlers and gamblers; 8,000 'thieves, pilferers and embezzlers'; 4,000 receivers of stolen goods; 3,000 coiners; while 2,500 preyed on docks and arsenals in the guise of 'Lumpers, Scuffle-hunters, Mudlarks, Lightermen, and Riggers'; and a mere 2,000 were conventional 'Professional Thieves, Burglars, Highway Robbers, Pick-pockets, and River Pirates'. Yet, when stripped of its lurid trimmings, Colquhoun's picture showed that, by this time, the more violent types of crime – armed robberies, murders and hold-ups – were on the wane and that his figures were largely inflated by a rising tide of 'economic' crimes or crimes against property. For these Parliament showed no mercy and the number of capital offences (stated by Colquhoun to be over 160 in 1795) had risen by the death of George III to 200 and more, of which

[1] Old Bailey *Proceedings*, 1762–77; *Wilkes and Liberty*, pp. 10–11; Wheatley and Cunningham, vol. 2, p. 301.

H

63 had been added between 1760 and 1810. Yet as the criminal code became more vindictive and repressive, the courts and juries, by an inverse process, showed a greater reluctance to convict and, where they convicted, a greater disposition to recommend the sentenced criminal to mercy. So the ratio of executions to capital convictions fell progressively, and sometimes dramatically. Thus, of 527 persons sentenced to death in London and Middlesex between 1749 and 1758 about two in three were executed; whereas between 1790 and 1799, only one in three of 745 capital convictions were carried out.[1]

But it was not only juries that showed a fine sense of discrimination between murder and theft or between one type of assault and another. All over the country ordinary men and women refused to see smuggling, poaching, assaults on game-keepers, tax evasion, or even arson, as offences worthy of death or transportation: and so, in London, as we have seen, there was a similar popular tendency to distinguish, and often brutally, between the child-murderer and the informer on the one hand and the highwayman or the house-breaker on the other. The common people had, in this as in other respects, a code of their own which often contrasted sharply with that of the people in authority. Another common attitude, stronger in the country though still surviving in the capital, was that wages and prices should be governed by the principles of 'justice' and tradition and not simply by the new-fangled laws of supply and demand; we shall see examples later in this book. Again, although the antagonism between capital and labour still remained muted, the 'meaner sort' had a strong sense of how far it was decent for the rich, or those living 'at the polite end of the town', to flaunt their wealth in the faces of the poor. We find this attitude expressed in the orgies of window-breaking that often accompanied popular disturbance; more particularly, we find it in the case of a barge-builder who, when arrested during the Gordon Riots, protested that 'no gentleman should be possessed of more than £1,000 a year'. This popular egalitarianism, so strongly at variance with the tenets of an aristocratic society, was no doubt fostered by the long tradition of religious freedom and democracy which the 'middling' and poor, through dissenting chapels and conventicles and tavern discussions, had inherited from the days of the great Revolution and the Good Old Cause. It was linked, too, with the strong popular belief that the English-

---

[1] Patrick Colquhoun, *Treatise on the Police of the Metropolis*, pp. vii-xi, 5, 230; E. P. Thompson, *The Making of the English Working Class*, pp. 60-1; J. L. and B. Hammond, 'Poverty, Crime, Philanthropy', in *Johnson's England*, vol. 1, pp. 314-22.

man, as a 'free-born' subject, had a particular claim on 'liberty'. While it could be taken for granted that foreigners – particularly Roman Catholic foreigners like Frenchmen and Spaniards, and even the Irish – would readily put up with 'tyranny', 'Popery' and 'wooden shoes', the Englishman had a natural 'birthright' which, in the last resort, in spite of press gangs, low wages and the oppression of magistrates and landlords, could never be taken away. This may help to explain the extraordinary and enduring chauvinism of Londoners in the course of the various wars with France and Spain; the war-makers, like William Pitt, were their natural heroes while they noisily condemned the activities of peace-makers, or would-be peace-makers, like Sir Robert Walpole, the Marquis of Bute or the Duke of Bedford. The hatred of the Scots, which was strong in the 1760s, no doubt stemmed from the Radical hostility to Jacobitism which, in turn, was associated with 'Popery' and France. Some of these attitudes became modified as a more conscious political ideology began to eclipse the old shibboleths towards the end of the century. So, during the American War, there was little of the old chauvinism expressed in relation to the colonists, though it was still reserved for the Spaniards and French. By this time, too, the Scots, having ostensibly cast off any suspicions of being either Jacobite or Roman Catholic, had ceased to be a bogey; and even the French, once they had had their revolution and shed their old 'wooden shoes', found considerable popular support, for a time at least, during the 1790s.[1]

In essence, these attitudes may be summed up as two: the Englishman's right to his daily bread and his right to his 'birthright' or 'liberty'. And these, as we shall see in later chapters, were the main motors (and at times the twin motors) of popular disturbance in Hanoverian London.

[1] George Rudé, 'The London "Mob" of the Eighteenth Century', *The Historical Journal*, vol. 2, 1959, pp. 1–18; E. P. Thompson, *The Making of the English Working Class*, pp. 55–68; *London Life*, pp. 124–39.

6

Religion and the Churches

THE RELIGIOUS life of the upper classes of Hanoverian London
was one of simple, placid and ostensibly pious conformity. Before
the evangelical revival, which in the capital gained little momentum until the 1770s, there was little in the practices of either the Church
of England or the main dissenting groups to arouse enthusiasm or to
imbue their congregations with a missionary zeal. The close connection
between Church and State, which had been so much in evidence under
Queen Anne, persisted, and the divisions within the established Church
between High Churchmen and Latitudinarians continued to reflect the
political divisions between Tories and Whigs; but as the conflict between
the parties lost its bitterness, or even a great deal of its relevance, so the
two wings within the Church settled down to a peaceful coexistence that
was only disturbed by mild theological controversies between Unitarians,
Trinitarians and Deists. In the fashionable churches of Westminster and
the City of London, congregations became more inclined to choose their
preacher for the polish of his oratory or the soundness of his training in
the classics than for the orthodoxy of his religious views. So, by the 1720s,
the old battle-cries had become muted and it seemed that an age had
passed since the stormy days of 1709 when Dr Henry Sacheverell, chaplain of St Saviour's Southwark, had set London by the ears with the
sermon he delivered in St Paul's on 'Perils from false Brethren'. The
Whig government of the day had suspended Sacheverell from preaching
for three years; but the sentence had been followed by the lighting of
bonfires, rioting in the City and attacks on Low Church and dissenting
houses and meetings. There had been a brief aftermath of 'High Church'
rioting and assaults on dissenters' meeting-houses in the months following

the accession of George I and the Jacobite rebellion of 1715; after which there was comparative tranquillity until the next great outburst – the most violent of all – against the Roman Catholics in June 1780.[1]

Yet one legacy remained from the religious turmoil of 1709. In 1710 the Tories had come to power after a general election and had decided to consolidate their victory by erecting a memorial to the triumph of High Church policy and practice. This was the Act of 1711, which provided for a tax to be levied on coal in order to pay 'for Building fifty new Churches . . . in or near the Cities of London and Westminster or the Suburbs thereof'; moreover, the churches were to be built of 'stone and other proper Materials with Towers or Steeples for each of them'. The number fifty was decided on as a House of Commons committee had advised that, with this addition, the average population of London's suburban parishes, long starved of new church buildings, might be reduced to 4,750: Stepney, in particular, with its neighbouring satellites of Limehouse, Wapping and Bethnal Green, was, as a rapidly expanding area, causing some concern. However, the target was never realized – possibly because the Tories, who had promoted the scheme, were out of office within three years and its execution was left to their less enthusiastic Whig successors. At any rate, over the next twenty years, only ten brand-new churches were erected while two were rebuilt on old foundations; in addition, certain contingent work was carried out as provided for in the Act's preamble: a number of towers and steeples, including the tower of St Michael's Cornhill, were constructed; Westminster Abbey was enlarged, and the outstanding debts owing to Sir Christopher Wren as Surveyor of St Paul's were finally honoured. Nevertheless, even though reduced in scope, the scheme was carried through on a lavish scale; and by 1718 the Commission in charge of the operation had incurred an expenditure of £161,000, which far exceeded the yield of the coal tax and had to be made up from annual grants from Parliament over a number of years.[2]

The designs of the churches were entrusted to five distinguished architects: Nicholas Hawksmoor, James Gibbs, John James, Thomas Archer and Henry Flitcroft. Six of the projects were carried through under the direction of Hawksmoor: St Alphege Greenwich, St Anne

[1] 'Ecclesiastical History', in *Victoria History of London*, ed. W. Page, 1909, vol. 1, pp. 351–2; and see pp. 111, 178-80, 221-4 below.

[2] *Georgian London*, pp. 84–5; Basil F. L. Clarke, *Parish Churches of London*, 1966, pp. 3–4.

Limehouse, Christ Church Spitalfields, St George in the East, St George Bloomsbury and the City church of St Mary Woolnoth. The first of these, St Alphege, was begun in 1712 and completed in 1730. St Anne's, at Limehouse, was built between 1712 and 1724 and consecrated in 1730. Christ Church, in Spitalfields, was begun in 1715, built for £19,418, and consecrated in 1729; it is of mixed Classic and Gothic inspiration. St George's in the East, in Cannon Street Road, was built between 1715 and 1723 at a cost of £18,557, and was consecrated in 1729; it, too, has Gothic origins. St George's, in Hart Street, Bloomsbury, whose Corinthian portico has been called the finest in London, was built in 1720-30 and consecrated in 1731. St Mary Woolnoth, the only church that Hawksmoor built in the City, was begun in 1716 and completed in 1727. Like its sister-church at Spitalfields it has a tower which, in plan, is much broader than it is deep. Hawksmoor's towers are, in fact, quite distinctive: admired by some, they have been sharply criticized by others. Thomas Pennant, for example, wrote of St Anne's Limehouse: '[It] has its awkward tower, a dull square rising out of another, embellished with palasters; heavy pinnacles rise out of the uppermost: the whole proves how unhappily Mr Hawksmoor . . . exerted his genius in the obsolete art of steeple-building.' St George's in the East fares no better; for 'square rises out of square to compose the steeple; its upper storey is incomprehensible, the outside stuck around with chimney-like columns, square at the lower parts, above making a sudden transition into the round'.[1]

Of the other church-builders under the Act, James Gibbs, a Roman Catholic pupil of Wren, built St Mary-le-Strand in the Roman Baroque style between 1714 and 1717; after which, being a Tory as well as a Catholic, he was dropped from the scheme. Thomas Archer designed St John's, in Smith Square (1713-28), and St Paul's, in Deptford High Street (1712-30); these, too, were in Roman Baroque. John James built the most fashionable of all these churches, St George's Hanover Square, and also (though here there appears to be some doubt as to its architect) St John's Horseleydown, which has since been demolished. Finally, Hawksmoor and James jointly designed St Luke's, in Old Street; it was begun in 1727 and completed in 1733. Meanwhile, the Commissioners had extended their activities and, under further Acts of 1730 and 1731, had churches built at Gravesend and Woolwich.

Other churches were built or renovated outside the 'Fifty-Churches'

[1] Thomas Pennant, *Some Account of London*, pp. 271-3.

scheme. Henry Flitcroft, who (unlike Hawksmoor) was much admired by Thomas Pennant, rebuilt the old Gothic church of St Giles in the Fields in 1731–3 in the Wren–Gibbs tradition, and built St Olave's Southwark under an Act of 1737. Meanwhile, Gibbs had transferred his talents to another enterprise and rebuilt the church of St Martin's in the Fields, which was completed in 1726 at a cost of £33,000, raised by private subscription and a sum twice that spent on any one of Wren's City churches. To this period, too, belong (the Elder) George Dance's St Leonard's Shoreditch (1735–6) and St Botolph's Aldgate (1741–4). St Leonard's was built with the aid of cheap Irish labour, which led, as we shall see in a later chapter, to serious rioting in Shoreditch, Spitalfields and Whitechapel.

Thus, about twenty churches were built or rebuilt in the thirty years following the Hanoverian Succession. The number fell far short of the target laid down by the Tories in the Act of 1711 and barely responded to the rise in the city's population. But it far surpassed anything undertaken in the next seventy-five years, when remarkably little was done to meet the church-going needs of the rapidly expanding metropolis. Church-building was, in fact, at a distinctly low ebb from the 1740s onwards. Around 1750, churches were built or rebuilt at Hampstead and Islington, and in Battersea and Clapham in the 1770s; George Dance (the Younger) rebuilt All Hallows London Wall, within the City, in 1777; and further churches were rebuilt in Paddington, Clerkenwell and Hackney in the 1780s and nineties. Meanwhile, in Middlesex, churches had been added at Teddington (1753) and Edgware (1764), and Feltham built a church in 1802. Ten years later, an official enquiry revealed that the 132 metropolitan parishes within the diocese of London had 186 Church of England churches and chapels with seats for 162,962 out of a population of 661,394. There were some notorious black-spots in the more recently developed areas: Marylebone, for example, had one single church (with seating for 900) for its 64,000 parishioners up to 1818; and St Pancras (with 32,000 parishioners in 1801) fared no better. Nor was the 1 in 4 ratio of church seats to potential worshippers particularly inspiring if it is compared with the proportionately greater facilities provided by the 'Free Churches' with their 265 places of worship to accommodate what was reputed to be only one-fifth of the number of Anglicans. Yet the situation in London, bad though it might be, was considerably brighter than it was in the expanding industrial and commercial cities of the north – such as Liverpool, Manchester and Leeds; and the balance would be further redressed in London's favour by the next big spurt in church-building provided by the 'Million' Church Building Act of 1818.[1]

So it may be argued that in London, as elsewhere, the laxity in building churches was but one reflection of the comfortable, placid and unhurried attitude towards religion that was predominant among the leisured classes of Hanoverian England. For there were greater abuses within the Church than a lack of seating for its real or hypothetical believers. Pluralism and non-residence were common in London, and continued to be so until the middle of the nineteenth century. London livings were both financially attractive (compared with most) and gave the preacher access to a large and educated public; so incumbents were loth, unless instructed to do so by their Bishop, to give up a London parish even when translated or promoted elsewhere. At the close of the seventeenth century, forty-three incumbents of City churches had country livings, and nearly all the most influential preachers of the eighteenth century were pluralists. In most cases, holders of City livings, on grounds of health, preferred not to live in their parishes, a practice that was often supported by the plea that the younger clergy could best win their spurs by serving 'non-residents' as licensed curates. But the practice was liable to grave abuse, as the curates were generally wretchedly paid and many, in spite of the strict rulings of the Church, remained unlicensed. An early nineteenth-century diocesan return reveals that, in 1810, there were 147 curates of non-resident incumbents in London parishes, of whom 93 only were licensed to the parishes they served (84 of them being also resident). Salaries had risen little in a hundred years. An Act of 1713 had provided that licensed curates should be paid not less than £20 a year and not more than £50: this was a few years after Gregory King had estimated the average income of a 'lesser' clergyman at £45 a year. A century later, Colquhoun had raised King's estimate from £45 to £120; but the law governing curates' salaries had not been amended in proportion. In fact, an Act of 1796 allowed bishops to pay their curates up to a maximum of £75. It does not appear to have been interpreted with any great liberality in London; for the return of 1810 showed that, of 47 cases cited, 19 were earning £20 to £40, 13 the old maximum of £50, three were earning £60, six £70, one £80, one £90, three £100 and one £110. This underpayment of

---

[1] *Georgian London*, pp. 85-97, 212-16; Nikolaus Pevsner, *London*, vol. 1, pp. 79-80, 159-60, 279-83, 448-9; and *Middlesex*, p. 19; Basil F. L. Clarke, *Parish Churches of London*, pp. 122-4, 153-6, 180-1, 219-20; Parliamentary Papers, 1812; E. Halévy, *England in 1815*, pp. 399-400, 428.

curates had, a generation before, been defended by Dr Johnson on the grounds that the curacy was 'the nursery of the church' and that 'if no curate were to be permitted unless he had a hundred pounds a year, their number would be very small'. However, an inevitable result was that a large part of the active London clergy was notoriously poor; their mean appearance had long been a standing joke in the coffee-houses, and few could afford to buy books to improve their education. And, equally, their very poverty made them all the more indispensable and resistant to promotion. To quote two examples from the beginning of our period: Smithies, one of the most influential of London's preachers at the end of the previous century, remained curate of St Giles Cripplegate for thirty-one years; and the curate of St Peter Poer had, in 1711, already held the office for twenty years.[1]

Other abuses (though not always accepted as such) related to the conduct of the services themselves. Prayers were read hastily and without reverence, so that Bishop Gilson felt constrained to remind his clergy that the mumbling of prayers made them so unintelligible that they might have been delivered in a foreign tongue. Sermons, as befitted a society to whom religious 'enthusiasm' appeared an abomination, were cold and uninspiring. Joseph Trapp, rector of Harlington, Middlesex, from 1733 to 1747, and a leading anti-'enthusiast', preached four discourses 'on the nature, folly, sin and anger of being righteous over-much'. Even so stalwart a champion of the Church as Dr Johnson was moved to criticize this trend. In particular, he thought the 'polished periods and glittering sentences' of the established clergy unsuited to anything but a sophisticated audience; and he even observed that 'something might be necessary to excite the affections of the common people, who were sunk in languor and lethargy, and therefore he supposed that the new concomitants of Methodism might probably produce so desirable an effect'.

Of a different order was the custom, most common in the earlier years of the century but still practised later, of baptizing infants in private houses; in 1785, William Wilberforce spoke of such a christening as 'very indecent, all laughing round'. Church attendance, too, in the more fashionable parishes, was often treated as a social rather than as a devotional exercise. Swift once asked whether churches were not dormitories of the living as well as of the dead; and Steele, in describing a morning

---

[1] *Victoria History of London*, vol. 1, pp. 354–7; Parl. Papers, 1812; M. Dorothy George, *England in Transition*, pp. 150–3; E. Halévy, *England in 1815*, p. 441; N. Sykes, 'The Church', in *Johnson's England*, vol. 1, p. 27.

service in his church in Kensington, relates how 'some pretty young ladies in mobs popped in here and there about the church, clattering the pew door after them, and squatting into whispers behind their fans'. Nor were services always offered with great frequency or regularity, and this abuse became greater as the century went on. In 1714 there were in London and Westminster seventy-two churches and chapels offering their worshippers two services daily; the number had fallen to fifty-eight by 1746. Similarly, the communion service, though generally held monthly, was held weekly in sixteen London churches in 1724 and only in eleven in 1728; while, by 1732, the guide-book of the London parish clerks makes no mention whatsoever of the service. Sunday services, which originally were held both morning and evening, also became more infrequent; and an enquiry of 1741-2 established that only 200 of 436 churches within the diocese of London were offering both Matins and Evensong on Sundays.

To maintain the social exclusiveness of their places of worship, wealthy Londoners endowed proprietary chapels and appropriated pews for high rents in parish churches. Proprietary chapels, owned and controlled by private patrons, were run, independently of the parishes, as commercial concerns. According to Maitland, there were sixty-nine chapels of this kind under the Church of England in 1738. Few free seats were provided and they charged high pew-rents to meet expenses. The annual income from pews in Queen's Square Chapel, Westminster, was £176; and the yearly rent of a pew in Grosvenor Chapel, Audley Street, was £15 0s. 2d. In parish churches, the increasing practice of letting pews for rent was an obvious deterrent against the regular attendance of the poor. The system, therefore, worked best when services were dull and unattractive. Conversely, it tended to break down whenever a popular preacher drew an unexpected influx of attendants; as when, in 1780, John Newton's preaching at St Mary Woolnoth, in the City, drew such crowds that not only were the aisles congested but the pew-holders, to their intense disgust, found their appropriated seats occupied by strangers![1]

It was this laxity and 'remoteness' within the Church that the Evangelicals – and in the first place the Wesleys and George Whitefield – set out to combat in the course of their long ministry after 1738. John Wesley's famous conversion to 'assurance by salvation' began in a house

[1] Michael Robbins, *Middlesex*, p. 113; N. Sykes, *Church and State in England in the Eighteenth Century*, 1934, pp. 255-6; and 'The Church', in *Johnson's England*, vol. 1, pp. 31, 35; *Victoria History of London*, vol. 1, pp. 359-67; Besant, p. 52.

in Aldergate Street in May 1738; and although the Methodist impact on London was never as great as it was in Cornwall, Staffordshire, the West Riding or the coalfields, the history of Methodism, during Wesley's lifetime, was always intimately connected with the Church in the metropolis. Some of John Wesley's earliest sermons were given, through his father's High Church influence, in the churches of St Andrew Holborn, St Clement Danes and St Lawrence Jewry, where he preached in 1738; and it was after such churches became closed to him that he followed George Whitefield's example and began, in April 1739, to preach to open-air congregations on Kennington Common. Whitefield went on to carry the Methodist message to Moorfields Fair, where he preached before 10,000 people on Whit Monday 1742, while the fair was at its height, and was pelted with stones, rotten eggs and dead cats. The same year, Wesley preached near Whitechapel and was struck between the eyes by a stone, while his assailants 'tried to drive in a herd of cows among them'; but, he added, 'the brutes were wiser than their masters'.[1]

Moorfields became the chosen headquarters, for several years, of both leaders. John Wesley took out a lease there in a disused foundry in 1740, and when the lease expired in 1778 transferred to the Wesleyan Methodist Chapel in City Road, where he stayed until his death in 1791. During his lifetime, other Wesleyan chapels were built at Snowsfields, Southwark (1743), Spitalfields (1750), Wapping (1764), Kentish Town and Lambeth Marsh (1790); and there were perhaps a dozen preaching-rooms besides. Whitefield, during his alliance with the Wesleys, built a Tabernacle at Moorfields (in 1741), but after their breach over the doctrine of Grace he formed his own separate group of Calvinist Methodists and moved to a new meeting-house in Tottenham Court Road, which he had built in 1756. And while the main body of Methodists remained within the Church as long as Wesley lived, Whitefield's organization declared its independence.

This is not the place to repeat the oft-told tale of the influence of Methodism on the churches of the eighteenth century. Suffice it to say that, in London as elsewhere, the results of this influence were three-fold: the winning of new recruits to Methodism, organized in Wesleyan 'connections' for work within and without the established Church; the revival of greater regularity, moral earnestness and 'enthusiasm' in the services of all the Protestant churches; and the gradual decline of the Latitudinarian outlook within the Church of England. This was achieved,

[1] *The Journal of the Rev. John Wesley. A.M.*, ed. N. Curnock, 1938, vol. 3, p. 45.

in part, from without by Wesley's and Whitefield's own Methodist preachers; and partly from within by the influence wielded within the Church by the Methodist converts among the London clergy. Among such converts, or followers, in London were Godden, a member of the Wesley's Oxford Society, who became rector of St Stephen's Coleman Street; William Romaine, a disciple of Whitefield, who became rector of St Anne's Blackfriars in 1764; Thomas Jones, chaplain of St Saviour's Southwark; Henry Foster, rector of St John's Clerkenwell; Richard Cecil, chaplain of St John's Bedford Row; and John Newton, lecturer at St Mary Woolnoth and a leading Wesleyan theologian. In 1783 Newton, Foster, Cecil and Eli Bates founded the Eclectic Society as a forum for discussion: by 1800 it had become the leading intellectual centre of the revivalist groups. Wesleyanism, after considerable effort, had also established itself in Middlesex. John Wesley had preached – and been heckled – at Brentford in 1742, and again in 1744 and 1746; he also preached several times at Hayes between 1749 and 1753, at Hillingdon in 1754, and at Uxbridge in 1758: on this last occasion he noted characteristically in his *Journal* that the Gospel 'is come to torment them at Uxbridge'. Meanwhile, a convert, Charles Manning, had been vicar of Hayes since 1739. Yet little was achieved until after 1760 ('the work of God is broke out afresh'); there was a relapse in the 1770s and 1780s, followed by a more massive revival, after the French Revolution, in the 1790s.

By this time, the Methodists had found allies among other evangelical groups. There was the Countess of Huntingdon's Connection, based on Calvinist Methodism, but remaining, like Wesley's own organization until after his death, within the Anglican Church. The Countess established a network of chapels, including the Northampton Chapel, in Spa Fields (1779), Sion Chapel, Whitechapel (1790), and a number of proprietary chapels of which the most notable was the Surrey Chapel, Blackfriars Road, built for Rowland Hill in 1783. More indirectly, the Methodists found allies among the small group of humanitarians and Members of Parliament, organized in the Clapham Sect, which counted among its leading members William Wilberforce and Hannah More. In addition to the role it played in the abolition of the slave trade, the Sect exerted a great influence within the Anglican Church and probably became the dominant force within the London Church by the 1830s; but it remained a small exclusive circle of intellectuals, never seeking to attract recruits from within a wider public. The Methodists alone quite deliberately opened their ranks to the people at large and rapidly increased their numbers. In 1790 the Wesleyans alone had 71,463 members in the British Isles, and three times that number, twenty-five years later, in Great Britain and the colonies.[1]

Meanwhile, the old dissenting groups – the Presbyterians, Independents, Baptists and Quakers – had, since the threatened Tory repression of 1709–14, increased their numbers but, like the established Church, declined in crusading vigour. In the High Church riots of 1709 and 1715–16, a dozen chapels and meeting-houses had been damaged or destroyed; but these had been quickly restored in the early years of the Hanoverian Succession. In 1695 there had been eighty-six dissenting congregations (excluding Quakers), served by eighty-nine ministers, in the metropolitan area; of these, the Presbyterians formed about one-half and the Baptists, the smallest group, about one-quarter. By 1730 only one new church had been built in London, but thirty older buildings had been enlarged and accommodation provided for a further 4,000 persons. The number of congregations, however, does not appear to have grown, for such figures as there are suggest that there were now eighty-four, the denominational proportions being roughly the same as before. But to this number (as to that of 1695) should be added the Quakers, who, according to Maitland, had a dozen meetings registered under the Toleration Act in 1738.[2]

In the second half of the century, this 'Old Dissent', both in London and Middlesex, entered into a period of decline: it lasted until late in the 1790s. Yet non-conformity as a whole increased considerably in the number of both adherents and congregations, largely owing to a proliferation of new sects and societies often stimulated by the Methodist and evangelical revival. Some of the old Presbyterian and Independent groups, in particular, disintegrated, either rent by the Unitarian controversy or seduced by the new Arminian or Calvinist ideas propagated by the rival Methodist societies. In the course of this development, eight of London's old Presbyterian churches disappeared, another four or five became Congregational and six became Arian or Unitarian. Meanwhile, four Independent churches expired, two having previously become Unitarian. But, in Middlesex at least, both Presbyterians and Independents began to

[1] *Victoria History of London*, vol. 1, pp. 368–9, 389–90; Michael Robbins, *Middlesex*, p. 113; H. S. Skeats, *A History of the Free Churches of England*, 1869, p. 367; E. Halévy, *England in 1815*, p. 415; Wesley's *Journal*, vol. 8, p. 83.

[2] *Victoria History of London*, vol. 1, pp. 383–9; H. S. Skeats, *A History of the Free Churches of England*, pp. 280, 335.

recruit, and even to build new chapels, after 1798. The Baptists increased their numbers; sixteen new groups replaced eight that expired; but they had, in the process, become more intensely divided between Calvinists and Unitarians. In Middlesex, they, too, had a revival at the end of the century and began to build new chapels after 1800. The Quakers, for their part, continued to hold meetings in the City, in Southwark, in Westminster and Ratcliff; in Middlesex they became increasingly active after 1770, recruiting prosperous millers and bankers in Uxbridge and Staines and founding a colony of Friends among professional men in Tottenham.

Meanwhile, some of the smaller sects had disappeared, but many more had been added. The small City communities of French Prophets, Muggletonians and Nonjurors had died out, but the Moravian Society in Fetter Lane (with which John Wesley had been closely connected in 1738), continued to flourish. The Sandemanians, an anti-Calvinist Scottish sect, established itself in Grocers' Hall in 1760, and moved in 1770 to a meeting-house in St Paul's Alley; a society of Baptist Sandemanians was formed in Red Lion Street in 1797. Another Scottish sect, the Bereans, met for a short time in Dudley Street, Soho. A group of Socinians (with a Unitarian bias) was founded by a former Anglican vicar, Theophilus Lindsey, in Essex Street in 1778. Universalism made its first appearance with James Relly, a former colleague of Whitefield, at the Coachmakers' Hall about 1765; he moved to a meeting-house in Crosby Square from 1769 to 1778; other Universalist congregations followed in Windmill Street and Parliament Court, Bishopsgate. The Swedenborgians formed a group in Great Eastcheap in 1788, and later built chapels in York Street, Westminster (1800), and Friars Street, Blackfriars (1803). At about this time, too, William Huntingdon proclaimed his extreme Calvinist views to large audiences in Providence Chapel, Titchfield Street, and the followers of Joannah Southcott, the 'Mother of God', established two lively congregations in Southwark. After all this activity, the enquiry of 1812 revealed that there were no fewer than 265 dissenting places of worship (compared with the Church's 186) in the metropolitan parishes of the diocese of London.[1]

The Roman Catholics had led a more precarious existence. Not only were their activities limited, like those of the Protestant dissenters, by the Test and Corporation Acts, but the Toleration Act did not apply to

[1] *Victoria History of London*, vol. 1, pp. 391–2; Michael Robbins, *Middlesex*, pp. 112–15; Parl. Papers, 1812.

them and an Act of 1699 condemned Catholics keeping schools to perpetual imprisonment and disabled them from inheriting or purchasing land. The next year, a proclamation had ordered the departure of all Catholics from the City and from within a radius of ten miles of it, and returns of Papists were successively called for in 1694–5, 1701–2, 1767 and 1780. (At the latter date there were 14,000 Catholic families in London.) Although the more barbarous penalties provided for by both recent and earlier laws were now seldom imposed, Catholics were therefore under constant observation, they could make few recruits, and the more prosperous of them confined their public worship to the chapels of foreign embassies, such as the Sardinian in Duke Street, Lincoln's Inn Fields, and the Bavarian in Warwick Street, St James's; others attended their own two chapels, of which the most conspicuous was in Ropemakers' Alley, in Moorfields. Catholics were natural targets of public animosity on occasions like the Jacobite rebellions of 1715 and 1745, but once the 'Forty-Five' was well past, there was little open persecution of the Catholic community, and in 1778 a Catholic Relief Bill, sponsored by Sir George Savile, Member for Yorkshire, was passed, unopposed, by Parliament. Its purposes were limited to removing the additional liabilities imposed by the Act of 1699. But in Scotland, before the new law was proclaimed, riots broke out in Edinburgh and Glasgow, and Roman Catholic schools and chapels were destroyed. The demand for repeal spread to London as soon as Lord George Gordon, a Scottish peer, became president of the newly formed Protestant Association, whose aim was to combat Popery in every form. The Association drew up a petition for repeal, which received the support of the Common Council of the City; and it was the presentation of the petition to Parliament on 2 June 1780 that provoked riots which lasted for a week and in the course of which a hundred dwellings and public buildings (including Catholic schools and chapels) were damaged or destroyed, prisons were broken into, the toll-houses on Blackfriars Bridge were set ablaze, and an attempt was made to storm the Bank of England.[1] But troops were mobilized, stern measures were taken against the rioters, and the Relief Act remained law. Yet it took time for the Catholics to outlive the hatred and prejudice which the riots had stirred to life, and it was not until 1792 that the first Roman Catholic chapel in Westminster was opened in York Street (though it was closed, for lack of funds, in 1798). At Tottenham, in Middlesex, the Church of St Francis de Sales was built in 1793; and the sympathy shown for French immigrant

[1] See pp. 221–4 below.

priests during the Revolution made it easier to recruit. By 1814 there were twelve Catholic chapels in London served by thirty-one priests, with a Catholic community now said to number 49,800.[1]

How did religion, canalized and dispersed through this wide variety of groups and denominations, touch the different social classes in London? It is, of course, impossible to answer this question with any degree of precision in relation to a period when there was no religious census; an answer must, therefore, at best be impressionistic. Perhaps one may claim, for a start, that the Church of England, until its evangelical revival at least, was essentially the church of the upper classes. The prevailing Latitudinarian theology, the high pew-rents and decorously muted ceremonies accorded well enough with the outlook and interest and sense of decorum of a social class to whom religious 'enthusiasm' had become abhorrent: it is the attitude expressed in the Earl of Chesterfield's injunctions to his son and in the voluminous correspondence of Horace Walpole. Horace's father, Sir Robert, was certainly not distinguished for his religious devotions any more than his political opponent, Viscount Bolingbroke; but against these non-believers, among statesmen, may be set such earnest religious practitioners as Viscount Percival (the later Earl Egmont), George Grenville and the Duke of Newcastle, who were all regular church-goers. To others, agnosticism and Deism were suitable subjects for social intellectual discussion; yet we have seen that such views found little support (in contrast with their French counterparts) in the 'blue-stocking' *salons*; and it may be that they remained largely philosophical exercises that had little effect on formal religious observance. This would seem to be borne out by the large and regular attendances at the more fashionable churches in London and Westminster.[2]

Similarly, Old Dissent had a close affinity with the mercantile community of the City of London. As the Latitudinarian Church of the eighteenth century harmonized with the social needs and attitudes of the aristocracy and gentry, so the Presbyterian, Independent and Baptist churches appear to have responded equally faithfully to those of the merchant and business class. The basic strength of Old Dissent in the City of London can best be illustrated by its extraordinary tenacity in

---

[1] W. E. H. Lecky, *A History of England in the Eighteenth Century*, 1906, vol. 4, p. 300; *Victoria History of London*, vol. 1, pp. 372-3; Michael Robbins, *Middlesex*, p. 116; House of Lords Record Office, Returns of Papists, 1767, 1780.

[2] N. Sykes, *Church and State in the Eighteenth Century*, pp. 255-6, 275-7; *Victoria History of London*, vol. 1, pp. 362-4.

40 Dame school, 1783 (*Victoria and Albert Museum*)

41 Dispersion of a Sabbath evening
school, 1799 (*Mansell Collection*)

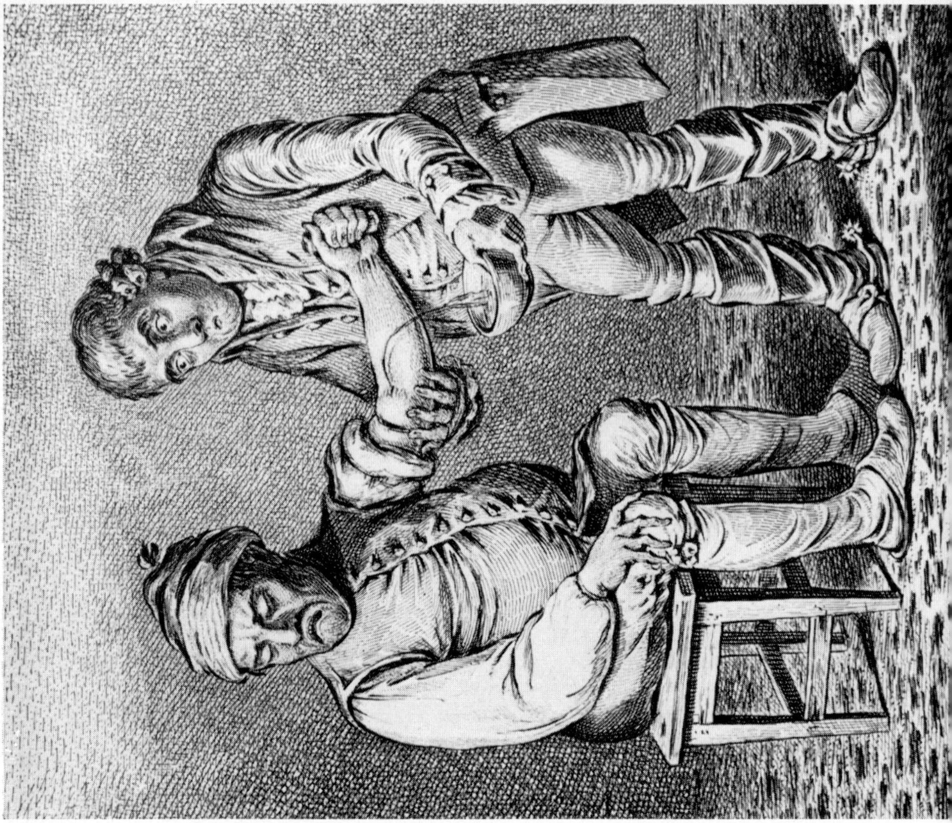

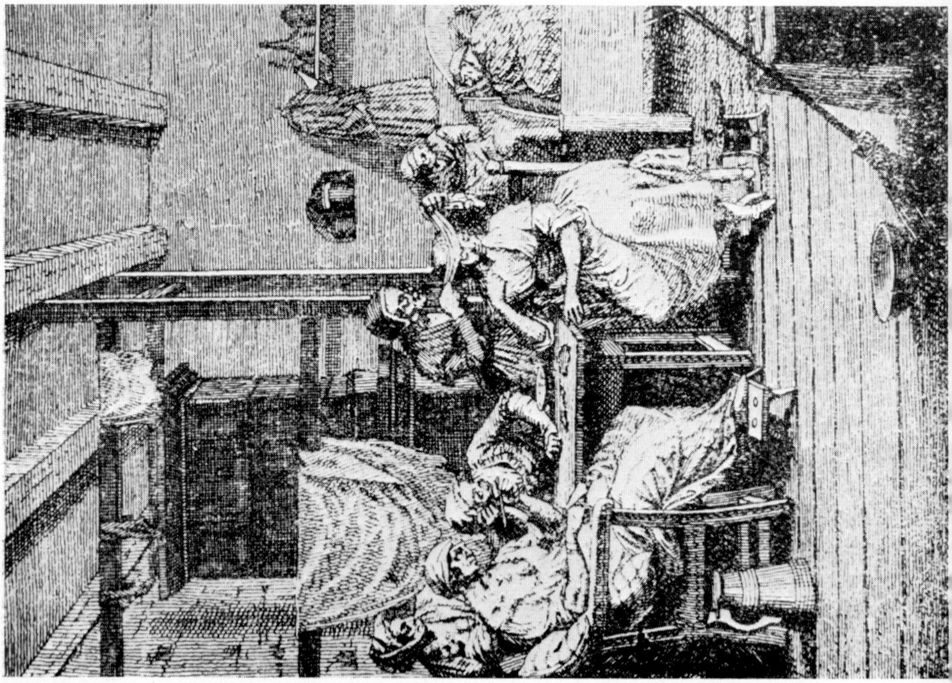

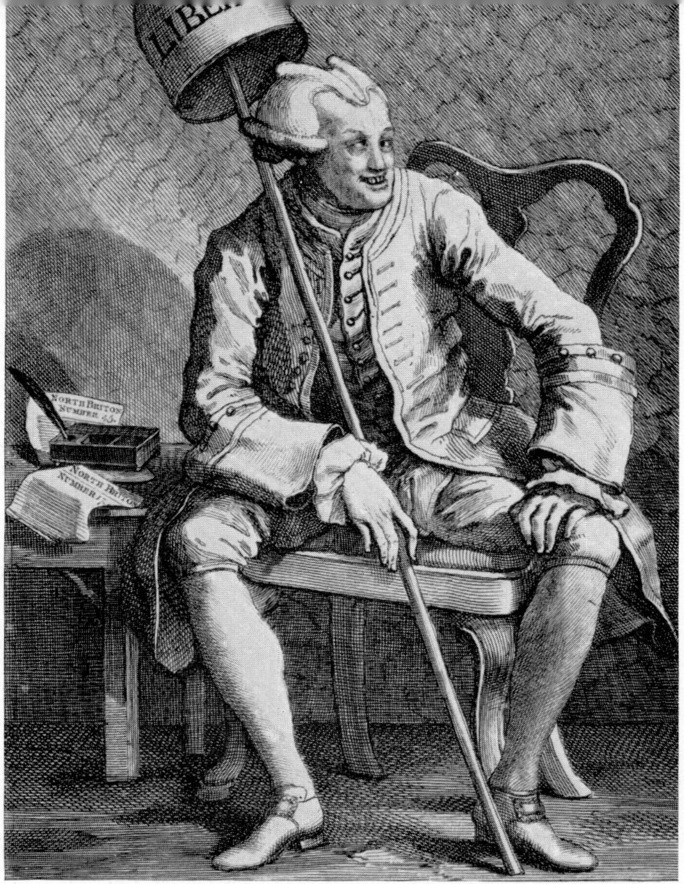
NORTH BRITON NUMBER 45.

44 John Wilkes, by Hogarth, 1763 (*British Museum*)

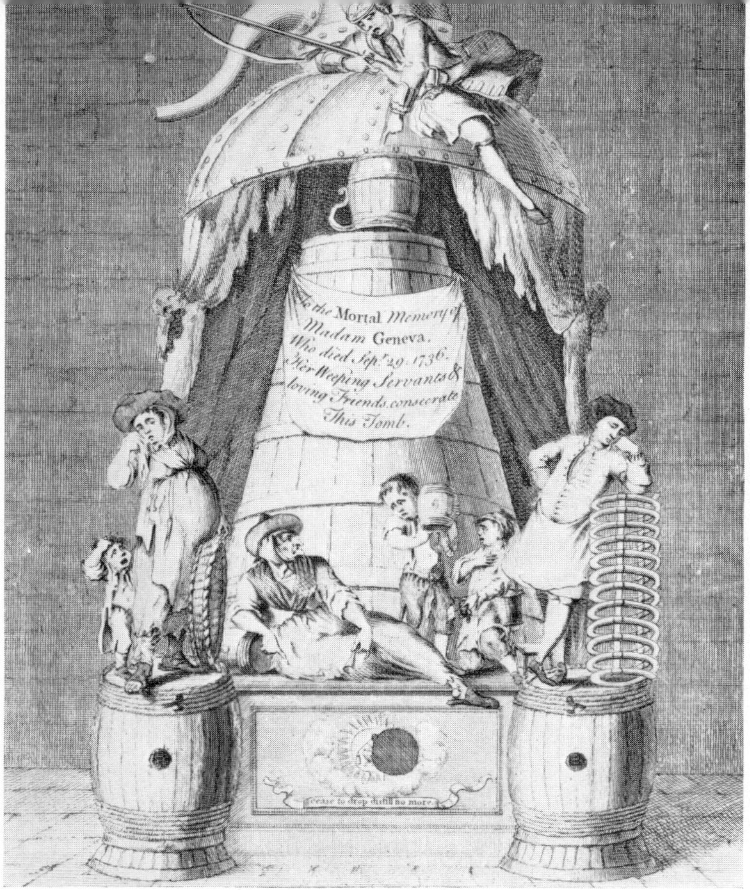
To the Mortal Memory of
Madam Geneva,
Who died Sep.r 29. 1736.
Her Weeping Servants &
loving Friends consecrate
This Tomb.
Cease to drop distill no more

45 Monument to Gin, 1736 (*British Museum*)

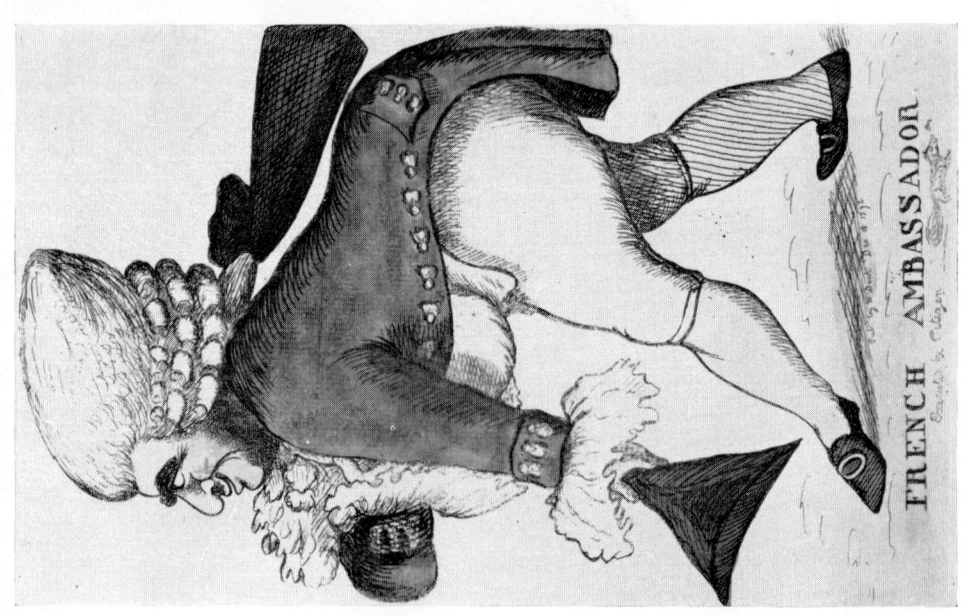

47 The Scotch Victory, May 1768 (*British Museum*)

FRENCH AMBASSADOR.

resisting, and surviving, the numerous and determined attempts made by High Church Tories in Charles II's and Anne's day to drive it from the City's precincts. As we have seen, with London's expansion, it built further meeting-houses and chapels in Westminster, Southwark and the out-parishes; but its essential bastion remained the City, where, in 1710, on the morrow of the Sacheverell Riots, it had thirty-eight places of worship. This association with City interests can also be illustrated by the close connection established between the City Companies and the dissenting groups to which they regularly let their halls for Sunday meetings. Thus, before 1689, a dozen Companies had been letting halls, as a regular fixture, to the various denominations. In the eighteenth century, several of these older tenancies continued; in addition, Curriers, Embroiderers, Tallow Chandlers and Turners let halls to Baptists; Founders and Brewers to Independents; Lorimers to both Independents and Baptists; and even the Universalists, a late-eighteenth century arrival, found a haven (like the Protestant Association in 1780), in the Coach-makers' Hall. And all these older bodies, as we have seen, settled, like the Church of England, into their own type of cosy and unruffled con-formity during a large part of the century, and may therefore be presumed to have made, at this time at least, little attempt to recruit members beyond the wealthy merchants and 'middling' groups.[1]

What, then, was the religion of the poor? To the Irish immigrant it was undoubtedly Roman Catholicism, which, in the eighteenth century, had far more followers among the poor Irish than among anyone else. At the time of the Gordon Riots, the largest Catholic communities were among the riverside workers, coal-heavers and weavers of Whitechapel, Wapping and St George in the East, the labourers of St Giles Cripplegate and St Luke Old Street, and the labourers, casual workers, barrowmen and poor lodgers of Saffron Hill, St Sepulchre Holborn and St Giles in the Fields. Compared with these the wealthy English Catholics of St James's and St George Hanover Square were, in point of numbers, of relative insignificance.[2] Among the native-born English, there was a considerable response to High Church Anglican principles in the early years of the century: this was evident in the Sacheverell affair and in the 'High Church and Ormond' riots that followed half a dozen years later. Again, the popular outcry, in the 1750s, against the Jewish Naturalization

---

[1] *Victoria History of London*, vol. 1, pp. 339 (map), 384.

[2] George Rudé, 'The Gordon Riots. A Study of the Rioters and their Victims', *Transactions of the Royal Historical Society*, 5th series, vol. 6, 1956, pp. 108–9.

I

Act appears to have been, in part at least, inspired from a similar source.[1] It may be, too, that the tenacity with which the small tradesmen and craftsmen of the City's Common Council, in the 1740s and 1750s, persisted in fining wealthy dissenters for refusing, on grounds of conscience, to assume high offices in the City's administration was motivated as much by an Anglican bias against nonconformity as by a desire to tax the rich.[2]

Conversely, the dissenting tradition itself found adherents among the more politically conscious of the City craftsmen and urban poor. It was bound up with the long and intangible tradition of 'Revolution principles' and 'the Good Old Cause', which entered into the new and popular Radicalism emerging in the City and in Middlesex in the 1760s. This tradition was reinforced, in turn, by the 'New' Dissent that sprang up in the wake of the Methodist revival. If the old dissenting bodies tended to become atrophied and failed to seek new recruits in the second half of the century, the same was not true of the new or transformed societies that appeared, as we have seen, in the City, Westminster and Southwark. There were the Unitarians (largely an offshoot of older Presbyterian and Independent groups) with their tradition of radical protest; the Sandemanians, among whom William Godwin's father was a minister; the Swedenborgians, the followers of Joannah Southcott, the Inghamites and Muggletonians; and strange sects like the Ancient Deists of Hoxton, who, with their talk of dreams and conversations with angels and departed spirits, had a close affinity with William Blake. Like Blake, many of these new converts were London craftsmen, whose training in the sects, with their egalitarian principles and revivalist, Messianic ritual, led them, with the advent of the revolution in France, to embrace Jacobin and radical political ideas.[3]

Wesleyanism and Calvinist Methodism, which served as 'triggers' for several of these dissenting groups, chose quite deliberately to bring their religion to the poor. Not that there was anything egalitarian (except with regard to the After-Life) in Wesley's teaching or organization: the 'connections' and 'circuits' he created were ruled and controlled by his mainly middle-class lieutenants with an iron hand. But, from the start, he had set out to save the souls of the poor and to bring them spiritual consolation for their earthly ills. To attempt this, their problems had to be studied at first-hand. And so we find Wesley making personal visits to

[1] See pp. 206–8, 210 below.
[2] *Victoria History of London*, vol. 1, pp. 390–1.
[3] E. P. Thompson, *The Making of the English Working Class*, pp, 51–3.

the filthy garrets and underground cellars of St Giles's, and Wesleyan ministers visiting the most wretched of the prisoners in Newgate and riding with the condemned on the execution-carts to Tyburn. And, as we have seen, both Wesley and Whitefield preached to the poor (at first in the face of considerable hostility) at open-air meetings at Moorfields and Whitechapel and on Kennington Common – a practice that was later followed by other popular evangelists at Spa Fields, Cold Bath Fields and Islington Green.[1]

Yet the 'enthusiasm' and personal involvement that the Methodists inspired, so utterly foreign to the practices of the other mid-century churches, had dangerous social consequences that Wesley himself had certainly never intended. It was seen in the great explosion of anger, directed against not only Roman Catholics but also Anglican bishops, Cabinet ministers and Members of Parliament, expressed in the Gordon Riots. This hornet's nest was one of the by-products of Wesley's teaching, with its lurid and morbid insistence on the wickedness of Popery. Admittedly, Wesley drew a fine distinction between inciting hatred against Catholics and actually doing them violence; and, in a sermon preached in his New Chapel a few months after the riots, he

> showed that supposing the Papists to be heretics, schismatics, wicked men, enemies to us, and to our Church and nation; yet we ought not to persecute, to kill, hurt, or grieve them, but barely to prevent their doing hurt.

But it is surely significant that two weeks later he accepted Lord George Gordon's invitation to visit him in the Tower, where he was held prisoner, and thought the indictment against him for high treason to be 'a shocking insult upon the truth and common sense'. Yet it is only fair to add that the Protestant Association, whose 'No Popery' petition directly provoked the disturbances, was composed rather less of Wesleyans than of stern Presbyterians and Calvinists whose anti-Catholic zeal had been equally stirred by the militant example of their co-religionists in Scotland.[2]

A rather different form of activity among the poor was that undertaken by both Anglicans and dissenters in the field of education. 'Dame' schools had existed since medieval times; but these were schools for the more prosperous workers and craftsmen who could afford to pay the fee of 3*d*.

[1] *London Life*, p. 26; R. E. Wearmouth, *Methodism and the Common People of the Eighteenth Century*, 1945, pp. 192–202.
[2] *Wesley's Journal*, vol. 6, pp. 299–302.

a week or £1 a year. The charity schools, on the other hand, were free and were intended solely for the children of the poor. They were started in London in the 1690s by an independent body, the Society for Promoting Christian Knowledge, but to which both Anglicans and Protestant dissenters contributed. The ages of the children ran from seven to twelve and it was held (in 1712) that a boy within this range might be clothed for 15s. 8d. and a girl for 16s. 1d. By 1704, there were fifty-four of these schools in London and Westminster, with over 2,000 children in attendance. By the end of the century these numbers had more than trebled; the *Account of Charity Schools* published in 1797 shows, further, that the 183 schools listed at this time were spread fairly evenly over the City, Westminster, Southwark and the out-parishes, while, in the City alone, there were thirty-two schools for boys and twenty-four for girls.

The aim of the schools was not so much to teach reading and arithmetic or to make good citizens; it was rather to preserve children from vagrancy or crime, to inculcate elementary Christian values, and prepare them for 'services of the lowest kind'. Consequently, there was no attempt to train scholars or craftsmen, but rather to train docile and humble servants, God-fearing and conscious of their lowly station in life. A charity sermon preached at the Orphan Working School at Hoxton in 1760 explained that the children were to be taught 'not to be able scholars or fine penmen . . . but so much reading as every Christian who values his Bible would wish them to have, and no more writing than would be useful in the meanest situation'. The books recommended by the Society to teachers and children in its various reports and *Accounts* eloquently bear this out. Among sixty titles, there are half a dozen on spelling (including 'The Charity Spelling Book'), three on arithmetic, and one on the 'influence of conversation'. The rest are entirely made up of catechisms, manuals on 'the whole duty' of man or of the Christian, 'principles of religion for charity children', 'pious instructions' to youth, and 'seasonal caveats' against Popery. In retrospect, this type of instruction appeared abysmal to some. 'Conceive,' wrote Francis Place in 1835, 'what a state London must have been in, when there was no provision for school teaching besides the charity schools, which taught the children next to nothing and nothing likely to be useful to them.' It is a harsh verdict, but was it justified? Specifically, did the schools help to bring a fuller measure of literacy to London's labouring population? Unfortunately, we do not know the answer, as the charity school records are silent on the point and as work at present being done on literacy in the eighteenth century, based on the signatures on marriage registers, has not yet been completed. But we may suppose that, whereas the 'dame' schools taught many craftsmen to read and write, the charity schools, with the curriculum and the priorities we have seen, gave little formal education to the poor in the alphabet or numbers.[1]

Yet out of the charity school movement, with its prejudices and limitations, it is undoubted that something better emerged. On the one hand there were the Sunday Schools which, under largely Evangelical guidance, opened in London in 1785. In these, too, reading and arithmetic fought an unequal battle against the catechism and moral injunctions; but out of them grew the first children's books, written both for the children's instruction and for their entertainment. On the other hand there were the 'Lancastrian' schools, the first of which was opened by their founder, Joseph Lancaster, a Quaker, in London in 1798. The Bible was still obligatory, but the catechism dropped out of the curriculum. In James Mill's phrase, they were 'schools for all, not for Churchmen only'. It was quite a big step forward.[2]

[1] Sir Charles Mallet, 'Education, Schools and the Universities', in *Johnson's England*, vol. 2, pp. 210–11; *London Life*, pp. 26, 217–20; M. G. Jones, *The Charity School Movement in the Eighteenth Century*, 1938, pp. 372–5; E. A. Wrigley, *Past and Present*, no. 37, 1967, p. 51.

[2] E. Halévy, *England in 1815*, pp. 528–31.

7

The Government
of London

WE HAVE seen how London, by the latter part of the century, while continuing to press outwards, was acquiring within its extending boundaries some of the attributes of a unified and compact metropolis. In this regard we noted that James Boswell, in visiting Wapping in the early 1790s, stressed the growing 'uniformity' of the capital where Addison, eighty years before, had looked on it as 'an aggregate of various nations'. To a large degree, of course, this uniformity was still more apparent than real. It was real enough in the sense that many of the internal gaps observed by Defoe in 1724 had been progressively filled in by builders and planners. It was also true that the capital was becoming increasingly unified by its economy – spreading outwards from the City and the Court – and that a common social and cultural pattern (though divided vertically between the classes) was observable not only in the Cities of London and Westminster but, increasingly, in the out-parishes of Middlesex and Surrey. Yet, in most other respects, London could still be seen – much as Addison had seen it – as a loose agglomeration of separate parts, each of which still retained its own distinctive identity and character. Thus, broadly speaking, the City of London, enclosed within its square mile of narrow streets and wharves, was the centre of banking, business and international trade; Westminster was the home of government, Parliament, justice, the Court, the arts and fashionable society; Southwark formed, across the Thames, a commercial extension of the City, as the 'five villages beyond the Bills' (Marylebone, St Pancras and the rest) were a residential extension of Westminster; while the out-parishes, half city and half village, were still thrusting their frontiers outwards into the countryside beyond.

But in no respect was this diversity of London more marked than in its government and administration. Each component of the capital had evolved its own form of government, a legacy that even the present Greater London Council has not yet entirely shed. And to add to the confusion, geographical unit and unit of administration did not closely correspond. The bailiwick of Southwark, for example, was administered by the City ward of Bridge Without, while its associated parishes came under Surrey. Middlesex, like Surrey and other counties, was largely under the control of its justices of the peace; but its assizes were held, jointly with London's, at the Central Court of Justice at the Old Bailey, and its judges were entertained and its Members of Parliament returned by Sheriffs appointed in the City. In return, the jurisdiction of the Middlesex J.P.s extended over Westminster. The City's ranged far farther beyond its own wards and precincts: it held a legal monopoly of markets in a radius of 7 miles; it levied coal duties in a radius of 12 miles, extending over an area of five hundred times its own; it administered and taxed the port of London, and it formed the sole governing authority for the River Thames over the whole 80 miles from Staines Bridge to the mouth of the Medway in Kent. Westminster was jointly governed by its Courts of Burgesses and the county justices of Middlesex. The 'five parishes' alone were largely independent of other local authority and were ruled by their separate vestries. In short, the government of the capital may be examined under four heads: the Corporation of the City of London; the Court of Burgesses of Westminster; the justices of Surrey and Middlesex; and the innumerable parish vestries (some 200 by 1801) that enjoyed a greater or lesser degree of authority within the metropolis.[1]

The constitution of the City was one of immense complexity. Even if we leave out of account the numerous manorial courts and the courts of each one of the eighty-nine Companies, there were still seventeen separate courts dividing between them the electoral, executive, judicial and legislative functions of the Corporation; moreover, in addition to the Lord Mayor, the two Sheriffs, the Recorder, the Town Clerk, the Remembrancer and the Chamberlain, there were, in the eighteenth century, over 150 official posts or sinecures, most of them purchasable and lucrative, associated with its multiform activities. But many of these had become obsolete or moribund, or were relatively unimportant; so that, for sim-

---

[1] For this and much that follows, see S. and B. Webb, *English Local Government from the Revolution to the Municipal Corporations Act. The Manor and the Borough*, 1908, pp. 569–692.

plicity, we may confine our attention to the Lord Mayor and Sheriffs and the four courts of outstanding importance, over which the Lord Mayor, nominally at least, presided: the Court of Aldermen, the Court of Common Council, the Court of Common Hall and the Court of Wardmote held within each one of the twenty-six wards. Between them, these discharged all the most important functions of the Corporation.

The Court of Aldermen consisted of the Lord Mayor, and the twenty-five other aldermen, who were elected for life by the freemen ratepayers in their various wards. Aldermen had to be freemen of the City and born of English father within the United Kingdom; but they were not required to be an either City householders or residents. Individually, they served as magistrates within their wards and, after 1742, they were enrolled on the commission of the peace, sometimes serving as justices in widely scattered counties. Collectively, they served as a sort of City cabinet and House of Lords, wielding a wide variety of executive authority and claiming a part in legislation as well. They appointed the Recorder and other senior City officers; they governed prisons, conducted the courts of law, appointed the Assize of Bread, issued ale-house licences, and authorized the payment of the City's accounts. They adjudicated in disputes between the Companies and in all matters relating to elections. By an extension of this right, they claimed the further right to select the Lord Mayor from two candidates submitted by the Court of Common Hall. And, most contentious usurpation of all, after 1689 they began to insist on a right of veto on all legislative acts brought forward by the Court of Common Council. This, as we shall see, proved a fertile field for disputes between the two Courts in the opening half of the century.

The Court of Common Council was composed of the Lord Mayor, the twenty-five other aldermen and some 210 Councilmen elected annually by the freemen ratepayers of the several wards. Like the aldermen, the 'commoners' had to be freemen of the City but, unlike the aldermen, they were also required to be householders resident within the wards that elected them. The Common Council came, in the course of the century, to acquire the attributes of a local House of Commons, while assuming important administrative duties in addition. Originally an advisory body to the mayor and aldermen, it had early been empowered to appoint certain City officers, such as the Town Clerk and the Common Serjeant. But since 1689 it had begun to present the Lord Mayor and aldermen with its by-laws and legislative acts, which it claimed (for long in the face of fierce aldermanic resistance) to be binding on the citizens. In the early decades, these had been largely concerned with matters submitted by the Companies, such as their continual complaints against the employment of 'foreigners' or non-freemen within the City. In these debates, the Common Council had moved from a total ban on 'foreigners' (in 1712) to a declaration of commercial freedom (in 1750), which allowed employers to hire non-freemen where freemen craftsmen made 'unreasonable' demands. But, by the latter date, this type of business had become less frequent and less important, and more pressing matters had arisen to take its place. There had been a great increase in the shipping and commerce of the port of London, which called for the legislative attention of both Parliament and City. New bridges would soon be built across the Thames; markets and prisons had to be enlarged; the Mansion House had been commissioned; new sites were being requested; new demands were being made on the watch and ward; above all, from 1765 onwards, new steps had to be taken to pave the City, to build sewers and cleanse its streets. Thus both the nature and the weight of the business handled by the Common Council became significantly changed; with the connivance of the Lord Mayor and aldermen and often at the expense of the ancient jurisdiction of the wardmotes, it gradually assumed a vastly enlarged legislative and administrative burden, set up an increasing number of committees, paid an increasing number of salaried staff and progressively assumed the responsiblity for the bulk of the City's day-to-day administration. In tracing this process from 1746 to 1832, Sidney and Beatrice Webb describe the growth in the Council's authority 'from a sort of consultative legislature, dependent for its Executive upon the Lord Mayor and the Aldermen, into a supreme organ of administration, itself wielding the whole power of government, and reducing the Lord Mayor and Aldermen to a mere magistracy'. The process was, however, far from being completed by the end of the eighteenth century.[1]

Moreover, the commoners' new authority had not been lightly won and its claims had long been contested by the Lord Mayor and the Court of Aldermen. The struggle for supremacy between the two Courts went back to the previous century. During the Commonwealth, the scales had been tipped in favour of the commoners; but, after the Restoration, the Lord Mayor and aldermen, as faithful servants of the Crown, had won back their authority and reduced the Common Council to filling a merely consultative role. After 1689 the Council made a new effort to redress the balance and claimed that, as an autonomous body, it had the right to

[1] S. and B. Webb, *The Manor and the Borough*, p. 637.

verify its members' credentials, endorse or annul its elections, regulate its own debates, disfranchise unqualified electors, and pronounce on the validity of its legislative acts irrespective of the attendance of the Mayor and aldermen. The latter, in return, riposted that, following parliamentary precedent, the legislative power was vested not in the Common Council alone, but jointly in 'the Lord Mayor, Aldermen and Commonalty'; and that therefore no legislation could be valid without the concurrence of the commoners' senior partners. After 1715 the struggle became all the sharper as the City became politically divided, the aldermen tending to be Whig and Latitudinarian and the Common Council to be Tory and High Church. And as Parliament reflected the views of the aldermen rather than those of the commoners, it is perhaps not surprising that when the aldermen appealed to Parliament it was their opinion that prevailed. An Act of 1725, in fact, limited the freeman franchise to £10 householders (thus disqualifying a large number of the less opulent, and therefore largely Tory, voters) and laid it down that enactments of the Common Council should only be valid if supported by a majority of the aldermen. Thus the City's legislative and executive power became vested in the Lord Mayor and aldermen alone and the aldermanic veto was imposed by Act of Parliament. The situation lasted for twenty years. For ten years the Common Council remained silent, and for over a year (between 1727 and 1729) it did not even meet. The political climate changed in the 1730s, when the two Courts combined their forces in common opposition to Sir Robert Walpole;[1] after the collapse of the 'Forty-Five' the Jacobite danger seemed past, and the Commons agreed in 1746 to a new Bill which virtually annulled the discriminatory provisions of the Act of 1725. And after this, as we have seen, new problems arose that compelled the Lord Mayor and aldermen to look on the legislative activities of the commoners in a more favourable light.

The contest, however, so happily resolved by the middle of the century, had not been due to political divisions, or to the absence of administrative pressures, alone. The factor of class had also undoubtedly played a part. The aldermen, as we saw, had no obligation to reside in the City and several of them (as noted in an earlier chapter) had houses in the fashionable streets and squares of St Anne's, St George's or St James's, in Westminster. Many more could have done so had they wished, for, although there was no formal property qualification for the post, they were almost without exception men of wealth and expected to hold

[1] See the next chapter.

property to the value of £15,000.[1] (There were admittedly 'outsiders' among them: men like John Wilkes and Edward Gibbon, the historian's father; but these were far less typical of the aldermanic body than wealthy or well connected men like William Beckford and the Rt Hon. Thomas Harley.) We have already seen, moreover, how frequently aldermen were connected with the aristocracy, or were bankers, directors of 'moneyed' companies or large holders of government stock. More precisely, if we take the six years of Wilkes's City ascendancy, between 1768 and 1774, we find that of the forty-three aldermen then holding office, no less than a dozen were or became bankers (two of them as directors or Governor of the Bank of England), one was a director of London Assurance, one the Governor of the Hudson's Bay Company, two were West India merchants, several were gentlemen of leisure, and only a handful followed the more common City crafts or trades. And there seems little doubt that a broadly similar pattern would apply to the earlier and later years of the century.[2]

The Common Councillors, however, were far more closely tied, both by residence and occupation, to the ordinary City voters and the ordinary City crafts. They were, in fact, predominantly retail shopkeepers and old-fashioned master craftsmen. (In this respect at least, they bore little resemblance to the members of the House of Commons!) In 1739, when the Council was engaged in strenuous opposition to the Ministry, a list of its members and their occupations was widely disseminated by the supporters of government in order to discredit their pretensions. It revealed that its 210 non-aldermanic members included 26 haberdashers and linen drapers, 14 druggists and apothecaries, 6 bakers and confectioners, 8 carpenters, cabinet-makers, masons and bricklayers, 2 cheesemongers, 5 grooms, 2 colourmen, 5 vintners, 3 plumbers, 7 coopers and about 70 other tradesmen and craftsmen; while there were among them only 4 bankers, 7 attorneys, 3 distillers, 1 brewer, 1 broker, 7 surgeons, 1 goldsmith and 6 merchants. Thirty-five years later the picture had not greatly changed; and of 311 Common Councilmen holding office between 1768 and 1774 and whose addresses and occupations appear in the *London Directory* for that year, 124 were wholesalers, brokers and merchants, 89 were shopkeepers (27 linen drapers, 39 in other textiles, 15 booksellers and stationers), 83 were craftsmen and manufactures (38 in sundry metal trades), 13 were professional men (11 of them lawyers), and 2 were company directors. And, in 1833, we find the Corporation Commissioners

[1] S. and B. Webb, *The Manor and the Borough*, pp. 656–8.
[2] *Wilkes and Liberty*, pp. 150, 217–19; Beaven, vol. 2, pp. 196–211.

elaborating on the same theme: the Common Councillors (they wrote) were 'generally responsible retail tradesmen or persons belonging to the same rank in life, including attorneys in many instances. . . . The Freemen householders, who alone can be elected, do not, generally speaking, comprehend the higher class of merchants[1].'

Traditionally, the local Court of Wardmote had played an important local role in City affairs. It was held separately within each of the wards, presided over by the alderman and open to all ward ratepayers, whether they were freemen or not. Its functions were threefold: to elect the ward officers, to nominate the ward's Common Councilmen (who, if freemen and unopposed, became automatically elected), and, with the Lord Mayor in attendance, to fill aldermanic vacancies as they arose. Closely associated with the Wardmote was the Inquest of the Ward, whose duties had long been to collect for the poor, to supervise paving and lighting, and to act as a watch-dog for public morals by closing down unlicensed ale-houses, gaming houses and houses of ill-fame. But even these comparatively modest duties began to be whittled away, after the early years of the century, as more authority passed from the rank-and-file citizen to the Common Council of the ward, formed by the alderman, his deputy and the resident Common Councilmen (whose number would range from four in a small ward to sixteen in a large). This local committee, besides conducting the current business of the ward, had the important tasks of directing the Night Watch, settling tax assessments, collecting rates and hearing appeals. To these were added, by two statutes of 1736 and 1737, the right to contract for street lighting, to appoint paid watchmen and to levy the appropriate rates. But this added importance was pared down, in turn, as the Guildhall extended its authority over the subordinate bodies. Thus the wards' responsibility for paving and lighting was taken over from the 1760s by the Court of Common Council, while the Court of Aldermen assumed the direction of the watch, leaving minor delegated powers to the local committees. So the wardmotes declined and, by the end of the Napoleonic Wars, had become little more than poorly attended debating clubs on public affairs.

The last of the four Courts, and one whose importance tended to increase rather than to diminish, was the Court of Common Hall, which was open to all freemen of the City's livery companies. A City Election Act of 1725 strictly excluded all non-liveried freemen (who may have amounted to one-third of the combined freemen body of 12,000–15,000); and, in the

[1] S. and B. Webb, *The Manor and the Borough*, p. 627.

elections of 1775 and 1776, energetic measures were taken to remove all gate-crashers from its meetings. The Common Hall was the essential backbone of City democracy, even more important, in terms of the political and electoral power that it wielded, than the freemen ratepayers of the twenty-six wards who elected the aldermen and Common Councillors. For it alone had the right of election of the Lord Mayor, the two Sheriffs of London and Middlesex, and the City's four Members of Parliament. Elections generally followed an agreed system of rotation by seniority and were seldom contested. The Sheriffs were selected from senior aldermen who had not yet held either the shrieval or mayoral office. The Lord Mayor tended to be chosen from the senior aldermen 'below the Chair', provided he had already served as Sheriff; and the Members of Parliament were, in nearly every case (following tradition rather than any written precept), elected from senior members of the aldermanic body. But there were moments of political excitement when elections did not proceed so smoothly. In 1739, for example, during the heat generated by the affair of 'Jenkins' Ear' (which eventually led to a war with France and Spain), Sir George Champion, M.P. for Aylesbury and a supporter of Sir Robert Walpole, was passed over in favour of John Salter, a 'patriot' candidate more acceptable to the liveried freemen. It was to avoid such situations that the Court of Aldermen had claimed the right to choose the Lord Mayor from the names of two candidates brought forward by the Common Hall. Yet the aldermanic veto which this implied was long held in abeyance, and the Court regularly 'scratched' for the one of the two candidates submitted who had the higher poll. But this practice was abandoned when John Wilkes presented himself for the first time for the mayoralty in 1772; though he headed the poll, the aldermen declared for his rival and runner-up, James Townsend. This led to violent scenes at the Guildhall on the following Lord Mayor's Day (9 November), when 3,000 demonstrators filled the yard and there were angry shouts of 'It's Wilkes's turn' and 'Damn my Lord Mayor for a scoundrel, he has got Wilkes's right, and we will have him out.'[1]

The office of Sheriff was less eagerly sought after except as a necessary stepping-stone to the mayoralty; it was therefore not frequently contested. But, as already mentioned in the previous chapter, a problem arose over nonconformist aldermen who, on grounds of conscience, refused to serve. In 1734 it was decided that, in such cases, a fine of £400 should be paid into the fund being raised for building the new Mansion House. The

[1] Old Bailey *Proceedings*, 1773, pp. 46–59.

most widely publicized case was that of Robert Grosvenor, who, when nominated, refused to take the necessary steps, provided by the Corporation Act, to qualify for office, and, in consequence, was fined. He appealed and eventually won his case; but other dissenters continued to incur fines which, in the space of a few years, amounted to £15,000.[1]

The most excited debates in the Common Hall were over parliamentary elections; this was particularly so in the high period of City Radicalism in the 1760s and 1770s. To ensure that the Members of their choice continued, after taking their seats at Westminster, to carry out their electors' wishes, the London liverymen had hit on the novel device of 'instructing' them as to how they should behave in Parliament. This had already been done, under William III, in the elections of 1696 and 1701, and the practice was resumed, under the first two Georges, in 1715 and 1741 and 1742. But, so far, these 'instructions' had been formal and not attended by lively debates and divisions within the Common Hall itself. This first happened in 1770 when, on Beckford's death, Richard Oliver was returned on the understanding that he should obey these 'instructions' as they arose and that he would resign his seat if he found himself unable to do so. Three years later, Frederick Bull was the first Member to enter Parliament after solemnly pledging himself to support a long list of popular demands; and, at the next election, in 1774, all four City M.P.s, Oliver, Bull, Hailey and Sawbridge, had to sign a pledge, before being elected, to obey their 'instructions' and specifically not to accept from the Ministry 'any place, pension, contract, title, gratuity, or emolument of any kind'. As long as the Common Hall kept to its brief and did not meddle in other affairs, it was able steadily to increase its authority; but when it attempted, as it did in the 1780s, to usurp the functions of the Common Council by claiming the right to elect to certain City offices and to control the Corporation funds, it met with a sharp rebuff and gained no success whatever.

At the base of the City's constitutional pyramid were the citizen householders, nearly all of whom had become freemen, either by the qualification of apprenticeship or by the purchase of the freedom of one of the liveried companies at a cost that might vary between £5 and £50. Freedom brought considerable advantages to its owner: it protected him from the 'press gang' in time of war, it gave him the right to vote for his aldermen and Common Councilmen and, most coveted prize of all, it entitled him to a licence for trading in the City. Equally, it entailed a number of obliga-

[1] *Victoria History of London*, vol. 1, p. 390.

tions. He had to pay his rates and taxes, hang out a lantern on moonless nights, and serve his turn as constable, scavenger or collector of the rates. Moreover, he was called upon to serve on a rota as a member of the Night Watch, to sweep the cobbles in front of his house, and to keep his part of the pavement in good repair. Such, at least, were his obligations during the earlier part of the century; but these became considerably whittled down with the Lighting and Paving and Watch Acts which, after 1736, began to transfer the more burdensome duties to more professional hands. So the London citizen enjoyed a considerable measure of democracy in local affairs (a 'ratepayers' democracy' as the Webbs have termed it), and that at a modest price.

Unlike the City of London, Westminster had never been allowed to become a municipality, to elect a Lord Mayor or a Court of Aldermen, nor to enjoy any sort of corporate status. Nominally it had, since Burghley's Constitution of 1585, been governed by a Court of twelve Burgesses appointed for life from its tradesmen by the City's High Steward. Initially, each Burgess had been put in charge of a ward where he exercised duties similar to those of the alderman's deputy in the City of London: he rooted out 'nuisances' and compelled citizens to serve their turn in the watch and ward, to put out lights and to keep the pavements in good repair. Later, more important duties had been added, such as supervising the operation of the watch and ward, paying the beadles and hiring the watchmen. Collectively, the Burgesses sat as a Court to try petty offences, not acting as justices (they were never on the commission of the peace) but as a kind of petty police magistracy empowered to fine, whip and imprison offenders against the City's by-laws. As a Court, they also appointed the constables and scavengers, the Leet Jury, the Jury of Annoyance, and the Wardmote or Christmas Jury (which looked after poor prisoners), and occasionally (as in 1710, 1735 and 1741) they set the Assize of Bread. In return for discharging these onerous duties the Burgesses and their twelve assistants received no reward other than such profits as they could make from the collection of 'fines' and the dignity and status that went with the office.

Yet, throughout the eighteenth century, and particularly after the 1720s, such authority as the Burgesses possessed was gradually pared down and transferred to the 'close' vestries of the nine parishes (of which more will be said later) and the Middlesex justices who sat on the Westminster Bench. Already in 1722, a resolution of the justices virtually questioned their right to survival; and, progressively, with the aid of

Parliament, the justices and 'open' vestries stripped them of any effective authority over the watch and ward (after 1736) and for paving and lighting the streets (after 1761). So that, by the mid-1760s, practically all that remained to the Burgesses was the dignity attaching to their ceremonial functions, which persisted until the office itself was abolished in 1901.[1]

So Westminster's government, from being for many years a jungle of rival jurisdictions, became little more than a bureaucracy in which the ordinary citizens, in sharp contrast to their fellows in the City of London, played a remarkably small part. In compensation, however, Westminster had a parliamentary franchise that, by being open to all resident house-holders or 'pot-wallopers', was even more democratic than the City's. We have seen, in earlier chapters, that even labourers, watermen and por-ters were listed in its poll books; and we shall see later how important a part the Westminster electors played in the Radical movement of the latter part of the century.

The out-parishes came under the usual county administration, in which the Lord Lieutenant and the High Sheriff (like the Burgesses in Westminster) played a largely decorative and ceremonial role and the real authority – apart from that exercised at parish level by the vestries – lay with the justices of the peace meeting in quarter sessions. In Surrey and Middlesex, as in other counties, the justices appointed and directed the activities of the parish officers – the constables, overseers and surveyors of the highways. They were responsible for the relief of destitution; they maintained roads and bridges; regulated wages and prices; maintained workhouses; licensed ale-houses; established and administered Houses of Correction; and sat in judgment in the courts of petty and quarter ses-sions. In the course of the century, these powers tended to become ex-tended at the expense of some of the old county officers; but the High Constable, generally a man of the 'middling sort' whose task it was to supervise a large part of the county administration, saw an increase rather than a diminution in his authority. The most influential person of all was the chairman of quarter sessions, formally elected at the beginning of each session but often holding office for several consecutive years. In Surrey, Lord Middleton held the post from 1798 to 1825, and in Middlesex, two successive incumbents held it between them for half a century: Sir John Hawkins, Dr Johnson's first biographer, from 1765 to 1780, and the formidable William Mainwaring, who was also a county Member of Parliament, from 1781 to 1816.

[1] S. and B. Webb, *The Manor and the Borough*, pp. 212–31.

Like the City's Common Councilmen, the Middlesex and Westminster justices were often recruited among men of comparatively humble or 'middling' origin: small professional men or tradesmen, of whom it was uncharitably said that they 'had picked up a little knowledge by attending on special juries, and thought themselves lawyers'. In 1744 we read of the Earl of Hardwicke, as Lord Chancellor, refusing to put the organist of St James's Church, in Piccadilly, into the Westminster Commission; and in 1780 Burke, with characteristic venom, denounced the justices of Middlesex as being 'generally the scum of the earth – carpenters, brick-makers and shoemakers; some of them were notoriously men of such infamous characters that they were unworthy of any employ whatever, and others so ignorant that they could scarcely write their own names'.[1]

When every allowance has been made for Burke's aristocratic preten-sions and his love of hyperbole, the fact remains that the promotion of men of humble means to unpaid positions of authority, often involving considerable out-of-pocket expenses, opened the way for the unsavoury scandal of the 'trading justice', an appellation that has gained considerable notoriety from its frequent use by eighteenth-century authors. The 'trading justice' made his appearance all over the country, but nowhere as conspicuously as in Middlesex, Westminster, the Tower Hamlets (on the outskirts of the City) and the metropolitan area of Surrey. He made his money not so much by accepting direct bribes as from charging a fee for every service that he rendered; thus he virtually acquired an in-built interest in promoting business and, in Samuel Butler's phrase, he 'used two equal ways of gaining, by hindering justice or by maintaining'. Some of these men were small-town operators who, setting up shop in Holborn or the Tower Hamlets, made a living from selling their 'protection' to prostitutes or swindlers. Others might, like Ralph Hodgson of Shadwell, promote a somewhat shady type of trade-union enterprise among the coal-heavers (of which more will be said in a later chapter); others, again, might achieve considerable renown, like Sir Thomas De Veil, who was the leading metropolitan magistrate from 1729 to 1747, served as a justice in four counties, enjoyed ministerial favour and was subsidized by Treasury grants. But the practice, whether covered by such a veneer of respect-ability or not, was widely condemned and was held up to contempt or opprobrium in the works of Swift, Steele, Gay, Fielding and Smollett.

[1] For this and much that follows, see S. and B. Webb, *English Local Government from the Revolution to the Municipal Corporations Act. The Parish and the County*, 1906, pp. 281–2, 325–42, 372–3, 435–6, 489–91, 557–80.

K

Moreover, the Middlesex quarter sessions, on numerous occasions between 1720 and 1780 (and never more vigorously than under the chairmanship of Sir John Hawkins), made representations to the Lord Chancellor to have such persons removed from the Commission; and at least a dozen corrupt justices of the kind were, during this period, struck off the lists. Such cases were, of course, comparatively rare; and against them must be set the long years of devoted service given to the Westminster Bench by men like Saunders Welch from his office in Litchfield Street, Soho, and the two Fieldings at their Bow Street office. But the reputation of the Middlesex Bench, still comparatively unblemished, received a severe setback when William Mainwaring, a banker of reputed piety, became its chairman, in succession to Sir John Hawkins, in 1781, and remained so for thirty-five years. Leading positions in the county were given to other members of the family, and under their rule there was erected an extensive system of corruption; significantly, no further cases of 'trading justices' and their malpractices were referred to the Lord Chancellor for his attention.[1]

The unit of government that was common to every part of the metropolis was the vestry. This, the meeting of the inhabitants in their parishes, was a feature as typical of the City of London as it was of Westminster, Southwark, the 'five villages' and the metropolitan areas of Surrey and Middlesex. Though the feature was common, it varied considerably in the importance that it played in local affairs. In the City of London, with its elaborate machinery of government based on the twin Courts at the Guildhall and the wards and precincts in the localities, the functions of the parish were limited to the election of churchwardens, the management and repair of the church and the distribution of parish charities; the more important business of government – such as lighting, paving, cleansing and sanitation – was handled, at various levels, by the Corporation. In other parts of the metropolis, a large part of these administrative duties fell on the parishes themselves. Yet, here, too, there were significant variations. In the out-parishes and in certain parishes of Westminster, the major responsibility for poor relief and highways, for example, fell on the county justices. Only in the 'five villages beyond the Bills' was there no general overriding authority to which the vestries were subordinate; though, here again, there were varying degrees of responsibility or competence. Thus Kensington and Chelsea depended for their roads and pavements on the Turnpike Trusts and Street Commissions for Paving; while the vestries of

[1] S. and B. Webb, *The Parish and the County*, pp. 372, 562–6.

Marylebone and St Pancras (like certain of the 'close' vestries of Westminster) had extensive powers of government, ranging over highways, poor relief, sanitation, and the assessment and levying of the various local rates.[1]

A feature of many London parishes during the late seventeenth and eighteenth centuries was the gradual concentration of power in the hands of a small number of 'principal inhabitants', while the mass of the ratepayers were stripped of all share in government. This is the story of the emergence of the 'select' or 'close' vestry, which, in about one quarter of the two hundred metropolitan parishes, superseded the old 'open' vestry whose meetings had, by long tradition, been open to all ratepayers wishing to attend. The open vestry had been typical of the older parish and, in most cases, continued to be so in Hanoverian London. In its extreme, democratic form there were parishes, like that of Whitechapel, in metropolitan Middlesex, which, in 1734, aroused the concern of the more respectable citizens by virtue of the 'clamorous proceedings and irregular behaviour of the great multitude of persons' who crowded into their meetings. There were other vestries which, while still 'open' rather than 'select', were more discriminating and excluded the ratepayers of 'the meaner sort'. Others, again, were 'mixed' in the sense that they were 'open' for some purposes and 'close' for others: such were St Leonard Shoreditch and St Stephen Coleman Street, in the City. There was also the remarkable case of Bethnal Green which, from being a hamlet of the manor of Stepney, became in 1742 a separate parish with a population of 15,000. The vestry was made open to all ratepayers occupying premises of a value of £15 a year and above; and until 1797 it was managed by a body of about 2,000 householders. At this point, the parish came under the control of Joseph Merceron, a justice of Brick Lane, who quickly established himself as a local dictator, combining the offices of chairman of the Watch Board and Street Commission with that of Treasurer, and owning or controlling a quarter of the parish's ninety beer-shops and public houses. By 1818, when justice caught up with him at last and he was sentenced to eighteen months in jail and a £200 fine, he had syphoned thousands of pounds of parish money into his private accounts. Yet far from behaving as an old-style autocrat or as the mouthpiece of the local rich, Merceron made the open vestry his base and the springboard of his authority, and won great popularity by keeping the beer-houses open through the night and organizing Sunday dog-fights and weekly bullock-hunts through the

[1] S. and B. Webb, *The Parish and the County*, pp. 170–243.

parish streets. In fact, it was only after this modern-type 'Tammany Hall boss' was toppled from power that the 'turbulent democracy' of Bethnal Green was replaced by the greater sedateness and greater social respectability of a select vestry.[1]

By the end of the century there were some fifty or sixty close or select vestries in London. They included several City parishes: among them St Giles Cripplegate, St Bartholomew the Great and St Botolph Bishopsgate; a majority of the parishes of Westminster; Marylebone and St Pancras among the 'five villages'; and a substantial number of parishes scattered over metropolitan Middlesex and Surrey. In these, there was no question of merely excluding the householders of 'the meaner sort': authority was vested in exclusive and self-perpetuating oligarchies, who might number thirty, forty, fifty or even a hundred persons empowered to fill vacancies by nomination. The nature of the 'principal inhabitants' thus selected would naturally vary with the social complexion of the parishes concerned. On the vestry of the aristocratic parish of St George Hanover Square, when it was first formed in 1725, there were 7 dukes, 14 earls, 2 viscounts, 7 barons and 26 other titled persons. The vestry of St Martin's in the Fields included, among its 48 members in 1724, 5 noblemen, 4 baronets or sons of peers and 13 mere esquires. That of St Margaret's, Westminster, was generally composed of a peer or two, several M.P.s, a number of gentry and the Speaker of the House of Commons. The close vestry that emerged in Marylebone in 1768 included the Rector, 2 churchwardens and 99 other local notabilities, with a further 20 nominated members, the whole being commonly composed (as it was later claimed) of 'as many noblemen and members of Parliament as we could get hold of'. St James's, Piccadilly, devised a more original scheme: it created a vestry evenly divided between the 'estates', one-third being noblemen, one-third gentlemen and Members of Parliament, and one-third composed of tradesmen and men of business!

The select vestry emerged in a variety of ways. Some evolved by immemorial custom, as was the case with St Martin's in the Fields and (until a 'revolution' overtook it in 1730) with St Saviour's, Southwark. Some became close under the terms of the transfer of land or authority made by the Bishop of the diocese: such were St Dunstan's, Stepney, and St Giles in the Fields, in Westminster. Others were made close bodies by Act of Parliament in order to build churches or administer the Poor Law in new areas, or as the result of the division of older parishes. Thus St

[1] S. and B. Webb, *The Parish and the County*, pp. 79–90.

Paul's, Covent Garden, had been given a select vestry when it was made a new parish by the Long Parliament in 1645; St Anne's, Soho, was created in this way in 1685, and St James's, Piccadilly, was endowed with a select vestry in the same year; and out of the 'Fifty Churches' Act of 1711 there grew the new parishes and select vestries of St George Hanover Square, St John Clerkenwell and St John the Evangelist, in Westminster. Others, again, developed from open into select vestries as the consequence of the emergence of new problems which the principal inhabitants felt that they alone were competent to handle, and then persuaded Parliament to change the old constitution by means of a Local Act. This is what happened in Marylebone and St Pancras. In Marylebone, the aristocratic proprietors began to become restive after an Act of 1756, endowing the old open vestry with a wide range of new powers, appeared to them to lead to widespread muddle and confusion. Following a four-year agitation, they managed to secure the Local Act of 1768 which gave them virtual control of the parish administration. Similarly in St Pancras, as the result of a population 'explosion' in the 1780s and 1790s, a campaign was launched by Thomas Rhodes, a rich landowner of the district, which, after nearly twenty years of stubborn fighting, led to the creation of a select vestry in 1819.[1]

There were other cases, too, where such a transfer of authority from the majority to a selected few led to bitter recrimination and to prolonged resistance by those dispossessed. This happened in the parish of St Botolph Bishopsgate, where two sets of complaints made against the select vestry by their opponents in 1710 and 1721 charged them with having engaged in a variety of malpractices reaching back to a whole century before. A complaint made in 1710, which clearly had political undertones (it was put forward at a time of intense hostility between Whigs and Tories), asserted that the vestry 'by an arbitrary power raise money upon the inhabitants . . . and clandestinely apply part of it amongst themselves, as they think fit'. In 1721 the complainants drew up a long list of grievances which they summarized under six main heads:

[that] they misspend the parish money, particularly in feasting themselves;
that they choose persons in office before their turns;
that they make all offices as burthensome as they can;
that they forced substantial citizens to pay fines instead of serving;

[1] S. and B. Webb, *The Parish and the County*, pp. 204–11; F. H. W. Sheppard, *Local Government in St Marylebone 1688–1835. A Study of the Vestry and the Turnpike Trust*, 1958, pp. 125–8.

that they coopted members without regard for their seniority; that they drew pensions from the dead.[1]

Yet this is perhaps only a picturesque incident of little more than antiquarian interest that made little difference to the future of the parish; still less to the future of the City or of London in the case of a vestry whose powers were strictly limited and strictly subordinated to a higher authority. And even in the case of vestries endowed with greater powers, like Marylebone, St Pancras and certain of the larger parishes of Westminster, it is not possible to judge with any degree of confidence whether the transfer of authority from a democracy to an oligarchy proved to be a blessing or not to the mass of the parishioners. It is certain that some select vestries enjoyed a high reputation for good government and for dealing with local problems in an efficient and forward-looking manner. Among such vestries were St Martin's in the Fields (at least, up to 1714) and Marylebone after 1768; and the Webbs considered St George's Hanover Square to have been 'by far the best-governed parish' in the eighteenth-century metropolis. But there is, of course, no means of knowing whether these parishes would have fared worse, or better, if responsibility had been shared by a larger number of inhabitants.[2]

This brings us to the greater problem: how did the authorities of London as a whole, in all their diversity, cope with the great task of administering and 'improving' a great metropolis over a period of a hundred years? One's general impression is one of a slow reaction to the enormous problems facing the city in the earlier decades and, after the 1750s, of a growing realization of the need for action that gained momentum as the century progressed. Let us look at these problems a little more closely.

At the beginning of the century, London's street-lighting, paving and sanitation were of the most primitive kind. Lighting was regulated by an Act of William and Mary which provided for lamps to be hung out during six months of the year – from Michaelmas to Lady Day – and then only from dark till midnight. But even this modest aim was not achieved. The City had its own regulations, governed by an Act of the Common Council of 1716, which obliged citizens, on a penalty of 1s., to hang out candle-

[1] S. and B. Webb, *The Parish and the County*, p. 250; G.L., MS. 4527A, London. Bishopsgate Vestry: 'The Case of the Inhabitants of Bishopsgate Parish London, in relation to the Select Vestry there, the legallity whereof they are now contesting' (c. 1721).

[2] S. and B. Webb, *The Parish and the County*, pp. 236–41; F. H. W. Sheppard, *Local Government in St Marylebone 1688-1835*, pp. 10, 131 and ff.

lights in the six winter months from 6 to 11 p.m. on 'dark nights' by the calendar, or on eighteen nights in each moon. Thus the City was plunged into total darkness an hour before midnight; and Maitland claimed that London had, until the 1730s, the unenviable reputation of being the worst lit of the great cities of Europe. It was also notorious that streets remained unpaved and unnumbered and that, outside the major thoroughfares, filth and refuse lay stacked almost shoulder-high at street corners and against the buildings. On the approaches to the City, Lincoln's Inn Fields, then unenclosed, had long become a public receptacle for rubbish; while the City itself endured the filthy open sewer of the Fleet, which stretched from Fleet Bridge to Holborn Bridge and was a constant threat to the health and survival of its inhabitants; even in 1748, a London newspaper wrote of the City's streets as 'a Hotch-Potch of half-moon and serpentine narrow streets, close, dismal, long Lanes, stinking Alleys, dark, gloomy Courts and suffocating Yards'. The condition of Westminster was little better; and Lord Tyrconnel, speaking in the House of Lords in 1741, referred to the 'neglect of cleanliness of which, perhaps, no part of the world affords more proof than the streets of London, a city famous for wealth, commerce, and plenty, and for every other kind of civility and politeness; but which abounds with such heaps of filth, as a savage would look on with amazement'. And he added that 'the present neglect of cleansing and paving the streets is such as ought not to be borne . . . and that this great grievance is without a remedy, is a sufficient proof that no magistrate has, at present, power to remove it'. And in 1750 John Gwynn listed in his *Essay on Improvements* some of the most notorious of the 'nuisances' which he believed could (unlike the greater evils of which Lord Tyrconnel spoke) be remedied without further statutory provision. These were: ordure left lying in the streets (he notes, as particular black-spots, the posterns of the City and the area to the north of the Royal Exchange); open cellar doors or stone steps projecting into the street; broken pavements; delapidated houses; streets blocked with sheds and stalls; the projections of newly built houses into the streets; the cluttering of the streets with mad dogs, beggars and bullock-carts; the 'deluge of profanity'; and the total absence of street lighting from such precincts as St Martin's le Grand, Cloth Fair and St Bartholomew the Great.[1]

Some steps had, of course, already been taken to remedy this depressing state of affairs. The Great Fire itself had helped to thin out the densely packed medieval city; and only about 9,000 of the 13,000 houses destroyed

[1] *London Life*, p. 109; *Three Tours*, p. 13; Besant, pp. 89-92.

had been rebuilt. New brick houses had begun to replace the old buildings of lath and plaster, and the inhabitants of London's newly built squares had taken steps to secure them against the threat of becoming refuse-dumps by seeking powers to 'enclose, adorn and beautify' them: these were the first steps towards a long succession of Improvement Acts. The City's nocturnal gloom began to be dispelled by an Act of 1736 which gave powers to rate the inhabitants to hang out lights throughout the year; and a similar Act was applied to Christchurch, Spitalfields, two years later. Lincoln's Inn Fields was enclosed by an Act of 1735, and the Fleet Ditch was filled, by order of the Common Council, in 1747. The Thames was embanked from the Fleet to London Bridge; and the building of West-minster and Blackfriars Bridges (completed, respectively, in 1750 and 1756) entailed the clearing away of old delapidated buildings and the opening of new thoroughfares on both sides of the river. The New Road through Marylebone and Islington opened up new building prospects to the north. And in 1760 the City embarked on a bold plan to widen its thoroughfares, a task that was carried out (though admittedly, without much speed) by the Committee of the City Lands. Far more decisive was the step taken in 1787, when all London roads south of the Thames were placed under a single authority. (Those north of the river had to wait for the Metropolitan Road Board of 1826.)[1]

But the real turning-point in the improvement of the capital was marked by the first Westminster Paving Act of 1762; it was quickly followed by other Acts applied to the City of London and other parts of the metropolis. Previous to these Acts, all measures relating to paving had depended, for their realization, on the civic duty of the householder to keep the street in front of his own door in good repair; the old methods of enforcement were cumbersome, slow and uncertain. Now paving commissioners were appointed with paid staffs at their disposal, and infringements of the Acts brought summary punishment by the magistrates. Moreover, gutters were built on each side of the road, and in the principal streets flat Purbeck stone replaced the old rounded pebbles. The Acts also provided for regular scavenging and cleansing and for the removal of the numerous obstructions – the stalls, the show-boards, unprotected coal-shoots, un-covered cellars and projecting balconies – that held up traffic and endan-gered lives. Further, houses began to be numbered, many of the old shop signs that shut out the light in narrow streets were taken down, sewers and drains were deepened, and the water spouting from rooftop gutters was

[1] W. A Robson, *The Government and Misgovernment of London*, p. 139.

channelled through pipes. In consequence, the old city began to acquire a neat and spruce appearance, and, twenty-five years after the first of the Paving Acts was passed, a commentator proudly described the whole enterprise as 'an undertaking which has introduced a degree of elegance and symmetry into the streets of the metropolis, that is the admiration of all Europe and far exceeds anything of the kind in the modern world'.

Street-lighting, too, had kept pace with paving. Since the first of the improved Lighting Acts of 1736 and 1738, a long succession of such Acts had been passed, many of them linked with the Paving Acts, so that paving and lighting powers were often vested in the same body of trustees or commissioners. Turnpike trustees also obtained powers to light and watch the highways into the city. The result was that the new oil-lamps of London, covered by crystal globes and hung on posts short intervals apart, became as much an object of admiration by foreign visitors as her pavements; Archenholtz, on his visit to the capital in the 1780s, wrote enthusiastically: 'In Oxford Road alone there are more lamps than in all the city of Paris. Even the great roads, for seven or eight miles round, are crowded with them, which makes the effect exceedingly grand.' Such a judgment would, of course, seem a little ingenuous when, only a generation later, gas-lighting made its first appearance in the streets of London. Gas was first used for lighting in Beech and Whitecross Streets in the City in August 1807; a year later, Winsor, a German Chemist, proved his point that it could be used for the general illumination of the capital by setting up a row of gas-lamps in Pall Mall. But, at the time that Archenholtz was writing, his claim that London's oil-lamps were more than a match for Paris was amply justified.[1]

Thus London, by the end of the century, could claim to be a pioneer among the world's great cities in her paving, her street-lighting and her public sanitation; possibly, too, in the excellence of her water supply,[2] her fire-plugs and her sewers. This was a solid achievement to which Parliament, the City Corporation, the justices of Middlesex and Surrey, and the city's innumerable vestries, and the initiative of their inhabitants, had made their varied contribution. But there were other matters to which the Paving, Lighting and Improvement Acts and hosts of Local Acts had not extended, or which they had barely touched. These had affected, above all, the more fashionable streets and squares, the central commercial districts,

[1] *London Life*, pp. 107–15; J. W. Archenholtz, *A View of the British Constitution*, p. 132; Besant, pp. 92–4.
[2] See pp. 10–11 above.

and the city's main thoroughfares; they had largely neglected the old courts and alleys, the markets, slaughter-houses and burial grounds, and (most notorious of all) the old slums and rookeries of Holborn and St Giles in the Fields. These were left as a legacy of filth, squalor and disease for the next century to deal with.

There was also the continuing, festering and corroding problem of London's poor for whom the old Poor Law of 1601 was still (with minor alterations) intended to provide. The Elizabethan Statute had entrusted the care of the poor to the churchwardens and overseers of the parish, authorized them to raise a poor rate, and instructed them to relieve the old and impotent, to train pauper children to follow a trade, and to provide the able-bodied unemployed with work. It had been the product of a largely rural society with a national population of at most four millions. Yet, with all the social and economic changes that had taken place and the great rise in population, especially in London, the law remained basically the same in the eighteenth century as it had been in the days of Elizabeth and James. Above all, the usual unit of administration was still the parish, and the parish had by now, in large urban communities at least, become quite unsuited for the job. In the City of London the wards levied and collected the poor rate, but the parish disbursed it; while, in Westminster and the out-parishes, the overseers were nominally responsible to the justices of the peace, but these latter had become increasingly reluctant to interfere, and in the course of the eighteenth century rarely did so except in matters in which public expenditure (as in litigation over 'settlements') and public 'morality' appeared to be involved. This was all the more unfortunate, as the parish officers held their posts for only a year, were unpaid and overworked, and consequently discharged their duties without enthusiasm. Moreover, there were poor parishes like Spitalfields and the dockside parishes of East London, which had a disproportionate number of persons requiring relief and where, in consequence, the rate levied on the local householders was quite insufficient to meet the needs of the poor. In Middlesex the justices had realized the problem, and late in the previous century had considered a number of remedies, including the creation of an overall corporate authority. But the discussions had come to nothing, and in the Hanoverian period the matter was allowed to rest until Gilbert's Bill of 1782 attempted to find a more rational solution.[1]

[1] E. G. Dowdell, *A Hundred Years of Quarter Sessions, The Government of Middlesex from 1660 to 1760*, 1932, pp. 58-9, 63-5, 86-8.

There were other problems besides. The fact that the work of the overseers was unpaid and uncongenial, and that their accounts were not subject to a proper inspection, frequently led to dishonesty and corruption. They might take the relatively innocent form of diverting a proportion of the monies collected for the poor into banquets and carousals in the local pubs: this was a frequent complaint of ratepayers in City parishes. A more serious form might be to add fictitious names or the names of persons deceased to the lists of those in receipt of 'casual' relief, or it might be to give lucrative contracts to parish officers or to their friends and relations: both these abuses came to light when an enquiry was held, in 1714, into the management of the poor rates in St Martin in the Fields, which had, up to then, enjoyed a reputation for honest and efficient administration.

More generally, the system was such as to induce the parish officers and justices to think of the poor as a 'nuisance' on which no more than the minimum public money should be spent. The Act of Settlements of 1662 here provided a useful expedient. For, under its terms, any person not apprenticed in a parish or not occupying a £10 tenement within it might, if he looked like becoming 'chargeable to the Parish' as a pauper, be removed by the justices within forty days and returned to the parish of his origin. So the justices of Westminster and the London out-parishes, prompted by the parish officers, became engaged, as they were in other parts of the country, in a constant game of shunting unwanted paupers across their boundaries: it was a barbarous sport in which the most frequent sufferers were poor working mothers and their children, abandoned by a husband or a father. Again, though the amounts paid in pensions and relief in London were higher than they were elsewhere, no attempt was made to adjust them to a rising cost of living; and Eden, in his *State of the Poor*, published in 1797, showed that, in spite of the rapid rise in food prices since the 1770s, weekly pensions of 1s. to 2s. 6d. were still being paid as they had been thirty years before. More notorious was the cutting of costs by allowing workhouses to become overcrowded or to fall into decay. Workhouses had originally been designed as suitable places for putting the able-bodied to work; but in this they had failed almost completely and had become, increasingly, dumps and doss-houses for the destitute and unemployable, including poor mothers and children. The Clerkenwell workhouse, in the middle of the century, had 320 inmates though it had been built for 150; and, in the 1770s, the parish workhouse of St Martin in the Fields continued to house the poor though it was said to be 'very ruinous and in Danger of falling'; and that of St Paul's, Shadwell, was 'so old and ruinous, that it is absolutely necessary the same should be taken down and rebuilt'. In consequence, the mortality in such houses, and infant mortality in particular, had become a public scandal. Jonas Hanway, the philanthropist, who was moved as much to anger as to pity by the condition of the poor, described the workhouse of St Giles in the Fields and St George Bloomsbury as 'the greatest sink of mortality in these kingdoms, if not on the face of the whole earth'; and a parliamentary enquiry which he inspired, held in 1767, produced evidence to show that of children under twelve months of age taken into workhouses whose records had been examined, only seven in a hundred appeared to have survived for more than three years.

In fact, the most notorious feature of the system was its treatment of the infant and adolescent poor. Poor infants were sent out to be nursed by pauper women or left, with their mothers, to the tender mercies of the workhouse. Those who survived these ordeals were apprenticed to a trade. The original purpose had been, quite properly, to turn the pauper child into a 'useful', productive member of society. But the Settlement laws being as they were, the parish officers – particularly those of the crowded London parishes – were too often tempted to bind out the children, in return for a modest premium, to masters in other parishes: thus, once the 'forty days' were over, the sponsoring parish would be rid of all further responsibilities, leaving the child to find a 'settlement' in the parish of his trade. This tempting prospect tended to make those concerned indifferent to the nature of the master or the suitability of the trade selected; and throughout the century there were complaints of the ill-treatment of pauper apprentices or of their being left destitute, in their new parishes, at times of trade depression. The Industrial Revolution in the manufacturing districts brought new temptations and offered a new solution: by the end of the century, long after the humanitarians had begun to rouse the public's conscience over the plight of the juvenile poor, cart-loads of London pauper children were being packed off to work in the cotton mills of the industrial north.

Inevitably, the system did not remain unchanged over the span of a hundred years. During the second half of the century, in particular, numerous improvements were made. The Foundling Hospital opened its doors in 1745, and, during the period of its greatest activity, in the 1750s and 1760s, was able to do something (though not as much as had been hoped by its supporters) to reduce the appalling mortality among the infant poor. In the 1750s, a number of London parishes – Marylebone, St Martin in the Fields and St George Hanover Square were among them – obtained Local Acts to transfer the care of the poor, along with other public services, to authorities operating over a wider field. Following Hanway's revelations, an Act of 1767 forbade any child of under six to be kept in a workhouse for more than three weeks, and it provided certain safeguards for the bonded parish apprentice: suitable employment should be found and 'binding-out' premiums might not be lower than £4 2s. 0d. In 1783 Gilbert's Act dented the parochial system of poor relief by allowing parishes to co-operate in building joint houses for the reception of the poor, to be administered by committees of local gentry; and in 1802 Peel's Act forbade some of the more flagrant abuses in the employment of young paupers in the cotton mills. Yet these were mainly palliatives. Gilbert's Act was only permissive and brought about no radical changes in London; the Settlement laws remained largely untouched; and the end of the scandal of the north-bound pauper children, which followed early in the nineteenth century, came in the good time of the cotton employers rather than in that of the humanitarian reformers.[1]

Another field in which London's record incurred the criticism of contemporaries, and may not have equalled that of Paris, was in the policing of her streets and in the tracking down of crime. Admittedly, there were important innovations, such as the Bow Street Office set up by Henry Fielding in 1749 and the Thames Police Office, promoted by Patrick Colquhoun in 1798; these laid the basis for the stipendiary police magistrate and police court of the future. But, beyond this, nothing was done (and, in view of London's diversity of jealously guarded local jurisdictions, perhaps very little could be done) to set up a metropolitan police force to cope with what had, in many respects, become a metropolitan problem. Whereas, in Paris, the lieutenant of police had jurisdiction over the whole extent of the capital, in London jurisdiction was strictly local, based on vestry, ward and precinct and subject to no overriding metropolitan or national authority. Throughout the century, the policing of London's streets was the task of local magistrates, marshals, beadles and constables, supported, at street level, by the watch and ward of the parishes and precincts, in which, nominally, all citizens played a part. While the system became to some extent professionalized by the levying of a regular

[1] Dorothy Marshall, *The English Poor in the Eighteenth Century*, 1926, esp. pp. 60–6, 90–100, 131–3, 144–5, 159, 165–6, 194–200, 204–6; and *Dr Johnson's London*, pp. 223–30, 270–4.

watch rate and the payment of a small number of salaried officials, it still bore, and continued to bear, the stamp of its medieval, strictly amateur and parochial origins. In the City, the number of constables and beadles had risen from 270 in Stow's time (1603) to 319 in the 1790s; while the number of peace officers in the whole metropolis (including police officers at Bow Street, Marlborough Street, Hatton Garden, Queen's Square, Whitechapel and Shadwell) amounted, at this time, to about 1,000; which, supplemented in turn by the watchmen and patrols, made up a total force, both amateur and professional, of a little over 3,000 unarmed men.[1]

Such a force had the advantage of drawing on local initiative and of being firmly rooted among the citizens. The right of local defence (of which policing was an important part) was a jealously guarded tradition, particularly in the City of London, where any attempt to impose a *metropolitan* system would have been sternly resisted as an invasion of local privilege. Moreover, the old system worked reasonably well in the case of purely local crime. But, of course, its essentially parochial nature impeded magistrates in tracking down offenders across the parish boundaries, and even more across such major administrative frontiers as those separating the City from Westminster or the old Bills of Mortality from the near-rural hinterland beyond. Even more, it proved quite incapable of dealing with major civil disorders, such as convulsed London during the Gordon Riots of 1780 – an occasion that prompted Lord Shelburne to complain in the House of Lords that 'the police of Westminster was an imperfect, inadequate, and wretched system . . . a fit object of reformation'.[2]

His Lordship was no doubt, like many other critics of the time, thinking of the hazards to which such disturbances exposed the properties of the more substantial citizens. But there was a graver, social aspect. The very inadequacy of the force immediately at their disposal compelled magistrates to summon the aid, as provided by law, of the troops stationed at the Tilt Yard, Westminster, or at the Tower of London; or, in extreme cases (as in 1780), of the militias of the neighbouring counties. From this could follow the sort of massacre that took place in the Gordon Riots, when 285 persons were killed by bullets. Peel's Metropolitan Police Act of 1829, though it roused intense hostility in London, had at least the merit of removing the probability of such a slaughter in the future.

[1] Besant, pp. 494–533.
[2] *Morning Chronicle*, 5 June 1780.

8

The Politics of London

A S LONDON was the centre of the nation's economic, social and cultural life, so it was the centre of politics and government as well. The hub of the nation's politics lay, moreover in Westminster, which housed not only the Court of St James's but also the two Houses of Parliament, the law courts and government offices, and lay within a stone's throw of the Archbishop's Palace at Lambeth. With few exceptions the politically active Lords – whose number may, in the eighteenth century, have been 200 or more – had residences in St George's, St Anne's or St James's; and the 558 commoners, who represented the country's boroughs and shires between 1707 and 1801, and the twenty-six Bishops who sat in the Lords, were also settled in the vicinity of Parliament for several months in the year. It was here, too, that the leaders of the great political factions or 'connections', who alternated between government and opposition, issued their directives from their mansions in Bedford Square, Berkeley Square, Arlington Street, Dover Street, St James's Square, Grosvenor Square, Cavendish Square or Leicester Fields.

But, in addition to being the centre of the nation's politics, London had its own distinctive political tradition and its own political representation in the House of Commons. The City of London had four Members of Parliament, elected by its liveried freemen in Common Hall; Westminster, with its even wider burgess franchise, returned two Members; as did the 40s. freeholders of the out-parishes of Middlesex and Surrey. There were occasions when the metropolis acted as one, as over Excise in 1733 and as in the period of 'Wilkes and Liberty', when City Radicalism, spilling over into Westminster and the out-parishes, harnessed the political energies of the capital as a whole. But such occasions were rare in the first half of the century; so, during this period at least, there is some justification for those many writers and historians who have treated political London not as one, but in its separate component parts.

Though Westminster was the centre of Court and Parliament, it was the City of London, with its corporate status, its concentration, its great economic power and merchant wealth – a combination that was unique throughout the world – that dominated the political life of the capital and most often gave a lead for others to follow. It was, therefore, a rich political prize for which both government and opposition greedily contended. London was justly proud of its charters and its ancient privileges, of which one was the rare distinction of being allowed to 'approach the Throne'. Moreover, the City had a long political tradition to uphold, a tradition that had more often than not brought it into conflict with the Crown and the government of the day. In the 1640s, supported by its train-bands, it had led the opposition to the 'tyranny' of Charles I and Laud; a generation later, at the time of the Exclusion Crisis, the Earl of Shaftesbury's 'country party', City politicians and London's *mobile vulgus*, with the Green Ribbon Club as its organizing centre, had formed a powerful extra-parliamentary pressure group. In the reaction that followed, London's charters had been revised and, after Monmouth's abortive rebellion of 1685, the City's influence had declined and it had ceased, for several years, to play an independent role. But the 'Glorious Revolution' had begun to restore its fortunes; by Anne's time, it was once again emerging as a powerful political force, and, with the accession of the House of Hanover, it had fully recovered its old independence and fighting spirit. The City welcomed the new monarch with a patriotic address and due protestations of loyalty and, almost overnight, its four Tory M.P.s of 1710 and 1713 were replaced by four Whigs sworn to uphold the Hanoverian Throne. Typical of this internal revolution was the rise to the mayoral office of Sir John Fryer, the son of a City dissenter. During the Tory 'reaction' of Anne's later years, Fryer had, in December 1709, been elected alderman of Queenhithe Ward; but (as he wrote) 'the Tory Ld Mayor (Sir Saml Gerrard) used such base tricks that I was not admitted into that Court till Feb. 6 1710'. His fortunes changed rapidly with the triumphal entry into London of George I in September 1714. In November he was made a baronet as a reward for his 'fidelity to the Protestant Succession in Ye House of Hanover'. In 1715 he was elected Sheriff and Master of his Company; he became a director of the East

India Company in 1719, Lord Mayor of London in 1720 and a South Sea Company director four years later.[1]

But this happy relationship between Court and City, epitomized by the career of Sir John Fryer, was to prove short-lived; and, even before Fryer took up his mayoral office, relations were beginning to become strained under the impact of the South Sea Bubble and the scandals that ensued. Shortly after, Sir Robert Walpole, who had lost money in the Bubble but retained his reputation, rose to office and, during the twenty years of his Ministry, the relations between City and Administration were at their worst. Indeed, it was said of Sir Robert that 'he is hated by the city of London because he never did anything for the trading part of it, nor aimed at any interest of theirs but a corrupt influence over the directors and governors of the great moneyed companies'.[2] Nor did Walpole's eventual fall, to which the City made its contribution, make things much better, as his successors incurred its odium in almost as full a measure as the great 'corrupter' himself. In fact, the greater part of the eighteenth century was marked by an almost unbroken state of hostilities between the City of London and the combined forces of Whitehall and St James's. It lasted, with brief intermissions, from the early 1720s to the middle 1780s; and it was not until the younger Pitt resurrected the Tory party after the fiasco of the Fox–North coalition in 1784 that the City found a Chief Minister to its liking. This time, the honeymoon lasted for over twenty years and survived the first dozen years of the late-century wars with France.

This is the general, and therefore a greatly over-simplified, picture. For to present the question in this way is to assume that the City spoke with one voice and to gloss over the very real political differences that not only separated the 'moneyed companies' from the 'trading' interest but separated the Common Council from the Court of Aldermen and the Court of Common Hall (on occasion, at least) from both. With such divisions within the City (and we have discussed the reasons for some of them already), it is hardly surprising that Court and Ministry, with ample means at their disposal for winning allies, should have been able to command, even in periods of their greatest unpopularity, a substantial nucleus of 'courtiers' within its walls – among the 'moneyed companies' and large government contractors in the first place. None of the great

[1] 'Some account of Ye Life &c of John Fryer & of severall of his Relations written by himself 1715 &c'; G.L., MS. 12,017.

[2] L. S. Sutherland, *The East India Company in Eighteenth Century Politics*, p. 21.

L

companies – neither the Bank of England, nor the South Sea and East India Companies, nor the large insurance offices – could ever afford to be at odds with the Ministry for long. Theirs was essentially a *national* interest, which ranged beyond the City limits, as they enjoyed privileges whose renewal and perpetuation depended upon the goodwill of government and made them extremely chary of taking sides on the controversial political issues of the day. It was a mutual arrangement of give-and-take and, in return for the government's protection, the great companies were always ready, in times of emergency, to place their considerable holdings at the government's disposal. Thus the companies were, almost invariably, the largest subscribers to government loans. In 1759–60, for example, there stood at the head of a list of a score of large private subscribers to a loan of £8 million the names of 'Mr Burrell for the Bank of England £466,000, Mr Bristow for the South Sea Company £330,000, Mr Godfrey for the East India Company £200,000'. And, in 1744, during the War of the Austrian Succession, the East India Company alone came forward with a loan of £1 million at 3 per cent, and thereby assured itself of a renewal of its charter until 1780. Of course, the situation was somewhat different when the Company's charter was under fire from the Ministry itself, as it was from the Fox–North coalition three years later.[1]

In consequence, there was a tendency for the City's moneyed interest to stand four-square against the City's own government when this threatened to take on an anti-ministerial, or (as later in the century) a Radical, complexion. In 1769, for example, when a large body of London merchants presented a loyal and anti-Radical address to George III, we find among its 600 signatories the names of 7 directors of the South Sea Company; 11 directors of the East India Company; the governor, sub-governor and 7 directors of the London Assurance Company; the governor, secretary and 11 directors of the Royal Exchange Assurance; 3 directors of the Sun Fire Office; and the reigning governor, 7 former and future governors, an ex-director and 10 present directors of the Bank of England. Yet very few of these men played any part in City elections or City government; in fact, of the sixty governors and directors of 'moneyed companies' involved in this affair, only eight are recorded as having voted in the parliamentary election of 1768.[2]

On this particular occasion, there was a conspicuous absence of

[1] L. S. Sutherland, *The East India Company in Eighteenth Century Politics*, pp. 16–31.
[2] *The Middlesex Journal*, nos. 9–11, 14, 18–28; 20 April to 3 June 1769; *The Poll of the City of London*, 1768.

aldermanic names, even among those most noted for their hostility to Wilkes and his Radical associates. And yet, as we have seen in earlier chapters, the aldermen were closely connected with the moneyed interest; this no doubt helps to explain why they, too, on other occasions, often found themselves opposed to the anti-government policies of the Courts of Common Council and Common Hall. So, even in the bitter disputes that ranged the City against Walpole, the Minister never failed to retain a solid body of support within the Court of Aldermen; and, remarkable as it may seem, he was still able to command a majority of 14 to 12 at the time of his fall from power in 1742. During the City's later Radical phase, the solid core of aldermanic loyalists had sadly diminished; but even in Wilkes's hey-day, when City offices were falling like ninepins to his followers, fifteen aldermen out of the forty-four holding office between 1768 and 1774 could generally be relied upon to cast their vote for George III and his ministers. It was, in fact, only on rare occasions, as over Excise in 1733 and the Printers' Case of 1771, when Lord Mayor Crosby and Alderman Oliver were clapped in the Tower by order of the Commons, that the City patched up its differences and faced a common enemy with undivided ranks.[1]

Yet, divided as the City generally was, its official voice, as represented by its various Courts and leading officers, was, through the greater part of the century, raised in almost constant opposition to government policies. And as the government sought to establish a firm foothold in the City by exploiting its divisions, so the City in turn allied itself with the reigning opposition faction of the day – whether it was the Leicester House party of the Prince of Wales, the 'Patriots' around Pulteney, Bolingbroke or Pitt, the Chathamites of the 1750s and sixties, the Rockinghamites and Shelburnites of the 1760s and seventies, or the Foxites of the 1770s and early 1780s. Each of these had, successively, their clients among the City Fathers, and each in turn used their following in the City to corrode or undermine the government's majority in the Lords or House of Commons. In addition to these powerful outside allies, the City had other resources of its own to advance its cause in its prolonged duel with Administration. Its own elected Members were naturally encouraged or briefed – in specific 'instructions' after 1770 – to promote its policies within the Commons. So, in the course of its context with Walpole, we find each one of the City's four M.P.s opposing the Excise Bill in 1733, three out of four supporting the motion to repeal the Septen-

[1] Beaven, vol. 2, p. lvii; *Wilkes and Liberty*, pp. 151, 217-19.

nial Act in 1734, and all four again opposing the Spanish Convention of
1739, which aimed to maintain peace with Spain after the tragi-comedy of
Captain Jenkins' ear. Thirty years later, three of the City's M.P.s opposed
the expulsion of Wilkes as the Member for Middlesex; in 1780 all three
City M.P.s in attendance voted for Dunning's famous motion deploring
the 'increasing influence' of the Crown; and, two years later, all four
declared their want of confidence in Lord North's administration as it
tottered to its fall.[1]

As the initiative, on such occasions, generally lay with the rank and
file in the Common Hall rather than with the Common Council – and
still less, of course, with the Court of Aldermen – means had often to be
found, in order to promote a popular cause, to shift the dead weight of
conciliar or aldermanic obstruction. This could rarely be done by merely
waiting on events, for the cards were generally stacked against the
newcomers by the firm control exercised over the various organs of City
government by the aldermen or councilmen. So it was often a case of
whipping up feeling for one's cause, lampooning one's opponents in the
press (whenever its columns were available), stacking the electoral meetings, blacklisting the obstructive candidates and driving them, if the
furore aroused was powerful enough, from office. This procedure was
followed, with remarkable success, during Wilkes's rise to high office in
the City. It was by such means, for example, that the Wilkite militants
within the Common Hall were, in the space of a few months between
1769 and 1770, able to convert an anti-Radical vote of 92 to 72 on the
Common Council into a pro-Radical vote of 112 to 76.[2]

There were other means as well whereby radical or anti-ministerial
opinions could be formed. One was to win support for the City's policies
across its boundaries or even in districts far removed from the metropolis
itself. Thus, City aldermen and officers often appeared on the commissions
of the peace of other counties; and, in Wilkes's day, among City opponents of government, William Beckford and James Townsend were justices
in Middlesex; John Sawbridge and Barlow Trecothick in Kent; Beckford
again in Wiltshire; John Glynn, the City's Recorder, in Cornwall; and
Brass Crosby and Trecothick in Surrey. This was also a great age of
political caricature, and the satirist's quill or brush was often used with
deadly effect to discomfort the City's opponents: among the most
notorious of the victims were Sir Robert Walpole (a frequent target),

[1] Beaven, vol. 1, pp. 319–20.
[2] *Wilkes and Liberty*, pp. 153–4.

Henry Fox, the Pelhams, 'Butcher' Cumberland, the Earl of Bute and (on occasion) even Charles James Fox. And finally – though this was considered a dangerous resort, and therefore to be used with caution – there was the alliance between the City and the streets; and, in later chapters, we shall see how, when a favourable occasion arose, the City's anti-ministerial policies, whether by accident or design, were reflected in the riots of the common people, as over Excise in 1733, gin in 1736, and Popery in 1780.[1]

The City's opposition to government falls into two main stages, with the year 1760 as a rough dividing-line. In the first half of the century, its opposition may be termed Tory-Radical, or even Jacobite; in the second half, when the old-style Toryism was all but dead until Pitt revived it in a new form in the 1780s, it assumed a new, Radical complexion, hostile to both of the old traditional parties, which will be discussed further in the following chapter. In the earlier period, it is not so much that the City's leaders were more Tory than Whig in their actual party affiliations (in fact, Tory and Whig Lord Mayors balanced one another in almost equal proportions between 1714 and 1759); but as a consistent champion of 'country' versus Court, the City (and the Common Hall, in particular) was more Tory than Whig in sympathy and its policies were more often coloured by Toryism, if not by Jacobitism, than by Whiggery. Moreover, its policies were given a certain degree of continuity by the long preeminence of the formidable Sir John Barnard, one of the most bitter of Walpole's opponents, who represented the City in Parliament from 1722 to 1761 and who, though nominally a Whig, maintained a firm alliance with the Tories. And it was under Sir John's leadership that the City allied itself with the 'Patriots' or 'considerable grumbling Whiggs' and the Tory remnants in the House of Commons to oppose Walpole over his Excise Bill, the Septennial Act and his efforts to maintain peace with Spain.

The purpose of Walpole's Excise Bill was to reduce the land tax, and thus appease the land-owning classes, by means of a new system of levying duties on tobacco and wine. It was the means to be employed, and not the tax itself, that was new. Hitherto, the duty had been paid on importation; now it was proposed to house the goods in bonded warehouses duty-free until they were removed for home consumption, when they might be sold only in shops that had been licensed for the

---

[1] *Wilkes and Liberty*, p. 5; M. Dorothy George, *English Political Caricature to 1792. A Study of Opinion and Propaganda*, 1959, pp. 73 ff.

purpose. Thus the old customs duties were transformed into an excise, a form of taxation which revived memories of Cromwell's interregnum and was the more obnoxious because it appeared to threaten the Englishman's liberty by letting loose on his home an invading army of revenue officers. Moreover, London merchants, farmers and distillers – not to mention smugglers – saw the measure as a serious impediment to trade. The *Craftsman*, which had been founded as a weekly opposition newspaper in 1727, got wind of the proposals long before they were put to Parliament and, in its issue of 4 November 1732, opened the attack on general excise as a threat to freedom, arguing that it was by such means that the French had lost their liberties and been reduced to slavery and wooden shoes. The more colourful popular press took up the cry, and *Mist's Weekly Journal* dwelt at length and with relish on the monstrous brutalities of excisemen, who would not merely rob the honest citizen of the fruits of his toil but violate his wife and daughters into the bargain. In short, Excise would lead inevitably to despotism, Popery and slavery. And so the slogan was devised, blazoned in banner-headlines in the press and chanted in the ale-houses: 'Excise, Wooden Shoes, and no Jury'; or, as a variant, 'No Slavery – no Excise – no Wooden Shoes!'; or, again, 'Liberty and Property and No Excise.' Ballads and prints followed in profusion. A well-known print shows Walpole, the Excise Monster, enthroned on a barrel and drawn by an emaciated British lion, shod with wooden clogs that trample the Magna Carta underfoot. A popular ballad bore the refrain:

> *See this Dragon Excise*
> *Has ten thousand Eyes*
> *And Five Thousand Mouths to devour us*
> *Its strong and sharp Claws*
> *With wide-gaping Jaws*
> *And a belly as big as a Storehouse.*

And to add a respectable note to the agitation, a large number of London merchants gathered at the Swan Tavern in Cornhill on 22 December and unanimously passed a resolution, pledging themselves to take action 'by all dutiful and lawful means' to ensure that the project should never become law.

Walpole bided his time, hoping the clamour would subside, and only presented his Bill in March 1733. It met with violent opposition, and more particularly from two of the City Members, Sir John Barnard and

Micaiah Perry. Their speeches were accompanied by a large and noisy demonstration at the doors of the House, and Walpole, in an unguarded moment, called the demonstrators a gang of 'sturdy beggars'. He was not allowed to forget the insult; and Barnard rose to his feet a second time to observe tartly that he 'saw none but such as deserve the name of sturdy beggars as little as the honourable gentleman himself, or any gentleman whatever'. Yet, as expected, the Bill was sent forward for a second reading. Meanwhile, the Common Council presented a petition to the House requesting to be heard against the Bill. The petition was refused, but only by a majority of seventeen votes. Appearing to yield to his critics, Walpole played for more time by persuading the Commons to postpone further consideration for two months. As he left the House, he was 'mobbed' by a large crowd and forced to dodge from one coffee-house to another to evade his pursuers. That night, both Walpole and Queen Caroline were burned in effigy and bonfires and fireworks celebrated, prematurely, a popular victory. The violence played into the Minister's hands and, next day, Barnard and Perry felt compelled to join with Wyndham and Pulteney, the opposition leaders, in repudiating the activities of their supporters. Yet, two months later, Walpole, having saved his face and won this temporary respite, withdrew his Bill altogether rather than court the possibility of a defeat in the Lords. So the City could chalk up a victory in this first major round of its struggle with Walpole, even though it was, in the event, only half deserved.[1]

The next round followed a year later, when three of the City's M.P.s, with the support of the Common Council, joined forces with the combined opposition of Pulteney's group and the Tories in an attempt to repeal the Septennial Act of 1716. The Act, which prolonged the life of Parliament from three to seven years, had been passed on the morrow of the first Jacobite Rebellion; and at that time it seemed reasonable to many in the House (including two of the London M.P.s) to adopt an emergency measure of this kind in order to ward off a Jacobite challenge at the pending elections. But, once adopted, the arrangement suited the governing party and its managers too well to be abandoned and, in the course of time, it came to be seen by Walpole's opponents as a corner-stone of his system of manipulation and 'corruption'. It was therefore a matter of the first importance and was treated as such by the Minister in his reply to the

[1] R. R. Sharpe, *London and the Kingdom*, vol. 3, 1895, pp. 35–8; J. H. Plumb, *Sir Robert Walpole*, vol. 2, pp. 250–75; M. Dorothy George, *English Political Caricature*, pp. 81–3.

debate. Walpole argued that to shorten parliaments would be to weaken the government's authority to make decisions and to expose it to the 'inconvenience' of 'factions, seditions and insurrections'. Above all, it would disturb the 'equal mixture' of the constitution by strengthening its 'democratical' at the expense of its 'aristocratical' and 'monarchical' ingredients. 'Therefore,' he concluded,

> in all the regulations we make, with respect to our constitution, we are to guard against running too much into that form of government which is properly called democratical: this was, in my opinion, the effect of the triennial law, and will again be the effect, if ever it should be restored.

With his assured majority, he easily outvoted his opponents. But the incident is an important landmark in the long history of parliamentary reform; and the demand for shorter parliaments became, with that for a 'more equal representation', one of the main planks in the programme of the Radicals and reformers of the later eighteenth century.[1]

Walpole's Gin Act of 1736 touched off another storm. To the gin-drinking poor whom it threatened with the loss of 'spirituous' consolation, it was hardly likely to be welcome; to the farmers and distillers, who prospered by the trade in gin, it was an infringement of rights and 'liberties'; and to Walpole's political opponents it appeared another of his devilish devices for smuggling in a general excise through the back door. The Act arose from a petition presented to Parliament on 20 February by the Middlesex justices, who called for action to restrict the excessive sales of spirits, 'by which means Journeymen, Apprentices, and Servants, are drawn in to taste, and, by degrees, to like, approve, and immoderately drink thereof'. Parliament acted promptly and resolved that, from 24 June of that year, all retailers trading in spirits should pay a duty of 20s. per gallon and that all ale-houses, brandy-shops and victuallers similarly engaged should be required to take out a licence at a cost of £50 a year. In brief, the purpose was to tax the drinking of cheap gin out of existence. A committee, whose members included Sir Robert Walpole and Sir Joseph Jekyll, Master of the Rolls, was ordered to prepare a Bill, which, though criticized by Pulteney and the 'Patriots', passed through its various stages unopposed, and received the Royal Assent on 5 May.

[1] William Coxe, *Memoirs of the Life and Administration of Sir Robert Walpole*, 1798, vol. 1, pp. 422–6.

So far, the City had raised no formal objection; and it was only between the Bill's enactment and its operation five months later that a campaign started, mainly based on London, to compel the government to change its plans. It took the form of prints, ballads and circulated letters and, in early September, a government informant wrote that 'it is the Common Talk of the Tippling Ale houses and little Gin Shops that Sʳ Robert Walpole and the Master of yᵉ Rolls will not outlive Michaelmas long'. The letters, many emanating from a common source, urged distillers and retailers to celebrate 'Madame Geneva's lying-in-state' by issuing free gin to the 'populace' on the night before the Act was due to operate. One such letter, addressed to a Westminster distiller, urged him to be generous in his supply of liquor to his retailers and added:

> If we are English men let us show we have English spirits & not tamely submit to the yoak just ready to be fastened about our necks. Let town and country Ring with the names of Sʳ Robert and Sʳ Joseph, let them see that wooden shoes are not so easy to be worn as they imagine.

And, in different parts of the capital, retailers, no doubt prodded by the distillers who appear to have played the main role in the affair, draped their signs with black to commemorate the demise of 'Mother Gin'. Yet the government, tipped off by its informants, was well prepared and such disturbances as there were amounted to very little; and it was not so much the agitation of the distillers and their associates that made the Act inoperative as the nature of the Act itself. The very severity of its provisions were self-defeating as they led to a wholesale evasion of the law. Walpole himself – a poor advocate for a measure with which his name was linked! – had foreseen, in a letter to his brother Horace, that the small gin-shops, whose suppression had been the main purpose of the Bill, would be virtually protected from prosecution by their poverty which would discourage legal action. He proved to be largely correct and, by 1743, the consumption of spirits had risen by a further 2½ million gallons. It needed another Gin Act in that year and a further Act in 1751, accompanied by Henry Fielding's *Enquiry* and Hogarth's 'Gin Lane', to stamp out the grosser evils of gin-drinking among the poor.[1]

Whereas the City had played only a minor part (if any official part

[1] George Rudé, ' "Mother Gin" and the London Riots of 1736', *The Guildhall Miscellany*, no. 10, September 1959, pp. 53–63; J. L. & B. Hammond, in *Johnson's England*, vol. 1, pp. 312–14.

at all) in the campaign against the Gin Act, it emerged once more as one
of Walpole's most spirited critics in his dealings with Spain. The country
had been at peace with Spain since the summer of 1718, but the Spanish
had insisted on the right of search of British vessels suspected of smuggling in the West Indies. Tension rose as reports and rumours became
more insistent of the ill-treatment of British crews by Spanish coast-
guards. A famous incident of the kind relates to a certain Captain Jenkins,
master of a trading vessel, who, in 1731, was reputed to have had one of
his ears cut off. This, however, only became a matter of public importance
when, some years later, London merchants began to demand that the
right of search be given up or, if refused, that war be declared against
the Spanish. Once more, it was the *Craftsman* that opened the attack. In
its issue of 29 October 1737 it accused the authorities of failing to protect
shipping and followed this up, in succeeding months, by exposing Spain's
alleged violations of its treaty obligations and with a call for war. The
matter was debated in the Commons in March of the following year,
when William Pitt made his first speech on behalf of the London merchants after Captain Jenkins, who had been summoned to attend, had
exhibited his severed ear wrapped in cotton wool. This dramatic gesture
naturally stoked up the campaign to new emotional heights, but Walpole,
who was anxious to maintain peace with Spain, persuaded Parliament, in
the face of a considerable opposition (which included Pitt, Pulteney and
all four of the City's M.P.s), to agree to a Spanish Convention. But as the
measure still left unsettled the right of search, the agitation continued;
and the Common Council, as spokesman for the City, warned Parliament
of 'the fatal consequences of leaving the freedom of navigation any longer
in suspense and uncertainty'; for (it was claimed) if the right of search
were not abandoned, 'the trade of his Majesty's subjects to America will
become so precarious as to depend in a great measure upon the indulgence
and justice of the Spaniards'. One citizen, Richard Glover, a Hamburg
merchant who was active in Common Hall, went further and expressed
his feelings in a poem entitled 'London, or the Progress of Commerce',
which carried the pathetic refrain:

> *Shall we now be more timid, when behold*
> *The blackening storm now gathers round our heads*
> *And England's angry genius sounds to arms.*

Glover also moved a vote of thanks in Common Hall to the City
Members for having opposed the Convention; and Walpole, whose

tenure of office was at this time precarious (Queen Caroline, his most trusty supporter at Court, had recently died), was swept into war with Spain against his own judgment. When Admiral Vernon, early in the war, captured Porto Bello, on the Isthmus of Darien, he was acclaimed by the citizens as a popular hero. The City's own contribution to these events was to prepare two petitions to Parliament – the one drafted by Glover on behalf of the merchants, the other emanating from the Common Council – which formed the substance of a Bill calling for the better protecting and securing the trade of the Kingdom in time of war. The Bill was sponsored by Sir John Barnard and Lord Mayor Godschall; it quickly passed through the Commons, but was rejected by the Lords. However, the City soon found ample compensation, as Walpole, following a defeat over an election petition from Westminster, resigned in February 1742. The event was celebrated in London with bonfires and general jubilation. A week before, the Common Council had urged their M.P.s to promote a Place Bill and a Pension Bill and to resume the attack on the Septennial Act, and so secure the Constitution 'against all future attempts either of open or secret corruption or any undue influence whatsoever'.[1]

The expectations were not realized, either under Carteret, who succeeded Walpole as George II's Chief Minister, or under the Pelham administration which followed shortly after. Soon after Carteret's rise to power, the City followed up its earlier 'representation' by urging its Members to refuse to vote supplies until the government showed that it meant business by taking a first step, at least, to end 'corruption'; London's initiative was widely commended in the national press. But other business soon arose to engage both the Ministry's and the City's attention: the war with France, which broke out in March 1744, and the second Jacobite Rebellion, with the Young Pretender's southward march to Derby, in 1745. As Charles Edward never came nearer to London than Derby, Londoners were never fully put to the test as to what their real feelings about the Jacobites were. Formally, the City and London merchants behaved with a commendable display of loyalty to the Hanoverian dynasty. The Lord Mayor assured the Duke of Newcastle, who had followed Carteret in office, that everything would be done to secure the peace and security of the City; the Courts of Aldermen and Common Council both presented loyal addresses to the King, and the Common Council, when

[1] Emmet L. Averye and A. H. Souter, 'The Opposition to Sir Robert Walpole, 1737–1739', *E.H.R.*, vol. lxxxiii, no. 327, 1968, pp. 331–8; Sharpe, vol. 3, pp. 40–9.

the danger appeared pressing, opened a defence fund with an initial donation of £1,000. In Westminster, 350 wealthy residents of St George's, Hanover Square, expressed their 'utter abhorrence and detestation of the present wicked and unnatural Rebellion carried on in favour of a Popish & abjured Pretender', and promised to contribute a considerable sum of money towards raising an adequate army to oppose him; among them were the Earl of Kildare, the Duke of Manchester and Horace Walpole, who each pledged twenty guineas.[1] Even more remarkable was the spirited response of the 'middling sort' in the person of the manufacturers of Spitalfields, where 133 master silk weavers (some employing as many as 70 or 100 men) offered the combined services under arms of nearly 3,000 of their 'workmen, servants and dependants'.[2] And the City's merchants and bankers, when the news of the Pretender's southward march caused a panic and a run on the Bank of England, issued a reassuring declaration that they would 'accept bank notes in payment of any sums of money to be paid to us'. Yet there were others whose response to the event was, to say the least, equivocal. According to Horace Walpole (whose political prejudices may, admittedly, have been engaged), both Carteret (now Earl Granville) and Pulteney (now Earl of Bath) refused to contribute to the defence fund launched by the Common Council. Others behaved, publicly, with greater circumspection while their Jacobite sympathies were hardly in doubt. In August 1746, after the Rebellion was over, the *Gentleman's Magazine* reported that, in the past six years, £700,000 had been collected in London on behalf of the Pretender and that the names of 1,500 subscribers had been discovered. A spy named Butler, working for the French, was taken in possession of a list of prominent Jacobite supporters, including the Lord Mayor, Richard Hoare, himself and ten other aldermen, two of whom had already served as mayor, while six others would do so in the next five years. Three of these, too, appear in a portrait called 'Benn's Club' (Benn was mayor in 1747), which hangs in the Goldsmiths' Hall and shows six subsequent Lord Mayors drinking a toast to the Pretender; the other three followed one another in the mayoral office between 1752 and 1754. This is not so surprising in view of the almost unbroken succession of Tory Lord Mayors from 1743 to 1754. There were also, at a lower social level, considerable Jacobite undercurrents in the ale-houses and beer-shops. Yet barely a ripple of this appeared on the surface. There was only a handful of arrests for

[1] W.L., C 765a.
[2] *London Gazette*, 5 October 1745.

toasting 'Charley across the water'; there were no public demonstrations of support; the Duke of Cumberland, the victor of Culloden, was applauded for his 'magnanimity' and had the Freedom of the City conferred on him in a golden box; and when the luckless rebels of the Forty-Five were drawn on hurdles to their execution, there was not the flicker of any public protest. But, as William Pitt reflected later, if the Jacobites 'had obtained a victory and made themselves masters of London, I question if the spirit of the population would not have taken a very different turn'.[1]

One further occasion arose when the City, led by a Tory (and suspected Jacobite) Lord Mayor, Edward Ironside, joined with the old Tory interest in a campaign directed against the government. The government was that headed by the Duke of Newcastle and his brother Henry Pelham, and the issue was the Jewish Naturalization Act of 1753. The measure was promoted by the Pelhams with the limited aim of making it easier for foreign Jews to become British subjects; its particular object was, no doubt, to reward men like Samson Gideon, the wealthy Jewish financier, and others of his co-religionists for their long-standing services to the Treasury. It was intended to apply to a comparatively small number of Jews, and it seemed a matter of relatively minor importance, which would meet with little objection, let alone arouse a storm of disapproval. Yet, as the Bill went through its various stages in Parliament, it stirred up a mounting storm of abuse and denunciation. Its original opponents – a combination of London merchants engaged in the Spanish and Portuguese trade and a group of Tory Members – at first objected on mainly economic grounds: that their trade would be undercut by rivals who, through British naturalization, would share their privileges and markets. Yet a new and more sinister note was struck when the Lord Mayor, aldermen and Common Council jointly blasted the Bill, in a denunciatory petition, as one that would 'tend greatly to the dishonour of the Christian religion, [and] endanger our excellent Constitution'. Once the bogey of religion was raised, a flood of anti-semitic tracts and ballads was let loose in both London and the provinces. The old anti-Excise slogan even was taken out of storage and adapted to read 'No Jews, no wooden shoes'. One of the cruder prints circulating in London, *Vox Populi, Vox Dei, or the Jew Act repealed*, shows Christianity menaced by 'a Mob of Jews & Deists' and by a bishop who holds a bribe of £1,000. The campaign continued,

[1] A. A. Mitchell, 'London and the Forty-Five', *History Today*, October 1965, pp. 719–26; Sharpe, vol. 3, pp. 50–6.

with increased venom, after the Bill became law. Fearing for its political future – a general election was imminent – the Ministry decided to beat an ignominious retreat; and so the 'Jew Act', passed in June, was repealed by its own authors in December. In the election that followed the issue was not allowed to rest and, in the City of London, Sir William Calvert, a Member of the previous Parliament, lost his seat for having supported the Bill.[1]

Meanwhile, the City had entered on its long partnership with William Pitt, the Great Commoner, in the course of which it gradually shed its former political orientation, disengaged itself from the old Tory connection, and struck out on a new 'radical' line of its own. As we have seen, Pitt and the City had joined forces in denouncing the Spanish Convention, and they had both helped to involve Britain in war with Spain over Jenkins' Ear and to drive Walpole from office four years later. The same belligerent spirit brought them together as partners on the eve of the Seven Years' War. In 1756 the Common Council once more clamoured for war and for Admiral Byng's execution after the surrender of Minorca to Spain. Pitt, newly appointed Secretary of State, aroused their enthusiasm by reorganizing the Militia and sending Hanoverian and Hessian conscripts out of the country. So, for a brief while, the City returned to an alliance with Whitehall and St James's. But when Pitt was dismissed a few months later, the City once more went into opposition and ostentatiously conferred on him its Freedom and named after him what was later called Blackfriars Bridge. With the City's help, Pitt was back in office, virtually as Minister of War, in June 1757 and received the citizens' enthusiastic support. When he fell from office again in October 1761, the Common Council, once more in opposition, voted him their thanks; and when he accompanied George III and his new favourite, the Earl of Bute, to the Guildhall a few days later, Bute was pelted and booed and Pitt and his brother-in-law, Earl Temple, were greeted by an ovation.[2]

But already the City of London stood on the threshold of a new 'radical' phase in its political life, which will be the subject of the next chapter.

It remains, however, to say a few words about the politics of the rest of London. What of Westminster and the out-parishes of Middlesex and

[1] Thomas W. Perry, *Public Opinion, Propaganda, and Politics in Eighteenth-Century England. A Study of the Jewish Naturalization Act of 1753*, 1962; M. Dorothy George, *English Political Caricature*, p. 100.

[2] Sharpe, vol. 3, pp. 58–65, 69–70.

Surrey? In the case of the out-parishes there is, for this first half of the century, nothing of any importance to be said, as they generally followed in the wake of the City of London – as over Excise, gin, the 'Jew Act', the Forty-Five and Jenkins' Ear. Westminster, however, with its broad burgess franchise, had a political life of its own and, like the City of London, on occasion displayed a sturdy independence of the government and Court. But having, unlike the City, no corporate status and no municipal authority, this it could only achieve momentarily at times of elections – as in the elections of 1741 and 1749. On the former occasion, the 'Independent and Worthy Electors of the Ancient City of Westminster', supported by Frederick Prince of Wales and his 'Patriots' and opposed by the Duke of Cumberland and the King's ministers, adopted as their candidates a certain Charles Edwin and Admiral Vernon, the hero of Porto Bello. The Court candidates, Sir Charles Wager and Lord Sundon, would undoubtedly have won the contest – they were leading by some 400 votes apiece shortly before the close of the poll – if Lord Sundon had not appealed to armed force and summoned a body of grenadiers to surround the hustings and persuaded the High Bailiff to close the poll and declare the Court candidates returned. The Independents appealed to the new Parliament against this obvious abuse; Wager and Sundon were unseated, and a new election was called for, of which the outcome was the return of the two 'patriot' candidates – this time, Charles Edwin and Lord Perceval, as Vernon, who had been elected in several constituencies, had already taken his seat for Ipswich. The result had, moreover, a by-product in the resignation of Sir Robert Walpole, the *bête noire* of all 'patriots' and Independents, from his office.[1]

The Courtiers had their revenge in the election of 1747. The Independents were liberally dubbed Jacobites by their opponents (with what shred of justice remains uncertain), and Admiral Sir Peter Warren and Lord Trentham, son of Earl Gower, a recent defector from the opposition, were returned. In 1749 there was a new (though only partial) contest, as Lord Trentham, recently appointed a Lord of the Admiralty, had to resign his seat and present himself for re-election. The Independents chose to oppose him a 'private gentleman', Sir George Vandeput. At the close of the poll, Lord Trentham was declared elected with a majority of 157 votes. But both sides accused each other of having returned large numbers of 'bad votes', and a parliamentary enquiry was held; it en-

[1] J. Grego, *A History of Parliamentary Elections and Electioneering from the Stuarts to Queen Victoria*, 1892, pp. 94–9.

gendered such heat that two witnesses were confined to the Tower for contempt of court; after a year's vituperative litigation and the invalidation of 700 votes on each party's score, the result was declared to be much the same as before: this time, Lord Trentham retained his seat with a margin of 170 votes.

So much for the bare results; but with the aid of the rate books and the poll books we can get a closer picture of how people voted and of what sort of people voted for which sort of candidate. As in all Westminster elections of the period, the Court candidate won his largest body of votes in the safe 'Court' parishes of St Margaret and St John: here, in the first count, he collected 1,313 votes against Vandeput's 550. His only other clear majority was in the 'genteel' parish of St George's, Hanover Square, where he outvoted his opponent by 937 to 520. In three parishes – St Anne's, St Paul's and St James's – the votes were fairly evenly divided; but, in two essentially commercial parishes, St Martin's and St Clement Danes (including the tiny parish of St Mary le Strand), the Independent easily defeated his opponent – by nearly two to one in the first and over three to one in the second.

So already we see a tendency to vote by class and occupation, a tendency that becomes all the more apparent if we now focus on a single district – the great trading and shopping district of the Strand, which, with its 472 houses, stretched across the two large parishes of St Martin's and St Clement's and the smaller parish of St Mary le Strand. Of the 140 Strand votes recorded in the poll box, 99 were cast for Vandeput and 41 for Trentham. So there appears to be a clear concordance between trade and 'independence'; and the pattern hardly varies as between grocers and cheesemongers, lacemen and carpenters, and (the largest group of all) the victuallers and publicans, of whom 16 voted for Vandeput and only 6 for Trentham. Even bankers gave support; and, at Mr Gissingham Cooper's banking house (which bore the sign of the Anchor and Crown), we read that a book was opened 'for receiving the subscriptions to carry on the expense of scrutinizing the late poll, on behalf of Mr Vandeput'. But if 'independence' went with trade rather than with 'gentility', was it more pronounced among the poorer than among the richer tradesmen? It may well have been so, for among the Strand voters in St Martin's, who account for three-quarters of those appearing in the poll book, those living in the poorer wards showed a distinctly greater tendency to vote for Vandeput than those living in the wealthier. Thus, in Spur Ward (the wealthiest, with an average rent of £48), the percentage of 'independent' votes cast was 59; in Exchange (£44) it was 64; and in Strand (the poorest, with an average rent of £38) it rose to 79.[1]

Even if we may assume (a bold assumption) that the picture here presented is valid for Westminster in general, the further question still arises: was this tendency to vote by class and occupation a phenomenon peculiar to Westminster, or did it apply to London as a whole? We shall return to the problem, in the wider context of the 'radical' London of the later eighteenth century, in the course of the next chapter.

[1] Westminster Poll Book, 1749; W.P.L., B.161 (St Clement's), F.525 (St Martin's), G.141 (St Mary le Strand), J.277 (Precinct of St Mary le Savoy); *Daily Advertiser*, 9 January 1750.

M

9

London Radicalism

WE HAVE already noted that the politics of the City, and of London as a whole, entered on a new phase somewhere about the 1760s. There was no sharp break with the past in that the City, as before, remained firmly anti-ministerial: the old conflict between City and Administration remained as vigorous as ever. But there were important differences. In the first place, where the City before had been inclined to take its cue from the opposition within Parliament, now it began gradually to detach itself from its old alliances, to take the initiative and formulate policies of its own that were often at variance with the traditional parliamentary parties and groups, whether ministerial or opposition Whigs, or Tory remnants. The old Tories, in fact, with the accession of George III (who 'gloried in the name Briton') to the throne, from being consistent critics of Court and Administration, became firm supporters of the Crown: this, in itself, had its effect on the old political alliances in London. Secondly, where the City in the past, while generally hostile to the Walpoles and the Pelhams, had had no clear and consistent programme of its own, now it began to elaborate a programme of parliamentary reform – at first against Rotten Boroughs, later for the rights of electors against the 'tyranny' of the Commons, for shorter Parliaments (as in 1734) and a 'more equal representation', and finally, from about 1780, for something like male adult suffrage. Thirdly, the spokesmen for the City – men like Wilkes and Beckford – did not confine their appeals to their own electors or to the men in Parliament, but directed them more and more to opinion 'without-doors', and even beyond the 'political nation' to the great majority who remained without a vote. Strictly speaking, this 'Radicalism' (as it has been called)[1] was not so much a novelty

[1] L. S. Sutherland, *The City of London and the Opposition to Government, 1768–1774,* 1959, pp. 5–7.

as a revival. For, during the struggle of King and Parliament in the previous century, Levellers, Diggers, Fifth Monarchy men and others had claimed it to be the right of every 'freeborn' Englishman to have the vote; and Colonel Rainborough, in the Putney debates of 1647, had even demanded full citizen rights for 'the poorest he that is in England'; these early 'radicals' had, like their successors, also made a deliberate point of enlisting support from the nation at large by appealing 'from the degenerate representative body, the Commons of England, to the body represented, the free people'. The point was not lost on some of the City's Radicals, like Catherine Macaulay, the republican sister of Alderman John Sawbridge, who, in her *History of England from the Accession of James I*, acclaimed the Levellers and 'the democratical system', while damning the more conservative Glorious Revolution of 1688 with faint praise. But this tradition had lain dormant, at least since Monmouth's rebellion of 1685, and was only now revived by the London Radicals of the 1760s.

There is a further feature distinguishing this new stage in London's politics from that we described in the last chapter. We then saw that it was reasonably appropriate to treat the politics of the City, as those of Westminster, within their own separate geographical context: it was only on occasion, as over Excise and Jenkins' Ear, that we could then properly speak of the politics of the metropolis as a whole. With the advent of mid-century Radicalism this is no longer the case. More and more we shall see a political line, generally (but now less frequently) emanating from the City, thrusting across the old boundaries and engulfing not only Westminster and Southwark but the urban (and even the rural) parishes of the neighbouring counties of Surrey and Middlesex. So, in this chapter, it will be more appropriate to abandon the old framework and discuss the politics of London within a wider metropolitan context, in which the new Radicalism was the most significant, if not the sole, common ingredient.

The first phase of this new development opened, more properly, around 1756, when the City of London entered into a firm and durable alliance with William Pitt. For it was Pitt's peculiar quality as a politician that, like the old Levellers and Independents, he was able to rouse the nation at large beyond the confines of the House of Commons; it was, in fact, the nation, and in the first place the City, rather than any party in Parliament, that hoisted him back to power, against the resistance of the King and his ministers, in 1757. And Pitt's chief lieutenant in the City, for a dozen years to come, was William Beckford, a wealthy Jamaica sugar-planter, who had entered City politics with Tory support in 1754. Under Pitt's influence and with his own experience of the nation at war, Beckford had moved from Toryism to Radicalism; he became a champion of the commercial and 'middling' classes against the aristocracy; and it was he who, in standing for election to Parliament in March 1761, took the first step to launch the City on its new Radical course, by denouncing the importance accorded in the Constitution to 'little, pitiful boroughs'. As Lord Mayor in 1763, Beckford led the City's opposition to the preliminaries of the Peace of Paris; and the Common Council, under his and Pitt's inspiration, instructed its M.P.s to ensure that there should be no surrender of Guadeloupe or any of the North American possessions. He was Lord Mayor for a second term (an unusual honour) in 1770, and then expounded what had by now become a fuller political creed: an end to 'little paltry rotten boroughs', fewer pensioners and placemen, shorter parliaments, and a more equal representation of the people.[1]

Meanwhile, what was to prove a greater influence than Beckford's had burst upon London's political scene. Like Beckford, John Wilkes had attached himself to Pitt and the 'Patriots' and, in his journal, the *North Briton*, he not only attacked the peace preliminaries of 1763 but also denounced the King's Speech made in support of them in such terms as to make it seem that George III was being called a liar. Although a Member of Parliament for Aylesbury, he was arrested on a general (or 'open') warrant and clapped in the Tower by order of the Secretaries of State on a charge of seditious libel; but, a week later, he was released by Chief Justice Pratt in the Court of Common Pleas on the ground of parliamentary privilege. As he left Westminster Hall, he was escorted to his house in George's Street by a large and enthusiastic crowd which chanted the new slogan of militant Radicalism, 'Wilkes and Liberty!'

Subsequently, Wilkes recovered damages, awarded by a London jury, for unlawful arrest and the confiscation of his private papers. Moreover, Pitt, in the House of Commons, and the Common Council, in the City, publicly defended his conduct. But, indiscreetly and against the advice of his patron, Earl Temple, he set up a private press to print copies of an obscene parody of Pope's *Essay on Man* for distribution among friends, as well as of the offending issue (No. 45) of the *North Briton*. Summoned to appear before the Commons, he evaded his pursuers by slipping across the Channel. While in France, he was expelled from Parliament and,

[1] L. S. Sutherland, *The City of London and the Opposition to Government*, p. 4.

when he failed to respond to a summons, was pronounced an outlaw by the Court of King's Bench. So he remained in exile in France and Italy – partly enforced and partly self-imposed – for the next four and a half years, awaiting a favourable moment for his return.

It came with the general election of March 1768. He reappeared in London and, although an undischarged outlaw, he had himself enrolled as a freeman member of the Joiners' Company and presented himself as a candidate in the City of London. He was received with enthusiasm by the small masters and craftsmen; but most 'Patriot' votes were already pledged to Beckford and Barlow Trecothick (the latter attached to the Marquis of Rockingham), and he emerged bottom of the list of seven candidates. So he presented himself in Middlesex where, a short while after, he defeated the Court candidate, Sir William Beauchamp Proctor, and was returned at the head of the poll. The result was greeted in the Cities of London and Westminster by a tremendous outburst of popular jubilation; crowds rampaged round the streets, ordered lights to be 'put out' for Wilkes, and smashed the windows of lords and ladies of fashion and government supporters, not omitting those of the anti-Radical Lord Mayor, the Rt Hon. Thomas Harley, at the Mansion House. But Wilkes had still to reckon with the law and, having surrendered to his outlawry in the Court of King's Bench, he was committed to the King's Bench prison in St George's Fields, where he was to serve a sentence of twenty-two months for his various misdemeanours. Yet the time was not wasted for his own and the Radical cause. While he was in prison, the government further damaged its reputation by shooting down demonstrators, who had come to catch a glimpse of the 'Patriot', in what became known as the 'massacre of St George's Fields'. Wilkes ably exploited the situation in a flood of letters to the press and manifestoes to his electors, and received in his cell visits from his principal supporters, the Rev. John Horne of Brentford (later known as Horne Tooke) and Serjeant John Glynn, and the City's emergent Radical leaders, Aldermen John Saw-bridge, James Townsend, Richard Oliver and William Beckford. With their support, he was elected, *in absentia*, alderman of the large City ward of Farringdon Without; and, when his fellow-Member for Middlesex, George Cooke, died in June 1769, Serjeant Glynn won the seat in a new contest with Sir William Proctor. Even more significant for the Radical cause was the creation, in February of that year, of the Society of Sup-porters of the Bill of Rights; among its founders were some of the most prominent, and wealthy, men in London public life, including Aldermen

Sawbridge, Townsend and Oliver (who were all Members of Parliament);
two other M.P.s: Sir Cecil Wray and Sir Joseph Mawbey, a malt-distiller
of Southwark; and Samuel Vaughan, a prosperous merchant of Mincing
Lane. While the Society's immediate purpose was to settle 'Mr Wilkes's
affairs' (it eventually paid out on his behalf some £20,000), it soon
assumed the even more important task of formulating a Radical programme, organizing petitions, conducting electoral campaigns and
harnessing support for Wilkes and Radicalism far beyond the frontiers of
the City and the metropolis.

Equally significant were the events that followed soon after in Middlesex which, for the next year, eclipsed even the City as the main focus of
the Radical challenge to government. In February 1769 Wilkes was
expelled for a second time from Parliament, and a few days later was
declared 'incapable of being elected as a Member of the present Parliament'. The Middlesex freeholders promptly re-adopted and re-elected
him as their Member, unopposed. The Commons riposted, as expected,
by declaring the election null and void. A month later, his second unopposed election was once more annulled by Parliament. The third time,
three candidates were put up to oppose him; two of these virtually withdrew, and when it came to the poll on 13 April 1769, it was a straight fight
between the absent Wilkes and the Court nominee, a young army colonel,
Henry Lawes Luttrell. Wilkes emerged the victor by 1,143 votes to
Luttrell's 296. Whereupon the Commons resolved that Luttrell 'ought to
have been returned a member for Middlesex' and, ignoring a petition of
protest from Middlesex, followed this up with the further resolution that
'Henry Lawes Luttrell is duly elected a Knight of the Shire to serve in
the present Parliament for the County of Middlesex'.

Opinion, ranging far beyond the boundaries of Radical London, was
outraged by this extraordinary decision. Whatever the legal niceties
invoked to justify it, it was widely seen as a serious infringement of the
electoral rights not only of the freeholders of a single injured county
but also of all county voters, if not of the electorate as a whole. The parliamentary opposition – the larger group led by the Marquis of Rockingham
and the smaller group led by Pitt (now Earl of Chatham) – who had
hitherto been extremely chary of doing anything to promote the cause of
Wilkes, now joined in the fray, marshalled their forces in the counties
and boroughs, and even held discussions with the City leaders to determine a common course of action. The outcome was a great campaign of
petitions conducted throughout the country, in which each of the three

parties, while formally co-operating, in fact marshalled and appealed to its own body of supporters. Thus, broadly speaking, the metropolitan Radicals of the Bill of Rights Society used their influence to win signatures not only in Middlesex, the Cities of London and Westminster and Southwark, but also, through the personal connections of individuals, in Surrey, Essex, Wiltshire, Devon, Cornwall and the cities of Bristol and Exeter. Meanwhile, the Rockingham Whigs tapped the political resources of Liverpool and the northern counties, in particular the Marquis of Rockingham's stronghold of Yorkshire, while the Chathamites confined their attention largely to Buckinghamshire and Kent. All the petitions had in common the central, minimum demand to redress the wrongs done to the Middlesex electors by unseating Luttrell and reinstating Wilkes. But the London Radicals went further: where their influence was greatest they appended to the text a more comprehensive set of grievances and Radical demands. So the London and Middlesex petitions both castigated the general conduct of George III's ministers and called for their removal, the Bristol petition denounced the taxation of the Americans, while the Middlesex petitioners listed a score of grievances, including arrests by general warrant, neglect of *habeas corpus* and trial by jury, attacks on freedom of the press, the outlawry and imprisonment of Wilkes, the murder of peaceful citizens by the military, the violation of the rights of electors, and the mismanagement of the American colonies. In all, some 38,000 freeholders from fifteen counties and 17,000 freemen of a dozen boroughs and cities appended their signatures; they represented between one-third and one-quarter of all the county voters of England and Wales and one in five of all the enfranchised townsmen. But, despite this impressive volume of condemnation, the Commons decided by a majority of sixty-nine that, in their treatment of the whole affair, they had acted 'in conformity with the laws of the land'.

The Wilkes–Luttrell affair did, however, have one immediate, tangible result: it led to an electoral victory for the Radicals in Westminster, where Sir Robert Bernard, a member of the Bill of Rights Society, was returned unopposed in a by-election in June 1770. Meanwhile, the London Radicals tried to counter the Commons' rejection of the petitions by promoting a campaign of remonstrances to the Crown. The City sent remonstrances in March, May, June and November 1770, Middlesex in March and Surrey in June of the same year. The Rockingham and Chatham groups made some attempt to do the same in Yorkshire, Buckingham and Kent, but they came to nothing. In fact, the whole undertaking aroused little response outside the capital; even in the City of London, which initiated the affair, the campaign is less memorable for any results it achieved than for the spirited performance put up by Beckford, when, as Lord Mayor serving his second term of office, he was presenting the second of the City's remonstrances to George III. Instead of merely delivering his address, kissing the Royal hand and bowing his way out (as was the prescribed custom on occasions of this kind), Beckford is reported to have firmly stood his ground, and to have lectured the Royal person in the speech which still stands engraved on his statue in the Guildhall:

> Permit me, Sir, to observe that whoever has already dared, or shall hereafter endeavour, to alienate your Majesty's affection from your loyal subjects in general, and from the City of London in particular, is an enemy of the public peace, and a betrayer of our happy Constitution, as it was established at the Glorious Revolution.

These bold words met with a mixed reception. The King stood speechless; Archenholtz, who witnessed the 'extraordinary scene', described 'the trouble and agitation' clearly visible on the faces of the courtiers. But the citizens were jubilant, and Lord Chatham congratulated his old henchman on expressing 'the spirit of Old England' on 'that never-to-be-forgotten day'.[1]

It was a few weeks earlier that John Wilkes, having served his full term, emerged from the King's Bench prison in April 1770. His political stock had appreciably risen during his confinement, and he was assured of a considerable following within the Common Hall and the Common Council, if not yet among the aldermen, as he turned his attention to the City, a career in Parliament being for the present denied him. A few months after Wilkes's release, relations between City and Commons became even further strained by their memorable duel over the reporting of parliamentary debates in the public press. The 'printers' case' arose from Members' complaints that, contrary to the Commons' regulations, a number of London newspapers were publishing reports of their speeches and proceedings. The printers were warned and, when the practice continued, eight of the most consistent offenders were summoned to the bar of the House. Two of the printers failed to appear, and when the Commons ordered that one of them should be taken into custody, the messenger sent to arrest him in the City was arrested in turn, brought

---

[1] J. W. Archenholtz, *A View of the British Constitution*, p. 151; L. S. Sutherland, *The City of London and the Opposition to Government*, pp. 2–3.

before Lord Mayor Crosby, Oliver and Wilkes (who, as if by chance, were concerting together at the Mansion House), charged with assault and ordered to answer to the charge at the next quarter sessions! The Commons were outraged. The Lord Mayor and Oliver, being Members of Parliament, were summoned to the House (Wilkes, who was waiting to take advantage of any precedent, it was thought best to leave alone) and, after a heated debate, during which the Commons were besieged by a crowd of 50,000 people, were confined in the Tower of London. It was a purely pyrrhic triumph for the House of Commons. The Common Council, recently divided between Courtiers and Radicals, united its forces to acclaim the services of Wilkes and the two 'martyrs' in supporting 'the privileges and franchises of this City'; and when Crosby and Oliver were released a few weeks later, they were escorted to the Guildhall in a triumphal procession of fifty-three carriages by almost the entire Common Council, and 'saluted with loud and universal huzzas'. The printers remained unpunished, and the newspapers resumed their printing of debates, virtually without further interference from the Commons. And Wilkes, who had probably master-minded the whole business, was elected Sheriff for the ensuing year, and thus stood already within striking distance of the mayoralty.

A few weeks earlier, John Sawbridge had moved in the Commons the first of a long series of annual motions calling for shorter parliaments; and, in June of the same year, the Bill of Rights Society drew up a list of eleven points to which it was recommended that all candidates to Parliament, in order to win the Society's nomination, should subscribe in writing. It was a kind of charter of Radical demands, which included a restoration of their fiscal rights to the Americans, the revival of annual parliaments, the establishment of a full and equal representation of the people, and the exclusion of all placemen and pensioners from the House of Commons. These formed the basis of the written 'instructions' accepted by Frederick Bull when he entered Parliament, after a by-election, in 1773.

It had been a momentous year for the City Radicals; yet it was marred by the divisions among them which had long lain dormant, but, with Wilkes's release from prison, had come into the open. Horne, Townsend, Oliver and Sawbridge broke with Wilkes; in the case of the first three it was a permanent estrangement. These dissensions naturally played into the hands of the Court party, and William Nash, a confirmed Courtier, was, much to George III's delight, returned Lord Mayor for 1772 in opposition to Sawbridge and Crosby (the latter standing for a second term of office). The next year, Townsend and Wilkes were sent forward for election by the Common Hall; but the Court of Aldermen, with its anti-Radical majority, in exercising its right to make the final choice, chose Townsend, although he had the lower vote, as the lesser of two evils. In 1773 Bull, a Wilkes supporter, was elected mayor over Wilkes by Town-send's casting vote. At last, in 1774, at his third attempt, Wilkes realized his ambition. The Court of Aldermen had, by a series of transfusions, become evenly divided between Wilkites and Courtiers; and when his name was once more sent forward at the head of the livery's poll, Saw-bridge, who had become reconciled, withdrew his own nomination, and Wilkes was elected with only two aldermen – the implacably hostile Townsend and Oliver – voting against him. It was a momentous occasion and marked a high-point in eighteenth-century London Radicalism. It was also the year of another general election, which, for the first time, gave the Wilkites the opportunity of testing their mettle on a national scale. In Middlesex, Wilkes and Glynn were returned without opposition. In the City, an anti-Wilkite Radical (Oliver) and three Wilkite Radicals – George Hailey, Frederick Bull and Sawbridge – were elected. Nathaniel Polhill, a Wilkite, was elected for Southwark. In Westminster alone, there was a clear victory for the Court: the Court candidates, Earl Percy and Lord Thomas Pelham Clinton, easily defeated the Wilkites, Lord Mountmorres and Lord Mahon – overwhelmingly (as could be expected) in St Margaret's and St John's and decisively in every other parish except St Anne's. So Radicalism had emerged as an electoral force in the metro-polis, with seven seats won (if we include Oliver's) out of ten.

Outside London the situation was somewhat different, and the high hopes raised by the petitioning campaign of 1769 had not yielded any substantial electoral result. In Surrey, Sir Joseph Mawbey, a founder-member of the Bill of Rights Society, was defeated, though he was returned in a by-election the next year. A Wilkite, John Trevanion, was successful at Dover; and there was a handful of other non-Wilkite Radicals and Wilkite sympathizers returned in a number of other bor-oughs. In all, there were at most, in the mid-seventies, a dozen Wilkes supporters (he called them his 'twelve apostles') among the 558 Members of the House of Commons. In electoral terms, at least, Radicalism re-mained at this stage, as it had begun, a largely metropolitan phenomenon.[1]

But this is not the whole story. While the hard core of Radicalism had

[1] Ian R. Christie, *Wilkes, Wyvill and Reform*, 1962, pp. 60–1.

such geographical limits as we have seen, it had achieved permanent results and had sown seeds which cannot be presented in purely temporary electoral terms. These results had been partly achieved by men like Beckford and Sawbridge, working through the traditional machinery of the City Corporation and the debating chamber of the House of Commons, and partly through the astonishing career, startling innovations and flamboyant personality of Wilkes. Wilkes has been accused of exploiting Liberty for the sole purpose of furthering his own career. There is some truth in this, but the result (whatever the intention) was permanently to extend the Englishman's liberties and to enrich his political experience. The issue of general warrants by the Secretaries of State in the case of persons suspected of treasonable or seditious libel had become a common practice in the course of the century, and had gone virtually unchallenged until Wilkes, with the powerful legal support of Chief Justice Pratt (soon to become Lord Chancellor Camden) questioned their validity in the affair of the *North Briton* – a challenge that led rapidly to the declaration of their invalidity in the case of Entick *v*. Carrington in 1765 and their subsequent condemnation by the Commons as being illegal and obnoxious. Again, the long-protracted dispute over the rights of the Middlesex electors ended in 1782, when Wilkes at last carried a motion (put forward every year since 1775) that the resolution of February 1769, declaring his 'incapacity' to sit in Parliament, be expunged from the Journals of the House 'as being subversive of the Rights of the whole body of Electors of the Kingdom'; it was a victory not only for Wilkes and the Middlesex freeholders but for the 'political nation' at large. Equally, Wilkes and the Radicals had played a part in helping to break down the wall of secrecy that separated the proceedings of Parliament from an increasingly curious reading public. This was the real significance of the 'printers' case' of 1771, which established the regular practice, if not yet the legal right, of the newspapers to print parliamentary debates. Again, it was the Wilkes affair which led to the launching of a new type of political machine in the form of the Society of Supporters of the Bill of Rights; for, as we saw, the Society soon extended its early, limited activities into the political field; and certain of these became models for later Radical politicians and groups to follow. Of particular importance for the future was its novel device of 'instructing' M.P.s on their conduct in Parliament; this set a fashion that was eagerly followed by the Radicals of the nineteenth century, and it became a feature of the election that preceded the passage through Parliament of the great Reform Bill of 1832.

It was in pursuit of this same objective of opening wider the channels of communication between Parliament and the 'political nation' outside that Wilkes and Sawbridge, following the initiative taken by Beckford and others in the City of London, supported within Parliament proposals for annual or triennial parliaments and a more equal representation of the people. In March 1776, as M.P. for Middlesex, Wilkes went further and became the first Member to propose to the House that the franchise should be extended to embrace 'the meanest mechanic, the poorest peasant and day labourer'. The same year, Major John Cartwright, a Westminster Radical, put forward, far more cogently than Wilkes, in a pamphlet called *Take Your Choice*, his programme for 'one man, one vote,' equal single-member constituencies, and a secret ballot. Thus, London Radicalism, through Beckford's initiative and the impact of the Wilkes affair, had advanced, in a bare fifteen years, from its first hesitant demand for the end of Rotten Boroughs to the far broader principle of male adult suffrage.

But some of this remained on paper and was of far greater significance for the future than for the immediate present. More tangible perhaps was the extension of the geographical boundaries of Radicalism beyond the City, where Beckford had launched it, to embrace the whole metropolitan area; and even occasionally, as we have seen, far beyond it. Equally, the *social* boundaries of Radicalism had been extended, and it is one of Wilkes's main titles to fame that he drew into political activity many thousands who had previously been considered to lie beyond the pale of the 'political nation' and gave them in 'Wilkes and Liberty' a cause which, however vaguely and incoherently, they believed to be their own. While we shall deal with this aspect of Wilkism in a later chapter, it is perhaps appropriate, at this stage, to return to the problem of the role played by class in politics. Specifically, what sort of people supported Wilkes and Radicalism in London in the 1760s and 1770s; and, conversely, who were their most vigorous opponents?

To begin at the top of the social pyramid. The Radicals, and Wilkes in particular, found only the most meagre of support among the aristocracy. There were exceptions, like Earl Temple, who, though never a Wilkite, gave Wilkes friendship and financial aid at various times in his career; but the opposition leaders within the Lords – Rockingham, Portland and Devonshire, and even Chatham – were remarkably lukewarm in their dealings with Wilkes and the Bill of Rights Society; and it was no doubt to please Chatham that Beckford, who was a Chathamite as well as a

Radical, never joined the Society. These peers were willing enough to use the Radicals as a stick to beat the government, but as Burke, who was one of Rockingham's principal lieutenants in the Commons, wrote of Wilkes: 'We had not the least desire of taking up that gentleman's cause as personally favourable to him; he is not ours.' Among the gentry and clergy, too, the Radicals found only occasional support. Again, there were exceptions, as in the case of the remarkably militant – though not always Wilkite – 'Parson' Horne; and Dr Thomas Wilson, the Prebendary of Westminster, was both a Wilkite and a devoted admirer of Catherine Macaulay, the Republican-Radical historian. But far more revealing was the record of voting of these groups in the various Middlesex elections contested by Wilkes and Glynn in 1768-9. Of 39 M.P.s who voted in one or more of these contests, only 2 voted for Wilkes or Glynn in two consecutive elections; these were the City Radicals, John Sawbridge, M.P. for Hythe, and James Townsend, M.P. for West Looe. Again, of 39 peers, sons of peers, baronets and knights whose votes were recorded, only 3 voted for the Radical candidates on any one occasion. The opposition of the churches was equally determined: of 42 clergymen, ministers and doctors of divinity, only 4 voted, in any contest, for either Wilkes or Glynn. And the pattern, in the case of local office-holders like justices of the peace, was much the same.

Far more solid was the body of support for the Radicals among shop-keepers and merchants – particularly among those of the 'middling' or lesser sort. In July 1763, after his first skirmish with authority over the *North Briton* affair, Wilkes wrote to Temple that 'the merchants are firm in the cause of liberty'. They included men of wealth: among those who later founded the Bill of Rights Society were men like Samuel Vaughan in the City and Sir Joseph Mawbey, the distiller, in Southwark; and Abraham Hake, a South Sea Company director, voted for Wilkes in Middlesex. But these, again, are exceptional, and the hard core of the City's moneyed interest remained implacably hostile to Radicalism and its leaders: we have noted the firm support given by the bankers and directors of the great City companies to the 'loyal', anti-Radical address of March 1769. The aldermen, too, while they gave no support to this particular address, remained a hard nut for the Radicals to crack; and we have seen that it was only on the very eve of Wilkes's election as Lord Mayor that the Courtiers and anti-Radicals lost their long-standing majority within their Court. For his more consistent and enduring support Wilkes had to look, in the City, to the small merchants, manufacturers and master craftsmen: among the liveried freemen in the first place and among the common councilmen in the second. Within the Council, during the years 1768–71, he could count on a firm core of about fifty to sixty activists, mainly of the typical City crafts and trades: packers, haberdashers, hatters, chinamen, saddlers, coopers, booksellers, ironmongers, brokers and petty tradesmen. And, outside the City, there were the 'independent' electors of Middlesex, whose obstinate and continuous support assured him of his seat in Parliament in the face of every attempt to dislodge him. Among these were a few wealthy men, a smattering of gentry and independent clergy; but the great bulk of Wilkes's and Glynn's support came from the lesser freeholders of both rural and urban districts, owning or occupying freeholds of 40s. to £10 a year. And here, too, as in the City, the great majority of merchants, tradesmen and manufacturers of the urban out-parishes (we have counted 130 out of 180 who voted) gave their votes to Wilkes and Glynn rather than to their anti-Radical opponents. And it was, broadly, the same people who signed the Middlesex petition in favour of the candidate of their choice in May 1769. So it appears to be firmly established – far more firmly than in the case of the Westminster contest of 1749 – that the electoral base of London Radicalism in the 1760s and 1770s was solidly of what Defoe had called the 'middle sort'. The composition of Wilkes's supporters in the streets is, of course, quite a different matter; we shall return to it in a later chapter.[1]

After Wilkes's return to Parliament and his election to the mayoralty in 1774, the Radical movement hung fire for a number of years. This was due, in part at least, to the general preoccupation with events in America, which, though initially favourable to Radicalism in England, entered on a new stage when the American colonists were proclaimed rebels against the Crown in August 1775. Yet Middlesex and the City continued, through their representatives in Parliament, to keep the issue of reform alive; and the City maintained, for some time to come, a steady flow of addresses and resolutions in favour of maintaining peace with America. The Radicals argued, in fact, that the two questions were closely linked, as the triumph of British arms and authority in America would, almost inevitably, be followed by an attack on liberty at home. It was not, however, a favourable moment for winning wide support for either; and, in 1775, no fewer than 141 addresses reached the King, condemning the Americans for their 'rebellion'. But the City persisted in its efforts long after the war had begun; and, even after the Americans' declaration of

[1] *Wilkes and Liberty*, pp. 82–9, 145–6, 152–3, 176–81.

their independence, Sawbridge, as Lord Mayor in 1776, and his successor, Sir Thomas Hallifax (though a Court-supporter), strenuously resisted the operations of the press-gangs within the City limits. As late as March 1778, on the very day the French signed a commercial treaty with the Americans, the Common Council presented an address to the King, renewing their demand for concessions to the colonists. But, after this, the City's attitude weakened, as first France and then Spain, the country's traditional enemies, entered the war on the American side; moreover, Chatham, whose opinions were widely respected, had, in his last speech in the Lords (he died in May 1778), called for a vigorous prosecution of the war to retain the colonies within the Empire. So for three years it was only a protesting minority within the Common Council that continued the attack; and it was not until December 1781 that the City, in a further address to the Throne, renewed its former demand, now made under far more favourable conditions, that the war be brought to an end.[1]

Meanwhile, there had been a Radical revival; but this time the initiative came not from London but from Yorkshire and, within London, from Middlesex and Westminster rather than from the City. In Yorkshire, Christopher Wyvill, a landowner and Anglican clergyman, set up a county freeholders' association pledged to parliamentary reform; his immediate purpose was to secure an 'economical' reform by the abolition of sinecures and unmerited pensions, while leaving open for the present such further questions as annual (or triennial) parliaments and a more equal representation. The Yorkshire 'associators' appealed for support in other counties and, as a preliminary step, sent forward a petition, signed by 8,000 gentry, clergy and freeholders, which Sir George Savile, as a Yorkshire County Member, presented to Parliament in February 1780. It was soon followed by similar petitions from 16 counties (they later grew to 28) and 11 boroughs; several of these, taking their cue from the Yorkshiremen, also formed committees and associations.

In London, the Yorkshire proposals were sufficiently ambiguous and open-ended to attract a mixed bag of supporters. The Rockingham Whigs, eager as ever to curb the 'influence' of the Crown, were attracted by the priority given by Wyvill to 'economical' reform. The Wilkite Radicals and the followers of Lord Shelburne (who had taken over the old Chathamite connection) saw new opportunities for promoting their old campaigns for shorter parliaments and a more equal representation, while the advocates of a more revolutionary programme, like Dr John Jebb, in

[1] Sharpe, vol. 3, pp. 149-61, 165-71, 193-7.

Middlesex, welcomed the proposal of associations as a first step towards achieving the old Levellers' idea of a People's Parliament based on 'an equal, annual and universal representation of the commons'. In the event, it was the Middlesex freeholders who set the pace; they were led by Jebb and by George Byng, a County M.P. and a close associate of Rockingham's ally, the Duke of Portland; and, in early January, having corresponded with Yorkshire, they appointed a committee with the aim of forming an association to promote both 'economical' reform and 'such other measures as may conduce to restore the freedom of parliament'. On 2 February, Westminster followed suit and adopted a petition for 'economical' reform and appointed a committee to promote it. The proposals were put forward by Sawbridge and Wilkes, but the star performer was Charles James Fox, who, having broken with the Court in 1774 and after a long period in the wilderness, was casting round for a political cause to champion. He now emerged on the scene as 'the idol of the people' by vigorously advocating parliamentary reform and even coming near, in his advocacy, to adopting Jebb's ultimate solution of a revolutionary popular assembly. So Fox became the chairman of a large unwieldy committee of a hundred, which brought together in an uneasy alliance Rockinghamite lords and gentry, old-style Radicals and new-style revolutionaries. Finally, in the City, a few days later, the Common Council set up a committee of twenty-four, all of them members of the Common Council or of the Court of Aldermen, and in which Wilkite Radicalism was the dominant trend. Wilkes himself and his brother-in-law, George Hailey, were occasional attenders; Brass Crosby, the chairman, and James Townsend and Sawbridge played leading roles, as did half a dozen common councilmen who, in the past five years, had been the main champions in the City of the American cause.

When Wyvill arrived in London to support the Yorkshire petition, a meeting of the various associations and committees was called for 11 March, to consider a Plan of Association 'for supporting the petitions, and other measures conducing to restore the freedom of parliament'. Only twelve counties and four cities responded, and it soon became evident that these 'other measures' were open to endless interpretations. The Rockinghams, when it came to the point, would have nothing to do with any measure other than a limited 'economical' reform; even the advocacy of shorter parliaments, they felt, might lose them support among the 'broad-acred' gentry. Wyvill and the Yorkshiremen, while initially in favour of annual parliaments as a second measure, settled in the end for the three-year formula; in this, they were closest to the Earl of Shelburne, who favoured triennial parliaments and (as a first step to a more equal representation) the addition of a further hundred county Members. This programme, too, was accepted by the Common Council in the Form of Association it adopted in April. More extreme views were expressed in Middlesex and Westminster – particularly in the latter, except when the Rockinghams were present in sufficient strength to counsel moderation. The Duke of Richmond, a member of the Westminster Committee, who had been an advocate of caution in March, had by June been won for a more comprehensive system of reform and moved a resolution in support of adult suffrage in the Lords. This line was expressed most sharply and coherently in the report of a subcommittee in Westminster which, in the absence of Rockingham supporters, put forward, over half a century before its time, the whole programme of the People's Charter of 1838. All of the Charter's 'six points' were there: equal electoral districts, annual parliaments, universal male suffrage, the payment of M.P.s, the abolition of property qualifications, the secret ballot; and, for good measure, the exclusion of all placemen from the Commons. The Westminster Committee decided, after some hesitation, two months later, to send the report to the other committees; yet, in the context of the time, it was more of an academic exercise (though one of considerable historical interest) than a serious call to action.

Thus divided, the movement entered, soon after, into the doldrums. But it had certain tangible results. One was the return of no less than nine Radicals or 'associators' in the twelve metropolitan seats (including the two for Surrey) in the elections of September 1780. Three of the four London M.P.s were former Wilkites or 'associators'. And Charles Fox, promoted by the local committee of association and at this time as much a Radical as an 'associator', made his *début* as Member for Westminster. He, and Sir George Brydges Rodney (who topped the poll), easily out-voted the sitting Court Candidate, the former Lord Clinton (now Earl of Lincoln), who, characteristically, led the field in the solitary parishes of St Margaret's and St John's.[1]

A second tangible result was the adoption by Parliament of a large part of the Rockinghams' (though not of the Yorkshiremen's) programme for 'economical' reform, skilfully engineered by Edmund Burke in the House of Commons. The Commons had already, in April 1780, by 233 to 215 votes, carried John Dunning's resolution that 'the influence of the

[1] Ian R. Christie, *Wilkes, Wyvill and Reform*, pp. 68–120.

Crown has increased, is increasing, and ought to be diminished'. Dunning was a friend of Shelburne, and he wished his motion to be only a first step towards meeting the wider grievances voiced in the numerous county and borough petitions, whose signatures corresponded, at the time he spoke, to about one-fifth of the electorate of England. But the Rocking-hams were less ambitious and, with their growing influence in Parliament in the final stages of the American War, were able to win a majority for a strictly limited measure of 'economical' reform: for Clarke's Bill to exclude government contractors, Crewe's Bill to disfranchise revenue officers, and Burke's own Bill which reduced the Pensions account to £90,000 a year, all passed in 1782. But it proved to be another pyrrhic victory (and this was the third tangible result of the events of 1779–82), as it helped to drive a wedge between the London and Yorkshire reformers and the opposition Whigs; for, as we shall see, London Radicals, like Yorkshire 'associators', when faced with the choice, preferred the younger Pitt's new Tories to Fox's old Whigs.

But, meanwhile, the London Radicals' hopes for a wider reform had been threatened from another quarter: the riots that followed Lord George Gordon's attempt to persuade Parliament to repeal the Catholic Relief Act of 1778. The measure, which removed certain of the additional liabilities imposed on Roman Catholics by William III's Act of 1699, had been introduced by Sir George Savile and had passed through both Houses without a division. It was not, in fact, until an attempt was made to apply the Act to Scotland that a public campaign started, at first in Edinburgh and Glasgow, to have the Act repealed. In London a Protestant Association was set up and, with Lord George Gordon as its president, decided to promote a petition to Parliament. By 2 June, the petition had been signed by about 44,000 people; and Gordon reviewed his Protestant supporters in St George's Fields before carrying the petition to Parlia-ment, followed by four contingents of marching Protestants, arrayed in their Sunday best and composed (it was said) of 'the better sort of trades-men'. When the Commons, refusing to deliberate under duress, adjourned the discussion to another day, a relatively peaceful demonstration was converted into a week-long orgy of rioting in which Catholic schools and chapels were 'pulled down' and their contents burned in the streets, prisons were fired and their inmates released, and the houses of prominent Catholics and supporters of the Act were threatened or destroyed. Such were the Gordon Riots, of which we shall say more in a later chapter.

Here we are primarily concerned with the part played by the City of

London in the affair. Already in March, long before Lord George
Gordon's petition, a motion had been made in the Common Council
against making any concessions to Roman Catholics. Discussion was
adjourned until the end of May. On the 30th, the Lime Street Ward
unanimously carried the following resolution:

> That it is the opinion of this Wardmote that Sir Watkin Lewes,
> Knight and Alderman, Mr Deputy Samuel Brown, Mr James Sharp,
> Mr John William Benson and Mr John Hardy, their representatives
> in Common Council, be desired to concur and assist in promoting
> any Resolutions of that Court to precure a Repeal of the late Act of
> Parliament in favour of Roman Catholicks so far as respects the
> establishment of Seminaries for the Education of Youth & Purchasing
> of Lands within this Realm of England.[1]

The next day the motion was adopted, virtually unaltered, by the Common Council as its own; a week later, when the riots were at their height,
the Council, far from being deterred by the spectacle of public disturbance, persisted in pursuing its course and resolved unanimously 'to
petition the Hon. House of Commons against the Act of Parliament
passed in favour of the Roman Catholics'. It followed this up the next
day by appointing a drafting committee of fifteen members, which included Alderman Frederick Bull, a close friend of Lord George Gordon.
And so the petition went forward.

So the City authorities found themselves in the equivocal situation of
being called upon to quell a disturbance with whose aims, if not with
whose methods, they were evidently largely in sympathy. How many of
them, in fact, had signed the Protestant petition? Lord George Gordon
later declared that the justices could not handle the crowds because 'many
of the magistrates had signed the petition and almost all the creditable
constables'.[2] Formally, Lord Mayor Brackley Kennet and his colleagues
acted correctly in marshalling the forces at their disposal and, when the
marshalmen and constables, many of whom were extremely half-hearted
defenders of Catholic properties, proved quite inadequate for the job, in
sending to the Tower for military assistance. But they acted tardily and
showed little enthusiasm for the task; it was not until the rioters, after
nearly a week's disturbance, turned their attention to the Bank of England
and the Mansion House that the City Fathers, realizing that more than

[1] Lime Street Wardmote Minute Book, 1780–1866, G.L., MS. 1169/2, p. 2.
[2] 'Lord George Gordon's Narrative', B.M. MS. 42, 129.

Catholic properties were at stake, ordered the Sheriffs to raise the *posse comitatus* to defend the properties of all. So Wilkes who, as a member of the London Military Association, had shouldered a musket in defence of the Bank, was not so far wrong when, in the House of Commons, he criticized the Lord Mayor for his lack of diligence and attacked his former friend and colleague, Frederick Bull, who had allowed the constables of his ward to 'wear the ensigns of rebellion in their hats' (the Protestants' blue cockade) and had been seen leaving the Commons arm-in-arm with Lord George Gordon.[1]

The riots had the effect, as in the case of Wilkes, of dampening the City's ardour for popular Radicalism, supported by the streets; and a City worthy was later reported as saying: 'From that moment, I shut my ears against the voices of popular clamour.'[2] But, though wrenched from its popular moorings, the City's own Radicalism – or, more properly in this case, its old hostility to Court and Administration – did not die a sudden death. In fact, in the aftermath of the riots, it revived and the City authorities fought a protracted duel with the government over their claim to form voluntary associations with their own appointed officers – rather as Parisians were to do with their National Guard in the summer of 1789. Ostensibly, the purpose was to protect City properties from further assaults by 'the rabble'; but it was also quite clearly an assertion of the City's ancient privileges and right of self-defence against the encroachment of the executive power, which, to quell the riots, had sent in a strong military force quite independent of the magistrates. This is what Wilkes and others had wanted to avoid; and Lord George Gordon, in his own account of the riots tells how, when he offered his services to quell them at the Guildhall, Wilkes refused the offer of 'an individual of Westminster' to quieten disturbance 'in their district' and feared that any military intervention by the government would spell the end of the City's 'liberties'.[3] The military authorities, for their part, objected to the City's claims on the ground that 'no person can bear arms in this country but under officers bearing the King's commission'. The City countered with the argument that, under the Bill of Rights, all Protestant subjects were entitled to bear arms for their own defence. Basically, it was the old dispute between 'country' and 'Court' which began with Charles II.

[1] Sharpe, vol. 3, pp. 178–90.
[2] L. S. Sutherland, 'The City of London in Eighteenth-Century Politics', in *Essays presented to Sir Lewis Namier*, eds R. Pares and A. J. P. Taylor, 1956, p. 73.
[3] 'Lord George Gordon's Narrative', fos. 41–2.

The citizens received no satisfaction; but, with the ending of the emergency and the withdrawal of the troops, the case lost its urgency and was allowed to lie in abeyance.[1]

But circumstances soon conspired to bring City and government closer together. Temporarily, the riots themselves, by raising doubts as to the wisdom of extending the franchise, may have played a part; but this was probably offset by the new government crisis of 1782, which brought Lord North's long Ministry to an end. More important, perhaps, were the respective activities of Charles James Fox and the younger William Pitt. Pitt entered Parliament, as an associate of Shelburne's, in 1781. Donning the mantle of his father, he called, in May 1782, when the air was once more thick with schemes for piece-meal 'economical' reform, for an enquiry into the state of the representation; it was defeated, though by only twenty votes. A year later, in May 1783, he moved three separate resolutions: for the disfranchisement of a number of Rotten Boroughs, for measures against bribery at elections and for an additional number of Members to represent London and the counties. These never came to the vote; but Pitt had already won a reputation as reformer and was being seen by London Radicals and by Wyvill and his Yorkshiremen as a more certain ally than Fox who, having entered the Rockingham–Shelburne Ministry of 1782, appeared now to think that, once Burke's 'economical' measures had been adopted, other reforms could be left to an uncertain future.

Rockingham died in July 1782; Shelburne and Fox, long at loggerheads over relations with the Crown, fell apart; and, to defeat Shelburne, Fox entered into a coalition with the old arch-enemy, Lord North. (Now that the American War was settled and further reform was temporarily held in abeyance, the alliance did not appear to Fox to be as unprincipled as it did to his former friends and supporters.) The coalition was, in itself, to many an affront that led to estrangement; but matters only came to a head with Fox's East India Bill, which the new partners presented to Parliament in 1783. Ten years before, the City had reacted sharply to North's Regulating Act of May 1773, fearing that any attempt to 'regulate' the charter of the East India Company might endanger its own; in a strongly worded petition to Parliament, it had denounced the Bill as 'a direct and dangerous attack on the liberties of the people' and a threat to 'the franchise of every corporate body in this Kingdom'. This time,

[1] G. Rudé, 'Some Financial and Military Aspects of the Gordon Riots', *The Guildhall Miscellany*, no. 6, February 1956, pp. 31–42; Sharpe, vol. 3, pp. 186–90.

the City went much further, and when the King used his influence with the Lords to get the measure defeated and subsequently dismissed the Ministry, it joined heartily in a national chorus of approval. And not only the City but also London: among eighty-four congratulatory addresses sent to the King from all over the country were addresses from Surrey, Southwark and Westminster, as well as from the City. The Common Council and Common Hall sent separate addresses, which applauded the use of the Royal prerogative to uphold 'parliamentary engagements' and chartered rights. So 'the successors of the Old Roundheads [to quote Macaulay's words] had turned courtiers'.[1]

Pitt was now called into office and, in February 1784, the Common Council voted him the Freedom of the City and a gold box for the part he had played in 'supporting the legal prerogative of the Crown and the constitutional rights of the people'. The general election that followed towards the close of the year ended in a sweeping victory for Pitt and George III, supported by a combination of 'old corruption' and a revulsion against the discredited Whigs. Fox and North lost 160 seats ('Fox's martyrs'). Yorkshire was carried for Pitt by the efforts of Wyvill and his reformers. In London, Wilkes declared himself for Pitt in Middlesex and, in the City, former Wilkite leaders like Brass Crosby followed suit, as did three of the City's M.P.s elected in 1784; John Sawbridge alone remained loyal to Fox (which nearly cost him his seat). In Westminster, Fox himself only just managed to retain his seat; in fact, the satirists claimed (and they may well have been right) that he was only saved from defeat by the energetic intervention on his behalf of the glamorous Duchess of Devonshire. So London Radicalism, disenchanted with Fox and Burke and the 'aristocratical' opposition, now pinned its hopes for reform on George III and Pitt. It proved to be a forlorn hope, for Pitt, having made one final but vain effort to have reform debated in 1785, abandoned the struggle altogether. But the new orientation in London's politics lasted, with minor intermissions, for over twenty years.

[1] Sharpe, vol. 3, pp. 204–6; *Commons Journals*, xxxiv, 343; P.R.O., H.O. 55/12–16.

10

Social Protest
'from below'

SO FAR, the politics we have been discussing have been almost exclusively those of the upper or middle classes, the politics of the gentry, merchants and the more prosperous craftsmen of the 'middle sort'. It is true that among the electors of Westminster and the freeholders of Middlesex there was, as we have seen, a smattering of wage-earners and petty craftsmen, or of those whom Defoe called 'the poor' or 'the working trades'. But their role was altogether marginal; for, even in Westminster, a man had to be a householder – and not a lodger or a mere member of the family – to have the vote; so that the great bulk of the 'lower orders' were strictly excluded from the political community, if we omit such activities as crowding the hustings at election times to huzzah the heroes of the day.

Yet, if denied the vote, the workmen and petty tradesmen found some degree of compensation in such popular outlets as strikes, riots or demonstrations. Of these the most familiar was the riot. In fact, eighteenth-century England, like France of the Ancien Régime, was constantly marked by riots; and it has even been argued that rioting, like resistance to oppression, was accepted as a part of the Englishman's 'birthright'.[1] (If so, it was a right that was strictly circumscribed – depending always, of course, on the force at the authorities' disposal!) In country districts and market towns, riots were generally concerned with the price of food, or they might be directed against enclosures, turnpikes, workhouses or Smuggling and Militia Acts. In big cities like London the case was rather different. Food riots, for reasons that we shall note, played very little part in Hanoverian London, at least until the time of the French wars at the

[1] Halévy, *England in 1815*, pp. 148–52.

end of the century; and London riots, like those of Paris and other capital cities, had two further characteristics: their great diversity (almost any issue might occasion a riot) and their tendency to become 'political' by reflecting the issues in debate between Tories, Whigs and Radicals or those dividing government from opposition or the City of London from both. Such issues were, as we have seen, Excise, gin and Jenkins' Ear, the Wilkes affair and the relief afforded to Roman Catholics. These were all reflected in the popular movements that we shall be considering in a later chapter. But there were other times when the people in the streets (or 'the mobbish part of the Town', as an observer once called them) were concerned with matters of more immediate moment to themselves – such as wages, working conditions or the price of food – when it needed no outside body, no political pressure group, no Common Hall or Common Council, to excite disorder or promote a riot. Such 'bread and butter' disputes, which might take the form of peaceful demonstrations but more often erupted into riots, were extremely common in Hanoverian times. It is with these that we are concerned in the present chapter.

Most commonly, such outbreaks arose in response to an evident threat to the worker's, or the small craftsman's or shopkeeper's, livelihood; even though, on occasion, the connection might not appear very close. In July 1749, for example, sailors from the *Grafton* man-o'-war wrecked Peter Wood's bawdy house, the Star Tavern, off Devereux Court, on the north side of the Strand. It was a bad time for sailors: the Treaty of Aix-la-Chapelle, bringing peace with France, had been signed only a year before; and three of these sailors, while frequenting the establishment, had been robbed of 'their watches, a bank-note value £20, four moidores and thirty guineas'. So, having failed to get immediate redress, they returned with reinforcements from the docks at Wapping, broke open the house, tipped the women almost naked into the street, ripped up the beds, broke the furniture to pieces and burned it in the street, and, returning a second time, proceeded to break up another brothel down the road. Honour being satisfied, the sailors made good their escape. But one young man, Bosavern Penlez by name, said to be of good character and a clergyman's son, was not so fortunate. Having drunk too much punch in a neighbouring tavern, he got mixed up with the rioters, was arrested by the Guards and, on the dubious evidence of Peter Wood, was tried and sentenced to be hanged at Tyburn.[1]

Another type of disturbance, which on occasion involved other classes

[1] Hugh Phillips, *Mid-Georgian London*, pp. 182-3.

as well, was the theatre riot – so common in the middle of the century that, at this time, the two largest theatres, the Covent Garden and the Drury Lane, had iron spikes along the front of the stage as a barrier against hostile spectators. Riots might arise over the price of seats or from dis- approval of the actors, particularly when they were French. They were accepted by the authorities as almost a matter of course; and, at a trial following a riot at the Haymarket Theatre in 1738 (the occasion was the visit of a group of French players), the judge pronounced that 'the public had a legal right to manifest their dislike to any play or actor'. But the public tended to decide for itself when such manifestations were called for; and there were riots at the Drury Lane in 1744 over an advance in prices and at the Covent Garden in 1763, when the old custom was abolished of admitting spectators at a lower price after the third act. The most destructive disturbance of all was at the Drury Lane in 1755, at a time of growing tension with France, when French dancers, invited by Garrick, were appearing in Noverre's ballet, *The Chinese Festival*. After five nights of noisy demonstrations by the pit and gallery, the more fash- ionable occupants left their boxes, sword in hand, and proceeded to lay about them among the 'groundlings'. But (so, at least, it was said) attackers and victims soon joined forces and, much to Garrick's speechless astonish- ment, they jointly tore up the benches and demolished the scenery to a cost of £4,000.[1]

Far more typical, of course, were protests and disturbances over wages and conditions of employment. These might take the form of riots over imported foreign goods or foreign labour, which, behind a nationalist or anti-foreigner façade, hid motives that were largely economic. Such were the calico riots in Spitalfields in 1719 and 1720 and the anti-Irish riots in Shoreditch, Spitalfields and Whitechapel in 1736.

The fashion of wearing printed calicoes had (like gin) been brought to England from Holland under William and Mary. Calicoes were a cool and colourful substitute for woollens and cost one-eighth of the price. The woollen trade protested and lobbied Parliament, and an Act of 1700 placed a total ban on the importation of printed calicoes. But the law left important loop-holes: plain calicoes could still be imported and, en- couraged by Parliament's protective measures, calico-printing began at home and, within the metropolis, there were presses set up at Lewisham. So the fashion grew and reached a peak soon after 1717, when a slump in the woollen trade – and in weaving in general – provoked the weavers to angry

[1] W. J. Lawrence, in *Johnson's England*, vol. 2, pp. 177–8.

retaliation and raised the cry for a total prohibition. In London, it was the silk-weavers who felt the pinch; they began their riots on 10 June 1719. Women wearing calicoes were attacked and insulted in the streets. Hand-bills were posted: 'Must the poor weavers starve?' and 'Shall the Ingy [East India] calicoes be worn whilst the poor weavers and their families perish?' The riots spread to Moorfields and weavers, dispersed from Bunhill Fields, were driven towards Southwark and took refuge in the old privileged sanctuary of the Mint, where two rioters were arrested. Some headed for Lewisham to destroy the presses, but were overtaken by the Guards and dispersed; one weaver was shot dead. Meanwhile, the Lord Mayor ordered the City gates to be closed. The London trained bands were summoned and a troop of Horse Guards was sent into Spitalfields, while a strong force stayed in the Tower as a reserve. So the first wave of rioting ended.

But the riots began again two days later and, in spite of arrests, con-tinued intermittently until the end of July. Small groups of weavers formed under cover of dark, and further attacks were made on women in the streets, particularly on Sundays when the new fashion was more blatantly paraded. Sometimes, stung to anger, the women riposted; and, at the end of July, four weavers sitting in stocks were jeered at by ladies wearing calicoes from a passing hackney coach. The press now began a lively debate, in which *Mist's Weekly Journal* took up the cudgels for the weavers, while *Read's Weekly Journal* blamed the master weavers them-selves for hiring too many workmen: their number, swollen by an influx of parish apprentices, had in fact doubled over the past ten years, and the frame-work knitters had rioted over this very issue in 1710 when a hundred frames had been broken in Shoreditch and Bunhill Row. A debate also took place between the masters and their journeymen. The former, in presenting through the Weavers' Company a petition to Parliament calling for a ban on all printed calicoes, reproved the journeymen for damaging their cause by violence; while the journeymen turned the tables neatly on their masters by charging them with being 'misled through the boundless ambition and pride of their wives', who themselves wore calicoes, thus setting the whole public an 'evil example'!

With the end of summer, woollens once more took over and the rioting momentarily abated. Meanwhile, Parliament had got busy and a new Bill passed through the Commons in February 1720, but it was held up for several weeks by the Lords. So a further spate of rioting followed in May. Weavers gathered in Spitalfields and Whitechapel, and calicoes were torn off women's backs on the approaches to Parliament. In Spitalfields, Dalby, a French calico-printer, had to take refuge in the City when his house was threatened with destruction. But the Lords came to heel soon after; and the Act of 1720 solved the weavers' problem, temporarily at least, by placing a total ban on the wearing of all calicoes, and even on their manufacture for household furnishings.[1]

It was perhaps inevitable that the journeymen weavers of Spitalfields should have been charged by their critics with having secret Jacobin designs. It appeared all the more credible as, by chance, their riots started on the Pretender's birthday, 10 June, when (it was reported in the *Plymouth Weekly Journal*) 'many people' in London were celebrating the event by wearing a white rose. But the weavers, for their part, appear to have had no share in it: in fact, a Jacobite, John Humphreys, who was alleged to have tried to turn the riots into a Jacobite demonstration, was handed over by weavers to the magistrates and committed to Newgate on a charge of high treason. But, on similar occasions, similar charges persisted. In the anti-Irish riots of 1736, they were made by no less a person than Sir Robert Walpole himself, who was inclined to see all challenges to his authority or to the stability of his government, whether by Tories, dissident 'Patriots', or striking working-men, in the context of a Jacobin conspiracy. He certainly had reason for concern. It was the year of the Gin Act and, in London, the watermen were further inflamed by the new Westminster Bridge Act. There had been riots over turnpikes at Hereford and Bristol and over smuggling (the Porteous Riots) at Edinburgh. There were reports of gun-running in Scotland and the North; and, to crown it all, Westminster Hall, on the very threshold of government, was rocked by an 'insolent' explosion of gunpowder, the presumed work of 'a sett of low Jacobites', who had concocted 'a preparation which they call a *phospherous*, that takes fire from the air'.[2]

So the air was charged enough, and it is possible that the riots against the Irish which broke out in East London in July of that year may have felt something of the backwash of some of these other movements; for as one of Sir Robert's informers wrote to him soon after the event, 'it is evident that there are great discontents and murmurings through all this

---

[1] D. C. G. Isaac, 'A Study of Popular Disturbances in Britain, 1714–1754', unpub. thesis for Ph.D. degree, Edinburgh, 1953, pp. 92–103.

[2] Archdeacon William Coxe, *Memoirs of the Life and Administration of Sir Robert Walpole*, vol. 3, p. 348.

Mobbish part of the Town'.[1] Yet these discontents were essentially social and economic; and so it was with the grievances of the rioting weavers and other workmen, who had been incensed by the employment of Irish labour at cheaper rates of pay; and we shall see that Sir Robert himself was to admit that this was 'a purely Irish incident'. The Irish, in fact, had been coming to London in larger numbers than usual and were competing with English workmen in a wide variety of trades. Specifically, they were being employed by master weavers in Spitalfields, and, in Shoreditch, the builders of the new church of St Leonard's dismissed a large number of English workmen and replaced them by Irishmen at one-half or two-thirds of their wages. It was these two facts which provoked the riots that broke out in the two parishes on 26 July, and which later spread to Whitechapel. Sir Robert Walpole, who was kept well informed of their progress by his agents, sent the following account of their earliest phase to his brother Horace:

> On Monday night last, there was an appearance of numbers being assembled in a very disorderly manner at Shoreditch, near Spital-fields. Their cry and complaint was of being underworked, and starved by the Irish: *Down with the Irish, &c.* But that night the numbers were not very great, and they dispersed themselves without doing any mischief. . . . On Tuesday evening they assembled again in bodies, and were about 7 o'clock thought to be 2,000 in number. They now grew more riotous; they attacked a public house, kept by an Irishman, where the Irish resorted and victualled, broke down all the doors and windows and quite gutted the house. Another house of the same sort underwent the same fate. By this time (those places being within the jurisdiction of the City), the Mayor and Deputy Lieutenant of the Tower Hamlets were assembled in order to disperse them. The proclamation was read; but the mob, wholly regardless of the proclamation, increased every minute, and were thought to be about 4,000 strong. The Magistrate upon this gave orders for raising the Militia; and in the Meantime the Deputy Lieutenant wrote to the Commanding Officer at the Tower to send to their assistance such a number of the Guards they could spare, upon which an officer with about fifty men was sent by Major White. Upon the appearance of the Guards the mob retired, shifted from one street and alley to another, and gave no resistance, and by break

[1] Camb. Univ. Lib., Cholmondeley-Houghton MSS., P/70, file 2/14.

of day were all dispersed. All Wednesday things seemed very quiet till evening, when the mob rose again to a great number; but the Militia of the Tower Hamlets being then raised, marched against them; but the mob in same manner retired before them wherever they came, and gave not the least resistance . . . and so dispersed themselves before the morning.

In a 'P.S.' he added a brief note on the events of Thursday, when the rioters, now numbering no more than three hundred, fled before the Militia, having defaced one weaver's house, 'who, they said, had employed Irish journeymen'.

From another eyewitness account we learn that the rioters in Holywell Lane had been assured by John Collet, a local publican and Militia lieutenant, that the builders of St Leonard's Church had 'already discharged his Irish Labourers and Employed English in their stead'; and that a Mr Chetham, who employed 'near 200 Irish', had promised him that he would discharge his Irish workmen 'as soon as they had finished the several pieces of work they had in hand'. So, in a further note, the next morning, Sir Robert assured his brother that there was 'now an end to this bustle'. But he was over-optimistic; the same evening, crowds began to re-form in Spitalfields and advanced down Brick Lane into Whitechapel, where they joined local rioters who, later that night, attacked Irish ale-houses and dwelling-houses in Goodman's Fields and Rosemary Lane. Surprisingly, Walpole has nothing to say about this phase of the disturbances, which was far more destructive and a greater threat to the security of the City than the one he had described before. The following account is from the evidence later given at the Old Bailey by Richard Burton, a brewer's cooper:

On Friday night, July 30, between 9 and 10, I was at the end of Red Lion Street, and I saw the Mob coming down Bell Yard, with Sticks and lighted Links. One of them made a sort of speech directing the rest to go to *Church Lane*, to the *Gentleman and Porter*. My Master serving Mr Allen who keeps the House with Drink, I ran down to inform him that his Sign was mentioned. There was about 50 or 60 of them then, and they had 2 or 3 Links with them. One read from a Paper the Signs of the *Gentleman and Porter*, the *Bull and Butcher*, and the Tavern in *Well Street*. I did not hear them make any Declaration what was to be done, but I went directly to Allen's to inform him they had great Sticks, like Stakes out of Bakers Bavins. While I was standing at *Allen's* Door, the Mob came down; I told them the House had been mine for a Fortnight, and the Man who kept it before was gone. One of them was called *Captain Tom the Barber*, and was in a striped Banjan. I would have taken notice of him, but he turned away and would not let me see his Face. I desired him to use me favourably and told him it was my House. They said they knew I was not Irish by my Tongue, and I should not be hurt. I made them set up Candles in the Windows, and pacify'd the Mob seemingly well, but a Woman telling them it was a Sham, and that I was only the Brewer's Cooper, the Sticks flew immediately and beat the Candle out of my Hand, as I stood at the Door; but Justice *Phillips* coming down, and the Captain with his Soldiers, they took some of them, and the rest made off immediately, and were gone as suddenly, as if a Hole had been dug in the Bottom of the Street, and they had all dropped into it at once.

The riots had a brief sequel in other parts of the capital; and, on 1 August, the *Gentleman's Magazine* reported:

Mobs arose in Southwark, Lambeth and Tyburn-road, and took upon 'em to interrogate People whether they were for the English or Irish? but committed no Violence; several Parties of Horse Grenadiers dispers'd the Mobs which were gathering in Ratcliff-highway, to demolish the Houses of the Irish.

Yet such incidents were short-lived; and writing three weeks later to Horace Walpole, Sir Robert assured him that 'the tumults and disorders here are quite at an end' and added, characteristically, that 'the industry of the Jacobites was not able to improve this truly Irish incident into a more general confusion'.[1]

This appears to have been the last occasion on which what was essentially a labour dispute was conducted in such a manner. However, wage-earners threatened with wage cuts or unemployment continued to put pressure on their employers by other 'pre-industrial' means, such as by intimidating letters, the destruction of machinery, and attacks on property and persons, as well as by more modern methods, more appropriate to an industrial age, including petitions, marches or peaceful demonstrations. In the disputes of 1763, there was a remarkable crop of threatening letters, vowing vengeance on employers who were slow to raise wages, who failed to find men work, or had recourse to the law to keep their work-people in order. So, in February of that year, we read of a 'numerous body' of

[1] G. Rudé, in *The Guildhall Miscellany*, no. 10, September 1959, pp. 53–63.

journeymen shoemakers conspiring together to have their earnings raised by 2*d.* a pair of shoes and addressing the following note to James Young, a master shoemaker of Cranborne Alley, Leicester Fields:

> Sir, Dam Your Blood if You do not Ryes Your Works Too 2 Pence a Pair moor We Well Blow Your Braines out For We Will Blow Your Brans our if You Doo not Do itt You slim Dog We shall sett You Houes on fier and You must Lay Sexty Pound in the Pawn Browker Ally earls Court Ropt in a Bitt Wyte Paper on Thursday Night att Ten a Clock Thee Second of Febr.

A fortnight later, a hosier and frame-work knitter, at the Bishop Blaze, Chiswell Street, received the following from his 'humble sevants':

> Sir, I am sorry to acquaint you that there are seven poor Families in great distress and we the fathers have come to a resolution to borry 50 pounds of you for Six months and then hope to pay you the principal and intrest if we do but get work wich you may suply us with but damn you are worst then a highwayman for you bete down prises and wont Lett us have any work neither if you do not Lay the Money at the place that we shall mention we will set your House and all that belongs to you on fire for it is in my power for to do it.

And, in October of that year, in the course of one of the numerous and violently conducted disputes of the East London silk-weavers (on this occasion between rival groups of journeymen), a journeyman weaver, whose silk had been destroyed in his loom and who had had the offenders issued with warrants for their arrest, was threatened that 'if you don't make your Wife discharge the Warrants your House shall be pul'd down and you all Murdered and Dead people'. Sometimes these blood-curdling threats (which, in fact, were extremely rarely carried out) were, as in the present case, tersely brutal; but, on occasion, they might be couched in almost lyrical terms, as the following message received by Peter Auber, a weaver of Spital Square who, in a later dispute of August 1769, had refused to comply with his journeyman's terms:

> Mr Obey, we give you now an Egg Shell of Honey, but if you refuse to comply with the demands of yesterday, we'll give you a Gallon of Thorns to your final Life's End.[1]

The 1760s were, in fact, the most remarkable decade of industrial

[1] *London Gazette*, 5-8, 15-19 February, 4-8 October 1763; P.R.O., Treasury Solicitor's Papers, T.S. 11/818/2696.

disputes of the whole century. In December 1761 the *London Chronicle* reported a simultaneous outbreak of 'combinations' for higher wages among journeymen cabinet-makers, peruke-makers, shoemakers and tailors. But this was far surpassed by the concentrated activity of the years 1768 and 1769, when there was a great crop of strikes, assaults on machinery, demonstrations, marches and petitions to Parliament, that thoroughly alarmed both ministers and magistrates, all the more so as they coincided with a major stage in the Wilkite–Radical agitation. In May 1768, as the price of wheat at the London Corn Exchange rose to 56*s.* a quarter, the authorities were faced by almost simultaneous demands and demonstrations by sailors, watermen, coopers, hatters, glass-grinders, sawyers, tailors, coal-heavers and silk-weavers. In fact, it seemed to contemporaries that the movement was bound to spread through the wage-earning population as a whole; as one Member of Parliament wrote to the Duke of Newcastle: 'So the evils, if not suppress'd, will go through all the inferior orders of men.' Thomas Harley, the Lord Mayor, reacting sharply to these and the other events of that month, took the extraordinary step of calling on master tradesmen to keep their journeymen and apprentices off the streets and reminding freemen of the City of their pledge to keep their journeymen from 'going abroad' in times of disorder. And, happening when they did, it was inevitable that the authorities should see more than a merely casual connection between these journeymen's and labourers' disputes and the popular political outbreaks that followed in the wake of Wilkes's first election victory in Middlesex; the Duke of Grafton, who was in all but name the Chief Minister of the day, noted long after the event that 'artisans of almost every denomination . . . combined for an advance of wages, and their discontents, and disobedience to the laws led them to join often, in numbers, these mobs which the consequences of the elections for Middlesex frequently produced'. And, taking their cue from contemporary opinion, historians have tended to treat the two movements as one; and it has even been suggested that these industrial disputes were an early example of 'political strikes'.[1] Yet, while there were points of connection between the two (there were certainly Wilkes supporters among coal-heavers and weavers), they were few and far between and by no means conclusive; and it is reasonable to suppose that these industrial movements were no more politically inspired than the riots of 1719 and 1736.[2]

[1] Raymond Postgate, *That Devil Wilkes*, 1956, pp. 90–104.
[2] For the argument and for much that follows, see *Wilkes and Liberty*, pp. 90–104.

It started with the sailors; and, on 5 May, the *Gentleman's Magazine* noted that

> a great body of sailors assembled at Deptford, forcibly went on board several ships, unreefed the top-sails, and vowed no ships should sail till the merchants had consented to raise their wages.

Sailors' disputes had been endemic since the discharge of many thousands at the end of the wars with France in the spring of 1763. That autumn, the justices were ordered by the Secretaries of State 'to take proper measures for suppressing the riots of sailors and others at Shoreditch'. The present agitation arose over wages and spread to London from northern ports. In April, sailors rioted at Newcastle, Tinmouth, Sunderland and Shields and compelled the shipowners to sign agreements with their representatives. The London seamen demanded a wage of 35s. a month and insisted that, until this was conceded, 'they would neither engage, nor suffer any ship to sail'. The sailors' committees visited all outward-bound ships and, on 9 May, the Navy Office reported that every single ship on the Thames had been disabled from sailing; one vessel had escaped, but was boarded at Limehouse Hole and made to heave to. Meanwhile, 5,000–6,000 sailors assembled at Stepney Fields to devise further measures. Some proposed to go to Richmond to see the King. Others gathered in St George's Fields and marched to St James's Palace, 'with colours flying, drums beating and fifes playing', and handed in a petition. A petition to Parliament followed on 10 May, when 'a great body of sailors' (some said 5,000, others 15,000) marched to Palace Yard, listened to speeches from the roof of a hackney coach, gave three cheers and dispersed. A week later, several shipowners appear to have come to terms with the sailors' committees and their ships were allowed to sail. Among them were the Hudson's Bay Company who, for the privilege, had been compelled to agree to a wage of 40s. a month, which they considered 'exorbitant', all the more so as their own sailors were (they claimed) quite ready 'to accept of moderate wages'. But further disturbances followed, and it was not until July, wrote Grafton, 'that the sailors took fairly to their work'.

Meanwhile, the Thames watermen, already a declining force and the victims of continuous irritations,[1] had followed suit. On 9 May 2,000 of them demonstrated at the Royal Exchange and Mansion House; and 500 were admitted to place their demands and grievances before Lord Mayor

[1] Henry Humpherus, *History of the Company of Watermen and Lightermen*, 1874–6, vol. 2, pp. 156–258.

O

Harley. These were that provisions were too dear, that private boats on Thames-side were competing with the watermen's craft, and that they were not allowed to work on Sundays. Harley gave them a friendly reception and advised them to draw up a petition, which he undertook to present on their behalf to Parliament. So, having given three huzzas for the mayor, they went peacefully away.

The same day, the hatters struck and (the press reported) 'refused to work till their wages had been raised'. The dispute must have lasted some weeks, as a hatmaker of St Olave's, Southwark, testified under oath on 21 June that, a few days previously,

> a Mob or Gang of Hatters to the number of thirty came to his house in the Maze . . . about one o'clock at noon, in a riotous manner, and insisted on this Informant turning off the men he then had at work, which he refused; and, upon such refusal, the said Mob or Gang of Hatters threatened to pull his house down and take this Informant thereout.

However, his house was saved by the intervention of a neighbour; and nothing further appears in the press about the dispute.

Charles Dingley, a prosperous Russia merchant, was not so fortunate; for his brand-new saw-mill in Fore Street, Limehouse, was 'pulled down' by a band of 500 sawyers on 10 May, the day of the 'massacre' in St George's Fields. It is tempting to see this as an act of political reprisal, as Dingley was an anti-Radical and known supporter of the Court: it was he, in fact, who, a few months later organized the ill-fated 'loyal' merchants' address to George III. But, on examination, it appears to have been, quite simply, an early instance of Luddism, or machine-breaking, by men threatened with a loss of work. 'The reason given for this outrage,' ran a press report, 'is that it deprived many persons in that branch from being employed.' The point is confirmed by Dingley's principal clerk, who, in giving evidence at the Old Bailey, stated that when he asked 'the mob of sawyers and other people' what they wanted, he was told 'the saw-mill was at work when thousands of them were starving for want of bread'.

A week later, glass-grinders, coopers and journeymen tailors all assembled to present their various petitions to Parliament. The authorities, after the events in St George's Fields, were no longer so willing to be co-operative as they had been in the case of the sailors and watermen; and Lord Weymouth, one of the Secretaries of State, commended the Westminster magistrates for their efforts 'to dissuade the tailors from proceeding to the House of Commons with a petition', and hoped the coopers would disperse peacefully. If not, his secretary, William Fraser, wrote to Sir John Fielding, 'you are already informed where to meet with support whenever you shall find it necessary to call for it'. No more was heard of the glass-grinders and coopers, but the tailors were more persistent and their past history was such as to cause the government more particular concern. For it was the London journeymen tailors who, as far back as 1720, had made one of the first attempts in history to form a stable trade union; that year, the master tailors complained to Parliament about their journeymen's 'combinations' over the past two years to raise wages and reduce working hours:

> and for the better carrying on their design [they] have subscribed their respective names in books prepared for that purpose, at the several houses of call or resort [being public-houses in and about London and Westminster].

A later petition by the masters records that, by 1751,

> they had formed into a kind of republic, holding illegal meetings at 42 different public-houses and appointing from each 2 persons to represent the body, and form the 'Grand Committee for the Management of the Town', which made rules and orders for the direction of the masters and the whole body of journeymen.

It was following the first of these two masters' petitions that an Act of Parliament of 1721 had proscribed all 'combinations' by journeymen and fixed their hours of work at 6 a.m. to 8 p.m. and their wages at 2s. from March to June and 1s. 8d. for the rest of the year. But the 'combinations' continued and, in 1744, 15,000 tailors made a concerted effort to advance their wages beyond this limit. They had no success, and, on this occasion, two masters were actually fined by the Middlesex justices for paying higher wages than permitted by the law. Seven years later, the masters once more complained 'that a great many journeymen tailors have . . . exacted and insisted to have much greater wages for their work', but supported their claim for a summer wage of 2s. 6d. and 2s. for the rest of the year.[1] The Middlesex justices refused it, but in January 1764 they agreed that wages should be 2s. 6d. all the year round and that hours should be reduced by one hour in the winter half-year. A further con-

[1] E. G. Dowdell, *A Hundred Years of Quarter Sessions. The Government of Middlesex from 1660 to 1760*, pp. 151–3.

cession followed: summer and winter hours were to be equalized; but when some of the masters refused to accept the award, a strike broke out in July, leading to a number of convictions to short terms of hard labour. The movement of 1768 was simply a further instalment in this long-protracted and highly complicated engagement. 'The tailors intend,' wrote Weymouth to the Lord Mayor, 'to assemble tomorrow evening and go round to the several masters in London to compel their journeymen to join them, in order to oblige the trade to raise their present wages.' But, this time, it proved to be a perfectly orderly movement. Two thousand tailors assembled, marched to Parliament and presented their petition. After receiving a few comforting words, 'they went away very quickly and peaceably'.

The coal-heavers' dispute was a far more violent and protracted affair; it went back to April of that year. The East London trade of coal-heaving (or unloading of coals from lighters) was, in the mid-eighteenth century, pursued by some 670 persons, resident in Shadwell and Wapping, of whom the majority were Roman Catholics. Partly for this reason, no doubt, they were viewed with the utmost suspicion by the authorities. 'A few . . . are quiet laborious men,' wrote the Treasury Solicitor in preparing a brief against a number of them, 'the rest are of a riotous disposition and ready to join in any kind of disorders.' The disturbances of 1768 had a dual origin. On the one hand, the men were demanding an increase of 4*d*. (later 8*d*.) on every score of sacks unloaded; and when the employers refused to comply, a total stoppage followed in the port of London. The other aspect of the dispute was a protracted 'war' between two groups of agents, or 'undertakers', operating rival schemes for registering coal-heavers. The 'undertakers' were generally publicans, who lodged and fed the men and provided them with liquor and whose pubs were used as houses of call. In 1758, after the men had complained of being cheated by the publicans, Parliament set up an official, regulated scheme whereby work-gangs were organized by recognized foremen, and all coal-heavers who registered and paid 2*s*. in the pound from their wages became eligible for sick and funeral benefits and for benefits for their widows and orphans. The administration of the scheme was entrusted to William Beckford, alderman of Billingsgate Ward; but a scandal arose over the malversions of Francis Reynolds, an attorney whom Beckford had appointed as his deputy; taking advantage of the confusion that ensued, Ralph Hodgson of Shadwell, a Middlesex 'trading' justice, set up a rival scheme of his own, which he ran on something like trade-union lines; wages were pushed up, and the coal-heavers began to flock into the new organization. Moreover, Hodgson supported the men in their dispute, while Beckford opposed them, and his agents, who were anxious to break the strike, advertised in the press in early April, inviting men willing to work to report to their office. In consequence, John Green, one of Beckford's principal 'under-takers', was besieged in his public house, the Round About Tavern in Gravel Lane, Shadwell, by angry coal-heavers armed with bludgeons, who demolished his windows but were repulsed by musket fire. The next day, Hodgson's men resorted to more violent measures: they made an armed assault on Green's house, taunted him with shouts of 'Green, you bouger, why don't you fire?', and swore that 'they would have his heart and liver, and cut him to pieces and hang him on his sign'. Green defended himself stoutly and, before escaping to safety over the rooftops, shot two of his assailants dead. As a result of this affray, seven coal-heavers were sen-tenced to death at the Old Bailey and hanged in Stepney before a crowd of 50,000, attended by 300 soldiers and 'a prodigious number of peace officers'.

The focus now shifted to the other aspect of the dispute. A settlement appeared to be in sight in early May; but the masters refused to consent to a rise in wages and engaged sailors to load and unload their colliers on the Thames. Further violence inevitably followed. On 23 May coal-heavers boarded the *Thames and Mary*, lying in Shadwell Dock, and said they would murder any sailor who continued to load. They were as good as their word, and the next day, when sailors came ashore from another collier, they were attacked with bludgeons and cutlasses. Two were wounded and a young sailor, John Beatty, was stabbed to death. At Wapping a week later, two collier captains who had come ashore to buy provisions were beaten up by fifty coal-heavers. Soon after, however, the military were called in to help the magistrates, several rioters were cap-tured and brought to trial, Beatty's murderer was hanged at Tyburn, and the movement appears to have collapsed.

Even more protracted was the weavers' dispute, which formed but an incident in the long, violent and colourful history of the silk-weavers of Spitalfields, Stepney and Bethnal Green, of which we have recorded certain episodes already. The weavers had a record of militancy second to none; it went back at least to the summer of 1675, when thirty-five 'engine weaving looms', recently imported from Holland, were smashed by rioting weavers in Hoxton, Stepney, Whitechapel, Shoreditch and Clerkenwell.[1]

[1] E. G. Dowdell, *A Hundred Years of Quarter Sessions*, pp. 61–6.

On occasion, when trade as a whole was threatened, masters and journey-men combined in common protest, as when in May 1765, 8,000 weavers marched to Parliament with black flags and besieged Bedford House because the Duke had defeated a Bill designed to protect the London silk-weavers' livelihood by excluding French silks (like the Indian calicoes of 1719!) from the English market. Again, in January 1768, masters and journeymen joined in a great march to St James's Palace to thank the King for reducing the period of Court mournings. Another joint approach to Parliament occurred in 1773, and we have already noted the weavers' common pledge of loyalty over the Jacobite Forty-Five. But such demon-strations of solidarity, though in their own way characteristic of eighteenth-century industrial relations, were more often overshadowed by bitter disputes over wages or the conflicting methods used by rival groups of tradesmen. So it was in this last phase of the weavers' stormy history – that of the 1760s and early 1770s. In October 1763, during a wages dis-pute, several hundred journeymen disguised themselves as sailors and, armed with cutlasses, broke into the houses of journeymen who had refused to join them, smashed their looms, wounded several and burned a master weaver in effigy. Such 'cutting' and destruction of looms had by now become a common form of reprisal, and Parliament in 1765, in addition to excluding French silks (as requested by the weavers), tried to end the abuse by making 'cutting' a capital offence; but we learn from an official report that the journeymen

> knowing their fate, if apprehended, . . . disguised themselves and performed all their exploits in the dead of night, procured arms and offensive weapons of all kinds, beat and abused persons of all ranks and denominations, whom they thought fit to visit for the purpose of cutting their looms and work.

And this was a constant feature of the weavers' outbreak of 1768–9. It started with a dispute between two groups of journeymen: the single-hand (or 'narrow') weavers and those operating the engine loom, which, as we have said, had been introduced from Holland. At the end of November 1767 the *Gentleman's Magazine*, in relating the first phase of the outbreak, spelled out the cause of the trouble: 'The engine-weavers were supposed to be ruinous to the narrow weavers, because, by means of their engines, one of them could do as much in one day as six of the other, and the same kind of work equally good; for which reason the narrow weavers were determined to destroy them.' In the following January there were three cases of assault by single-hand weavers on their opponents' looms in Stepney; one of the assailants was later hanged for the offence. Meanwhile, to add fuel to the flames, the masters had reduced the price of work by 4*d.* a yard, so a three-cornered fight ensued, in which it is often difficult to distinguish one aspect from the other. After a few months' lull, we read that, on 26 July 1768,

> a great number of evil-disposed persons, armed with pistols, cutlasses and other offensive weapons, and in disguise, assembled together about the hour of twelve in the night . . . and entered the houses and shops of several journeymen weavers in and near Spitalfields . . . and cut to pieces and destroyed the silk works then manufacturing in nine different looms there.

And, on 20 August, the Spitalfields weavers 'rose in a body', broke into the house of Nathaniel Farr, in Pratt's Alley, cut to pieces the silk in two looms and shot dead Edward Fitch, a lad of seventeen. Rewards were offered, but no prosecution followed.

Shortly after, a partial agreement was reached between masters and journeymen, and some firms drew up new price lists providing for earnings of 12*s.* to 14*s.* weekly and more. But as the Middlesex justices refused to endorse the agreement, it was soon broken by a number of the masters and reprisals began again. Meanwhile, the journeymen weavers, to promote their cause, had, like the sailors and tailors, formed committees for the different branches of the trade; they called themselves the Bold Defiance and levied a monthly contribution of 2*s.* to 5*s.* a loom to build up a strike fund and meet all expenses. These contributions were collected in conspiratorial fashion at a number of public houses in the weaving districts, to which committee members came in disguise and armed with pistols, swords and cutlasses. Summonses were sent out to masters and journeymen couched in such terms as these:

> Mr Hill, you are desired to send the full donation of all your looms to the Dolphin in Cock Lane. This from the Conquering and Bold Defiance, to be levied at 4*s.* per loom;

and contributors were handed receipts made out as follows:

> Independent and Bold Defiance
> Received . . . shillings . . . Looms.
> Success to Trade.

The 'cutters' reopened their campaign in the spring of 1769 – both, it would seem, to bring wage-cutting employers to heel and to intimidate those defaulting on their subscriptions. On 10 March we read that Spitalfields throwsters had 'extorted money from the masters and committed many outrages'. On 10 April William Tilley of St Leonard's, Shoreditch, cut and destroyed a loom and 'a warp of thread therein of the value of ten shillings', the property of Lydia Fowler. Further attacks followed in the summer and autumn. During the night of 7 August, Thomas Poor, a self-employed journeyman weaver of Stocking-Frame Alley, Shoreditch, was visited by a number of 'cutters', headed by two of their leaders and committeemen, John Doyle and John Valline. Though Poor protested that he had paid his weekly contribution of 3s. 6d. for the seven looms that he worked with his journeyman for the master weavers, the intruders 'cut a large quantity of bombazine silk in the loom'; his looms were 'cut' again on two subsequent occasions, and, for fear of more drastic reprisals, he was eventually compelled to leave his house and seek nightly refuge 'under hedges in the fields'. A more substantial victim was Lewis Chauvet of L. Chauvet & Co., silk handkerchief weavers, of 39 Crispin Street, Spitalfields Market. (Chauvet had pledged 65 men for anti-Jacobite defence in 1745.) The house was besieged by John Valline at the head of a crowd of 1,500 weavers, who 'cut' seventy-six of his looms as a reprisal for his failure to contribute to the committee's funds. He only escaped further damage by handing over £2 2s. for beer-money and consenting to pay his subscription.

Meanwhile, the authorities had decided to take more vigorous action. At the end of September, the magistrates, supported by the military, made an armed raid on the Dolphin Ale-House in New Cock Lane, in the course of which a soldier was shot dead by the weavers, two 'cutters' were killed in the taproom and one of their leaders, Daniel Murphy, found in the landlord's bed, was arrested and later sentenced to death. Publicans who put their houses at the disposal of the 'cutters' ' committees were threatened with the loss of their licences. Troops were quartered in Spitalfields, and Lewis Chauvet and 150 other master weavers undertook to lodge the officers at their own expense and to feed their men at the Three Tuns Tavern at a cost of 9d. a head per day. The City Radicals were incensed and the Sheriffs, James Townsend and John Sawbridge (both staunch Wilkites at this time) protested energetically and held a meeting with Sir John Fielding at Bow Street. Radical opinion was further outraged by the decision to terrorize the weavers by hanging two of their leaders, Valline and Doyle, in the neighbourhood of their crimes. The Sheriffs, who had raised no protest against the execution of the coal-heavers in Stepney, at first refused to execute the warrant, but they were overruled and, on 6 December 1769, Doyle and Valline were hanged before a great crowd of weavers near the Salmon and Ball, in Bethnal Green. It was the last, and bloodiest, of the great weavers' outbreaks of the century.

Industrial movements continued into the 1770s, but they were never again on this scale and were never again attended by the same degree of violence. In February 1770 there was a strike of journeymen hat-dyers in Southwark, and 'at all shops they came to they obliged the men to strike in order to have their wages raised'; the hatters were involved in a further dispute in 1775. During the months of rising food prices in 1772, the tailors petitioned the London magistrates for a further increase in wages 'on account of the dearness of provisions', and won an increase of 6*d*. a day 'at ordinary times' and of 1*s*. a day 'in times of general mourning'. In October of that year, sailors assembled on Tower Hill and demanded a restoration of wage cuts imposed by their employers; and ten journeymen curriers were charged (and acquitted) at the Old Bailey for conspiring to raise their wages. In 1773 there was a recurrence of something of a combined movement of trades, when coal-heavers, watermen, carmen, porters and silk-weavers drew up petitions to the King. This time the magistrates, fearing disorder, forbade any march. But the weavers, at least, who were going through a period of massive unemployment, received some satisfaction. After a revival of riots in the weaving districts, masters and journeymen combined to make a joint approach to Parliament. The result was the Spitalfields Act, which, by empowering magistrates to fix wage-rates and enforce their observation, marked a return to the old Tudor protective legislation which had been allowed to fall into disuse. It also brought with it an interesting innovation. To keep the magistrates fully apprised of the state of trade, the weavers – both masters and men – formed a permanent body known as the 'Union'; and through it the weavers' case was presented to the justices and piece-rates were periodically determined.[1]

After this there was remarkably little industrial disturbance until the outbreak of the long wars with France; and Francis Place, writing in 1834, specifically recalled that the years 1777–94 had been lean in both

[1] *Annual Register*, 1770, p. 74; *Gentleman's Magazine*, 1772, pp. 241, 492, 596; S. and B. Webb, *The History of Trade Unionism*, 1896, pp. 46–9.

strikes and wage-increases.[1] There was at least one exception. The end
of the American War brought the usual problem of distress and unemployment among sailors discharged from the fleet. So once more, as in the
years following the peace of 1763, there were sailors' riots in 1783; and that
year sailors 'stopped all the outward-bound ships, many of which they
entirely unrigged; they compelled the merchants to discharge all foreign
seamen and engage English, at an advance of 12s. per month before they
were allowed to proceed'.[2]

We return to a phenomenon already noted in passing: the almost
complete absence of food riots in eighteenth-century London, at a time
when provincial cities and market towns were periodically convulsed by
them. There were certainly years of shortage and bad harvests, particularly frequent after the 1750s, when prices rose sharply and living standards were threatened. We have seen, too, that certain of these wages
movements arose directly in response to 'the dearness of provisions'. This
was evident enough in the case of those of the early months of 1768 (when
the cost of living was abnormally high) and of 1772 and 1773; and it is
perhaps significant that the East London riots against the Irish in 1736
occurred at the end of a month during which the price of the quarter of
wheat had risen from a range of 20s. to 25s. to one of 26s. to 36s. The
impact of food prices on popular disturbances was particularly marked
during the Wilkite agitation of 1768. On 18 April of that year, a few weeks
after Wilkes's triumphant election in Middlesex, the *Annual Register*
carried the following news item:

> Yesterday a ½-penny loaf, adorned with mourning Crape, was hung
> up at several parts of the Royal Exchange, with an inscription, con-
> taining some reflections touching the high price of bread and other
> provisions.

And, three weeks later, during a demonstration at the House of Lords, it
was reported that while some cried 'Wilkes and Liberty!', others cried
'that bread and beer were too dear & that it was as well to be hanged as
starved'.

So concern for the price of bread was, undoubtedly, on occasion, a
stimulus to popular disturbance; but, properly speaking, these were not
food riots, such as those that broke out in provincial centres in 1727,

[1] *London Life*, p. 361.
[2] Henry Humpherus, *History of the Company of Watermen and Lightermen*, vol. 2,
p. 357.

1740, 1756 or – most spectacularly – in 1766. The nearest London ever got to an outbreak of this kind before the wars with France was in April 1772; it was a time when the press reported that 'letters from almost every part of the Kingdom bring melancholy accounts of the distress of the poor and of their readiness to rise and to do mischief'. Not far from the capital, angry crowds besieged flour-mills and food-convoys at Chelmsford and Sudbury. Once more, 'inflammatory' hand-bills appeared in the city's streets: this time 'in Spitalfields & the points adjacent, with a view to excite the populace to rise on account of the high price of provisions'; and in the City of London itself, Lord Mayor William Nash, as he drove back from church, 'was roughly used by the populace for not lowering the price of food'.[1] Yet this never developed into a proper riot and certainly bore no resemblance, in either form or intensity, to those affecting other capital cities: even Paris, which was relatively free of them before the Revolution, had, in addition to more frequent 'murmurs' and 'commotions', serious outbreaks of bread-rioting in the near-famine years 1725, 1740 and 1775.

Why, then, was London, while so prone to other types of disturbance, so singularly exempt from these? We will offer only a few tentative explanations. In the first place, London, like Paris, was remarkably well favoured by its easy access to supplies. As Defoe observed in the 1720s, the whole Kingdom was employed 'to furnish something . . . to supply the city of London with provisions'. Wheat, in particular, reached the capital in ample quantities, except in the leanest years, from the granaries of Lincoln, East Anglia and Kent. Not only were London's markets well supplied but the authorities also kept a watchful eye on the price of wheat and bread, and the Assize of Bread, imperfect as it was, kept its fluctuations under some control. Such protective measures London shared with other capital cities, whose provisioning was considered a matter of national concern. But she had others besides. England, unlike France, was no longer a country of small peasant producers; and where Paris was ringed by and exposed to the frequent invasion of peasant communities that flocked into the capital to buy or sell in its markets, London was, at her most vulnerable point, cut off from the countryside by the protective shield of the near-urban county of Middlesex. So that a massive grain riot, such as that which almost literally swept into Paris from its rural belt in 1775, was impossible in a city like London. Moreover, for all the poverty of London's 'poor' (not to mention those whom Defoe termed 'the miserable'), the numbers of people whom a sudden rise in bread prices might

[1] *Wilkes and Liberty*, pp. 53, 188–90.

drive to utter destitution was probably at no time as great as in Paris. It may be, too, that the London journeymen's ability to form their own committees (we have noted the case of sailors, tailors and weavers) provided a further safeguard against food riots; for London must have been one of the very few places in which, as early as this, workers could hope for any measure of success in striking (or petitioning) for better wages at a time of shortage and rising prices.[1]

However, such safeguards could only be effective in relatively normal times. We shall see, in a later chapter, that even in London they were inadequate to withstand the shock of the inflation that followed from the wars with Revolutionary France.

[1] See George Rudé, 'Paris et Londres au XVIIIᵉ siècle: société et conflits de classes', shortly to appear in *Annales historiques de la Révolution française*.

11

The Political Riot

IN THE last chapter we considered movements of social protest involving the common people of London; here we shall be dealing with the more specifically 'political' riots or disturbances in which they became engaged. Of course, there is no strict division, no wall of Babylon, separating the one from the other. We already saw how London theatre rioters, for example, were inclined to be as hostile to French visiting performers (thus reflecting the political realities of the day) as to managers who charged higher prices for their seats. Equally, there were moments when the rioting weavers and coal-heavers of 1768, though mainly concerned with their own working conditions, showed a distinct political sympathy for Wilkes. Conversely, we shall see that political riots nearly always had undertones of social hostility. The main difference between them, in fact, is not so much the degree of social or political protest we can find in the one or the other as the extent to which the protesters were acting on their own initiative and in a cause that was essentially their own. This independence is evident enough in the case of the workers' riots, the industrial disputes and incipient protests over food prices that we have just been considering. It will not be so much in evidence in the more 'political' disturbances that are the subject of the present chapter. In these the initiative and the inspiration will be seen to come from others and the cause that is being promoted, though willingly adopted by the people in the streets, to come to them at second hand. Thus, in all such movements, there was an element of collusion between the 'middling' and 'inferior' classes, in which the latter played the role of a junior partner; and we shall see that this applies as much to High Church, gin and Excise as it does to 'Wilkes and Liberty' and the outburst against Popery in 1780. It is only in the course of the Revolutionary Wars that the roles became to some extent reversed and that we shall find the 'inferior set' (or, at least, the 'working trades' among them) setting up political organizations of their own and even setting the pace without waiting for the initial impetus to be given them by others.

The nature of this 'collusion', however, calls for a word of caution. It has too often been supposed that the rioters, as a junior partner, were an inert mass, willing to set their hand to any mischief provided that there was some prospect of easy loot or the satisfaction of some lurking criminal or destructive instinct. Such a picture in no way corresponds to the realities of Hanoverian London. There was never a mindless 'mob' willing to do any person's bidding; or, rather, this only happened on very rare occasions. In the so-called 'mug-house' riots of 1715 and 1716, there may have been a mercenary element among the rival gangs of 'loyalists' and 'Jacks' who fought it out with clubs and staves or muskets in and about the ale-houses of Fleet Street and the Strand. Again, there was a recognized political device known as 'raising a mob' and, as Burke wrote in a speech he drafted about 1769, 'many in the House find an use in Mobs'. It was a device used, in fact, by the Court candidate, Sir William Beauchamp Proctor, in his contest with Serjeant Glynn at the Brentford hustings, when he hired a gang of butchers, prizefighters and chairmen as a protection against his Radical opponents. But this has little to do with the riotous crowds whose activities are the subject of our present chapter.[1]

Let us begin with these activities in their 'High Church', Tory or Jacobite phase, which broadly covered (as in the case of the Common Hall of the City of London) the first forty years of the Hanoverian period. We saw, in an earlier chapter, how the Tory revival during the last years of Anne's reign had been marked by assaults on dissenters' houses and chapels during what became known as the Sacheverell Riots. A similar outbreak occurred soon after George I's accession. There were riots in Scotland at the end of the year, but, in London, Jacobite activity was at first confined to the distribution of anti-government tracts and ballads; among these, one tract in particular, entitled 'English advice to the freeholders of England', caused so much concern that a reward of £50 was offered for the discovery of its printer. There were also proclamations issued against rioters, though as a purely precautionary measure; for in the capital there were no riots until the elections of 1715 had been followed by punitive measures against the old Tory ministers, when

[1] Besant, pp. 75-6; *Wilkes and Liberty*, pp. 59-61, 196.

Lord Oxford was committed to the Tower and Bolingbroke and Ormond, threatened with impeachment, fled to France. On 23 April the anniversary of Queen Anne's coronation was noisily celebrated by supporters of the late ministers: wine was drunk round a barrel draped in a flag, householders were ordered to 'put out lights' and crowds paraded from Snow Hill to Holborn Bar to shouts of 'God Bless the Queen' and 'High Church' – a slogan that had developed by early May into 'High Church and Ormonde'.

The authorities expected trouble at the end of May, as the 28th was the new King's birthday and the 29th marked the anniversary of the restoration of Charles II. So precautions were taken to meet them: they proved to be effective in Westminster, where the justices decided to meet on successive days in the various parishes; they proved to be less so in the City and its neighbouring out-parishes. On 28 May crowds, chanting the slogan 'High Church and Ormonde', broke windows that were illuminated for George I. At Highgate, a Presbyterian meeting house was damaged and, at Aldersgate Church, the bell ropes were cut to prevent the ringing of the bells. Yet it all amounted to comparatively little; and the constable of Cheap, who reported a plot to raise 'mobs' at Cheapside, Whitechapel and Smithfield and claimed to have routed them single-handed and taken twenty-eight prisoners, may have been giving rein to an over-active imagination! And it is surely significant that London – unlike Worcester, the west midlands and the North – remained quiet on the Pretender's birthday which followed ten days later.

Six months later came the 'mug-house' riots, which lasted intermittently from November 1715 to July 1716. They took the form of ale-house fights between rival gangs of youths, enrolled respectively under the Hanoverian and Jacobite banner, who braced their muscles for the fray on a succession of Royal anniversaries. So there was a fight on 3 November, when the Jacobite Bridewell Boys (otherwise known as the 'Birds' or the 'Jacks'), who were smashing windows illuminated for the Prince of Wales's birthday on Ludgate Hill, were set upon by loyalists from the nearby Roebuck Inn. There was another fight on 16 November, when thirty 'Jacks' in Newgate Street were attacked by loyalists who had been celebrating Queen Elizabeth's birthday anniversary in St Martin's-le-Grand. This time there was bloodshed: 500 'Jacks' who attacked the Roebuck Inn were met by musket-fire, which killed two of the assailants. A lull followed till February, when the 'Jacks', commemorating the accession of James II, attacked Newcastle House in Leicester Fields. On 8

March, to mark the death of William and the accession of Anne, loyalists drove the 'Jacks' off the streets at Aldersgate, Newgate and Ludgate Hill. Similar affrays followed on the anniversaries of Queen Anne's coronation (also St George's Day) and of Charles II's restoration. Finally, at the end of July 1716, the 'Jacks' attacked Read's Mug-house (another loyalist stronghold) in Salisbury Court, off Fleet Street. As the police were slow to appear, Read took the law into his own hands, fired at his assailants and shot dead one Daniel Vaughan, whose funeral was attended by a large crowd; meanwhile, to shouts of 'High Church and Ormonde', Read's Mug-house sign, wrenched from its socket, was paraded round Fleet Street by the triumphant 'Jacks'. But, this time, the authorities decided to set a stern example. Five of the Jacobite rioters were arrested, sentenced to death and hanged at the end of Salisbury Court. This brought the 'mug-house' riots to an end and, with them, all open Jacobite agitation in the streets of the capital.[1]

After this, Jacobitism appears to have lost such attraction as it had as a rallying point for the common people of London. It is of course tempting – and certainly entertaining – to follow Sir Robert Walpole in looking for the Jacobite hidden hand in the various riots of the 1730s, but it seems to be a vain quest. At the time of the anti-Irish riots, for example, his informers were never able to give any genuine substance to their repeated talk of the activities of 'high church' or 'the lower sett of Jaco-bites'; and it seems perhaps a little far-fetched to suspect (as one of them did) that among those inciting the Shoreditch labourers to riot against the Irish were 'many cunning, Intriguing Persons of the better sort . . . in disguise, particularly several who are strongly suspected of being popish priests'![2] This is not to discount such Jacobite influences altogether; and in view of the known Jacobite sympathies of several City aldermen at the time of the Forty-Five, Pitt may well have been right to suppose that, had the Pretender succeeded in reaching London, the 'spirit of the population' might have 'taken a very different turn'. But, failing this eventuality, we have very little to go by. There was certainly no public display – at any social level – of pro-Jacobite sympathy; and the government's round-up of Papists, down-at-heel actors and beer-house tipplers turned up nothing more promising than the case of Joseph Payne, who was sentenced at the Old Bailey in December 1745 to pay 5*s*. with two

---

[1] D. C. G. Isaac, 'A Study of Popular Disturbances in Britain, 1714-1754', pp. 143-85; Sharpe, pp. 4-5.

[2] G. Rudé in *The Guildhall Miscellany*, no. 10, September 1959, p. 62.

months' gaol for having said 'Damn you and your king too!' to a couple of soldiers in a Bishopsgate pub![1]

But if London crowds shed their Jacobitism by 1716 or soon after, they certainly did not shed their hostility (any more than the City's Common Hall) to Walpole or the Pelhams; and this 'country' versus 'Court' attitude continued, for some years to come, to be Tory rather than Whig. We have already seen that Londoners, incensed by Sir Robert's plan for an Excise, adopted such slogans as 'No slavery – no excise – no wooden shoes!' and 'mobbed' him at the House of Commons, when he presented his Bill. There were also demonstrations and bonfires all over the capital, reaching a climax when it was known that the Bill would be withdrawn. It was most certainly a political protest in which the 'lower order' of people followed the lead given them by the City's livery and Common Council. But it was also a form of social protest of the poor against the rich, against those who lived at 'the polite end of the town'. So much is evident from an incident recorded by Viscount Perceval in his diary on 9 April 1733. 'The City is so inflamed,' noted Perceval, 'that some ladies were rudely stopped and the cry was: "We know this coach, it comes from St James's end of the town; knock the coachman down." One of the ladies having presence of mind, saved her servant by calling out: "Though we live at St James's end, we are as much against Excise as you." On which the mob said: "Are you so? Then God bless you. Coachman, drive on." '[2]

When the Minister withdrew his Bill, not only was the event celebrated with a further round of bonfires but it was proposed in the following year to commemorate it as a public anniversary in years to come; in the City, subscriptions for this purpose were invited through the press. At this stage, the Lord Mayor, Sir William Billers, and the Court of Aldermen parted company from the Common Hall and their supporters in the streets. Billers, advised by the aldermen, issued a precept for a special watch to be kept and ordered the arrest of any persons attempting to light bonfires or to create a disturbance. In consequence, a riot broke out in which Billers had his windows broken and, as he patrolled the streets, was pelted with dirt and stones. Moreover, as he went out of office shortly after, crowds pelted him again and tried to smash his coach. However, the Court of Aldermen stood by him, accorded him a heartfelt

---

[1] A. A. Mitchell, in *History Today*, October 1965, p. 724.
[2] Dorothy Marshall, *Eighteenth-Century England*, p. 151.

P

vote of thanks, and offered a reward of £50 for every offender brought to justice.[1]

Two years later, as we have seen, the agitation against Walpole's Gin Act followed hard on the heels of the anti-Irish riots in Spitalfields and Shoreditch. We noted, too, that there were no actual riots on the occasion of 'Madam Geneva's lying-in-state', in spite of the undoubted attempts made by some of the distillers to incite them. But, a full year after the Act had been passed, disturbances broke out in the summer of 1737. They were not directed against the Act itself, which was largely being ignored by the small retailers, but against the growing army of informers, who, attracted by a £5 reward, brought several of them to justice. On 28 July an informer was stoned to death in New Palace Yard, and two more three weeks later. In November, when Westminster's chief magistrate, Sir Thomas De Veil, convicted six retailers of breaking the new law, the informer concerned was seized and De Veil's house was threatened with destruction. Soon after, a fourth informer was done to death, and in December a crowd engaged in stoning a further two informers had to be cleared from Somerset House by the Guards. Another skirmish took place in Pulteney Street in January 1738, and in February one informer was killed and several were injured. The situation was now so serious that the government had to promise special protection to informers, and in May distillers, victuallers and coffeemen – so suspect had they become to the authorities – were made ineligible for service as constables or headboroughs. But, meanwhile, the occupation of informer had become so hazardous that informations against retailers were falling off, and by March 1739 they had ceased altogether. And by this time the Act itself, in all but name, was a dead letter.[2]

After the 1730s there was a considerable lull in popular political activity. Undoubtedly, the 'inferior set' of citizens supported the Corporation in its demands for war with Spain, they huzzaed for Admiral Vernon when he captured Porto Bello, they applauded the execution of the luckless Admiral Byng, and they could hardly fail to be impressed by the arguments used by the Common Council and the *London Evening Post* in condemning the Jewish Naturalization Act of 1753. But there appear to have been no considerable street demonstrations, and certainly no riots. These only revived, though at first in a muted form, with the swing of the City's political affiliation from Toryism to Radicalism with the advent of

[1] Sharpe, vol. 3, p. 38.

[2] D. C. G. Isaac, 'A Study of Popular Disturbances in Britain, 1714–1754', pp. 222–7.

William Pitt, aided by his lieutenant William Beckford. And before the arrival of Wilkes, Pitt was undoubtedly the most popular of all the politicians and statesmen of the eighteenth century with the tradesmen and small craftsmen of the capital. We have seen that the ordinary Londoner was easily given to religious intoleration, had a considerable contempt for foreigners (including the Scots and Irish) and felt a passionate concern to defend his 'Englishman's liberties' against both 'tyranny' at home and despotism (particularly when linked with Popery) abroad. This made him a natural ally of the Great Commoner who, as we have seen, lacking support within Parliament and Ministry and being an object of aversion to the King, only succeeded in 'storming the Closet' with the aid of the newly awakened opinion 'without-doors', and, in particular, that of the City of London. So when Pitt, failing to persuade his new colleagues to make war on Spain, resigned from office in October 1761, he was assured of a hero's welcome in the City, which shared his belligerent 'patriot' views. It became, in fact, an object of public scandal that the King's visit to the Guildhall, on 9 November (Lord Mayor's Day), was turned, on the initiative of Beckford, into a public demonstration – and near-riot – in support of the fallen minister. For Pitt was also a guest, and driving with Temple (who, too, had resigned his office), he was greeted with noticeably greater warmth in the City streets than George III himself. As for the King's Chief Minister, the new favourite, the Earl of Bute (a Scot, to make matters worse), he was pelted with mud and hooted and might, it was believed, have suffered serious injury if he had not hired a force of 'butchers and bruisers' to protect his carriage from direct assault.[1]

But, by this time, Pitt was already a declining force as a popular hero and leader of the streets: his acceptance of an earldom and a pension, on his retirement from office in 1761, was never quite forgiven him, and he became a virtual invalid soon after. And, eighteen months after the incident at the Guildhall, John Wilkes appeared on the scene in the *North Briton* affair; for nearly a dozen years, he was able to command on the hustings and in the streets, around the slogan of 'Wilkes and Liberty', a degree of personal loyalty and enthusiasm that Pitt, even in his heyday in the 1750s, had never quite attained. We have already told the Wilkes story in terms of its impact on the politics of the City; here we shall tell it briefly again in terms of the political riots and disturbances that sprang up in London in the wake of his remarkable career.[2]

[1] Sharpe, vol. 3, p. 69.
[2] For most of what follows, see *Wilkes and Liberty*, pp. 26 ff.

In both cases, it began with the *North Briton* in 1763. Wilkes himself struck the right note when, brought to Westminster Hall on 6 May, he prefaced his remarks to his judges by identifying his cause not only with 'the liberty of all peers and gentlemen' but also 'that of all the middling and inferior set of people, who stand most in need of protection'. The response was immediate; and when he rose to thank his judges after the verdict, 'the mob [as the Duke of Portland reported to Newcastle] could no longer refrain from expressing their approbation in the loudest & strongest terms'; and they appear at this stage to have been composed of both the 'middling' and the 'inferior' sorts, for George Onslow, another of Newcastle's numerous informants, told him that 'many thousands' of those who accompanied Wilkes to his Great George Street house after the hearing, to cries of 'Wilkes and Liberty' and 'Whigs for ever', were 'of a far higher rank than common Mob'. Soon after, Wilkes's successful claim for damages against the servants of the Crown was greeted by 'bonfires & rejoicing', and when his *Essay on Woman*, a parody on Pope, scandalized the Lords and estranged him from Chatham, his supporters of both the 'middling' and 'inferior set' remained unshakeably loyal. So when the Lords and Commons jointly ordered the Common Hangman to burn the offending No. 45 of the *North Briton* at the Royal Exchange, his followers in the streets intervened forcibly on their hero's behalf. At the appointed time, a large crowd of Londoners, 'to the number of 500 and more', gathered at the entrance to Cornhill, pelted the Sheriffs, Thomas Harley and Richard Blunt, with 'hard pieces of wood and dirt', smashed the glass of Harley's coach, rescued the *North Briton* from the flames, and made it impossible for hangman and Sheriffs to discharge their duties. Later, at the Old Bailey, John Franklin, a ship's steward, was fined 6*s.* 8*d.* for his part in the affair. The Commons duly voted the Sheriffs their thanks for attempting to carry out their wishes, but the Common Council pointedly refused to do so.

On his return from exile for the elections of 1768, Wilkes met with an immediate and enthusiastic response. While a candidate in the City, his sedan-chair was constantly carried shoulder-high to and from his headquarters at the King's Arm Tavern in Cornhill and the hustings at the Guildhall, and he was continually followed by eager supporters, both voters and others, 'huzzaing and crying *Wilkes and Liberty*'. But this was as nothing compared with the outburst that greeted his election in Middlesex a fortnight later. The election itself was orderly enough, but there were disturbances at Hyde Park Corner, through which the main body of voters passed on their way to Brentford. According to Horace Walpole, the Spitalfields weavers – as always champions of the 'Patriot' party – had mustered in strength in Piccadilly, giving out blue cockades and papers inscribed 'No. 45, Wilkes and Liberty', and objection was raised to two blue silk standards carried by Proctor's supporters, bearing the provocative inscriptions, 'No Blasphemer' and 'No French Renegade', which (it was said) 'raised an unhappy resentment in the populace'. A scuffle ensued in the course of which the glass on one of Proctor's coaches was broken and a Mr Cooke, son of the City Marshal, was pelted and knocked off his horse, and had the wheels stripped off his carriage and his harness slashed.

For the next two days Wilkes's supporters of 'the inferior set' held the streets and noisily celebrated his victory. Citizens were obliged to light up their windows at night, every door from Temple Bar to Hyde Park Corner was chalked with 'No. 45', and the Austrian ambassador (again, according to Horace Walpole) was dragged from his coach and had the slogan chalked on the soles of his boots! At night, wrote the *Annual Register*,

the rabble was very tumultuous; some persons who had voted for Mr Wilkes having put out lights, the mob paraded the whole town from east to west, obliging every body to illuminate and breaking the windows of such as did not do it immediately. The windows of the Mansion-house, in particular, were demolished all to pieces, together with a large chandelier and some pier glasses, to the amount of many hundred pounds. They demolished all the windows of Ld Bute, Lord Egmont, Sir Sampson Gideon, Sir William Mayne, and many other gentlemen and tradesmen in most of the public streets of both cities, London and Westminster. At one of the above gentlemen's houses, the mob were in a great measure irritated to it by the imprudence of a servant, who fired a pistol among them. At Charing Cross, at the Duke of Northumberland's, the mob also broke a few panes; but his Grace had the address to get rid of them by ordering up lights immediately into his windows, and opening the Ship alehouse, which soon drew them to that side.[1]

The next night, an eyewitness spoke of 'a Mob of about 100 men and boys' setting out from Charing Cross about nine o'clock in the evening and smashing windows in Leicester Fields, Covent Garden, Russell

[1] *Annual Register*, 1768, p. 86.

Street, the Strand, Long Acre, Oxford Street and Piccadilly. Before becoming lost to view in Southampton Street, they had broken the Duke of Newcastle's windows off Lincoln's Inn Fields and the lamp over Sir John Fielding's door in Bow Street, and drunk two gallons of beer to 'Wilkes and Liberty' at the Six Cans Tavern in Turnstile, Holborn. Among those arrested as the result of this incident was one Matthew Christian, a 'gentleman of character and fortune', late of Antigua, who was alleged to have spent £6 or £7 on filling the rioters with beer in a number of ale-houses.

The Common Council was indignant (the repair of the damage to the Mansion House alone was to cost more than £200) and, meeting at the Guildhall on 30 March, the Councilmen resolved to prosecute the rioters with the utmost rigour, offering rewards of £50 upon conviction. They met with remarkably little success, and the riots continued, with inter-missions, until nearly the middle of May. After Wilkes's appearance at the Court of King's Bench on 20 April, his temporary release was cele-brated by the rioting coal-heavers of Shadwell with shouts of 'Wilkes and Liberty, and coal-heavers for ever!'; further cries were heard of 'Damn you, light up your candles for Wilkes'; and soon every house along the Ratcliffe Highway was lighted up in his honour. A week later, as he was being escorted by the tipstaff across Westminster Bridge to the King's Bench prison, 'a number of persons [ran an official report] took off the horses, turned the coach round and, with expedition beyond conception, drew the coach through the Strand, and through Temple Bar, and into the City' – with Sir John Fielding and his clerk in hot pursuit. And so on to the Three Tuns Tavern by Spitalfields Church, where Wilkes appeared at an upper window and was acclaimed by his supporters before vanishing in disguise and under cover of dark to surrender to his jailers in St George's Fields. From now on riots were continuous for almost a fort-night. 'The next day,' a local chronicler noted,

> the prison was surrounded by a prodigious number of persons, but no disturbance happened till night, when the rails which enclosed the footway were pulled up to make a fire, and the inhabitants of the Borough were obliged to illuminate their houses, but a Captain Guard arriving soon after 12 the Mob dispersed.

The climax came on 10 May. It was the day of the opening of Parlia-ment and large crowds gathered outside the prison, many hoping to see their hero escorted to the Commons to take his seat. Shortly before midday, some of the demonstrators broke through the ranks of the Foot Guards surrounding the prison and affixed to the wall a paper bearing the lines:

> *Venal judges & Ministers combine*
> *Wilkes & English Liberty to confine;*
> *Yet in true English hearts secure their fame is,*
> *Nor are such crowded levies at St James's.*
> *While thus in Prison Envy dooms their stay,*
> *Here, O grateful Britons, your daily homage pay.*
> *Philo Libertatis no. 45.*

When, at the instance of the justices, the paper was removed, the demonstrators grew restive: there were shouts of 'Give us the paper' and 'Wilkes and Liberty for ever!' and stones were thrown at the soldiers. A captain and three grenadiers chased one of the stone-throwers, 'a man in a red waistcoast', off the Fields, and in a nearby cowhouse they shot dead William Allen, a publican's son, whom they mistook for their assailant. Other casualties followed. After the Riot Act had been twice read, the foot soldiers, by now reinforced by Horse Guards, opened fire and killed and wounded a score of persons, several of them casual spectators. The 'massacre' (as it became called) was followed by riots in the City and in Southwark. In Southwark, two magistrates, believed to have played an active part in 'suppressing the tumults', had their houses 'pulled down' in the traditional manner; they later recovered damages from the Treasury in two amounts of £491 5s. 6d. and £69 4s. 7d. In the City, crowds threw stones and 'damned the Lord Mayor', and more windows were broken at the Mansion House. There was also a noisy demonstration in Palace Yard followed by a riot outside the House of Lords.

After the May riots there was a considerable lull, only broken by the street celebrations accompanying Wilkes's birthday on 28 October and the excitement roused all over London in December by John Glynn's election to fill the vacancy left by George Cooke in Middlesex. In fact, it was not until 22 March 1769 that another great popular Radical demonstration took place. The occasion was the presentation of the 'loyal' merchants' petition to the King at St James's Palace, of which some mention has already been made. It was, for the merchants, a humiliating fiasco, for of the 130 who set out that morning from the City in their coaches only a mud-bespattered dozen got through to the Palace after what became known as 'the Battle of Temple Bar'. Their cavalcade, as the *Annual Register* tersely reported:

[was] interrupted by a desperate mob on passing through the City, who insulted, pelted and maltreated the principal conductors, so that several coaches were obliged to withdraw, some to return back, others to proceed by bye-ways, and those who arrived at St James's were so daubed with dirt, and shattered, that both masters and drivers were in the utmost peril of their lives.[1]

A far more detailed and more colourful account of the event was sent by Mrs Harris, the wife of James Harris, M.P., to her son, the future Earl of Malmesbury, at Madrid. She related how the merchants' passage was blocked by 'a hearse attended by an immense Mob' coming down Pall Mall. This hearse, which was 'decorated with prints and two pictures, one of which represented the killing of Allen in St George's Fields, the other the killing of Clarke in the riot at Brentford', was drawn by one white and one black horse and driven by a coachman dressed in black, who drove it close to Palace Gate and then up St James's Street, arriving just ahead of the battered merchants' procession. In shocked tones but not without malice, the lady continued:

During this period all the shops in the neighbourhood were shut. The merchants, when they got to St James's, could not find their address. The gates of Temple Bar having been shut against them, a most infamous riot took place there. Mr Boheme, the chairman, was insulted and forced to quit his coach, and got into a coffee-house; in the bustle he left the address in the coach, which was then carried back to his coach-house; this was made known to His Majesty, who said he *would wait for it, if it was till the next day*. At last, I believe, it was brought privately by water from Whitehall; it was four o'clock before it could be presented. . . . Your father was in St James's coffee-house all the morning, so saw the whole. Your sisters and I were at Clapham in the morning, and came down to Pall Mall in the midst of the mob. We let down our glasses, they cried Wilkes and Liberty enough to us, but did not insist on our joining them, so we got safe home, though I was a great deal flurried at the time. Many of the mob cried Wilkes, and no King, which is shocking to think on.

'Tis reported some of these rioters are sent to Newgate, and that seventeen are taken.[2]

[1] *Annual Register*, 1769, p. 84.
[2] *Letters of the First Earl of Malmesbury from 1745 to 1820*, ed. J. H. Harris, 1870, vol. 1, pp. 176–9.

But only five came up for trial, and they were all discharged by a Grand Jury in Westminster, a week later. The decision infuriated George III, who wrote angry notes to Lord North condemning the 'partial conduct' of the jurymen and demanding an enquiry.

There followed, soon after, the affair of the Middlesex election; but this was fought out in other terms: by the petitions and remonstrances of 'respectable' gentry, freeholders and burgesses, in which the street demonstrations of the 'lower order' of citizens played little or no part. So there was another lull until the 'printers' case' of 1771, with its head-on-collision between the City and the Commons, once more made rioting the order of the day. When Lord Mayor Crosby, summoned to attend the House with Richard Oliver, set out for Westminster on 19 March, he was attended by a considerable escort of citizens. Handbills had been distributed in the City, inviting 'Liverymen, Freemen and Citizens' to assemble at the Mansion House and give him a good send-off. In fact, the *Gentleman's Magazine* reported:

> a prodigious crowd of the better sort were at the Mansion House and in the streets near it, who testified their approbation by repeated huzzas, which were continued quite from the Mansion House to the House of Commons. On his arrival there, one universal shout was heard for near three minutes; and the people, during the whole passage to the House, called out to the Mayor as the *People's Friend*, the *Guardian of the City's rights and the Nation's Liberties*.[1]

And when the Lord Mayor, who was suffering from a bad attack of gout, was allowed to retire, he was 'attended by a great number of people', many of whom unharnessed his horse at St Paul's and drew his carriage in triumph back to the Mansion House. A week later, when the sitting resumed, there was a further 'prodigious concourse of people about the Mansion House' to see the magistrates off and great crowds, who had gathered volume and momentum from the City to Westminster, surged round the Houses of Parliament, many wearing labels inscribed 'Crosby, Wilkes, Oliver, and the Liberty of the Press'. Members had difficulty in entering St Stephen's Chapel and were subjected to insults (wrote Mrs Harris) 'by a most blackguard set of shabby fellows', who were eventually dispersed by the High Constable and the Westminster justices. Oliver was put in the Tower forthwith, but Crosby, still swathed in bandages, was again allowed to go home. Two days after, he was escorted once

[1] *Gentleman's Magazine*, 1771, pp. 139-40.

more by vast crowds to Westminster for the final act in the drama. At St Martin's Lane, the horses were removed and the carriage was drawn to Palace Yard, where 50,000 people ('most of whom appeared to be respectable tradesmen') were waiting. Members, particularly those of the Court party, had the greatest difficulty in getting through to the Commons. Lord North's hat was taken off and cut to ribbons, his 'chariot glasses' were shattered, his carriage was broken to pieces, and he was only rescued from serious injury by the intervention of an opposition Member, Sir William Meredith. Similar treatment was reserved for the 'two Cubs' – Charles James and Stephen Fox – who (according to one report) had their carriages broken and their clothes torn and (according to another) were 'greatly insulted and pelted with mud'. The King, too, was insulted the next day as the State coach passed down Parliament Street, and Gregory Brown, a hosier of Coleman Street, is reputed to have shouted, 'No Lord Mayor, no King!' Meanwhile, pandemonium reigned, for several hours, within and without the House as Crosby's fate was being decided. Eventually, with the aid of the London Sheriffs and various opposition Members (including Edmund Burke), the crowd was persuaded to disperse and Crosby, found guilty of a breach of privilege, was sent to join Oliver in the Tower.

Further popular demonstrations followed. On 1 April a hearse and two carts appeared on Tower Hill, and figures representing the Princess Dowager, Lord Bute, the Speaker and the two Foxes were beheaded by a chimney-sweep in clerical garb, and burnt. A few days later a similar fate befell the stuffed dummies of Lord Halifax, Lord Barrington, Alderman Harley, Colonel Luttrell ('the usurper'), Colonel Onslow ('cocking George') and William de Grey, the Attorney-General. In short, all the most prominent 'enemies of the people', since the affair of the *North Briton*, were taken care of, one by one. A few weeks later, when Parliament was prorogued and the prisoners were released from the Tower, they were given an impressive escort back to the City, to the accompaniment of 'loud and universal huzzas'. The City was illuminated in their honour and, as a final gesture of defiance against the enemy entrenched in Westminster, Sir Fletcher Norton, the Speaker, had his windows smashed by an angry crowd.

A year later, Wilkes, having served his term as Sheriff, made his first bid for the mayoralty. When the Court of Aldermen cast precedent aside and 'pricked' for Townsend, despite his lower vote, his supporters were outraged and staged a violent demonstration against the successful

candidate on Lord Mayor's Day. That evening, when the new Lord
Mayor returned to the Guildhall after his inaugural procession, a crowd
of 3,000, 'headed by some sailors', filled the yard. The constables were
forced to beat a hasty retreat, while the crowd attacked the iron gates at
the entrance to the Hall 'and pulled down and burnt the different temporary erections for the day'. Ladies arriving for the Lord Mayor's party
were asked for money 'to drink Mr Wilkes's health' and there were angry
shouts of 'It is Wilkes's turn' and 'D—n my Lord Mayor for a scoundrel,
he has got Wilkes's right, and we will have him out.' Distinguished guests
were molested: 'One gentleman I saw,' stated a witness, 'had a part of
his head of hair cut off.' Bonfires were lit and the riot continued until
two in the morning. The Hon. Artillery Company, whom the crowd
(after first mistaking them for the Guards) treated with scant respect,
took seven prisoners, of whom one was later sentenced to five weeks in jail.[1]

Two years later, Wilkes's election was received in the City with tumultuous acclaim. The horses were taken from the mayoral coach and he
was drawn in triumph to the Mansion House. The unpopular Alderman
Harley had his windows broken once again, and the Lord Mayor-elect
had the duty – and, no doubt, the grim satisfaction – of committing the
culprit for trial at the Old Bailey. It was the last of the Wilkite riots. In
December Wilkes regained his seat in Parliament, and from now on his
career was divided between the House of Commons and the Guildhall
(where, having served his mayoral term, he held the post of Chamberlain
after 1779). Thus, having achieved his ambitions and found a safe haven,
he had little more use for 'Wilkes and Liberty'.

So the crowd had to find other heroes. For a brief while in 1779 it
was an Admiral of the Fleet, Augustus Keppel, who later, with Radical
support, became M.P. for Southwark. Keppel, in an engagement with
the French off Ushant in July 1778, had quarrelled with his second-in-
command, Sir Hugh Palliser. As Palliser was a Lord of the Admiralty
and Keppel a member of the Rockinghamite opposition, the quarrel
inevitably took a political turn. Keppel was sent before a Court Martial
at Portsmouth, whose findings were anxiously awaited for a month. At
last, late on 11 February, news reached London that Keppel had been
honourably acquitted. The capital became a blaze of lights, guns were
fired and bells were rung. Palliser, seen as the villain-of-the-piece, had to
escape to Portsmouth while a house he had once occupied in St James's
Square was stripped and its contents burned in the street outside. Lord

[1] Old Bailey *Proceedings*, 1773, pp. 46–59, 68, 114–15.

George Germain's house received the same treatment. The gates of the Admiralty were taken off their hinges and a bonfire was made of its plush sedan-chairs. Lord North and the Earl of Sandwich (both seasoned enemies of the crowd) had their windows broken. The next day, the Common Council played its part in the affair by rewarding Keppel with the Freedom of the City and a highly 'loaded' vote of thanks

> for his spirited behaviour on the 27th of July last in his attack on the French fleet, for his glorious and gallant efforts to renew the engagement in the afternoon of that day, efforts rendered unsuccessful thro' the want of obedience to his orders by the Vice-Admiral of the Blue.[1]

Another short-lived hero was Lord George Gordon; yet he provoked a disturbance which, in its scope and destructiveness, far exceeded any of the riots associated with the name of Wilkes.[2] Two questions immediately arise: why should Lord George, a man of limited political capacity and one little known to the public at large, have been able to provoke, whether deliberately or not, such an extraordinary outburst of destructive fury? And why should a cause so repugnant to liberals and Radicals of later generations have been so eagerly embraced not only by the people in the streets but also by the Radical politicians of the City? The same answer applies to both questions. Popery remained, two hundred years after Philip of Spain and the Spanish Armada, associated in the popular mind with 'wooden shoes' and foreign enslavement. There had been the dread of a massacre of Protestant Englishmen by Irish Catholics on the eve of the Civil War; again, there was the panic aroused by James II's reputed Catholic army of 1688, following hard on the heels of the scare fomented by Titus Oates at the time of the Popish Plot. So anti-Catholicism was not only part of the stock-in-trade of Protestant bigots (such as flocked into Lord George's Protestant Association) but also a part of the political tradition of the people, which had been consecutively nourished by Republican, Whig or 'Patriot' agitation, and most recently by the new Radicalism in London. Moreover, in 1780, England was at war, not only with the American colonists – for whom there was a large measure of sympathy – but with the old traditional enemy, the Catholic Powers of France and Spain. And only a half-dozen years before, the passage of the

---

[1] Sharpe, vol. 3, pp. 172-3; Besant, pp. 480-1.
[2] G. Rudé, in *Transactions of the Royal Historical Society*, 5th series, vol. 6, 1956, pp. 93-114; J. P. de Castro, *The Gordon Riots*, 1926.

Quebec Act, which gave a new constitution (including 'French laws') to Canada, had been greeted by angry crowds with shouts of 'No Popery!', and its terms had been denounced by a combination of Whig politicians, the Earl of Chatham and the City of London. Though the bishops of the Established Church remained singularly unmoved, the Common Hall and Common Council (prompted by Wilkes and Bull) presented a strong petition against the Bill as 'unduly favouring Roman Catholics', and begged the King to withhold his assent after the Bill had been accepted by both Houses.[1] So there was no lack of continuity between the Whig and Radical agitation of 1774 and the chorus of disapproval, voiced in their various ways by the City, the Protestant Association and the rioting crowds, against the Catholic Relief Act of 1778. And, clearly, the tradition within which their protests lay was Radical and 'levelling' and decidedly not Tory.

To return to the riots of which only a brief mention was made in an earlier chapter. We saw then that Lord George Gordon, on that morning of 2 June, brought his Protestant followers to the House of Commons, in four great marching columns, to support their anti-Catholic petition. They were said to be composed of 'the better sort of tradesmen'; and Lord George had previously insisted that they should be 'decent' and 'dressed in their sabbath days cloaths'. So the whole affair started with respectable persons of 'the middling sort', who, as Lord George was to assure Lord Hilsborough, were 'of a different description' from the rioters in the streets;[2] and the same could, without much doubt, be said of the 44,000 signatories to the Protestant petition (though this, unfortunately, has long disappeared). But the crowd, as it waited in Parliament Square, underwent a transformation. It had earlier been reported that the Spitalfields weavers were mustering, and it may be supposed that many others of the 'inferior set' attached themselves to the demonstrators who, to shouts of 'No Popery!', hustled and buffeted the members of both Houses as they arrived in their coaches. But it was only late at night, after the Commons had adjourned and the Guards had cleared a passage for the imprisoned Members, that the demonstration itself changed its character. At this point, one section of the crowd moved off towards the private chapel of the Sardinian ambassador in Duke Street, Lincoln's Inn Fields, another to the chapel attached to the Bavarian Embassy in

[1] Sharpe, vol. 3, pp. 142–3; *Gentleman's Magazine*, 1774, p. 444.
[2] 'Lord George Gordon's Narrative', fos. 6–8, 60; B.M., MS. 42, 129 (transcript in G.L.).

Warwick Street, St James's. The first, known to be frequented by English Catholic gentry, was burned to the ground; both were plundered and ransacked and their contents burned in the streets. Fourteen persons were arrested, of whom five were later committed to Newgate.

The next evening, crowds gathered in Ropemakers' Alley, Moorfields, where there were known to be a Catholic mass-house and the houses of a number of prosperous Catholics. At first they were dissuaded or dispersed by the constables, but the next night and the day following, doubtless encouraged by the supineness of the Lord Mayor, Brackley Kennet, and the reluctance of the constables to intervene, they pulled down the Roman chapel, destroyed the personal property of the priest, Mr Dillon, and of four of his lodgers, and damaged a number of neighbouring houses, not all of them occupied by Roman Catholics. The same day, the houses of Messrs Maberley and Rainsforth, two justices who had played a part in the arrest of prisoners, were pulled down in Westminster, and in Leicester Fields Sir George Savile, the promoter of the Act, was threatened. An expedition was made to Virginia Street, by Wapping, where, in spite of the efforts of the local Irish to rally in support of their priest, Dr Copps, the mass-house was destroyed and neighbouring Catholic dwelling-houses were attacked. In adjoining Spitalfields rioters damaged the houses of a number of Catholic brokers and manufacturers.

Parliament reassembled on Tuesday, 6 June, at three o'clock. Crowds had once more gathered at its approaches wearing blue cockades and shouting slogans; and Sir George Osborne told the Commons that 'people from Wapping were just then arriving with large beams in their hands and seemed determined to make an attack on the soldiers'.[1] So it was decided to adjourn till Thursday morning. At five o'clock, Justice Hyde attempted to overawe the demonstrators by reading the Riot Act and ordering the Horse Guards to disperse them. He was rewarded for his pains by having his house destroyed in St Martin's Street, off Leicester Fields. And from there the cry went up 'To Newgate!' While a smaller party made off to Bow Street to 'pull down' Sir John Fielding's house and office, the mass of the rioters headed, through Long Acre and Holborn, for Newgate Gaol. Preceded by thirty men armed with bludgeons, crowbars and chisels, they arrived at the Old Bailey shortly before eight o'clock. Having fired the house of the keeper, Mr Akerman, they wrenched open the prison gates, released all prisoners and set fire to the buildings. When Dr Johnson went by the next morning, he found the prison 'in

[1] 'Lord George Gordon's Narrative', fos. 45–6.

ruins, with the fire yet glowing', while 'the protestants' (he wrote to Mrs Thrale) were quietly plundering the Sessions House at the Old Bailey, 'as men lawfully employed in full day'.[1]

The next point of attack was Lord Mansfield's house in Bloomsbury Square. Lord Mansfield had earned the particular hostility of the rioters both as Lord Chief Justice (as such he had committed Wilkes to the King's Bench prison a dozen years before) and as a warm advocate of the Catholic Relief Act; in fact, the rumour had been spread 'that he had advised the Dragoons to ride over the Protestants, that he was a Roman Catholic and that he had made the King one!' An orgy of looting and destruction followed; Mansfield's residence and his library of precious books and manuscripts were gutted or pulled to pieces; firemen, called to the scene, were forced to stand idly by. It was here that the military fired for the first time and, when the crowds dispersed at daybreak, they left several dead behind them.

The next day ('Black Wednesday', Horace Walpole called it), the riots reached their climax. Destruction was widespread: in Westminster, the City and the Middlesex out-parishes, houses, shops and offices occupied by Catholic merchants, businessmen, shopkeepers and justices were attacked and pulled down or damaged; public houses were destroyed in Golden Lane and Whitechapel. But, in the evening, the main centre of disturbance lay to the west and south of the City. At about six o'clock, a band of rioters arrived at the premises of Thomas Langdale, a wealthy Roman Catholic distiller, who occupied two great blocks of buildings between Holborn and Field Lane. It was said that 'there was a Roman chapel in the house'; and whether it was due to this or to the attraction of the vast quantities of gin (estimated at 120,000 gallons and valued at £38,000) stored in their cellars, the two distilleries were broken into and fired. The result was appalling: the vats ignited and the fire spread to adjoining buildings. While men, women and children struggled to collect or lap up the flaming liquor, twenty-one neighbouring houses caught fire. To onlookers it seemed that the whole city was ablaze, and, recording the scene on the following day, Walpole wrote: 'I remember the Excise and the Gin Act and the rebels at Derby and Wilkes' interlude and the French at Plymouth, or I should have a very bad memory; but I never till last night saw London and Southwark in flames!'[2]

[1] Wheatley and Cunningham, vol. 2, p. 592.
[2] *The Letters of Horace Walpole, Earl of Orford*, ed. P. Cunningham, 1891, vol. 7, p. 388.

And more was to come. The Fleet prison, a few hundred yards from Langdale's, was attacked, the dwelling-house of the keeper was fired and the prisoners were released. Marchers crossed the river to St George's Fields and joined local rioters in setting fire to the King's Bench prison, the New Gaol, Southwark, and the Surrey House of Correction; the Marshalsea – a debtors' prison – was attacked and its inmates turned loose. In East Lane, Bermondsey, a Roman mass-house was destroyed and neighbouring Catholic houses damaged or pulled down. Blackfriars Bridge was taken by storm, the halfpence removed from its tills and the toll-houses set ablaze. As a climax, an attempt was made to capture the Bank of England; but this time the City wards had begun to organize themselves for defence, and the London Military Association (in whose ranks Wilkes played a conspicuous part) and regular troops made a stand at the Royal Exchange and repulsed the rioters with heavy casualties.

The next day, the riots continued in Southwark and Bermondsey; the public houses and dwellings of Roman Catholics and others were attacked in a dozen streets. A Catholic pastry-cook's shop was destroyed in the City; in Bishopsgate and Holborn, men were arrested for soliciting with threats. Fifty persons were arrested in the ruins of Newgate. There were bloody skirmishes in Fleet Street and St George's Fields. But the riots were all but over. The military, by now numbering more than 10,000 men, were in full possession of the streets. On the 9th, Lord George Gordon, still protesting his innocence in the whole affair, was escorted to the Tower from his house in Welbeck Street. Nothing remained but the judicial and financial reckoning and the counting of the dead.

On all accounts the cost was considerable. Of 450 prisoners taken, 160 were brought to trial; and of these 25 were hanged and another 12 were imprisoned. The toll taken by the military was far greater: 210 persons were killed outright, 75 died in hospital and 173 others were treated for wounds. The damage to property was perhaps less than might have been expected: some fifty buildings, both private and public, had been seriously damaged or destroyed and something over £100,000 was paid in compensation to a host of claimants. Such were the Gordon Riots, perhaps the most violent and the most savagely repressed of all the riots in London's history.

Indeed, all these disturbances had their own distinctive features: they varied in their scope and intensity and in the causes and issues they were seeking to promote. Yet, in certain other respects, there is a common

48 'The Tars Triumph' or 'The Bawdy House Battery', showing the destruction of the Star Tavern in 1749 (*British Museum*)

49 The mob assembled to pull down the bawdy-house kept by Peter Wood in the Strand, 1749

pattern to which they all conform, a pattern which marks and distinguishes the urban riots of eighteenth-century England. First, as to the methods used by the rioters. We have noted their tendency to operate in itinerant bands, marching (or running) through Shoreditch, Holborn, the Strand, the City of London, Westminster or Southwark, gathering fresh forces on the way, but always retaining a strong nucleus of local men who were readily recognizable to publicans and other eyewitnesses. This feature applies as much to social-protest movements such as that against the Irish in 1736 as to the 'High Church' disturbances of 1715, the Wilkite episode of 1768, and the 'No Popery' riots of 1780. And these bands were frequently 'captained' by men enjoying temporary authority – men like Tom the Barber, who led a contingent in Goodman's Fields in July 1736, or Thomas Taplin, a coach master, who directed the collection of money 'for the poor Mob' in Great Russell Street during the Gordon Riots; similar leaders were described to the police in the Wilkite riot of March 1768. These men may also have passed to their followers the slogans of the day: 'No slavery – no Excise – no wooden shoes' in 1733, 'Wilkes and Liberty!' in 1768, and 'No Popery!' in 1780. They may, too, have been the bearer of 'lists' of houses that were to come down or whose windows were to be smashed. Whether such 'lists' existed in fact or were merely figments of the imagination of informants, it is certain enough that the houses of selected victims were picked out for special treatment. By such direct-action methods considerable damage was done, as we saw; but it is also important to note that it was strictly discriminating and directed against carefully selected targets. This goes without saying in such limited operations as those directed against Lord Mayor Billers in 1734 or in support of Admiral Keppel in 1779. But even in the Gordon Riots, considerable care was taken to avoid damage to neighbouring property, and where the wrong targets suffered it was due to the wind rather than to the rioters' intentions. Violence was discriminating in another sense as well. It was generally limited (though we have seen that there were exceptions) to property and, of all the lives lost in 1780, it is remarkable that all were from the side of the rioters and not one from among their victims.

Nor were the rioters, on these occasions, the 'criminal elements' or 'slum population' imagined by those writers who have taken their cue from the often prejudiced accounts of contemporary observers. An anonymous informer of 1780 gave the following description of the Gordon rioters:

Q

200 house brakers with tools;
550 pickpockets;
6,000 alsorts;
50 men that . . . gives orders what to be done; they only come att night.

In a similar vein, an eyewitness of the assault on the Bank describes the assailants as being composed of 'thieves of every species'.[1] But the picture, for all its apparent authenticity, turns out to be largely fanciful. From the records of those brought to trial at the Old Bailey, at the Southwark Sessions House and at the Surrey Assizes, we may be reasonably confident that the rioters were a fair cross-section of London's working population: two in every three of those tried were wage-earners, journeymen, apprentices, waiters, domestic servants and labourers; a smaller number were petty employers, craftsmen and tradesmen. In the anti-Irish riots of 1736, as we might expect from their nature and origins, wage-earners formed an even larger proportion; whereas the Wilkite rioters appear again to have been a similar mixture of wage-earners, small employers and independent craftsmen. Such elements, too, although seldom appearing on the lists of householders assessed for the poor rate, were rarely vagrants, rarely had criminal records of any kind, generally had settled abodes, and tended to be 'sober' working men rather than slum-dwellers or the poorest of the poor. It is also perhaps a surprising fact that the most riotous parts of London, not only on these occasions but on others, were not the crowded quarters of St Giles in the Fields or the shadier alleys of Holborn but the more solid and respectable popular districts of the City, the Strand, Southwark, Shoreditch and Spitalfields.[2]

Another constant element (we have already noted the point in passing) is that of an underlying class hostility of the poor against the rich. We saw how the Excise rioters of 1733 quite naturally selected their targets from the coaches coming from 'the polite end of the town'. In March 1768 Wilkes's supporters celebrated his election to Parliament by smashing the windows of lords and ladies of opulence and fashion with gay abandon; and they made little distinction, in picking out their victims, between government and opposition members. Another good opportunity for socially selective window-breaking was provided by the vindication of Admiral Keppel. But this concern to settle accounts with the rich was

[1] P.R.O., State Papers 37, no. 20, fo. 200; Besant, p. 492.
[2] G. Rudé, in *The Historical Journal*, vol. 2, 1959, pp. 1–18.

even more strikingly displayed in the Gordon Riots. Overtly, the rioters proclaimed their abhorrence of Catholicism in general; but, as it turned out, the Catholics and Catholic sympathizers whose houses were attacked were not those living in the densely populated Catholic districts (whether in St Giles in the Fields, Saffron Hill or the dockside parishes of East London), but in the more salubrious and fashionable areas of Westminster or the City; and it was not the Catholic craftsmen and labourers – men similar to themselves – who engaged the rioters' attention, but gentlemen, publicans, manufacturers and merchants.

And it was precisely this socially discriminating attitude that worried the City Fathers in the later stages of the Gordon Riots, particularly when they developed into an attack on Blackfriars Bridge, the Royal Exchange and the Bank of England. So they saw the red light and, as one of them said, began to 'shut their ears against the voices of popular clamour'. In so doing, they snapped the threads that had so long linked the activities of the streets with the debates and resolutions of the Guildhall. The result was to put a damper on popular Radicalism and all forms of popular street activity for a dozen years to come. They revived; but, as we shall see in the next chapter, the old collusive partnership was never quite restored.

12

London and the French Wars

THE HANOVERIAN century may, for convenience, be divided into three main periods: that extending from the death of Queen Anne to the end of the 1750s, the thirty years from the accession of George III to the outbreak of the French Revolution, and the period of the wars with Revolutionary France and Napoleon. Each brought important changes to London, to its growth and appearance and its pattern of life; but none affected it so deeply and transformed it so quickly as the twenty-two years separating the outbreak of war with France in 1793 from the fall of Napoleon in 1815.

In the first place, these years were years of a quite unprecedented economic expansion, which, though it affected the north and the midlands more than London, made a considerable impact on the capital as well. Yet this general 'boom' was by no means continuous and was offset by periodical crises that were often alarming and left in their wake a trail of hardship, misery and distress. Thus, in 1793, a few months after the wars started, there was a severe financial and economic crisis. County banks (though none of the London banks) closed down; there was a sharp decline in foreign trade; in 1794, only 714 new ships were built where 1,156 had been built in 1787; and the number of bankruptcies (in 1793) was over double that in each of the three preceding years. After a distinct recovery in the next three years, there was a greater recession in 1797. It was a year of military defeats for Britain's allies, of mutinies, invasion scares and of a general loss of business confidence; besides, the Bank of England's stocks of bullion, due to large-scale loans and foreign shipments, had become dangerously depleted. In February, the Bank declared a moratorium on all cash-payments; there was a further slump in foreign trade, a further upward curve in the number of bankruptcies, and the crisis in shipbuilding, which particularly hit the Thames-side shipyards, obstinately persisted. Meanwhile, the poor had, in certain years, to suffer a double burden by a disastrous rise in the price of food. The quarter of wheat rose from an average of 60s. 6d. in 1794 to 91s. 8d. in 1795; and, in 1800, it reached the then fantastic price of 142s. 10d. So that, in that year, a London family who had been paying 6½d. for the quartern loaf (4 lb) at the outbreak of war were now paying nearly 1s. 4d.

Once more, trade revived: in foreign trade, there was a great boom in the last two years of the century and even shipbuilding (the most persistently depressed of the nation's industries) had a temporary recovery. But a third, and a far more serious, crisis developed between 1808 and 1812, largely as the result of Napoleon's economic blockade and Britain's own retaliatory measures. The Emperor launched his Continental System, intended to bring Britain to her knees by sealing her off from Europe, at Berlin in 1806. At first, its purpose failed: Britain's sea-lanes remained open, new markets were found or old markets reopened in the Baltic, America, Portugal and the Near East. But, as long as Napoleon held a firm grip on the European coastline, Britain's cross-Channel trade inevitably declined; her total exports fell from a value of £48 millions in 1805 to £41 millions in 1806 and £35 millions in 1808. The decline was marked by the closure of further shipyards on the Thames; and, once more, bullion was drained off, in payments to Europe, from the Bank of England: £6 millions in 1808, £9 millions in 1809, and £14 millions in 1810. To make matters worse, relations with the United States steadily deteriorated due to British insistence on searching neutral merchant ships, leading to a war with America in 1812; and, after two disastrous harvests, the country faced near-famine conditions in 1811–12, when the price of the quartern loaf in London rose to a new record of 1s. 5d. – a predicament from which, ironically enough, she was partly saved by Napoleon's willingness (as a true Mercantilist) to barter European grain for English gold!

Yet, grim and dramatic as these disasters were, they were offset for many by the general stimulus given to the nation's trade and industry by the long years of war and industrial revolution. France emerged from the wars with her economy badly dented; but Britain did not. Napoleon's blockade may have slowed down the rate of her industrial expansion and diverted her investments into other fields, but of the reality of that expansion there can be no doubt at all. Her output of pig-iron rose from

68,000 tons in 1788 to 300,000 tons in 1815. Imports of raw cotton, for her expanding cotton mills, rose from 32½ million pounds to 60½ million pounds between 1788 and 1802. Exports of made-up cotton cloth increased from £1 million in 1785 to £5½ million in 1800 and £18½ million in 1809. The total value of foreign trade, which had been £41½ million in 1792, had risen to £69 million in 1800 (a year of boom) and, after severe set-backs in 1808 and 1811, rose again to £65½ million in 1812 and £68 million in 1815. Banking continued, in or out of crisis, to be a profitable under-taking; and the Bank of England's profits from discounts rose from £193,000 in 1792-3 to £633,000 in 1806-7, and to a record figure of over £900,000 in 1809-10; as the wars ended, it was paying an interest of 10 per cent on a capital of £11,642,400.

Yet shipbuilding had, as we noted, suffered from a series of depressions, which, with a three-year intermission after 1800, extended over the greater part of the wars. But there was a revival in 1814 and, with the peace, there came a further forward leap in the construction of ships for the merchant navy. This expansion, however, did not apply to London; for new building had, since the wars began, become increasingly centred in Scotland, Tyneside and Wales and new contracts were being placed with Newcastle, Sunderland and Leith (or, in the case of warships, with Portsmouth and Plymouth) rather than with the old shipyards of the Thames-side at Blackwall, Deptford and Chatham. So one of the economic effects of the war had been to shift the focus of shipbuilding, as of shipping in general, away from London to the rapidly expanding shipyards of the west and the north. But while London's share of the nation's shipping and shipbuilding declined, there was no absolute decline in the number of vessels that docked in her harbours or the volume of goods that was loaded or un-loaded at her wharves. The opposite, indeed, was the case; and the tonnage of shipping entering London from foreign ports from 235,000 in 1751 had risen to 620,000 by 1794. The expansion of coastwise shipping entering the port of London was of a similar order, rising from 512,000 tons in 1750 to 1,176,000 tons in 1795; and the number of ships of both kinds using the port rose from 14,000 in 1794 to 15,600 in 1795 and to 20,700 in 1822. And it was, as we have seen, largely in response to this added pressure of both foreign and coastwise trade that Parliament decided, at long last, in the early years of the wars, to take the first steps to give London an up-to-date system of docks. In the teeth of considerable opposition from the City's Lord Mayor and Court of Aldermen – not to mention the Company of Watermen – an Act to build the West India Dock was passed in 1797. Three years later the dock was opened; by 1808 it was handling close on 600 ships. The West India Dock was followed, in the course of the next five years, by the London, East India and Surrey Commercial Docks; so that, with the exception of St Katharine Dock (completed in 1828), the foundations of London's present dockland had been firmly laid by the end of the Napoleonic Wars. Moreover, the war and the countless activities it promoted inevitably found work for hands that might otherwise have been idle; and even so confirmed a pessimist as Patrick Colquhoun was led grudgingly to concede that the new avenues of employment that the war had opened up along the riverside had led, temporarily at least, to an abatement in crime in the dockland areas. For, as he wrote early in the wars, 'the resource afforded by the present war gives employment, for a time only, to many depraved characters and mischievous members of the community'.[1]

The war years brought other material improvements besides: for example, in the supply of water and the lighting of streets. Iron water pipes, which had first been introduced in western residential districts in 1756, came into general use after 1810. Gas-lighting, as we saw in an earlier chapter, made its first public appearance in the City of London in 1807; in 1810, after Winsor's successful experiments in Pall Mall, a company was formed to promote his ideas, and Westminster Bridge was the first of the London bridges to be illuminated by gas in 1812. The spread of the new method was rapid in the residential and main commercial districts and, twenty years later, there were 39,504 public gas-lamps, lighting 215 miles of London's streets.[2]

But it was not until later in the new century that such devices did much to touch the lives of the ordinary people of the metropolis; meanwhile, the small shopkeepers, craftsmen and working people continued to live and work by oil or candle-light; and the humble residents of the East End and south of the River continued to live in overcrowded homes and to draw their water from the pump across the street. Yet there seems little

[1] T. S. Ashton, *The Economic History of England. The Eighteenth Century*, 1964, pp. 140–5, 239, 252–4; Steven Watson, *The Reign of George III, 1760–1815*, 1960, pp. 466–70, 504–20; M. Andreades, *History of the Bank of England*, 1966, pp. 187–202; Sir John Clapham, *The Bank of England*, vol. 2. pp. 14–15, 433; A. Briggs, *The Age of Improvement*, 1959, pp. 162–9; Sir Joseph G. Broodbank, *History of the Port of London*, vol. 1, pp. 80–1, 156; Henry Humpherus, *History of the Company of Watermen and Lightermen*, vol. 3, pp. 7–112; Patrick Colquhoun, *Treatise on the Police of the Metropolis*, p. 100.

[2] *Three Tours*, p. 95; Besant, pp. 93–4.

doubt that, in other ways, their lives had been touched and their condition improved by the advances made in public health and sanitation. After 1790, the death-rate fell and it became normal to expect the annual number of births within the metropolis to exceed the number of burials. Francis Place, writing thirty years later, attributed the change to a number of factors, among which he picked out for special mention 'the increased salubrity of the Metropolis', the advance in surgical and medical knowledge, the higher wages consequent upon the Napoleonic Wars, and 'much also to the change that has taken place not only in London, but all over the country, in the habits of the working classes'. Those contemporaries, medical men and philanthropists among them, who shared his optimism were inclined to lay the main emphasis on the improvement in medical care, particularly of mothers and young children, and on the benefits arising from the 'opening' of London streets and a more general concern for ventilation and hygiene. Among the most significant developments were the building of lying-in hospitals for poor working mothers and the growth of the dispensary movement, both products of the later eighteenth century. The first maternity hospital, the Lying-in Hospital for Married Mothers, had been opened in 1749 and was followed by half a dozen others (catering for both married and unmarried women) before 1765. By the 1770s, these hospitals were delivering an annual average of between 4,000 and 5,000 women; but the proportion of deaths remained high until the last decade of the century. The records of the first of the hospitals illustrate the rapid decrease in deaths of both women and children during these years: the proportion of deaths among women falling from 1 in 60 in 1779-88 (it had been 1 in 42 in the first decade following the hospital's foundation in 1749) to 1 in 288 in 1789-98 and to 1 in 914 in the single year 1799-1800; meanwhile, among children it had fallen progressively from 1 in 44 to 1 in 77 and 1 in 115. Another late-century feature was the opening of a score of public dispensaries, intended mainly for the treatment of the poor, between 1769 and 1810, half of them being built after 1790. But already in 1775, it was claimed that whereas 1 in 13 of all patients admitted to St Thomas's and St Bartholomew's hospitals died annually, less than 1 in 33 patients died in the best-known of these dispensaries, the General Dispensary (founded in 1770). It was a revolutionary development, a first step towards wresting the indigent sick from the clutches of the parish workhouse; and John Feltham, in his *Picture of London in 1802*, wrote enthusiastically and with perhaps pardonable exaggeration:

From the eastern extremity of Limehouse to the western of Millbank on the north from Islington and Somers Town to the south as far as Lambeth . . . a system of medical relief is extended to the poor, unknown to any other part of the globe. About 50,000 persons are thus supplied with medicine and advice gratis, one-third of whom at least are attended at their own habitation.[1]

Also associated with the dispensary movement was the war that was being methodically waged against two of the main killer-diseases of the century, smallpox and 'the fever', or typhus. Smallpox had, in mid-Georgian times, accounted for something like one in every thirteen deaths, but it declined after the beginnings of inoculation in the 1770s. In 1779, Dr Lettsom, a pioneer of the dispensary movement, opened an inoculation dispensary in London specifically intended for the treatment of the children of the poor; and in 1796 Edward Jenner, a Gloucestershire country doctor, introduced the modern method of vaccination by injecting a child with cowpox. During the next ten years, numerous centres were opened, which gave free vaccination; and in 1806, for the first time on record, one whole week went by in London without a single death from smallpox. Even more successful was the battle fought against typhus, which Dr John Hunter, the most eminent of London's eighteenth-century medical practitioners, had, in a report to the College of Physicians in 1779, singled out as a disease of the poor, the result of poverty, filth and overcrowding, and one that was particularly prevalent in workhouses, prisons and public hospitals. To combat it, the London House of Recovery was established in Gray's Inn Road in 1802, and steps were taken to isolate the patients, to whitewash infected houses with hot lime, and even to cleanse wholesale the most severely stricken parishes. These measures were supported by a Treasury grant of £3,000 in 1804; and the number of fever cases fell dramatically in the next few years. Where the average annual mortality from typhus had been 3,188 through the eighteenth century, deaths fell to 2,201 in 1802 and to 1,033 in 1815. In the House of Recovery itself, only one in nine of all typhus patients admitted during its first nine years had died; and Dr Lettsom considered that, by 1810, typhus was 'almost extinct' in London. And Francis Place, looking back in 1824 on the improvements that had been made in the medical treatment of London's poor over the past forty years, observed that 'there are no such groups of half starved, miserable, scald-headed children with rickety

[1] *London Life*, pp. 60-3, 72, 326-30.

limbs and bandy legs as there were in the days of my youth, neither is there anything like the same mortality amongst them'; and he added that whereas the working people of his youth 'were to a great extent, drunken, dirty, immoral and ignorant', people now 'were better dressed, better fed, cleanlier, better educated, in each class respectively, and much more frugal, and much happier'. Yet, while insisting on the general improvement in the health and living standards of the poor, he conceded that there was still a great 'mass of poverty and misery of places along shore from the Tower to the Isle of Dogs'. Even so, his picture of almost unrelieved improvement and progress was almost certainly overdrawn, if not tendentious. What of the brutal operation of the Poor Law, the conditions in Newgate and the debtors' prisons, the old rookeries and slums and alleys of Holborn and St Giles, or of Southwark and Bermondsey, that still persisted in the writer's old age? Yet his optimism provides perhaps a useful corrective to the sombre picture painted by some of the more recent historians who, looking back on the improvements of the hundred years before their time, have been as apt to blacken the picture of the early nineteenth century as Place was to blacken that of the half-century before.[1]

The wars also brought changes to the lives and the social activities of the wealthier classes. Some of these were spectacular, others were muted and restricted by the exigencies of war: income tax was introduced, after the second financial crisis, in 1798, and the trebling of the window tax and the house tax discouraged the old type of private luxury building. So there was little housing development either for the rich or for the poor; and several building ventures that were launched after the American War, such as the laying out of Sloane Street and Sloane Square by Lord Cadogan and the construction at Camden Town and Somers Town, had to be temporarily abandoned; other projects, including the development of the Foundling and Bedford estates in Bloomsbury, continued at a reduced pace. Yet there were improvements. The houses of the gentry were now more inclined to be freshly painted, floors to be washed and scrubbed, and the footpaths to be cleared by paid sweepers: these were certainly innovations. But the kitchen, at least, retained some of its mid-century squalor; and a young French visitor, the Duc de la Rochefoucauld, was prompted to observe that, even in a nobleman's house, where servants were plentiful, napkins and dishcloths decidedly were not![2]

[1] *London Life*, pp. 327–30, 363–71; S. E. Ayling, *The Georgian Century 1714–1837*, 1966, pp. 289–90, 472–4, 497.
[2] *Three Tours*, p. 95.

Even public building was generally confined to naval and military purposes; the great exceptions were the building (by private enterprise) of the London docks between 1800 and 1812 and the building of the Bank of England on its present site in Threadneedle Street (though not in its present form) by Sir John Soane between 1792 and 1833. Soane's structure consisted of an interlocking system of halls, in which flat segmented arches, grooves and panels took the place of the old academic-classical rounded arches, columns, cornices and architraves; it has been described as 'the Gothic miracle rediscovered at the heart of the Roman tradition'.[1] Soane also built the Art Gallery and Mausoleum at Dulwich College (in 1811-14) and, for himself, a private mansion, Fitzhanger Manor, at Ealing, in 1801-2 and a house in Lincoln's Inn Fields in 1812. The war also saw the building or rebuilding of a handful of churches: an old-style church at Feltham in 1802; the more original French-style tower of St Anne's, Soho, by S. P. Cockerell, in 1802-6; and St John's, Hackney, by James Spiller, a friend of Soane's, in 1792-7. (The large parish churches of Marylebone and St Pancras belong to the immediate post-war years.) Yet, paradoxically, it was private house-building, which, though so patently discouraged, provided the most daring innovation in urban development. For in the plans drawn up for the Eyre estate, covering a part of the present St John's Wood (originally sketched in 1794, though not realized until the 1820s), the terrace house, that standard product of the eighteenth-century builder, was abandoned for the semi-detached villa of the future.[2]

Another feature of the times, though not strictly confined to the period of the wars, was the gradual disintegration of the social pattern of some of London's fashionable streets and squares. We have already noted the case of Holles Street, in Marylebone, where the speculative landlord, letting on a rising market, had made his appearance by the first decade of the nineteenth century. Similar, if not identical, developments could be found elsewhere. Soho and Golden Squares, for example, which had, already before the mid-eighteenth century, been largely deserted by the aristocracy, began, soon after, to be invaded by commercial interests. In Golden Square, Joseph Mahoon, a harpsichord maker, had already established himself in 1742, and an army contractor and a firm of wholesalers followed in the 1770s. Soho Square continued, until late in the century, to be largely inhabited by country gentry, dowager ladies and

[1] *Georgian London*, p. 157.
[2] *Georgian London*, pp. 175-6.

Members of Parliament, with a leavening of professional men, such as Dr George Armstrong, the paediatrician, and Sir Joseph Banks who, as a young man, bought himself a house there (no. 32) in the late 1770s. But, in the mid-1780s, commerce, in the person of John Trotter, an army contractor, made its appearance. Trotter occupied no. 5 between 1785 and 1790, and in 1793 he rebuilt nos 4 to 6 as a warehouse (this was converted into the Soho Bazaar in the last year of the wars). Perhaps it is no coincidence that the Duke of Portland, responding to the winds of change, chose the same year to dispose of all his freeholds in the square! Meanwhile, Leicester Fields too (by now called Leicester Square) had undergone a transformation. The wealthy county families who, during the greater part of the century, shared the Fields with the artists and remaining aristocrats, now tended to move out as the reigning head of the family died; and one of the last of the distinguished 'county' residents, Sir George Savile, died there in 1784. Leicester House, which had ceased to be a Royal residence in 1764, was demolished in 1791–2; its grounds were divided up and sold in smaller lots. Already in 1775, Sir Ashton Lever's Museum was set up at the original Leicester House, and in 1793 Barker's (later Burford's) Panorama was opened in the grounds at what had become no. 16; while, in 1809, Mary Linwood's gallery of needlework was established in a part of the long-deserted Savile House. Meanwhile, as in Hanover Square, there had been a steady influx of professional residents, notably of doctors, since shortly before the wars. John Hunter lived at no. 28 from 1783 to 1793, and was followed by half a dozen other medical men, who were living in the Fields between the outbreak of the French Revolution and the end of the wars. St James's alone, of the older fashionable quarters, retained something of its old hold on the aristocracy: St James's Square remained obstinately aristocratic or 'genteel', or merely 'ministerial'; and the Duke of Bedford, when he deserted Bedford House and Bloomsbury Square to make way for his new 'middling' tenants in 1810, came to live in Arlington Street, St James's.[1]

Fashions were changing, particularly among the wealthy and professional classes. In dress, for a while, there was a turn towards a greater simplicity. Young men of fashion had given up the use of powder, partly as a protest against the powder tax, which was another of Pitt's devilish devices for financing the war; and with powder wigs had been abandoned and had given way to mops of shaggy hair: it was a 'levelling' of nobility,

[1] *Survey of London*, vol. 29, pp. 78–81; vol. 31, pp. 143–5; vol. 33, pp. 45–50; vol. 34, pp. 428–31.

in Horace Walpole's phrase. Beards had not yet come in, though the eccentric Lord George Gordon grew one in Newgate prison shortly before he died of jail-fever in 1793. Men wore round hats with wide brims in place of the old three-cornered hats; umbrellas were ousting swords and trousers breeches; and Pastor Moritz, in his *Travels in England* in 1782, had been astonished to see how many people were wearing spectacles. Another novelty – and this was by no means confined to the rich – was the wearing of stockings. In George I's time, it has been said that only one person in fifty wore stockings, whereas now they were almost universal except among the poor; and even among them Place would claim ten years after the wars that, in contrast to his own youth, 'multitudes were wearing shoes and stockings'.

Women, too, had gone through another sartorial revolution. The notorious 'walking steeples' of the 1770s, which had provoked the sarcasm of Hannah More, had disappeared, as had the pads, hoops and long-waisted stays of the pre-war period. The *décolleté* bodice was all the rage, the waistline had risen (and would rise still further), skirts were thin and light, and the former elaborate head-dresses had been replaced by the simple ostrich feather. This tendency to a greater freedom of style was, no doubt, a reflection of the greater freedom that gentlewomen now enjoyed in society. The 'blue-stockings', with their insistence that women should play a more active social role, had made a contribution to this, as had writers like Catherine Macaulay, the historian, and the remarkable Mary Wollstonecraft who, on the eve of the wars, had engaged Burke in spirited controversy over the revolution in France and written a *Vindication of the Rights of Women*. So it was now unthinkable that a noblewoman, like Lady Mary Coke in 1748, should be locked up by her husband for refusing to have children; and it had even become fashionable for ladies to boast of their proficiency in the Classics, hitherto the jealously guarded preserve of the other sex![1]

There had been, similarly, something like a revolution in the arts and sciences and in the attention paid to them by a wider public; and here the war (so restrictive in the case of architecture) acted as a stimulus rather than as a brake. Paradoxically, London began to play a central role in the sciences just as she was losing her virtual monopoly in literature and the fine arts. During the greater part of the eighteenth century, the Royal Society had been little more than a fashionable debating society, which promoted little or no research; while the more serious business had been

[1] *Three Tours*, pp. 96–8, 104–5.

conducted by the Scottish universities, the Nonconformist academies, and, more recently, such middle-class and largely nonconformist bodies as the Lunar Society in Birmingham (associated with Joseph Priestly, who discovered oxygen) and the Literary and Philosophical Society of Manchester (which gave the Quaker, John Dalton, a laboratory and a chair in Mathematics). But it was only a matter of time before London responded to the intellectual challenge of the provinces. An educated reading public had been steadily growing and was constantly having its thirst for knowledge whetted by the more reputable of the many newspapers that were by now in circulation. By 1807 there were eight daily newspapers (including *The Times*, the *Public Ledger* and the *Morning Post*); five evening papers, of which two – the *Star* and the *Sun* – appeared daily; nine Sunday papers (including the *Observer*), and six weekly papers (including Cobbett's *Register*); and we have seen that some of these papers at times attained a circulation of 4,000 or 5,000 copies, and presumably reached a far larger number of readers. To satisfy the demand for 'useful knowledge' in the sciences, William Nicholson began to publish his *Journal of Natural Philosophy*, *Chemistry*, *and other Arts* in 1797 and achieved an immediate success. Meanwhile, in 1788, the Linnaean Society had been founded in London to promote the study of natural history, or biology; it was followed, soon after the turn of the century, by a Geological Society (in 1807), a Zoological, a Horticultural, a Medico-Surgical and an Astronomical Society, and other learned bodies of the kind. Most important of all, perhaps, was the creation by Count Romford in 1799 of the Royal Institution, which was patronized by high society and offered the public a series of lectures given by eminent men of science. Here Dalton came to lecture on atomic theory in 1804 (though he found a more responsive audience in Edinburgh, where he moved soon after). But the star performer was Humphrey Davy, the later inventor of the miner's safety lamp, who lectured at the Royal Institution between 1807 and 1810 and presented to a wider public than had ever been admitted to witness such mysteries before his important discoveries in the interrelations of chemistry and electricity, the use of the electric arc-lamp and the new elements of potassium, magnesium, chlorine and iodine. And, even more significant for the future, Davy trained in his laboratory Michael Faraday, the great pioneer of electro-magnetic induction and the progenitor of the electric telegraph and dynamo.[1]

[1] *Holden's Triennial Directory*, 1805-7; S. E. Ayling, *The Georgian Century*, pp. 495-7.

In literature and the fine arts, London had played an all-important role. The culture of Pope, Swift and Johnson, as of Hogarth and Reynolds and many of the early novelists, had been essentially urban and metropolitan. In this sense, the death of Dr Johnson in 1784 almost literally marked the passing of an era; the old classical-Augustan age, which drew its inspiration from the city, was now gone for ever. In poetry, William Blake's *Songs of Innocence* appeared in London in 1789 and his *Songs of Experience* in 1794; Jane Austen wrote (though she did not yet publish) her *Sense and Sensibility* in 1797, and, the same year, Coleridge and Wordsworth submitted their manuscript of the *Lyrical Ballads* to a London publisher. Yet three things had changed, or would shortly change. One was that the new poets and writers, with the exception of Blake, were not really Londoners: even if they lived at various times in London (like Coleridge, Crabbe, Southey, Byron and even Wordsworth), they sought their themes in the Lakes, like Southey and Wordsworth, in the Highlands or Lowlands of Scotland, like Burns and Scott, or in Greece, Italy or the Middle East, like Shelley and Byron. Another was that they quite consciously rejected the modes and art-forms of their predecessors. Whether they argued for a new poetic simplicity, as Wordsworth and Coleridge did in the Preface to their *Lyrical Ballads*, became 'Romantics' (like Byron, Keats and Shelley), sought refuge in the medieval (like Scott) or in the Old Testament (like Blake), or promoted the Oriental verse-tale (like Byron), there was a quite sharp, deliberate and self-conscious break with the immediate past. And, thirdly, the new poetry and the new novel were immensely popular and reached audiences, both in London and the provinces, that had rarely, if ever, been touched by the great poets and writers of the eighteenth century.

In music and painting, there was also a turn to new forms and new patrons, though the break was not so sharp as in the case of poetry and it came at different times: earlier in music and considerably later in the case of painting. The musical 'revolution' went back to the early 1760s and was associated with the visit then paid to London by Sebastian Bach's youngest son, John Christian, whose concertos and symphonies, conceived in what was called the *galant* style, were attended by large audiences, including a new middle-class audience that had had no part in the small aristocratic and 'genteel' musical societies of the earlier Hanoverian period. The main features of the 'revolution' were a turn from the concerto to the symphony, a faster tempo, greater drama and passion, larger and more highly professionalized orchestras, a greater use of wind instruments and, above all, the subscription concert (often held in the open air, as in the Vauxhall Gardens), which drew ever larger audiences. The 'revolution' was already well under way in London by the early 1790s, when Joseph Haydn came on a four-year visit and delighted his listeners with his 'Surprise' and other symphonies. In 1796 an essay appeared in London which firmly established the contrast between the 'ancient' and the 'modern' styles of music; it noted that the 'ancient' was favoured by the *elderly* and the 'modern' by the *young*.

The older generation of painters, on the other hand, still held the field until the end of the Napoleonic Wars. Gainsborough died in 1788 and Reynolds in 1792; but the Royal Academy which they had created survived them and there was no passing of an era on their departure as there had been, in literature, on the death of Johnson. For one thing, historical painting, which had been the main challenger to portraiture for the past twenty years, lived on in the canvases of Benjamin West. West, who succeeded Reynolds as president of the Academy, was still selling pictures to George III in 1801 (they had, it was said, already earned him £37,787) and, as late as 1811, sold his 'Christ Healing the Sick' to the British Institution for £3,000. Moreover, several portrait painters still carried on the tradition established by Gainsborough and Reynolds. Romney died in 1802 and Hoppner in 1810; but Henry Raeburn lived till 1823 and Sir Thomas Lawrence till 1830. In 1815 Lawrence sold a portrait for £700, and had just been commissioned by the Prince Regent to commemorate Britain's recent victories in a series of portraits at Windsor Castle. It was only after this that an entirely new school of painting, represented by the landscape art of Turner, Constable, Cotman and Crome, came into its own. Both Turner and Constable exhibited in 1815, but their main works, and the influence that they had on others, belong to the post-war generation. And they, too, like the poets, from the very nature of their chosen themes, belonged to the country rather than to London.

One of the arts, however, remained a peculiarly London phenomenon. This was the art of political caricature, which continued to depend, as it did at the time of Hogarth, both for its inspiration and its public, on a metropolitan environment. The most prominent of the new political caricaturists who had inherited the mantle of Hogarth were Isaac Cruikshank (the only R.A. among them), James Gillray and Thomas Rowlandson. Such 'revolution' as they brought about in their satirical prints and illustrations occurred in the period between the American and French revolutions. In their case, there was no sharp break with the past. Like

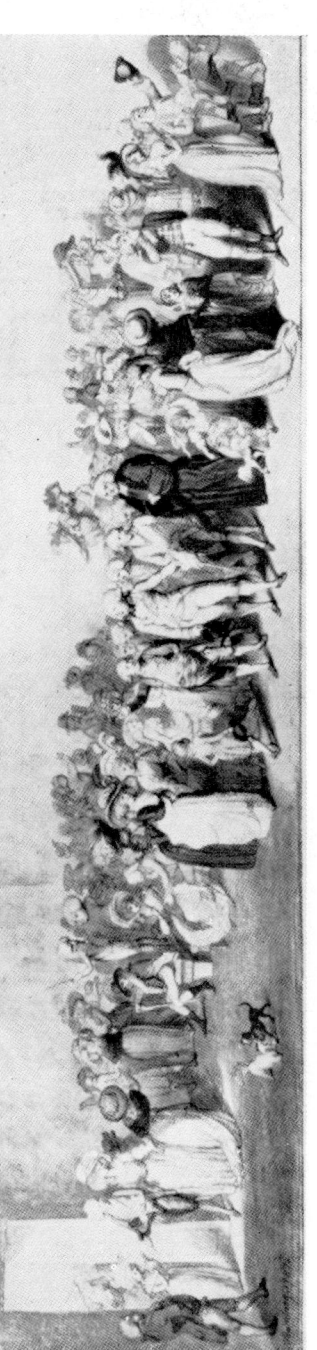

51　The Royal Academy Exhibition in 1771, held in Dalton's Print House, Pall Mall

52　Taste à la Mode in the year 1735, by L. P. Boitard
(*British Museum*)

53　Taste à la Mode in the year 1745, by L. P. Boitard
(*British Museum*)

Hogarth, they were realists, who specialized in realistic portraiture; and they rejected the conventional symbols (representing Fox as a fox, North as a badger and so on) that Hogarth's immediate successors had made use of in the 1760s and 1770s. They were also – with the exception of Rowlandson, whose real strength lay in the portrayal of the daily lives of the people – highly 'political' and class-conscious and they tended, particularly after the outbreak of the revolution in France, to place their talents at the service of the government rather than of the opposition: Gillray, for example became a pensioner of Pitt's in 1797. The most prolific and probably the most popular among them was Gillray, whose John-Bullish brand of Torysim commended itself to a large public during the wars. His art was biting, cruel and often malicious; and he was a bigoted anti-Papist, anti-Radical and anti-Gallican. His targets lay generally on the Left (whether Radical or Whig): among his favourites were Dr Price, Sir Francis Burdett, Tom Paine, Horne Tooke, and Sheridan and Fox; yet (on the other side) he displayed a consistent hostility towards Burke. Of the three artists, only Rowlandson survived the wars; Cruikshank died in 1811, and Gillray was declared insane in the same year.[1]

Meanwhile, London's political scene had also changed and a new generation of politicians and leaders was emerging to replace the old. Lord North and the Earl of Bute (by now almost forgotten) died in 1792, Alderman Brass Crosby and Lord George Gordon in 1793, John Sawbridge in 1795, and Wilkes, Burke and Horace Walpole in 1797. Of the old City leaders, the Rt Hon. Thomas Harley (a member of the Privy Council since 1768) and Sir Watkin Lewis survived till 1804; Pitt and Fox lived till 1806, and 'Parson' Horne (now become Horne Tooke), Wilkes's old ally and opponent, till 1812. Among the new men and future Prime Ministers were George Canning, who lived in London since student days in 1792 and began to edit his *Anti-Jacobin*, with government support, in 1797; and Henry Addington, Viscount Sidmouth, who was also living in London in 1792 and became Speaker of the House of Commons in 1789; and among the most prominent of the City's wartime leaders were Harvey Christian Combe, a Whig, who became alderman for Aldgate Ward in 1790, and Sir William Curtis, a Tory, who was elected alderman for Tower in 1785.

[1] S. E. Ayling, *The Georgian Century*, pp. 490–3; Owain Edwards, 'Revolution in 18th-Century Music', *History Today*, November 1968, pp. 755–9; E. Halévy, *England in 1815*, pp. 494–8; M. Dorothy George, *English Political Caricature to 1792*, pp. 171–223.

R

We have seen that the City, with the general election of 1784, entered into a firm alliance with the younger Pitt. The alliance lasted, with minor interruptions, for the duration of Pitt's two periods in office (1784–1801 and 1804–6) and, for two years after his death, the City generally supported his Tory (or mainly Tory) successors. In the crisis of 1808, the spell was broken and the citizens returned to something like their old opposition, or Radical, policies; and this opposition lasted, almost continuously, until the wars were over. In short, the City during the wars was more often a supporter of the government and its policies than its opponent. Yet this was far more true of the leaders than of the rank and file, more true of the Courts of Alderman and Common Council and the Lord Mayors (in whose election the aldermen had the deciding vote) than of the liveried freemen of the Court of Common Hall. So we find that of twenty Lord Mayors holding office between 1789 and 1808, 15 were Tories and only 5 were Whigs; of the 34 aldermen (out of 39) elected to office during those years, and whose political affiliations are known, 22 were Tories and 12 were Whigs. After 1808, as we should expect, the balance shifted; but even then the Court of Aldermen was sufficiently Tory-inclined to ensure that of the 7 Lord Mayors elected during the remaining years of war, 4 were Tory and 3 were Whigs.

This behind-the-scenes tussle between a predominantly Tory Court of Aldermen and a predominantly Whig Court of Common Hall is well illustrated by the case of Harvey Christian Combe, a wealthy brewer who led the City Whigs for many years and represented the City in the House of Commons from 1796 to 1817. Having served as Sheriff in 1791–2, Combe presented himself for the mayoralty in 1793, a few months after the war began. He was returned by the livery with the highest poll, but passed over by the Court of Aldermen. The same thing happened in each one of the next five years. Eventually, in 1799, he was elected to the mayoral chair on his seventh attempt, when a fellow-Whig and former mayor, Thomas Skinner, whose name was put forward with his, refused to accept office. Two other fellow-Whigs, William Newman and George Mackenzie Macauley, both of them aldermen since 1786, were less fortunate than Combe. Though repeatedly returned by the livery during the wars, they were on each occasion passed over for mayoral office by the aldermen owing to their unfashionable political views.[1]

To return to the City's relations with government since Pitt took office after his election victory in 1784. During the pre-war years, rela-

[1] Beaven, vol 2, pp. 138–41.

tions were generally cordial and were only marred by disagreements over financial matters. Pitt's final attempt, in 1785, to achieve a modest measure of parliamentary reform was supported by the City; as were his championship of Wilberforce's proposals to abolish the slave trade (first put forward in 1788) and his sponsorship of the Regency Bill of 1788–9, which left the choice of a Regent, during George III's first illness, to Parliament: on this occasion, the Common Council congratulated Pitt on his victory over Fox and, on the King's recovery a few months later, greeted the event with a congratulatory address and public illuminations. But the City opposed Pitt's Shop Tax of 1785 and worked energetically for its repeal; when the tax was withdrawn four years later, it opposed with equal energy its successor, an excise duty on tobacco, which revived unpleasant memories of Walpole's Excise of half a century before.

During the French Revolution and the wars with France, the City remained at first obstinately Tory. In May 1792 a Royal proclamation suppressed seditious publications; it was opposed by Fox in Parliament, but the City gave it its support and, later in the year, the Common Council thanked the mayor, Sir James Sanderson, for suppressing 'seditious' assemblies and urged other corporations to follow his example. When France declared war in February 1793, the Council offered bounties to seamen, pledged its support to the King and the Constitution, and voted £500 to a merchants' fund being raised in support of privateers. Further sums were voted by the City to support the campaigns of 1793 and 1794; but when, at the end of that year, there was a shortage of bread and a threat of famine, the first public signs appeared of a rift between government and City, and within the City itself, between leaders and rank and file. In January 1795, an emergency meeting of the Common Hall condemned the war as wrong in principle and urged Parliament to disclaim any right to interfere in the internal affairs of France and to conclude an early peace. Even the Common Council, while proclaiming its continued loyalty to the King, trimmed its sails sufficiently to express a desire for an early peace with 'dignity and honour'. But the livery and Common Council expressed directly opposite views on Britain's subsidies to her European allies: the Common Council approved them, while the Common Hall condemned them. Again, when peace negotiations, opened tentatively in 1796, failed to achieve results, the Council applauded the government for its efforts, whereas the livery demanded the instant dismissal of the ministers, and even attempted to present their views directly to the King.[1]

[1] Sharpe, vol. 3, pp. 209–33.

The discussion was temporarily cut short by the panic engendered by the naval mutinies and the financial crisis of 1797. Responding to the mutiny at the Nore, which appeared to be a threat to London, the Common Council resolved on 6 June to invite the wards to form volunteer associations for 'preserving the peace' of the City. These associations, which were sponsored by the government and were eventually formed all over the country, were intended as a civilian police force to combat 'sedition' from within rather than as an auxiliary defence corps against an enemy from without. So much was made clear by a 'model plan', circulating in London in 1798, which defined their major tasks as being 'to contribute to the due execution of Laws, maintenance of Civil Order and Government' and 'the immediate Suppression of all Riots and Tumults under what Pretence so ever they may be excited'. They were first put forward in London in April 1794, when it was proposed to raise a volunteer regiment of infantry and a troop of cavalry under the imposing title of 'The Loyal London Volunteers'; this, however, appears to have come to nothing. Even now, on the second attempt, the response in the City was remarkably half-hearted, and only one association, the Cornhill Military Association, composed of fifty-three members, had been formed before the current emergency was over; though, a year later, there were reports of similar bodies in Bishopsgate and Farringdon Within. Neighbouring Marylebone did better: here a corps of 800 volunteers, popularly called the 'Blue Bottles', had been formed by 1801.[1]

As the war continued, the Common Council made further patriotic contributions, and it rewarded the heroes of the war at sea, Admiral Duncan and Lord Nelson, with swords of honour. Yet, characteristically, the Council opposed the Income Tax Bill in 1798 and, after bread riots had broken out in the City in September 1800, it petitioned the King (though without success) to summon a special session of Parliament to consider the high cost of food. Pitt's retirement from office in 1801 made little difference to the City's political allegiance, and it was under the Addington Ministry that the Peace of Amiens, signed with France in March 1802 and bringing the first round of the wars to a close, was greeted with general jubilation in the streets of London.

[1] Corp. Lond. R.O., P.A.R., vol. 4 (1702–1827), bk 1, p. 291, bk 4, p. 27; M.P.L., G. Daniell, 'Volunteers' (folio, n.d. [1848?]); Thomas Smith, *A Topographical and Historical Account of the Parish of St Marylebone*, 1833, pp. 264–6; J. R. Western, 'The Volunteer Movement as an Anti-Revolutionary Force, 1793–1801', *E.H.R.*, vol. 71, 1956, pp. 603–14; Sharpe, vol. 3, pp. 224, 233–6.

When war broke out again a year later, the Common Council firmly pledged its support to meet 'the insatiable ambition of the French Republic'; and when volunteers were again called for to meet a new emergency, the response was noticeably greater than it had been six years before. It was now proposed by the government to build up the army of reserve to 50,000 men and the militia to 70,000, and to raise the strength of the volunteers to 300,000. The City's quota of 800 (later 1,600) men for the army of reserve was poorly subscribed: by February 1804 only 300 men had come forward and, in September, additional financial inducements had to be offered. But there was no similar reluctance on the part of the householders to parade in the uniforms of scarlet cloth ('with such facings as each district Regiment many determine among themselves') which were now prescribed for the regiments of volunteers; and, in July 1803, a mere fortnight after the first call for volunteers had been made, the Court of Aldermen observed 'with inexpressible Satisfaction the Alacrity with which their fellow Citizens have yielded to its Recommendation'. Eleven regiments of infantry, in addition to a corps of cavalry, came forward; and these were grouped in four divisions (Royal Exchange, St Paul's, North-East and South-East, according to the location of the wards) and were duly presented with their colours (supplemented by two field-pieces for the cavalry) in October 1803, at a cost of £385 7s. 0d. Meanwhile, the employees of the Bank of England and the East India Company, and the Harbour Marines and River Fencibles (recruited mainly from the watermen and lightermen), had formed their own separate corps and received the City's thanks and congratulations.

The combined City contingents amounted to a force of about 10,000 men; they were supplemented, in turn, by a further 17,000 volunteers from Westminster, Marylebone and Knightsbridge, Southwark and the out-parishes of Middlesex and Surrey. In Westminster, in addition to a score of cavalry and other separate units, 954 volunteer infantrymen enrolled in St James's, 663 in St George's, 625 in St Margaret's and St John's, 245 in St Clement Danes, 167 in St Anne's and 70 in the Liberty of the Rolls (the latter, however, disbanding in August when informed by the Lord Lieutenant that the Middlesex quota had already been exceeded!). Among the 'five parishes', Knightsbridge raised 124 men and Marylebone (where the former 'Blue Bottles' had become 'the Royal York St Marylebone Volunteers') 905; but St Pancras had its problems – a volunteer corps, formed in 1798, was on the point of dissolution, 'serious difficulties having arisen among its officers and men'. In addition, the

East London parishes raised some 2,300 men, Holborn and Clerkenwell a further 1,000, and Southwark and the Surrey out-parishes perhaps another 1,800. In all, a total of a little over 27,000 metropolitan volunteers of every sort paraded in their scarlet uniforms in a great review that was held in Hyde Park on 28 October 1803. There were watermen and artificers among them, as there were at the further review of City volunteers held on Blackheath in May of the following year; but, predominantly, these were men of the solid 'middling sort' from which the 'inferior set' and the labouring poor were largely excluded. In Marylebone, the vestry deplored the fact that its volunteers were 'composed principally of master trades-men, and officered by gentlemen'; in St Anne's, Westminster, only 'householders and their connections' were admitted; and in St George's, Hanover Square, the registers reveal a significant absence of both gentry and common working men. In short, these were essentially parades of loyalist London tradesmen, who had been summoned to bear arms (in the words of the City's Court of Aldermen) 'for the purposes of protecting Property, and preserving the Peace of the Metropolis on occasions of Rebellion, Insurrection, Civil Commotion, and all other Cases of ex-traordinary emergency'. But, as it turned out, such dangers were already past.[1]

Pitt returned to office in May 1804; the new Ministry was as solidly Tory as before, as the King, pursuing an old vendetta, had refused to admit Fox to office. But by now Pitt's alliance with the City was wearing thin and it only needed a further crisis to disrupt it. The City objected to the Additional Forces Bill (June 1804), which raised its quota for an army of reserve from 800 to 1,600 men. Relations became more strained when Pitt's old friend Lord Melville (Henry Dundas) was removed from the Privy Council after being acquitted at Westminster Hall of a charge of peculation; the Common Council, with little concern for the Prime Minis-ter's feelings, congratulated the King on having rid himself of an obnox-ious minister. Even Nelson's funeral in the City, a few weeks after Trafal-gar, was disturbed by a squabble over the Lord Mayor's place in the funeral

[1] Corp. Lond. R.O., *Journal of the Common Council*, 81, fos. 166–72, 204–5, 219, 231–2; P.A.R., vol. 4, bk 1, p. 381; MSS. 113.5: Minute Bks of Militia Cttee, 3 vols 1794–1808, entries July 1803–September 1804. W.P.L., Vestry Minute Bks and Registers, St Anne, A.2303, 2307; St Clement Danes, B.1359, 1363, 1367; St George, C.1102, 1104, 1105; St Martin, F.3314–17; Liberty of the Rolls, K.392. M.P.L., G. Daniell, 'Volunteers'. F. H. W. Sheppard, *Local Government in St Marylebone 1688–1835*, pp. 183–4. Sharpe, vol. 3, pp. 251–2, 256–7. Henry Humpherus, *History of the Company of Watermen and Lightermen*, vol. 3, pp. 33–40.

procession. Pitt himself died a few days later and, like his father, was given a State funeral in Westminster Abbey, but on this occasion the Common Council expressed no desire, as it had done on the death of Chatham, to attend in a body; and it carried a motion to erect a monument to Pitt in the Guildhall by a majority of only six votes. That the City's Tory loyalties were waning became all the more apparent when the Council extended a warm welcome to the Coalition Ministry 'of all the talents', in which Fox served (briefly) as Foreign Secretary. However, there was a sharp reversal of opinion when, after Fox's death, Lord Grenville, the Prime Minister, proposed to open commissions in the armed services to Roman Catholics. The King refused to co-operate and dismissed the Ministry, and the City once more, as over the Fox–North India Bill of a quarter-century before, congratulated the King on having vindicated 'the glorious independence of the Crown'. It was the last of the City's loyalist demonstrations. The Common Council applauded when the new Tory Prime Minister, the Duke of Portland, promised arms and money to the rebellious Spaniards, but it was outraged when, by the Convention of Cintra in August 1808, the French army was allowed to withdraw un-hampered from Portugal and, having voiced its indignation to the King, was sternly reprimanded for its pains. This was the turning-point, and from now on, the City, having loyally supported a succession of pre-dominantly Tory governments for over twenty years, returned to opposi-tion. And matters went from bad to worse. In February 1810, the Com-mon Council, having been refused an audience of the King, accused ministers of placing 'a barrier between the King and the people'. The same year, Sir Francis Burdett, the Radical Member for Westminster, was committed to the Tower for a breach of parliamentary privilege; and the Common Hall responded with a petition to Parliament that revived memories of Wilkes: it condemned the Commons' action as an attack on liberty and called for an immediate and radical reform. In April 1812 the Common Council followed suit: in a petition to the Prince Regent, it made a frontal onslaught on the government's policies, denounced 'influence and corruption', and demanded 'radical reforms' and the re-moval of the ministers.[1]

But it was in Middlesex and Westminster, rather than in the City, that London Radicalism, having lain dormant or succumbed to persecution, was reborn in the course of the Napoleonic Wars. The first stirrings of

[1] Sharpe, vol. 3, pp. 257–85; S. Maccoby, *The Radical Tradition 1763–1914*, 1952, pp. 75–7.

Radicalism, on the electoral plane, after its virtual burial in 1784, appeared in Westminster in 1790, when Horne Tooke (the former John Horne), standing as an Independent Reformer, won 1,779 votes in a contest with Fox, who was supported by the Westminster Committee and the official Whigs, and the Treasury candidate, Sir Samuel Hood. Both of his opponents scored twice his vote; yet it was a significant achievement, as the Treasury and Westminster Club had concluded what amounted to an electoral truce by agreeing to put forward only one candidate each. After this, the main energies of London Radicals were directed into other channels: notably into furthering the aims and activities of the various Reform societies that sprang up or revived under the impact of the French Revolution and the writings of Tom Paine and his fellow-democrats. Of these, the most significant was the London Corresponding Society, founded by Thomas Hardy, a master shoemaker, at the Bell tavern in Exeter Street, Strand, on 25 January 1792. The L.C.S. was remarkable in that it was largely composed (to use Hardy's own phrase) of 'tradesmen, mechanics and shopkeepers'. While opening its doors to all – to 'members unlimited' – it directed its main appeal to the lower 'middling' and working classes and charged a weekly subscription of 1*d.* with an entrance fee of 1*s.*, where the middle-class Society for Promoting Constitutional Information (sponsored by Major Cartwright) charged up to 5 guineas a year with a guinea entrance fee, and the aristocratic Society of the Friends of the People (of which the future Earl Grey was a member) charged 2½ guineas on both counts. It was also remarkable in that it provided a national forum for discussing its aims of annual parliaments and universal suffrage and corresponded with similar societies in Manchester, Sheffield, Leeds, Norwich and other centres. At the height of its activity and influence, early in 1794 and late in 1795, the Society probably had over 5,000 paying members. Burke once termed it, in a speech in the Commons, 'The Mother of all Mischief'; and it was inevitable that when, after the wars had started, repressive measures were taken against reformers, revolutionaries and friends of France, the Society should become a main target of persecution. Hardy and Tooke of the L.C.S. and John Thelwall of the Constitutional Society were tried at the Old Bailey on a charge of high treason in October 1794. But they were acquitted by the jury and carried in triumph through the streets of London; and the Society continued to lead a vigorous life, reaching the peak of its activities in October 1795, when it drew a crowd of 200,000 people to listen to its speakers in the Copenhagen Fields. But, meanwhile, other repressive measures had been taken:

Habeas Corpus was suspended annually, in the case of persons suspected of high treason, between 1794 and 1801; and a Treasonable and Seditious Practices Act and a Seditious Meetings Act were adopted in 1795. And, in July 1799, an Act against Unlawful Combinations and Confederacies specifically named and 'utterly suppressed and prohibited' the L.C.S. and half a dozen other smaller, republican societies, as well as a number of trade unions, as 'unlawful combinations'. So, from now on, the Society led a purely clandestine existence and probably ceased all organized activity by the end of 1800. By this time, too, even the more 'respectable' of the Reform societies had closed shop or taken cover, waiting for a better day.[1]

It came with the conclusion of the peace of Amiens with France in March 1802; that year, in Middlesex, Sir Francis Burdett, a Radical, joined George Byng, the sitting Whig Member, in unseating William Mainwaring, the corrupt old manipulator of the local Bench, who had represented the county in the Tory interest since 1784. (It is perhaps of interest to note that, in Enfield, Mainwaring received the vote of William Cobbett, the future Radical, who was then still a Tory.) But in 1804 Burdett's election was declared void on the ground that several of his supporters had no right to claim freeholds in the country; and, in a fresh contest, Mainwaring's son defeated him by five votes: the scene is depicted by James Gillray in a famous cartoon, 'The Middlesex Election, 1804 – a Long Pull, a Strong Pull, and a Pull All Together'. In 1806, the year of the Whig–Tory Coalition, Burdett was decisively defeated by George Byng, the Whig, and a Coalition-Tory, William Mellish. Meanwhile, in Westminster, the Radicals put up a newcomer, James Paull, a master tailor, who led the field at first but was eventually defeated by the joint Whig–Tory combination of R. B. Sheridan and Sir William Wood. In 1807 there was a new Westminster election, and both Paull and Burdett, having failed to reach an agreement, contested. Burdett won handsomely, out-voting his fellow-victor, Lord Cochrane, who was standing as an Independent, by 5,134 votes to 3,708; poor Paull was deserted by his former Radical supporters and came bottom of the poll. The election was a memorable one in more than one respect. In the first place, Burdett, who had declared his intention to withdraw from politics after his last Middlesex defeat,

[1] Add. MSS. 27808; Henry Collins, 'The London Corresponding Society', in *Democracy and the Labour Movement*, ed. John Saville, 1954, pp. 109–11; E. P. Thompson, *The Making of the English Working Class*, pp. 19–21, 152–6; Gwyn A. Williams, *Artisans and Sans-Culottes*, 1968, pp. 68–78.

refused to canvass and to appear on the hustings, and even to contribute a penny to his own election fund; in the event, his supporters raised a mere £1,720 for his expenses compared with the several thousands (Cobbett actually named a figure of £12,000) paid out by Lord Cochrane. Moreover, his election committee was composed almost exclusively of Westminster tradesmen: bootmakers, tailors, curriers and coachmakers. Only two of its twenty members claimed to be 'gentlemen' and six at least (Francis Place among them) had been members of the London Corresponding Society. So it was in every sense a victory for 'Reform' against 'old Corruption'. Besides, it marked a decisive break-through for the Radicals. Burdett continued to represent Westminster in Parliament for the next thirty-seven years; and from now till the Reform Bill of 1832 Westminster remained the acknowledged headquarters of Radicalism both in London and the country as a whole.[1]

The wars also brought new experiences to the London 'working trades' and labouring poor. In the first place, there was a general rise in the cost of living; yet it was by no means continuous. In 1795, after two years of war, prices were 30 per cent above their level in 1790. They fell back to 20 per cent in 1797-8, rose sharply to 70 per cent in 1800 and 74 per cent in 1801, fell again to 54 per cent in 1805, rose again to 76 per cent in 1810, fell again after 1813, and ended up, at the end of the wars, at 50 per cent above the level of 1790. Wages, meanwhile, after trailing wretchedly behind prices in the 1790s, may have caught up between 1805 and 1810, and, after a serious set-back in 1811-12, ended with a fairly comfortable lead over prices in 1815.[2] But these are national figures based on a national index, and they do not correspond at all closely to those in Rufus Tucker's index of real wages of London artisans for the period of the wars. According to Tucker, the money wages of London craftsmen barely changed until 1795, when they rose slowly until 1806, after which they took a sharp upward turn, reaching their war-time maximum in 1814-15. But their *real* wages fell sharply after 1794, reaching their lowest point in 1800; they picked up after 1806 yet still lagged slightly behind their pre-war level in 1815.[3] So here there is a discrepancy; yet there is general agree-

[1] *Poll of the County of Middlesex*, 1802; Michael Robbins, *Middlesex*, p. 100; J. Grego, *A History of Parliamentary Elections*, pp. 311-23; J. M. Main, 'Radical Westminster, 1807-1820', *Historical Studies: Australia and New Zealand*, vol. 12, April 1966, pp. 186-203.

[2] Steven Watson, *The Reign of George III*, pp. 525-6.

[3] Rufus S. Tucker, 'Real Wages of Artisans in London, 1729-1935', *Journal of the American Statistical Association*, vol. 31, 1936, pp. 73-84.

ment that money wages rose substantially after 1805 or 1806; and this picture broadly corresponds to that given by Francis Place, of which mention was made in an earlier chapter.

How were these increases in money wages brought about? Partly, no doubt, they resulted from the economic situation itself: particularly after the renewal of war in 1830, there was a great drain of men and boys to the army and navy, with a consequent shortage of labour in the workshops and offices and on the docks. Secondly, there was a great increase in the number and in the activities of the friendly societies, which, though nominally intended to give support in times of sickness, accident and old age, often developed into associations for the improvement of wages. In 1797, Eden, in his *State of the Poor*, estimated that there were 600 such societies in London with an average of 80 members in each; and these played, without much doubt, an important part in helping to improve working-class earnings after the formal proscription of trade unions by the Combination Laws of 1799. Moreover, we have the further testimony of Place that, between 1793 and 1815, there were numerous strikes (where there had been few in the late seventies and the eighties) conducted by the journeymen in a wide variety of trades; these were often remarkably successful, in spite of the general ban on 'combinations', above all in those trades in which the workers were well organized in clubs and associations. (In fact, Place himself led a strike of journeymen breeches-makers in 1793.[1])

Occasionally, however, when prices rose particularly sharply, strikes gave way to other forms of protest, and in 1795 and 1800, two of the years in which food prices rose most steeply, the capital had its first bread riots since the Hanoverians came to the throne. In August 1795, following two bad harvests, the average national price of a bushel of wheat rose to 13s. 6d. where it had been 6s. 6d. in August of the previous year; there were riots all over the country. In London, the price of the quartern loaf rose to over 1s. (it had been 6½d. at the outbreak of war), and the City's Common Councilmen, following the example of the Lords of the Privy Council, solemnly pledged themselves and their families to reduce their consumption of flour 'in other Articles of Food'. Matters came to a head at the end of October, when the King, driving in state to open Parliament at Westminster, was besieged in the Mall by an angry crowd, who shouted 'Bread, bread, peace, peace!' and broke a window of his coach.

[1] E. Lipson, *The Economic History of England*, vol. 2, pp. 391–2; *London Life*, pp. 361–2.

The incident had two sequels, neither of which was directly concerned with the price of bread: the Common Hall renewed its demand for an early peace, while Pitt presented his Sedition and Treason Bills to Parliament. This was, however, a minor and short-lived affair compared with the disturbances that broke out, following an even sharper rise in food prices, in 1800. That year there were two separate outbreaks in London. The first took place in early July when John Rusby, a Mark Lane jobber, was tried at the Court of King's Bench on a charge of 'regrating', or reselling oats, in the same market on the same day at a higher price than he had paid for them. After Lord Kenyon had summed up with a violent denunciation of all forestallers, engrossers and regraters, Rusby was found guilty, and a crowd marched on his house and 'pulled it down' in the traditional manner. But, as the *Annual Register* put it, 'the discontents of the people were not sufficiently allayed' by the trial of a single offender; and there was a second, and more prolonged, outbreak in September. On the night of Saturday, the 13th, a placard was stuck up on the Monument, announcing that 'Bread will be sixpence the quartern loaf if the people will assemble at the Corn Market on Monday'. Crowds duly assembled that morning in Mark Lane, and Harvey Combe, the Whig Lord Mayor, was met with cries of 'Bread, bread, give us bread, and don't starve us!' when he came to address them with other City officers; yet he was cheered when he left for the Mansion House. But riots followed in Mark Lane the same afternoon and evening; the Riot Act was read, a suspected corn factor was manhandled, a City marshal was attacked with bludgeons, four rioteers were committed to the Compter and the Loyal London Volunteers made their first appearance as an anti-riot force when they came to relieve the Militia. The next day a crowd gathered in Bishopsgate Street and threatened the warehouse of Messrs Wood, Fossick and Wood, but were dispersed by the Artillery Company. Other minor riots followed in various parts of the City during the next three days, but were confined to the breaking of street-lamps. In short, these London disturbances were small-scale affairs and far less violent and extensive than many of the food riots that broke out in other cities and market towns. And it is remarkable that there was no outbreak at all in London in the far greater crisis of 1811-12.[1]

More significant, in fact, than bread rioting was the revival, during these years, of a popular Radicalism which had virtually disappeared since

[1] Walter M. Stern, *Economica*, vol. 36, 1964, pp. 168-87; D. G. Barnes, *History of the English Corn Laws*, pp. 81-2; Sharpe, vol. 3, pp. 226-7, 241-5.

the Gordon Riots of 1780. But the French Revolution and writings like Tom Paine's *The Rights of Man* (published in two parts in 1791–2) provoked a great crop of Radical pamphlets and tracts which, by 1794, were causing the government considerable concern. In August of that year there were riots in London directed against the 'crimping houses', or houses used for recruiting to the armed services, and several of these houses were attacked and destroyed in Holborn, the City, Clerkenwell and Shoreditch. The rioters, according to one of the Lord Mayor's dispatches to the Home Office, were 'a mixed multitude of men, women and boys', but it took several days to disperse them with the aid of the Militia, the Guards and the Artillery Company. Unlike the disturbances of 1800, the riots had political undertones: they were accompanied by tracts and handbills which protested against the 'tyranny' of ministers and the invasion of the Englishmen's 'liberties'; one even raised the nostalgic question: 'Would such atrocious acts have been suffered in the days of Alfred? . . . Did Sydney and Russel bleed for this?'[1] After this, apart from minor skirmishes between 'loyalists' and 'Jacobins', there was only one other considerable disturbance which may reasonably be termed 'political' in the course of the wars. This occurred in the City in April 1810, when Sir Francis Burdett was being escorted by a troop of Guards to the Tower of London. Though the escort had been ordered to take a roundabout route, it was waylaid and attacked by a protesting crowd. The soldiers opened fire, and one man, Thomas Ebrall, was killed and several were wounded. Local opinion was outraged and a jury returned a verdict of murder against a guardsman, 'name unknown'. The Court of Aldermen, however, after holding an enquiry, decided that the soldiers had been justified – an opinion that could hardly have been fully shared by the Common Hall, which chose the occasion, as we saw, to mount a general attack on the ministers and to call for a thorough reform.[2]

So perhaps we may trace in these events the revival of a certain degree of collusion – though it is far less evident than in the 1760s and 1770s – between the riotous London crowd and an increasingly Radical Common Hall. But this was nothing new, and nothing like the old relationship developed until the protests against the Corn Law in the last year of the wars. What *was* new, and also far more important for the future, was the emergence of a political movement, entirely independent of the City Corporation, among the craftsmen and 'working trades' themselves. For

[1] Old Bailey *Proceedings*, 1794, pp. 1326–32.
[2] Sharpe, vol. 3, p. 277.

the London Corresponding Society, the product of the Revolutionary wars, while open to all, deliberately set out to recruit 'tradesmen, mechanics and shopkeepers'. At the height of its activity, in 1794-5, its members were, overwhelmingly, craftsmen of the typical London trades; and even its committeemen, though they included doctors and journalists, were mainly artisans and tradesmen: shoemakers, silversmiths, plumbers, booksellers, print-makers, hatters, hairdressers, tailors, turners and bookbinders.[1] Moreover, members were organized in groups of eighty or less, so that there was ample opportunity for study and discussion of the problems of the day. The Society did not last eight years, but it left a fruitful legacy of working-class political education and self-help.

By and large, then, the French wars had brought important changes to the metropolis. It had become the first city of Europe (though probably not of China or Japan) to contain a population of over a million. The wars had brought a great expansion of the economy; the London docks had been built; the City of London stood unrivalled as the leading centre of the world's money market as well as of its trade. By an inverse process, the revolution in the arts accompanying the wars had tended to end London's old cultural monopoly, as the new generation of poets and painters began to seek inspiration in the Highlands or the Lakes, on the Norfolk coast, in cathedral cities or in the English countryside. Architects, though temporarily frustrated, would soon be finding new outlets for their talents in Regency terraces and a new spate of elegant churches. Meanwhile, there had been something of a revolution in building and domestic technology: there was a greater and more subtle use of cast iron in the construction of bridges, docks and public buildings; stucco had become fashionable with John Nash; the iron water-pipe and the gas-lamp were already in evidence before the wars were over; and the water-closet (invented in the 1770s) would soon be on the order of the day. There was a new concern for hygiene, fresh air and sanitation; the houses of the 'middling' and richer classes were cleaner and more spacious; and, for all, the expectation of life was certainly greater than it had been thirty years before. London's politics, having been firmly geared to the policies of a Tory Prime Minister for over twenty years, had entered on a new Whiggish, even Radical phase; middle-class Radicalism, firmly centred on Westminster, was ready to reach northwards, beyond the old chartered boroughs, into the new factory and industrial towns; while among the London craftsmen there were already germinating the elements of a

---

[1] E. P. Thompson, *The Making of the English Working Class*, pp. 152-6.

working-class political movement. So, as this page of her history ended, the city could look forward with some confidence to what the new century might bring.

Yet, in many respects, there had been no change from the older Hanoverian London, or even from the days of Queen Anne. In an age when so much was new, the new still rubbed shoulders uneasily with the old. The old verminous rookeries remained, as did the old police and the barbarous treatment of the parish poor. The prisons were still filthy, overcrowded and fever-ridden, awaiting the reforms prompted by the selfless labours of John Howard and Elizabeth Fry; and judges could still, among nearly two hundred capital offences, condemn a man to death for planting a tree in Downing Street or impersonating a Chelsea pensioner! In the new age of steam and gas, old beliefs and habits died hard: in April 1801, the year of the first census and of the first steamboat on the Forth–Clyde Canal, a woman was ducked in the Thames at Kingston, on the periphery of the new 'greater' London, in the traditional 'scold's' chair.[1]

[1] Henry Humpherus, *History of the Company of Watermen and Lightermen*, vol. 3, p. 17.

Bibliography

References to *manuscript sources* consulted are given in the footnotes, as are references to *contemporary printed sources*, such as newspapers, directories, poll books and Old Bailey Proceedings; they are not listed here.

The first date given is that of the original edition; the place of publication is London, unless otherwise stated.

Works marked * are those considered to be of particular importance for the present volume.

1. *Works of Contemporary Writers and Observers*

Archenholtz, J. W. von, *A View of the British Constitution and of the Manners and Customs of the People of England. 1794.*

Boswell's London Journal 1762–1763, ed. F. A. Pottle, New York, 1950; 1966.

Colquhoun, Patrick, *A Treatise on the Police of the Metropolis*, 1796.

Defoe, Daniel, *The Complete English Tradesman*, 1726.

  A Tour Through the Whole Island of Great Britain. 1724–7.

Eden, Sir William M., *State of the Poor*, 1797.

Fielding, Henry, *Enquiry into the Causes of the late Increase of Robbers . . .,* 1751.

Fielding, John, *An Account of the Origin and Effects of a Police set on Foot by his Grace the Duke of Newcastle in the Year 1753 . . .,* 1758.

  A Plan for the Asylum for Orphans and other deserted Girls of the Poor of the Metropolis, 1758.

Gwynn, John, *London and Westminster Improved,* 1766.

The Journal of the Rev. John Wesley, A.M., ed. N. Curnock, 8 vols, 1909–16; 1938.

Letters of the First Earl of Malmesbury from 1745 to 1820, ed. J. H. Harris, 2 vols, 1870.

The Letters of Horace Walpole, Earl of Orford, ed. P. Cunningham, 8 vols, 1891.

Lysons, D., *The Environs of London . . .,* 1792–7.

Maitland, William, *The History and Survey of London*, 1739; 1756, 1760, 1772.

Pennant, Thomas, *Some Account of London*, 1805; 1813.

Smith, Adam, *Inquiry into the Nature and Causes of the Wealth of Nations*, Glasgow, 1776.

Strype, John, *A Survey of the Cities of London and Westminster*, 1720.

Voltaire, *Letters Concerning the English Nation*, 1759.

2. Later Works of General Reference

Ayling, S. E., *The Georgian Century, 1714–1837*, 1966.
Besant, Sir William, **London in the Eighteenth Century*, 1902.
Briggs, A., *The Age of Improvement, 1783–1867*, 1959.
George, M. Dorothy, *England in Transition*, 1931; 1953, 1964.
  *London Life in the Eighteenth Century, 1925; 1930, 1965, 1966.
Halévy, Elie, *A History of the English People in the Nineteenth Century. Vol. 1: England in 1815*, 1924; 1949, 1960–1, 1964.
Lecky, W. E. H., *A History of England in the Eighteenth Century*, 7 vols, 1892.
Lewis, W. S., **Three Tours through London in the Years 1748, 1776, 1797*, New Haven, 1941.
Marshall, Dorothy, *Eighteenth Century England*, 1962.
  Dr Johnson's London, 1968.
Mitchell, R. J. and Leys, M. D. R., *A History of London Life*, 1963.
Namier, Sir Lewis B., *England in the Age of the American Revolution*, 1930; 1961.
Plumb, J. H., *England in the Eighteenth Century*, 1950; 1966.
Robbins, Michael, **Middlesex*, 1953.
Turberville, A. S. (ed.), **Johnson's England*, 2 vols, Oxford, 1933; 1952, 1965.
Watson, Steven, *The Reign of George III 1760–1815*, Oxford, 1960.
Wheatley, H. B. and Cunningham, P., **London Past and Present*, 3 vols, 1891.
Williams, Basil, *The Whig Supremacy 1714–1760*, Oxford, 1939; 1962.

3. Later Works on Particular Aspects of London Life and History.

(1) *Topography, Population* (see Chapter 1)

Glass, D. V., 'Notes on the Demography of London at the end of the Seventeenth Century', *Daedalus*, Spring 1968.
Jones, P. E. and Judges, A. V., 'London Population in the late Seventeenth Century', *Economic History Review*, vol. 6, 1935–6.
Spate, O. H. K., 'The Growth of London, A.D. 1600–1800', in *An Historica. Geography of England before A.D. 1800*, ed. H. C. Darby, 1948.
Wrigley, E. A., ***'A Simple Model of London's Importance in Changing English Society and Economy 1650–1750', *Past and Present*, no. 37, 1967.
See also D. M. George's *London Life*, and works by Maitland, Strype (above).

(2) *Town Planning, Building, Architecture* (Chapters 1, 3, 12)

Olsen, Donald J., *Town Planning in London in the Eighteenth and Nineteenth Centuries*, Yale, 1964.
Pevsner, Nikolaus, **The Buildings of England. London*, vol. 1, 1957; 1962.
  Middlesex, 1951.
Rasmussen, Steen Eiler, *London the Unique City*, 1961.
Summerson, Sir John, **Georgian England*, 1945; 1962.
Survey of London, ed. F. H. W. Sheppard, vols 26–34, 1956–66.
See also Gwynn (above).

S

(3) Economic Life (Chapters 2, 12)

Andreas, M., *History of the Bank of England*, 1966.

Ashton, T. S., *The Economic History of England. The Eighteenth Century*, 1955; 1964.

Barker, Theodore, *'London and the Great Leap Forward'*, *The Listener*, 29 June 1967.

Beales, H. L., 'Travel and Communications', in *Johnson's England*, ed. A. S. Turberville, vol. 1.

Broodbank, Sir Joseph G., *A History of the Port of London*, 2 vols, 1921.

Clapham, Sir John, *The Bank of England. A History*, 2 vols, 1944.

Clarke, William M., *The City in the World Economy*, 1967.

Davis, Ralph, *The Rise of the English Shipping Industry*, 1962.

Dickson, P. G. M., *The Financial Revolution in England. The Story of the Development of Public Credit 1688–1756*, 1967.

Humpherus, Henry, *History of the Company of Watermen and Lightermen*, 3 vols, 1874–6.

John, A. H., 'The London Assurance Company and the Marine Insurance Market of the Eighteenth Century', *Economica*, vol. 25, 1958.

Joslin, D. M., 'London Private Bankers 1720–1785', in *Essays in Economic History*, ed. E. M. Carus-Wilson, 1962, vol. 2.

Lipson, E., *The Economic History of England*, 3 vols, 1947.

Smith, Raymond, *Sea-Coal for London*, 1961.

Sutherland, L. S., *The East India Company in Eighteenth Century Politics*, Oxford, 1952.

See also Pennant, A. Smith, Strype (above).

(4) Society and Social Classes (Chapters 3, 12)

George, M. Dorothy, *'London and the Life of the Town'*, in *Johnson's England*, ed. A. S. Turberville, vol. 1.

Habakkuk, H. J., 'England', in *The European Nobility in the Eighteenth Century*, ed. A. Goodwin, 1953.

Mingay, G. E., *English Landed Society in the Eighteenth Century*, 1963.

Phillips, Hugh, *Mid-Georgian London*, 1964.

Plumb, J. H., *Sir Robert Walpole*, vol. 1, 1956.

Robson, Robert, *The Attorney in Eighteenth-Century England*, 1957.

Sutherland, L. S., *A London Merchant 1695–1774*, 1962.

Thomson, G. S., *The Russells in Bloomsbury, 1669–1771*, 1940.

Trevelyan, G. M., *A Social History of England*, 1944, chaps. 10–16.

Wheatley, H. B., *Hogarth's London*, 1909.

See also M. D. George's *London Life* and *England in Transition*, Defoe's *Complete Tradesman*, and Besant, Clapham, Dickson, Wheatley and Cunningham (above).

(5) Social Life, the Arts, Press and Entertainment (Chapters 4, 12)

Ashton, J., *Social Life in the Reign of Queen Anne*, 2 vols, 1882; 1925.

Chancellor, E. Beresford, *The Annals of Covent Garden*, 1930.

Crane, R. S., and Kaye, F. B., *A Census of British Newspapers and Periodicals 1620–1820*, 1927.

Ellis, Aytoun, *The Penny Universities. A History of Coffee-Houses*, 1956.

Ford, Boris (ed.), **The Pelican Guide to English Literature*, vol. 4: *From Dryden to Johnson*, 1957; 1965, 1966.

Handlist of English and Welsh Newspapers, 1620–1920, 1920.

Lillywhite, Bryant, *London Coffee Houses*, 1963.

Tinker, Chauncy Brewster, *The Salon and English Letters*, 1915.

Watt, Ian, **The Rise of the Novel. Studies in Defoe, Richardson and Fielding*, 1957; 1966.

See also articles by R. W. Chapman (authors and booksellers), E. D. Cuming (sports), M. D. George (London life), Sir Henry Hadow (music), W. J. Lawrence (*theatre), A. Shirley (*painting), O. Sitwell and M. Barton (taste), N. Nichol Smith (*press) in *Johnson's England*, ed. A. S. Turberville; *and see* Boswell's *London Journal*, and Besant, Lewis, Phillips, Voltaire (above).

(6) *The 'Other' London, Food Prices, Wages, Health, Gin, Crime and Punishment* (Chapters 5, 12)

Barnes, D. G., **A History of the English Corn Laws from 1660 to 1846*, New York, 1961; 1965.

Cole, G. D. H. and Postgate, R., **The Common People 1746–1938*, 1938; 1947, 1949, 1956.

George, M. Dorothy, **London Life in the Eighteenth Century* (above).

Hammond, J. L. and B., 'Poverty, Crime, Philanthropy', in *Johnson's England*, ed. A. S. Turberville, vol. 1.

Herbert, A. P., *Mr Gay's London*, 1948.

Rudé, George, ' "Mother Gin" and the London Riots of 1736', *The Guildhall Miscellany*, no. 10, September 1959.

Stern, Walter M., **'The Bread Crisis in Britain, 1795–96', Economica*, vol. 36, 1964.

Thompson, E. P., **The Making of the English Working Class*, 1963; 1968.

Tucker, Rufus S., 'Real wages of artisans in London, 1729–1935', *Journal of American Statistical Association*, vol. 31, 1936, pp. 73–84.

Webb, S. and B., 'The Assize of Bread', *Economic Journal*, vol. 14, 1904.

See also T. S. Ashton, Besant, Colquhoun, H. and J. Fielding, Lewis (above).

(7) *Religion, the Churches, Education* (Chapter 6)

Abbey, C. J. and Overton, J. H., *The English Church in the Eighteenth Century*, 2 vols, 1878; 1896.

Clarke, Basil F., *Parish Churches of London*, 1966.

*'Ecclesiastical History', in Victoria History of London, ed. W. Page, vol. 1. 1909.

Jones, M. G., **The Charity School Movement in the Eighteenth Century*, Cambridge, 1938.

Mallet, Sir Charles, 'Education, Schools and the Universities', in *Johnson's England*, ed. A. S. Turberville, vol. 2.

Skeats, H. S., *A History of the Free Churches of England*, 1869.
Sykes, N., *Church and State in England in the Eighteenth Century*, Cambridge, 1934.
  *'The Church', in *Johnson's England*, ed. A. S. Turberville, vol. 1.
Wearmouth, R. E., *Methodism and the Common People of the Eighteenth Century*, 1945.
See also *Wesley's *Journal*, *Halévy, Pevsner, Summerson, *Thompson (above).

(8) *Local Government, Poor Law, Police* (Chapter 7)

Beaven, A. B., *The Aldermen of the City of London*, 2 vols, 1908, 1913.
Dowdell, E. G., *A Hundred Years of Quarter Sessions. The Government of Middlesex from 1660 to 1760*, Cambridge, 1932.
Marshall, Dorothy, *The English Poor in the Eighteenth Century*, 1926.
Robson, William A., *The Government and Misgovernment of London*, 1939.
Sheppard, F. H. W., *Local Government in St Marylebone 1688-1835. A Study of the Vestry and the Turnpike Trust*, 1958.
Webb, S. and B., *English Local Government from the Revolution to the Municipal Corporations Act. The Parish and the County*, 1906. *The Manor and the Borough*, 1908.
See also Archenholtz, Besant, Colquhoun, *H. Fielding, Robbins and D. Marshall's *Dr Johnson's London* (above).

(9) *Politics, Radicalism* (Chapters 8, 9, 12)

Christie, Ian R., *Wilkes, Wyvill and Reform*, 1962.
George, M. Dorothy, *English Political Caricature to 1792. A Study of Opinion and Propaganda*, Oxford, 1959.
Grego, J., *A History of Parliamentary Elections and Electioneering from the Stuarts to Queen Victoria*, 1892.
Maccoby, S., *The Radical Tradition 1763-1914*, 1952.
Main, J. M., 'Radical Westminster, 1807-1820', *Historical Studies: Australia and New Zealand*, vol. 12, April 1966.
Mitchell, A. A., 'London and the Forty-Five', *History Today*, October 1965.
Perry, Thomas W., *Public Opinion, Propaganda and Politics in Eighteenth Century England. A Study of the Jewish Naturalization Act of 1753*, 1962.
Plumb, J. H., *Sir Robert Walpole*, 2 vols, 1956, 1961.
Postgate, Raymond, *That Devil Wilkes*, 1930; 1956.
Rudé, George, *Wilkes and Liberty. A Social Study of 1763 to 1774*, Oxford, 1962.
Sharpe, R. R., *London and the Kingdom*, vol. 3, 1895.
Sutherland, L. S., *'The City of London in Eighteenth-Century Politics', in *Essays presented to Sir Lewis Namier*, eds R. Pares and A. J. P. Taylor, 1956.
  The City of London and the Opposition to Government, 1768-1774, 1959.
Veitch, G. S., *The Genesis of Parliamentary Reform*, 1913; 1965.
See also *Beaven (above).

(10) *Social Protests, Political Riots, Popular Radicalism* (Chapters 10, 11, 12)

de Castro, J. P., *The Gordon Riots*, 1926.

Collins, Henry, 'The London Corresponding Society', in *Democracy and the Labour Movement. Essays in Honour of Dona Torr*, ed. John Saville, 1954.

Isaac, D. C. G., 'A Study of Popular Disturbances in Britain, 1714–1754', unpub. thesis for Ph.D. degree, Edinburgh, 1953. (By permission of the Librarian, the University of Edinburgh.)

Rudé, George, 'The Gordon Riots. A Study of the Rioters and their Victims', *Transactions of the Royal Historical Society*, 5th series, vol. 6, 1956.

'The London "Mob" of the Eighteenth Century', *The Historical Journal*, 1959, vol. 2, i, 1959.

Webb, S. and B., *The History of Trade Unionism*, 1896; 1920.

Williams, Gwyn A., *Artisans and Sans-Culottes. Popular Movements in France and England during the French Revolution*, 1968.

See also M. D. George's *London Life*, and Barnes, Besant, Dowdell, Halévy, Humpherus, Sharpe, *Thompson, Wearmouth (above).

Index